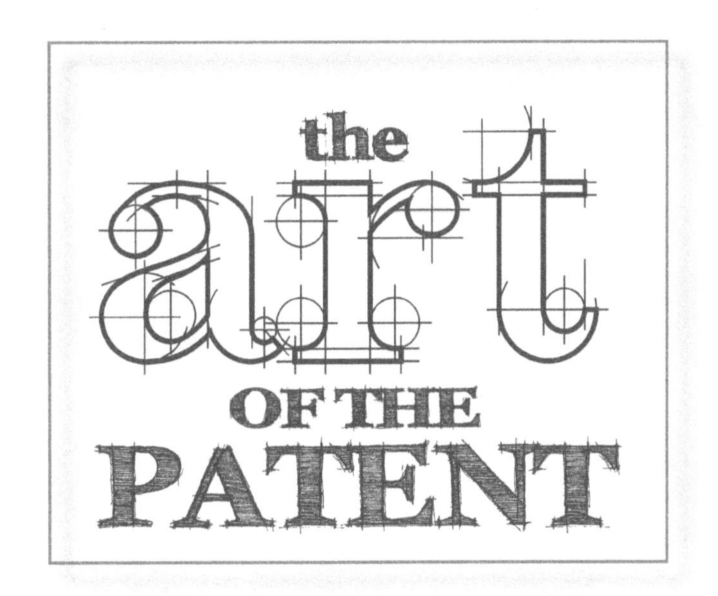

Kevin Prince

GLASSKO PRESS

Published by:

Glassko Press
San Juan Capistrano, California, USA
www.glassko.com

ISBN-13: 978-0-9839640-0-1 (soft cover)
ISBN: 0-9839640-0-9

Cover design by PureFusionMedia.com
Book Layout by BryanPrince.com

Printed in the United States of America

TABLE OF CONTENTS

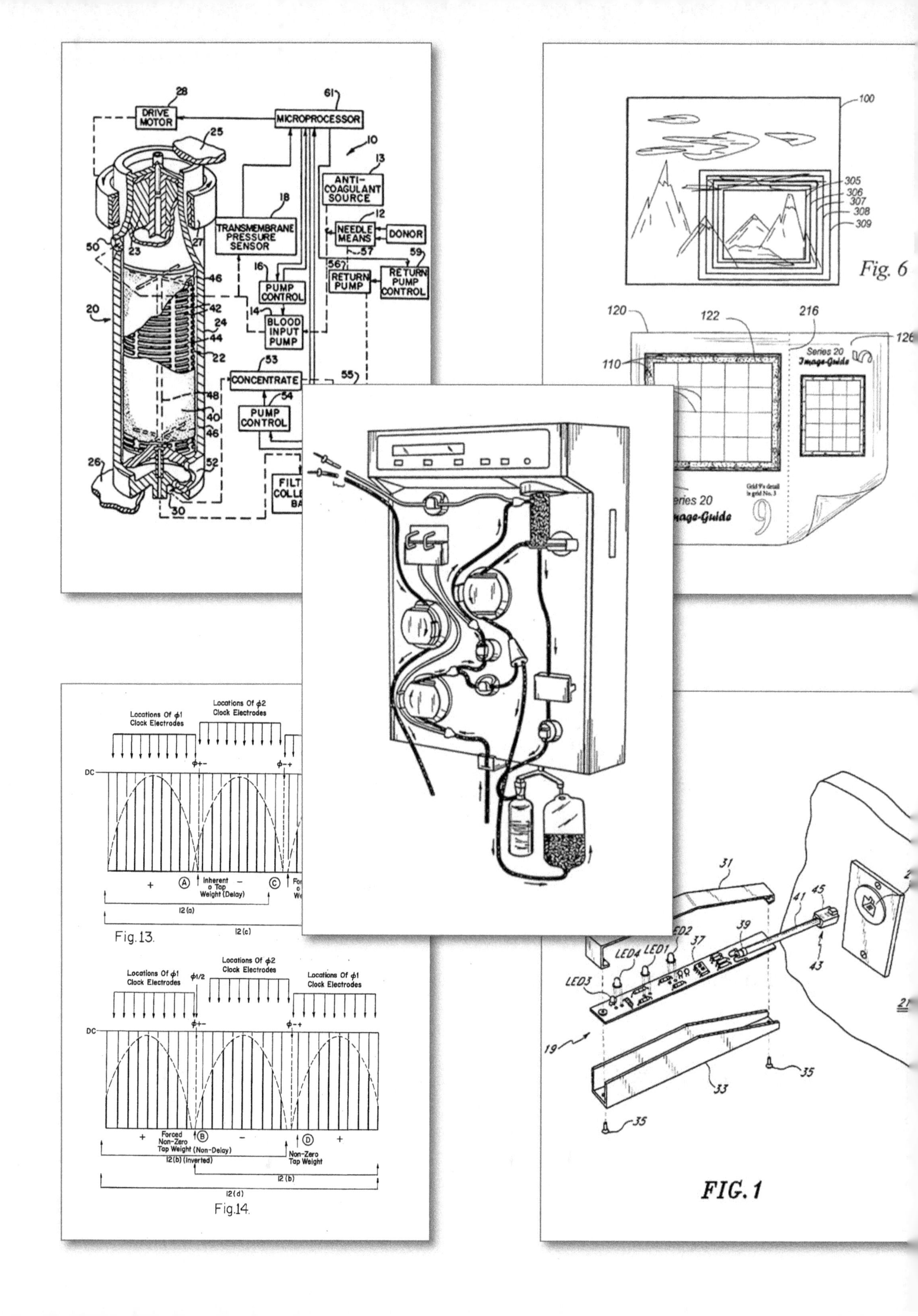

DRIVE MOTOR
MICROPROCESSOR
ANTI-COAGULANT SOURCE
TRANSMEMBRANE PRESSURE SENSOR
NEEDLE MEANS
DONOR
PUMP CONTROL
RETURN PUMP
RETURN PUMP CONTROL
BLOOD INPUT PUMP
CONCENTRATE
PUMP CONTROL
Fig. 6
Series 20
Image-Guide
Locations Of ϕ1 Clock Electrodes
Locations Of ϕ2 Clock Electrodes
DC
Inherent o Tap Weight (Delay)
Fig.13.
Forced Non-Zero Tap Weight (Non-Delay)
Non-Zero Tap Weight
Fig.14.
LED1
LED2
LED3
LED4
FIG.1

For my dad...

Paul R. Prince

- Prolific Inventor, 26 patents (and counting).

- Encourager (filed a patent application on my behalf at 12 years old... how many kids get that?)

- Entreprenuer (US Patent 4062070... didn't quite work out, except that the trademark "Bull's Eye" was sold for $2,500, which my dad used to buy one of the first Apple II computers in 1976, launching my love affair with computers and anything tech!)

- Financier (my first venture, www.cdsnaps.com, US Patent 5088674... didn't quite work out, except I learned a lot about inventing and marketing a new product... thanks for the $15K dad!)

- Partner... my dad now works for me drafting patent drawings, from the comfort of his recliner and three 19" displays

Thank you, Dad... you have fulfilled Proverbs 24:3 and 4!

Introduction

Behind nearly every patented invention lies a series of illustrations designed to explain its details. These "patent drawings" must conform to the legalistic guidelines of the United States Patent & Trademark Office (PTO), and typically include multiple figures that show the inventive device from different angles, in different configurations, and disassembled bit-by-bit to reveal the inner workings of the invention. Each lever, bolt, and flange is numbered so that it can be described in painstaking detail in the written patent "specification." As one might expect, many times these illustrations are extremely simple, unremarkable, and downright boring to all but those few who are somehow involved with the product.

Yet, in many cases, the patent illustrator's sense of artistry jumps out between the rigid requirements of the patent law. Drawings that go well above and beyond the call of duty have been enshrined in long-expired patents that are now only referenced by a functional title and a consecutive patent number. The name of the illustrator is not included in the historical record, and thus all such illustrations are effectively anonymous. This book is a tribute to those draftsmen who, over the last two hundred years or so, have spent countless hours drawing (and no doubt re-drawing) figure after figure with what at times can only be described an elegant mastery of the pen (or mouse), and an uncanny ability to bring beauty to a dry field.

US Patent 659,856

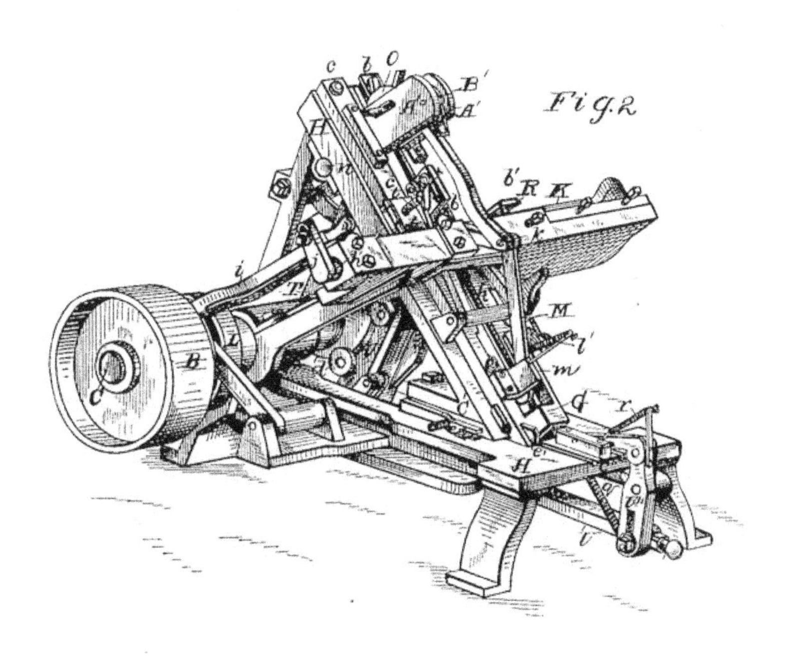

US Patent 377,376

For the first 200 years of patent history in the United States, drawings were done with ink on paper. Accurate reproduction of patent documents was difficult for most of this history, and printing presses could not easily reproduce photographs, gray-scale drawings, colors, or other multi-tone illustrations. As a result, the PTO limited patent illustrations to basic line art drawings, black lines on a white background. Such drawings are easier to replicate with basic offset printing, as there were no scanners, laser printers, .pdf files, or other ways of easily reproducing gray-scale or color illustrations before about 1980. As with most government institutions, old habits die hard. Many outdated drawing requirements still exist, even though now we have the technology to reproduce color and gray-scale photographs with ease. Hence, we still file patents, with few exceptions, with black and white line art drawings.

That is not completely undesirable, however. In the following pages, you will see that such line-art drawings can lend themselves extremely well to describing an invention, how it is put together, and how it works. The right choice of angle, drawing type, and subject can render a complex machine understandable at a glance. Patent professionals frequently look at the drawings of a patent first, before even reading the abstract or other portions of the patent document. With patents, if the drawings are well executed, they can paint not just a thousand words, but two thousand!

As a registered patent agent and an inventor, I've had the privilege of working with several patent illustrators who have shown me that patent drawings can be so much more than just stick figure drawings of a material object. Choice of shading, angles, line thickness, and subjects can make even the most complicated machine understandable. Hats off to those who, for no fame and little fortune, endeavor to create beauty and understanding in what should rightly be called Patent Art.

Kevin Prince, 2011
San Juan Capistrano, CA

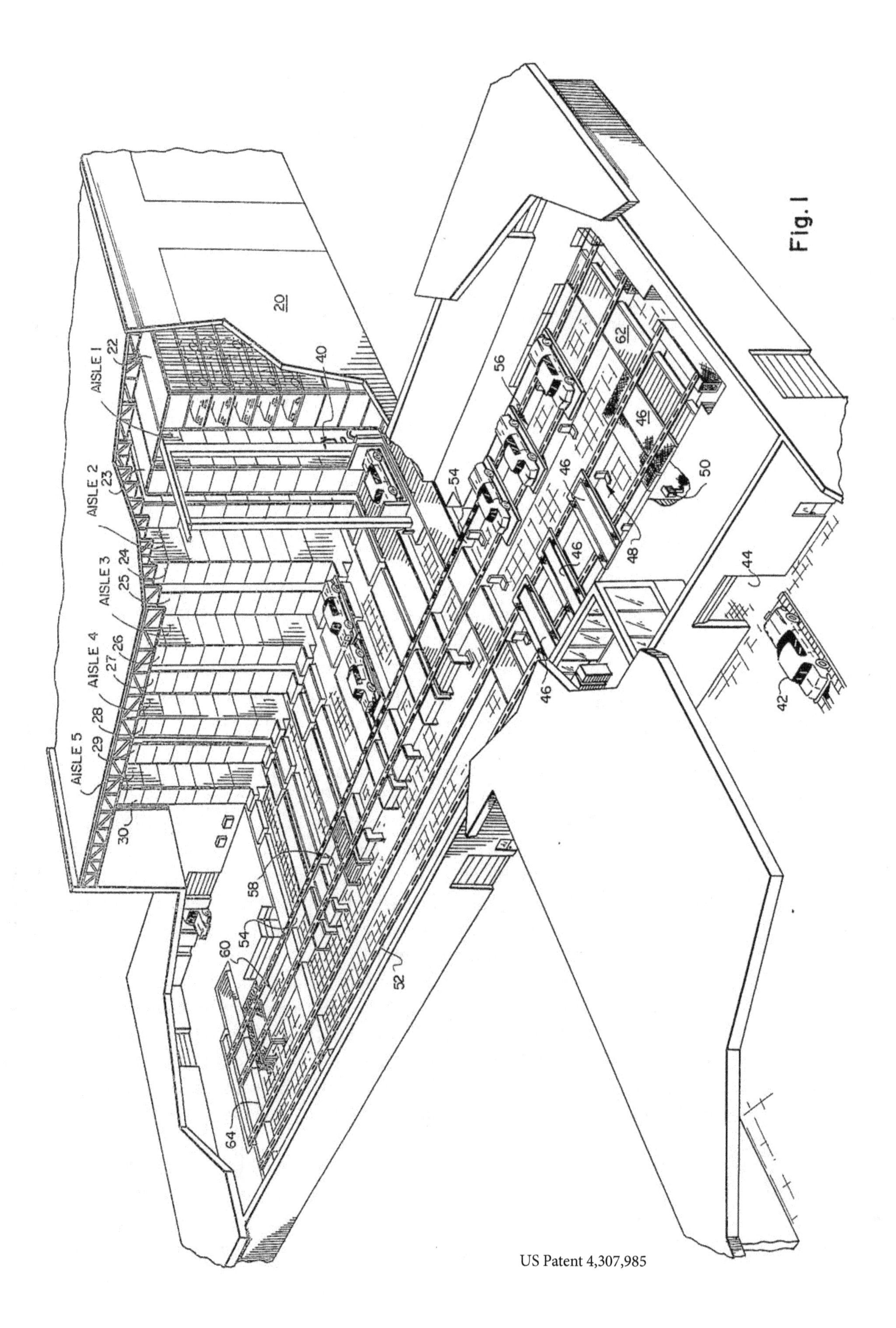

US Patent 4,307,985

Chapter 1

Patents as Art

Written within the depths of the driest of government manuals are the requirements and guidelines for submitting and securing patent rights to new inventions. Some, like the light bulb, became everyday fixtures; others have taken more circuitous routes to fame, or died in bud form on the vine of an active if not practical imagination. Yet it's within these government regulations and abiding by a plethora of bureaucratic and counterintuitive laws, that an art was born.

From the most mundane everyday container to intricate machines promising intergalactic travel, the ink drawing has been at the core of almost every patent application. The United States Patent & Trademark Office (PTO) requires patent drawings to be included with written patent applications when such drawings are necessary to understand the invention. Only in rare cases are drawings not needed, such as with chemical compositions where a chemical formula is sufficient for a
full understanding.

Welcome to the wonderful world of patent art! Within these pages I'll guide you through not only the whys and what-fors, but also the purely artistic side of patent drawings.

Fig.1. Fig. 1 Fig.10. Fig. 1 Fig.1.

Fig.1. Fig.1. Fig.1. FIG.1.

Fig.1. Fig.1 FIG—1 Fig. 1. Fig.1

FIG. 1 Fig.1. Fig. 1. FIG. 1 Fig.1.

Fig.1 Fig.1 Fig.1. Fig.1. Fig. 1

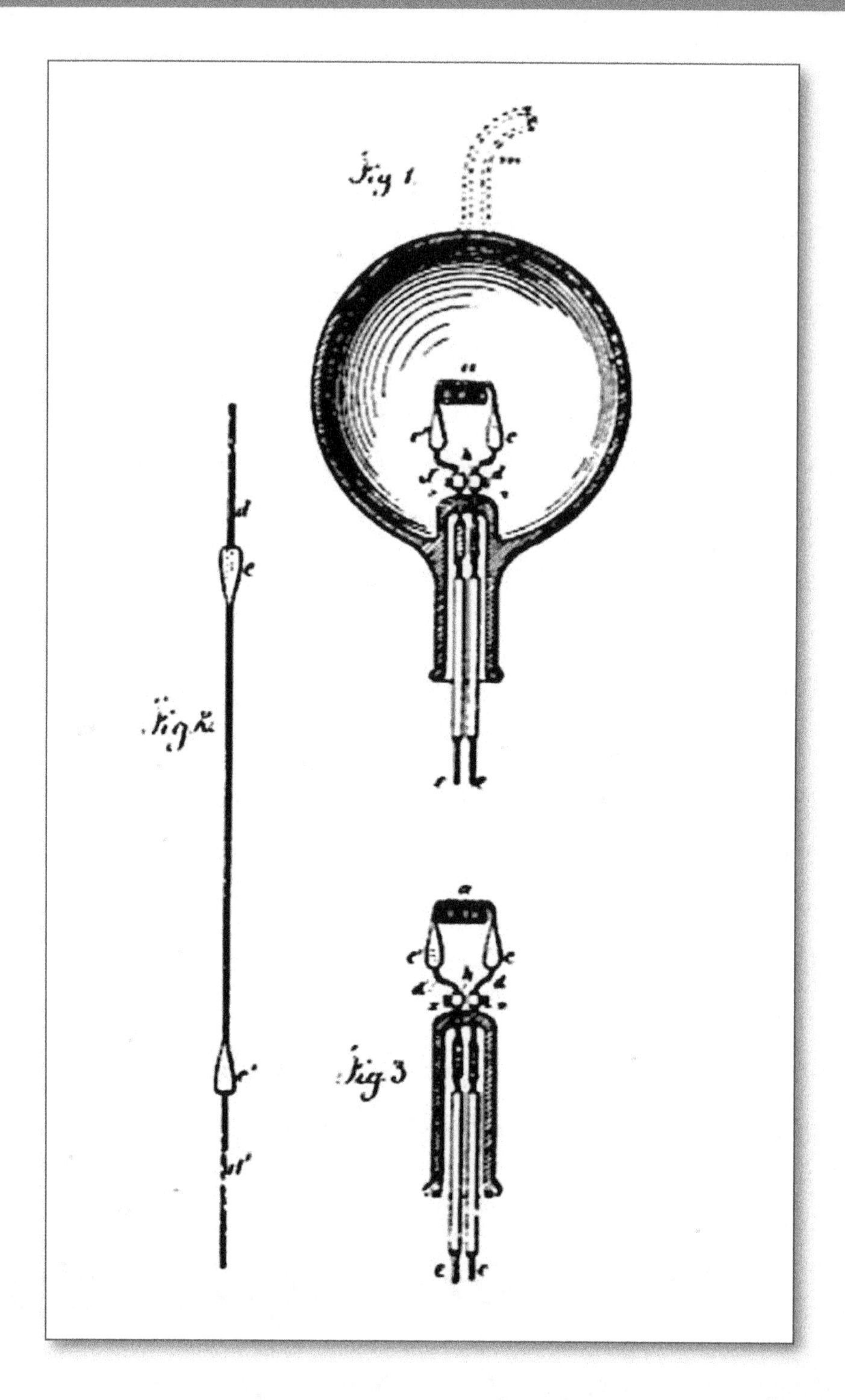

Above is Thomas Edison's electric lamp. The drawing is simple yet adequately descriptive of the apparatus beneath which you're probably sitting while reading this book. Chances are you were born within the rays of one or more light bulbs, you read your first books by them, studied, grew up, got into all kinds of trouble, and worked, all within line-of-sight to one of these little glass bulbs. This single invention is, in fact, the icon of all inventions, the very picture of one's thinking while inventing. The impact of this one document, US Patent 223,898, is immeasurable.

Edison has over one thousand patents in his name, which exemplifies his famous quote: "Genius is one percent inspiration, ninety-nine percent perspiration."

Not all patents achieved the fame and longevity of Edison's light bulb, of course. Have a look at this obscure Seed Planter idea from 1900. Note the attention to detail in both the apparatus and the man's clothing and face. The artist could easily have made a rudimentary figure drawing of the man and left out the ground detail. Note the perspective used with the long grass in the background. This drawing clearly shows how the artist, whoever he may have been, went beyond the prescribed duty of just accurately depicting the seed planter. Figures 2, 3, and 4 on the next page are cut away details of the main invention. At the bottom of the page, and nearly works of art themselves, are the signatures of the witnesses and attorneys involved.

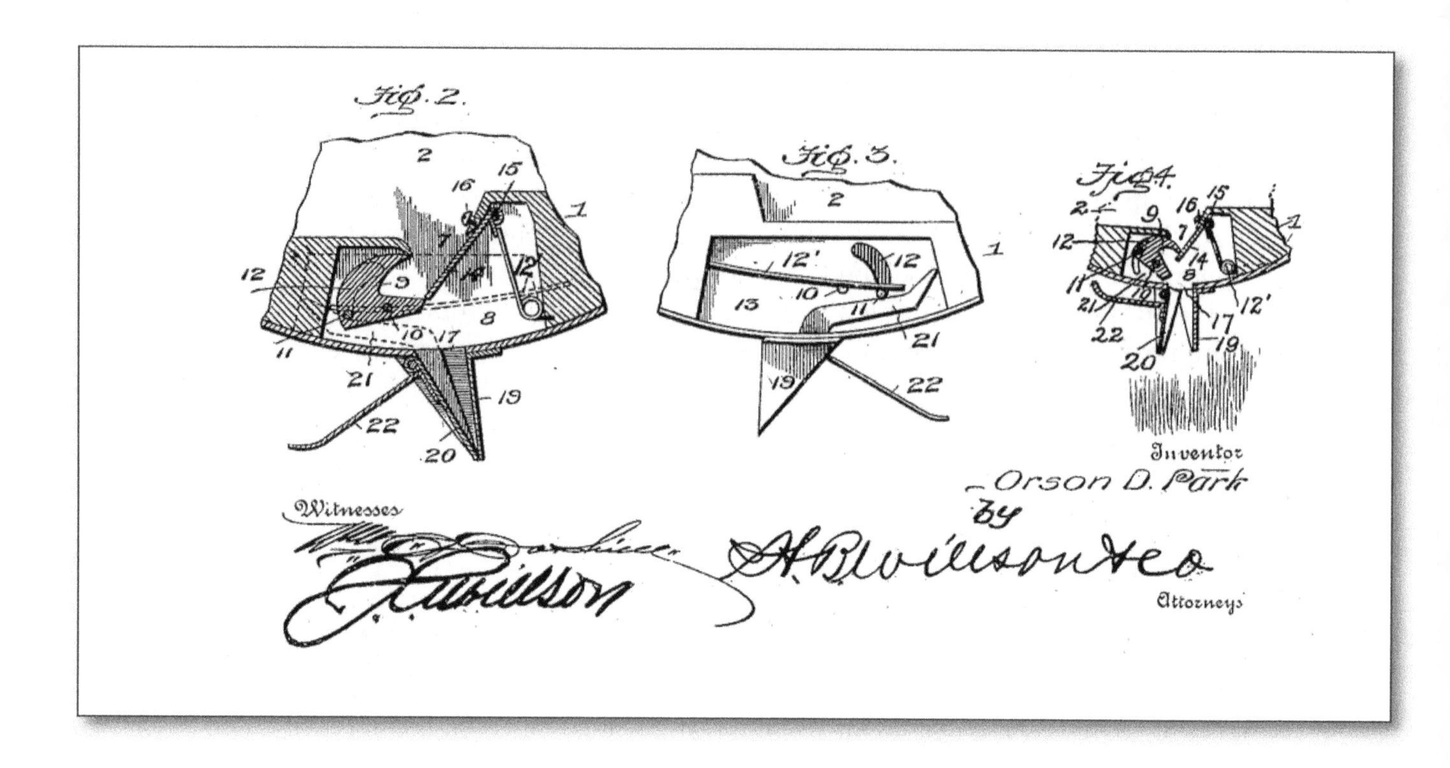

So why are drawings used at all? Why not just describe the invention? After all, in theory a good description would cover all the nuances the artist might leave out.

Or, why not use a photograph? I'll go into the modern uses of digital photography in a later chapter. Given today's technology, high resolution digital images are seen now in certain types of patent applications. However, for most of the history of the PTO, photographs couldn't be reliably reproduced. Black and white ink drawings, as time consuming as they are to make, are more easily and reliably replicable and are still required today. Color photos are seldom used unless special permission is given by the patent office. Once again, reliability of reproduction is the gremlin. Red might come out as black, and green as blue, and then where would our fluorescent garden gnome design be?

So the standard for clarity and ease of reproduction in patent drawings had been and continues to be black and white ink drawings.

On the next page I have excerpts from just the written description of the invention. Notice the picture that forms in your mind when you read the words first without looking at the drawing. Then, have a glance at the drawing on the subsequent pages. It's no contest as to which one is easier to understand and quicker to visualize.

O.D. PARK SEED-PLANTER May 8, 1900 No. 649,257

My invention relates to toys primarily intended for amusement of children, but also for family use as parlor games and the like, and for advertising purposes.

A purpose of my invention is to provide a helical spring toy which will transfer its turns from one end to the other in an entertaining manner when it is bent into general semi-circular form and the ends are moved up and down.

A further purpose is to provide a helical spring toy which will walk on an amusement platform such as an inclined plane or set of steps from a starting point to successive lower landing points without application of external force beyond the starting force and the action of gravity.

A further purpose is to design a helical spring toy of essentially low natural frequency, suitably between 10 and 100 cycles per minute, having substantially no compression between turns in closed position when no external force is acting, and having dimensions and proportions which permit manual handling.

A further purpose is to design a helical spring toy adapted to walk and oscillate, consisting essentially of a helical spring having substantially no compression or tension between turns in closed position when no external force is acting, and in which the spring cross section has substantially lower torsional stiffness than a square cross section of the same cross sectional area, thereby producing low natural frequency.

A further purpose is to design a helical spring toy having substantially no compression or tension between turns when no external force is acting, having a radial cross sectional dimension between 1.1 and 10 times (preferably between 2 and 6 times, and most desirably about 4 times) the axial cross sectional dimension, with an outside diameter of coil between 4 and 100 times (preferably between 10 and 50 times, and most desirably about 30 times) the radial cross sectional dimension, and having a solid height between one-half and 5 times (preferably between ¾ and one and one-half times, and most desirably equal to) the diameter, the coil being capable of bridging an axial semi-circle without external force holding it in position.

Further purposes appear in the specification and in the claims.

This application is a continuation in part of my application Serial No. 625,996, filed November 1, 1945, for Toy and process, copending herewith.

In the drawings I have chosen to illustrate one only of the embodiments in which my invention might appear, with a minor variation, the form

Having read the above, what picture do you have in your mind–if any? Compare it to this...

It's the Slinky® toy!!

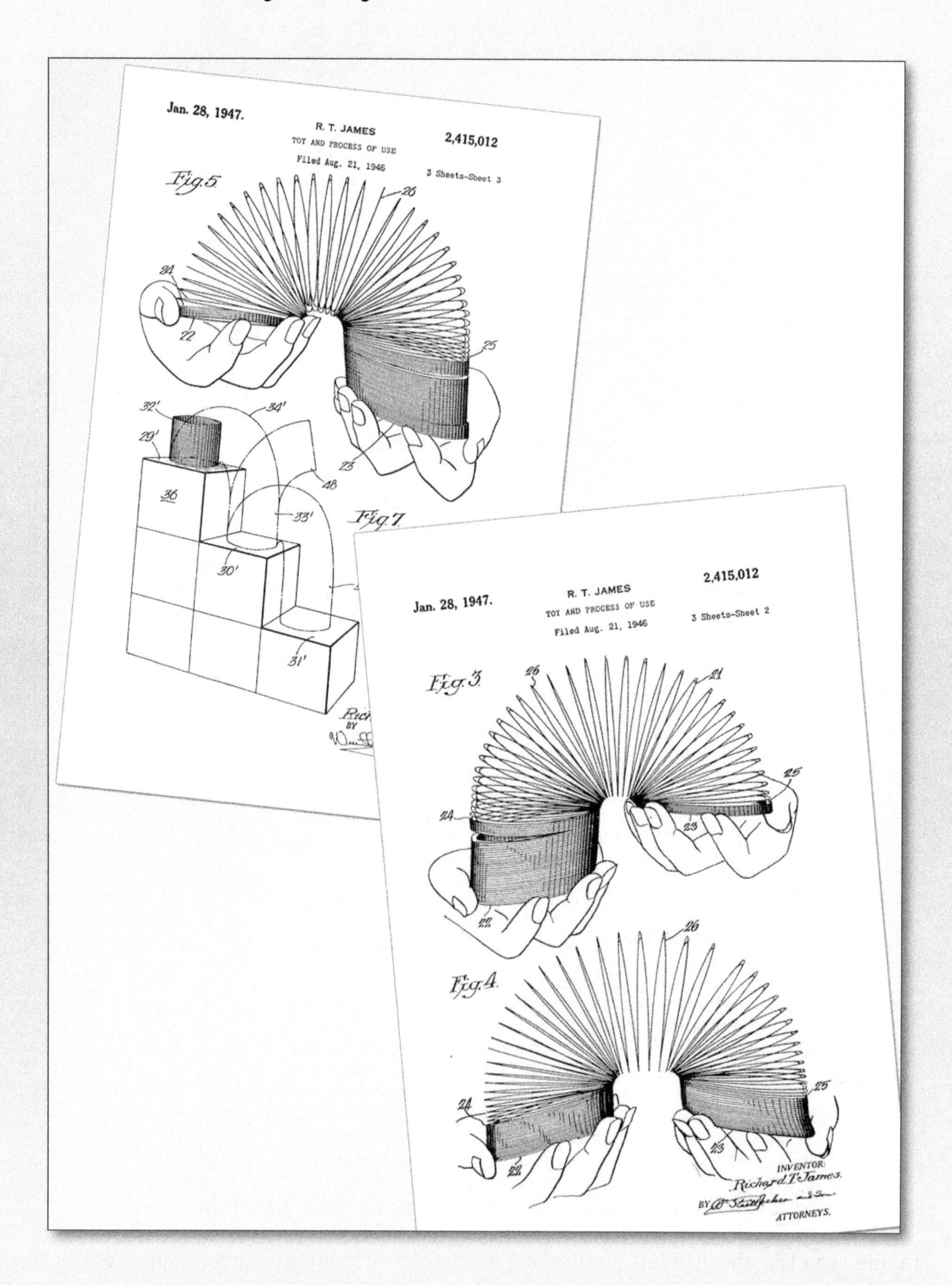

It's much easier to get the idea with a rather simple drawing. Notice how in the "step" figure at left it's easy to "see" the action involved as the toy makes its way down the blocks. Can it be described verbally? Yes. But how much more efficient to have a clear and concise drawing impressed straight from the page into our minds and imaginations.

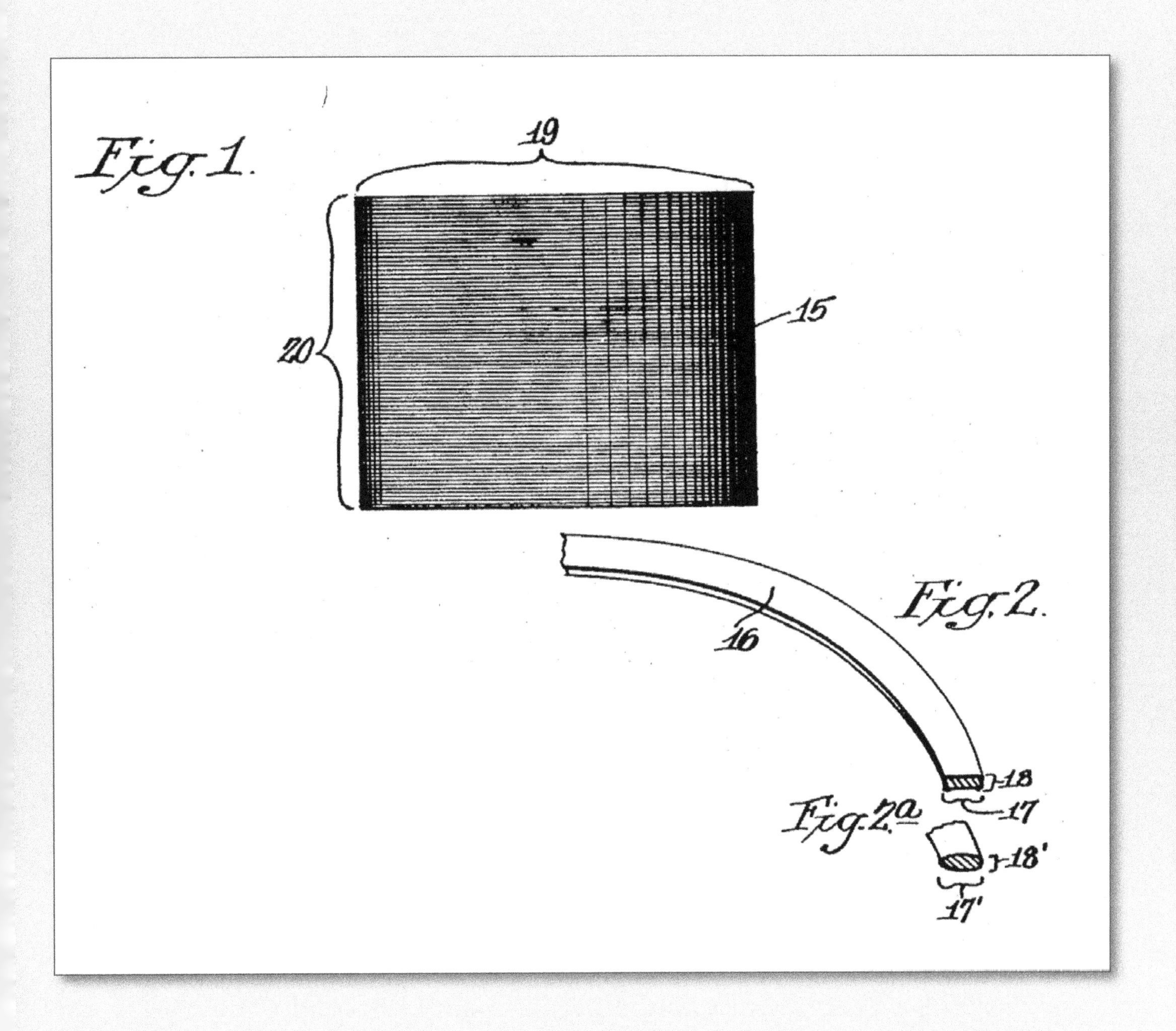

Let's try it again...

Read the following description and pay attention to the mental image that appears.

Would you be able to understand and utilize the product based on this?

My invention has for its object a velvet fabric including a foundation structure constituted by a weft and a warp incorporating threads that are cut at a predetermined length so as to form a raised pile. My novel fabric distinguishes from the other similar fabrics by the fact that the raised pile is made of artificial material, while at least part of the threads in said pile is provided near its end with material-engaging means, as required for adhering to a similar fabric or for scouring purposes.

My invention has for its further object a method for producing a fabric of the above type, according to which the raised pile is provided with its material-engaging means by forming loops round a carrier and submitting the loops formed on the carrier to a thermic action with a view to giving them their final shape, after which the loops are cut on one side of the carrier so that each loop produces at least one pile thread having a hook-shaped end.

Fabrics of the type referred to are intended primarily for use as closing means or fasteners for garments, curtains and the like as substitutes for the usual slider-operated closing means or fasteners or for buttons or the like attaching means, whenever a yielding invisible closing arrangement is of advantage.

Fabrics of the type referred to may also be used to advantage as cleaning implements. As a matter of fact, it is possible to lay them on a support made of wood or of plastic material so as to produce a clothes or shoe brush.

I have illustrated diagrammatically and by way of example in accompanying drawings various embodiments of the fabric according to my invention. In said drawings:

Fig. 1 is an explanatory diagram of a preferred method of production of such a fabric.

Fig. 2 shows two pieces of fabric executed according to a first embodiment of my invention and laid over each other so as to interengage and to adhere to each other.

Turning to Fig. 1, it is apparent that the velvet fabric, illustrated in the making, includes a foundation structure constituted by a weft **1** and by a warp **2.**

The foundation structure also carries the warp thread **3** in addition to the warp thread **2**, said thread **3** being adapted to form the raised pile **9**, **10**, some of the pile threads showing near their ends material-engaging means; in the example illustrated, the threads **9** of the pile are bent downwardly to form a hook **4.**

Obviously, the weft and warp threads forming the foundation structure may be arranged otherwise than in the manner illustrated.

Furthermore, the raised pile is made of artificial or a synthetic resin material so that it is possible to give the pile threads the desired shape and to make them retain the said desired shape. I may use as an artificial material any suitable plastic material, such as that sold in the trade as "nylon", which is a generic term for any long chain synthetic polymeric amide which has recurring amide groups as an integral part of the main polymer

Now look at the drawing....

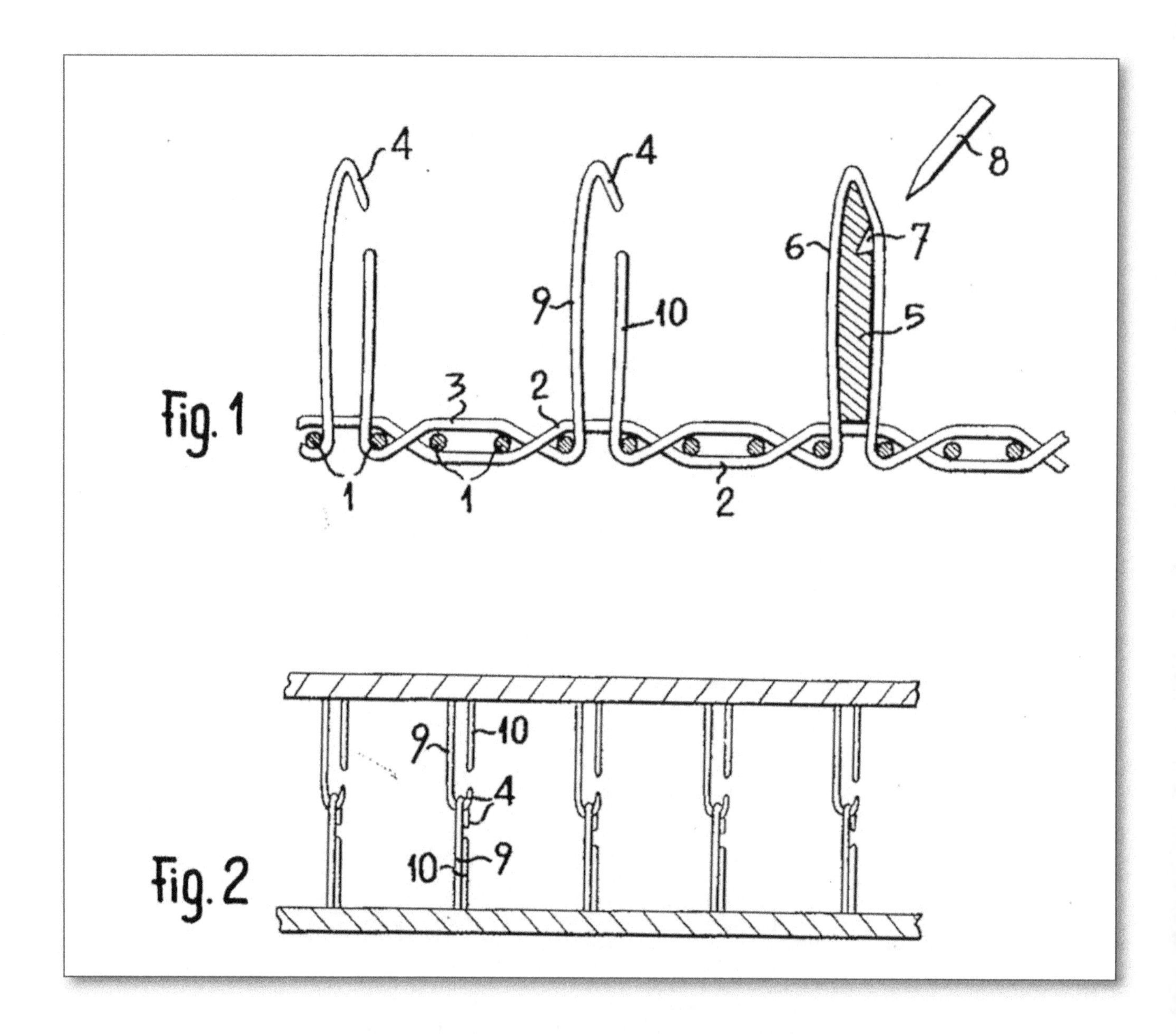

Both the written description and the drawing are of a household object we now call Velcro®, or what we patent practitioners refer to as a "hook-and-loop" type fastener.

Many times, as we begin the project of writing a patent application, we will study the sketches or photos provided by the inventor. We'll mark-up these photos or sketches with numbers and alternate views, and then deliver a jumbled mess to our draftsman, hoping for a magical transformation from illegible disaster to elegantly clean formal patent drawing. More often then not, the magic occurs. Each numbered feature or item is explained in detail in the text, if necessary. But the reader doesn't have to try and picture the invention from words if the image is already there.

VELVET TYPE FABRIC AND METHOD OF PRODUCING SAME
G. DE MESTRAL Sept. 13, 1955 No. 2,717,437

Let's look at another example of magic. The following drawing is of an Apparatus for Manufacturing Glassware. Note how many items are tagged for further description in the patent application text. From G^2 to d^7 to m^3 there are nearly 150 items to be detailed in the application. Imagine if you could only rely on words—these words—to decipher how this incredible machine is assembled and functions.

The plunger-rod *d* moves in the guide c^6, formed at the outer end of the extension c^3 of the frame *c*. Pivoted to the upper ends of said guide c^6 at the point c^7 are the two levers *g*, one at each side thereof. To the outer ends of said levers *g* at the points g^2 are pivoted the two levers *g'*, which at their lower ends are pivoted to the block d^8, said block being secured to the plunger-rod *d*. Links f^4 are pivoted to the inner sides of the segmental plates *f*, as at f^5, said links also being pivoted at their other ends to the pivotal point g^2 of the levers *g* and *g'*. It will thus be seen that as the lever *f'* is moved in the direction of the arrow, Fig. 2, the plates *f* will rock upon the shaft *c'* and by means of the links f^4 will draw the point g^2 of the levers *g* and *g'* toward the standard C. The two sets of levers *g* and *g'* each form a toggle, and as the points c^7 are stationary the pivotal points d^9 of the levers *g'* are forced downwardly, thus forcing the plunger into the mold. As the two segmental plates *f* are fixed

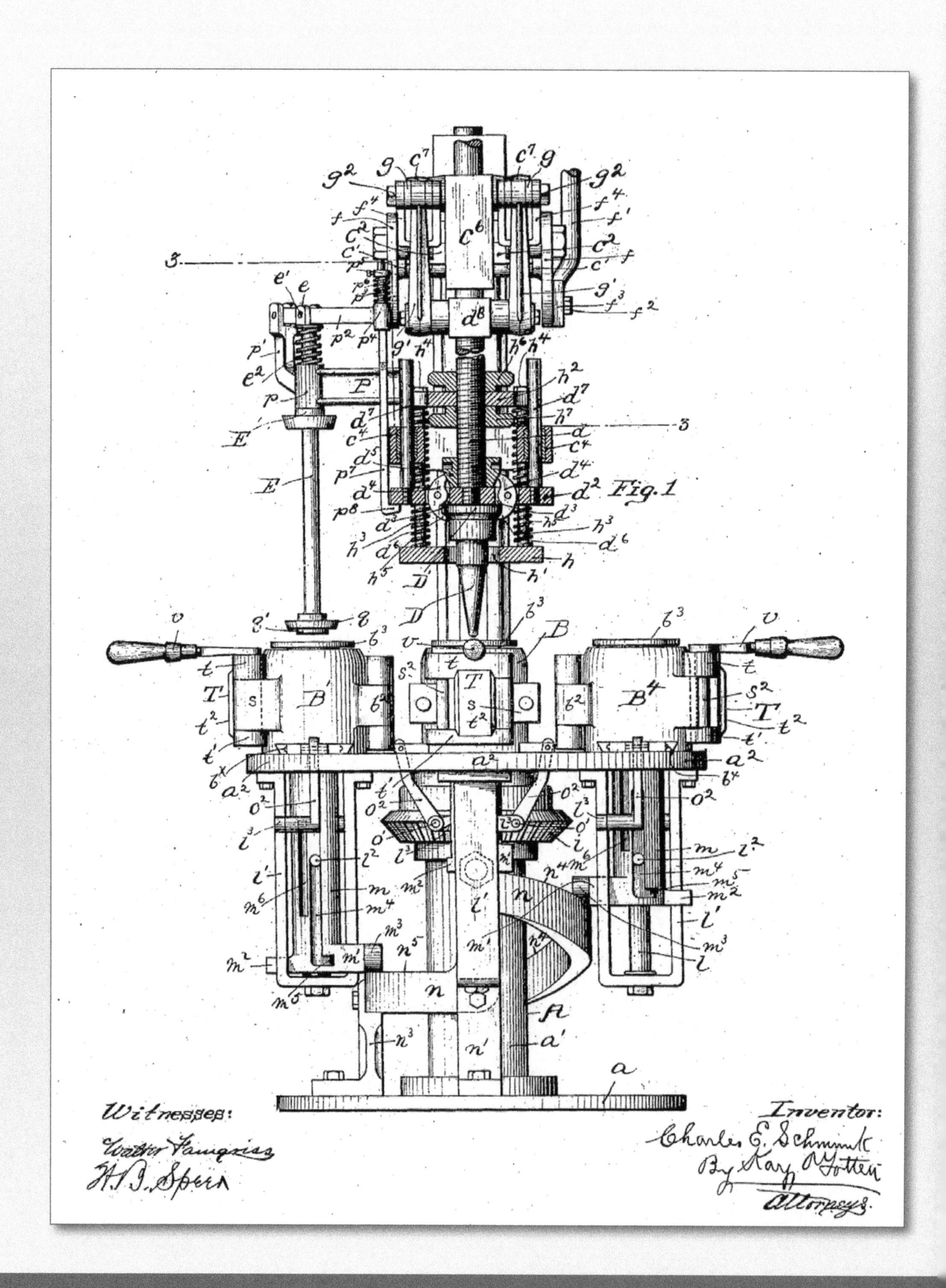

APPARATUS FOR MANUFACTURING GLASSWARE
C.E. SCHMUNK May 31, 1898 No. 604,907

Through the image the drawing provides, the reader is better able to discern the features and workings of the invention. Moreover, and as is true with so much patent art, the drawings are eerily satisfying to study. You may have no idea how a glass-making machine works or even a desire to learn, but looking at the art is a reward all itself.

The drawings on this page also incorporate many technical drawing tools, such as shading and cross sections, which we'll cover in the next chapter.

It's important to note that a typical patent, especially one as complex as this, will have many drawings associated with it. Each will be designed to visually express the invention in such as way as the structure, functionality, and originality can easily be understood.

This Schmunk patent has a total of eleven drawings. Have a look at a few more of them that follow. Note how each brings out a different angle or aspect of the structure. Yet each is uniquely beautiful. in its own right.

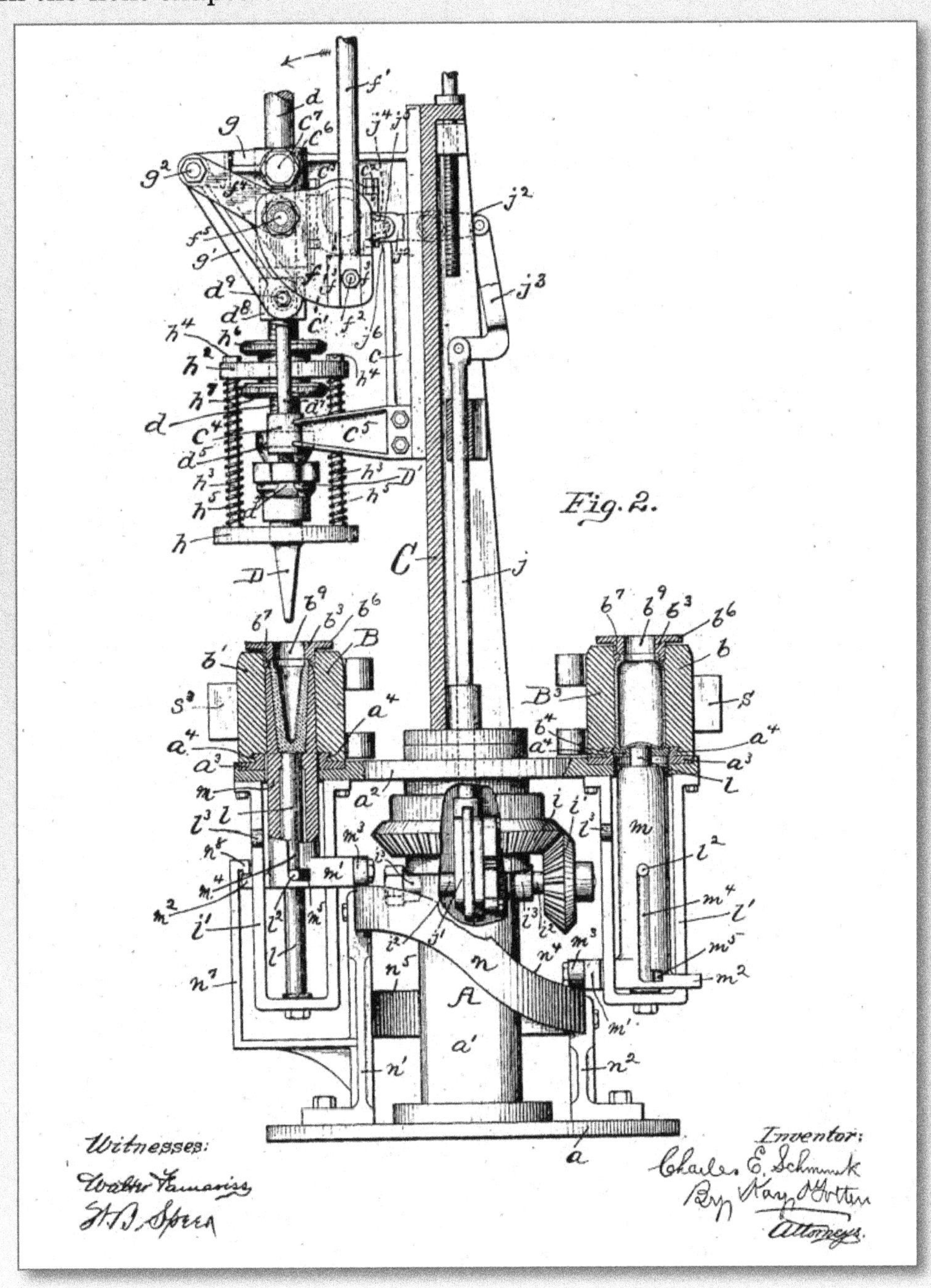

APPARATUS FOR MANUFACTURING GLASSWARE
C.E. SCHMUNK May 31, 1898 No. 604,907

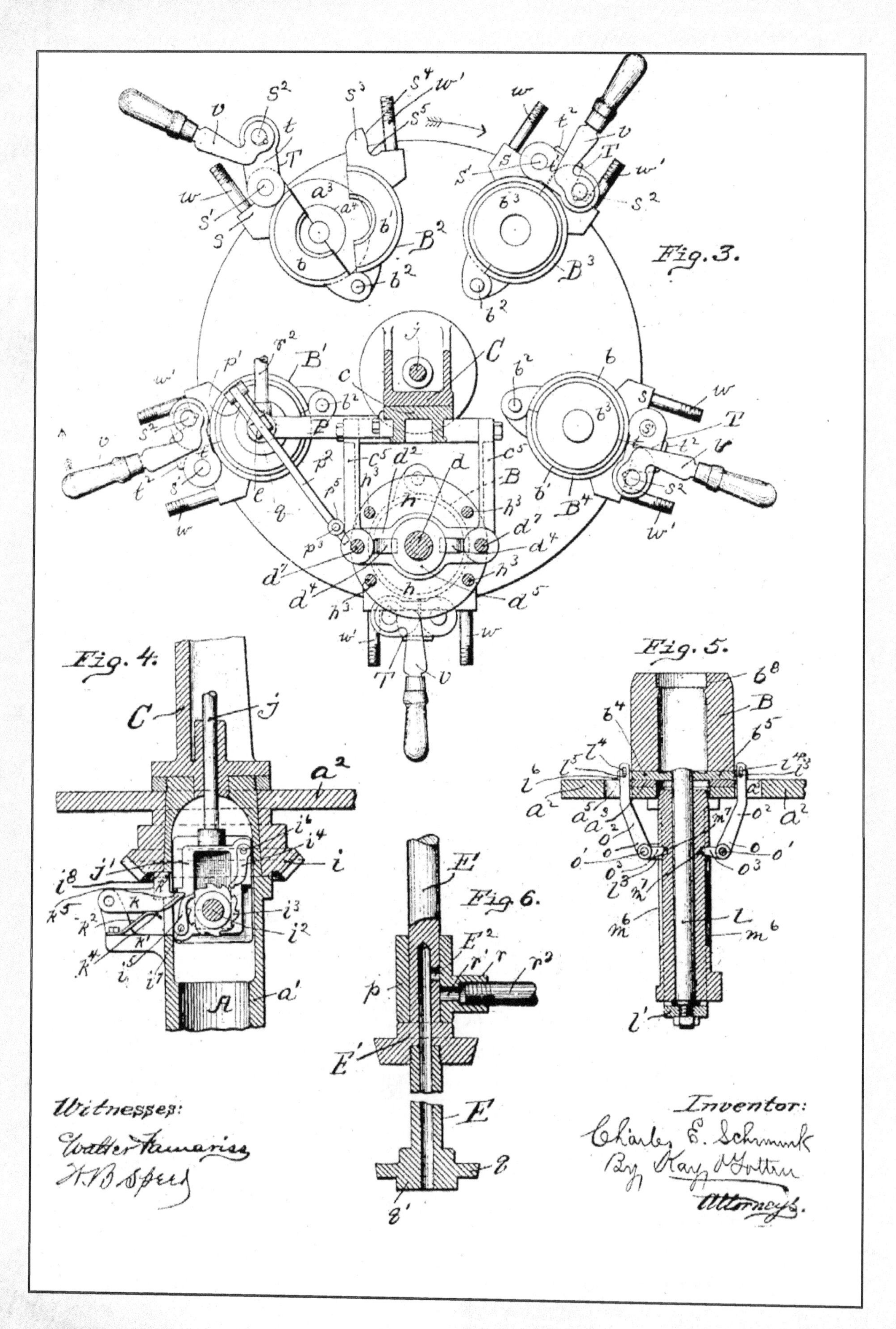

APPARATUS FOR MANUFACTURING GLASSWARE
C.E. SCHMUNK May 31, 1898 No. 604,907

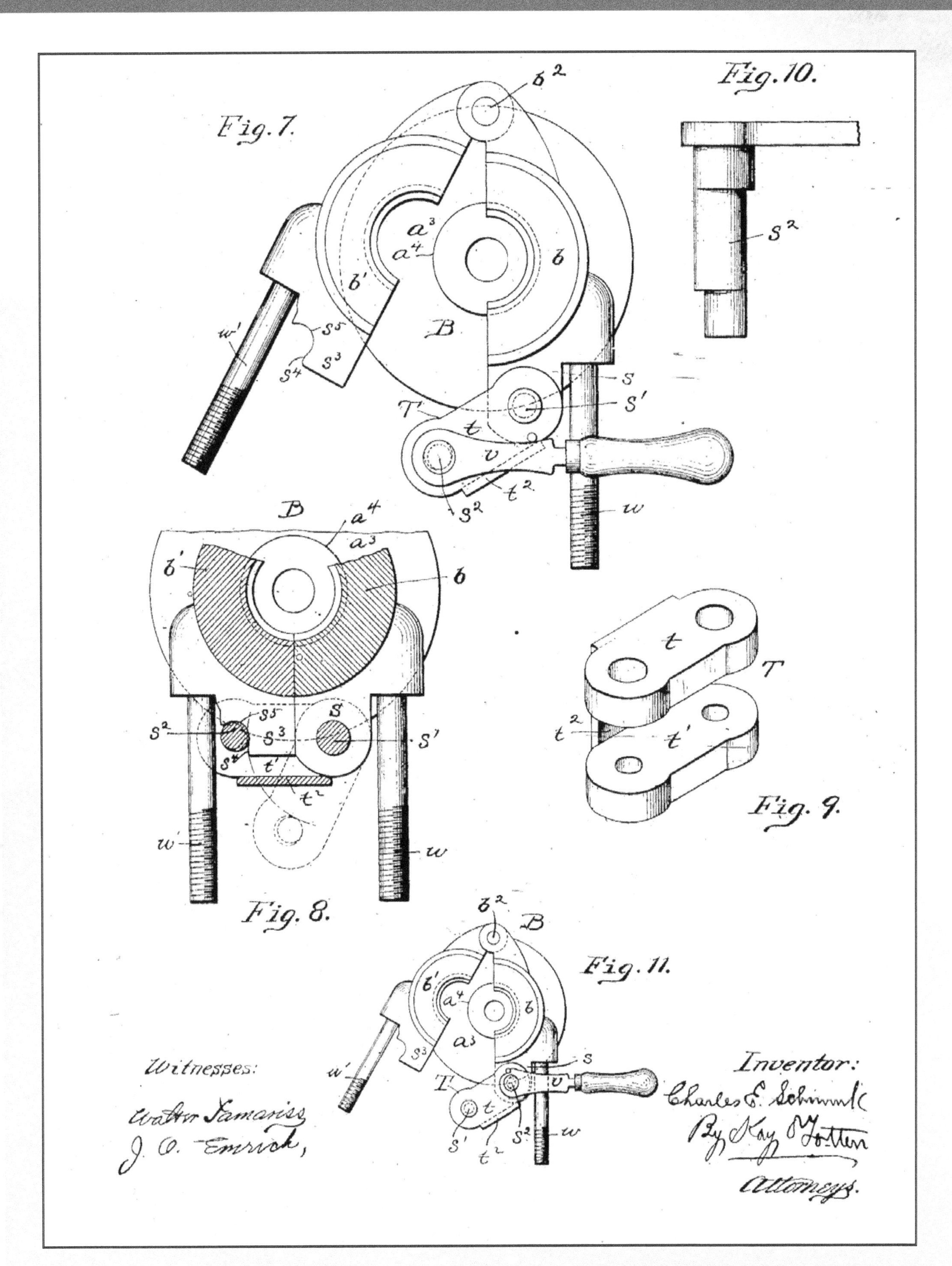

APPARATUS FOR MANUFACTURING GLASSWARE
C.E. SCHMUNK May 31, 1898 No. 604,907

You will notice that very rarely are words used directly on the drawings. We'll see exceptions to this in subsequent examples, but for the most part the drawings are meant to stand alone, text-free, with only numerical call-outs used for reference in the specification. In fact, the PTO manual for patent drawings clearly states that the rule of "as few words as possible" guideline should be used for the drawings themselves:

> "37 CFR 1.84(o)
> (o) Legends. Suitable descriptive legends may be used subject to approval by the Office, or may be required by the examiner where necessary for understanding of the drawing. They should contain as few words as possible."

In other words, special approval is needed if the author wants to add words. A drawing must stand by itself, and it's within this confine that the art can really shine through.

We refer to the "state of the art" when speaking about current technology, and "prior art" when referring to what's come before. Sometimes prior art patents really are "art" in both senses of the word. The following drawing is titled the Art of Coloring Wood, and depicts a clever way to color wood while the tree at right is still growing.

Look at the enormous detail given to the crown of the tree when the mechanics of the invention actually happen farther below.

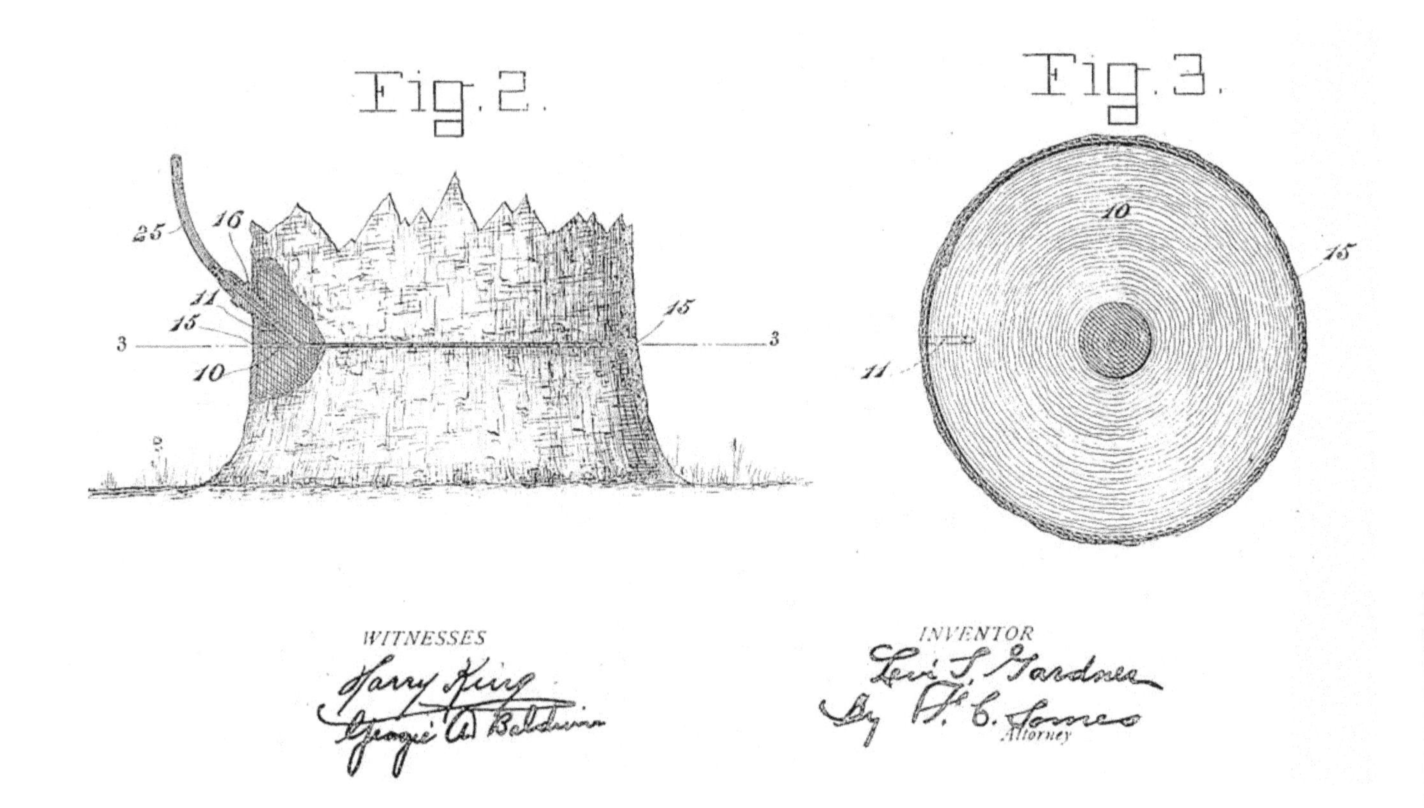

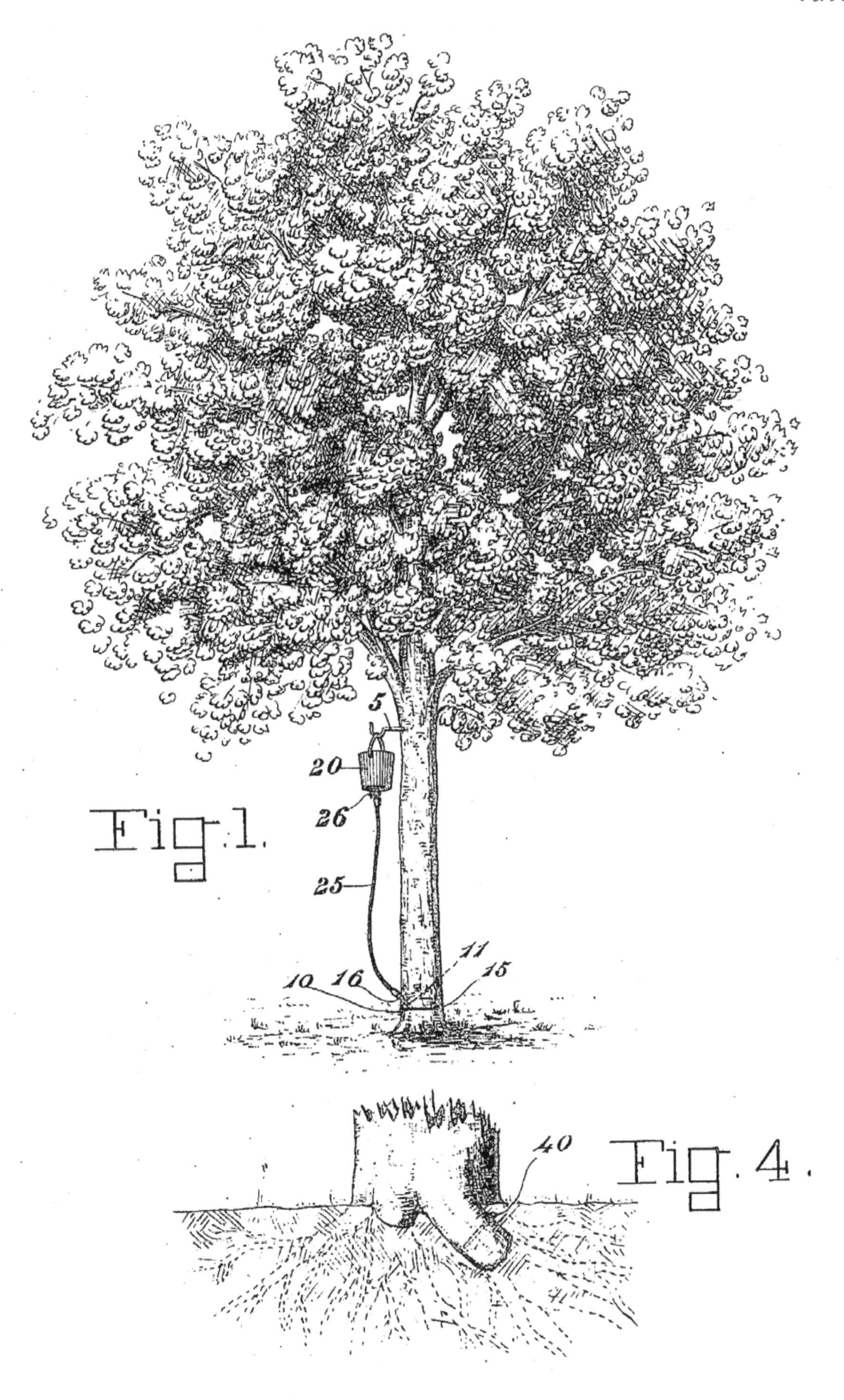

ART OF COLORING WOOD
L.S. GARDNER Mar. 15, 1910 No. 952,245

The following drawing is another beautiful example of the pride taken in the application and presentation of the patent. It's titled the Art of Compiling Statistics and was meant to be used in organizing population census numbers. One doesn't usually associate statistics and census numbers with art, but the illustrator for this patent did, and the drawings are beautiful representations of the machine his client created.

Note how six drawings, each with a different view, can be used to illustrate the invention on just a single page.

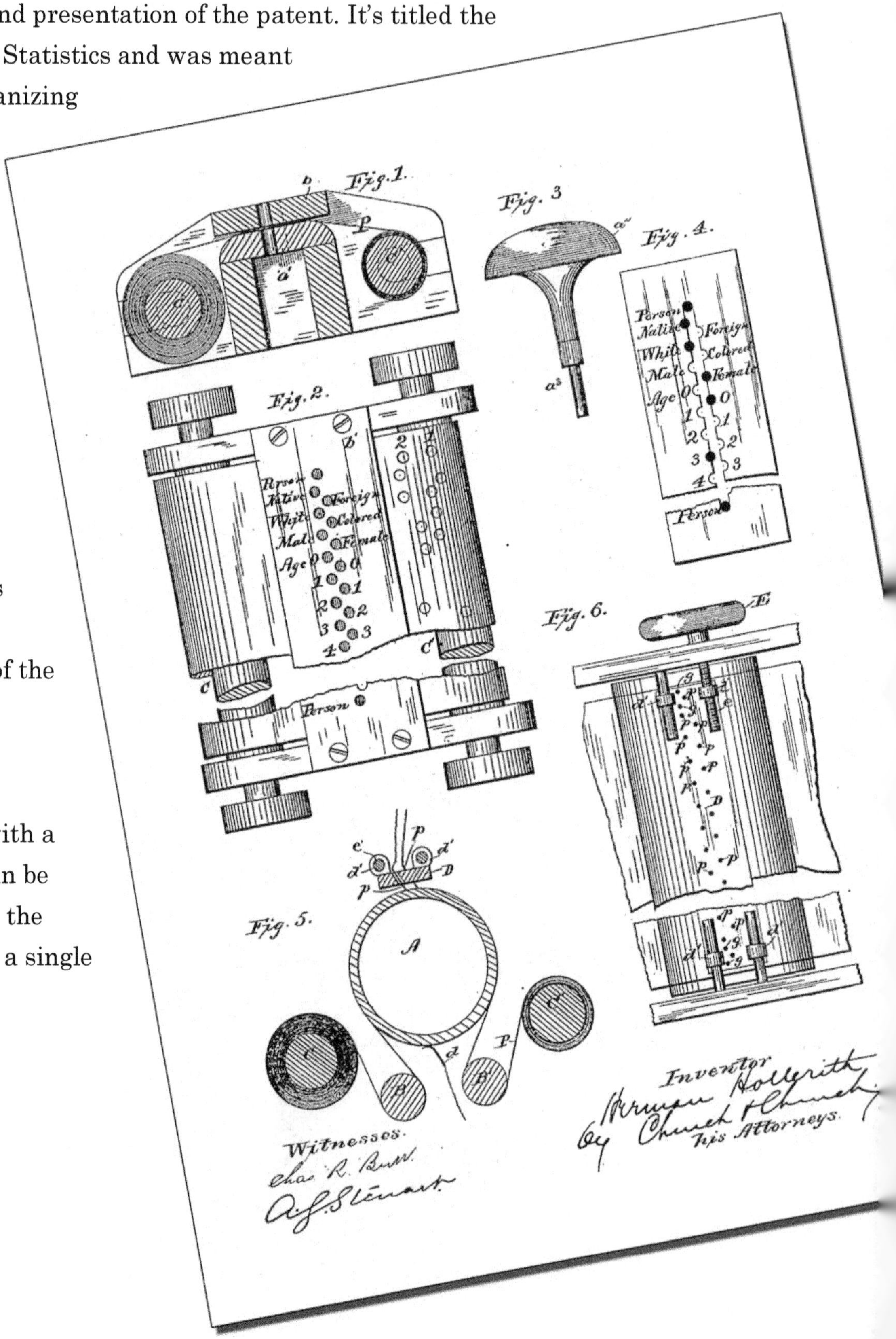

ART OF COMPILING STATISTICS
H. HOLLERITH Jan. 8, 1889 No. 395,782

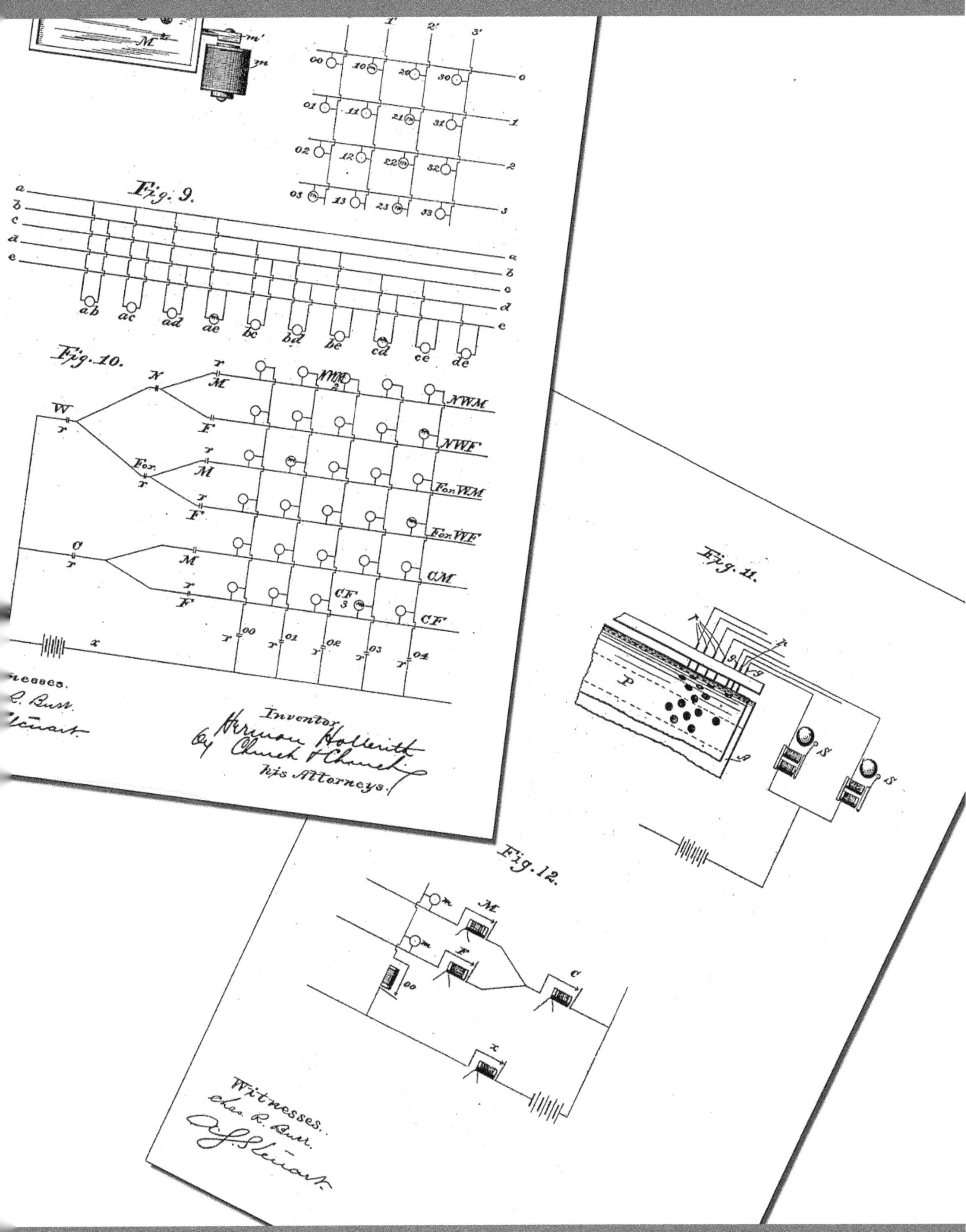
Fig. 9.
Fig. 10.
Inventor
Herman Hollerith
By Church & Church
his Attorneys.
Fig. 11.
Fig. 12.
Witnesses.
Chas. R. Burr.

Three different flavors of patents exist; utility, design, and plant (which we'll explore in a subsequent chapter). A utility patent teaches and protects how something works, the way it operates, and it's "theory of operation." The Art of Compiling Statistics patent above is an example of this. It clearly explains, visually and in writing, how the invention works.

A design patent protects how something looks, or its ornamental appearance. One could obtain a design patent on a vehicle wheel, for example, but not how a wheel works. There's no way to get a utility patent on the wheel since the wheel—that is, the way it works—is already in the public domain. However, the specific appearance of a wheel, or vehicle rim, for example, can certainly be patented with a design patent.

For example, look at these beautiful drawings of a Harley Davidson motorcycle engine. This patent does not protect how the engine works, but rather how it looks. Design patent drawings are richly detailed and often beautifully rendered because it's the look of the object that is being protected. Again, several different angles are shown in order to show every side and feature of the object being patented.

Notice the attention to the design detail and shading. In design patents there is very little text because the drawing does virtually all the talking. These are truly drawings you can frame and display.

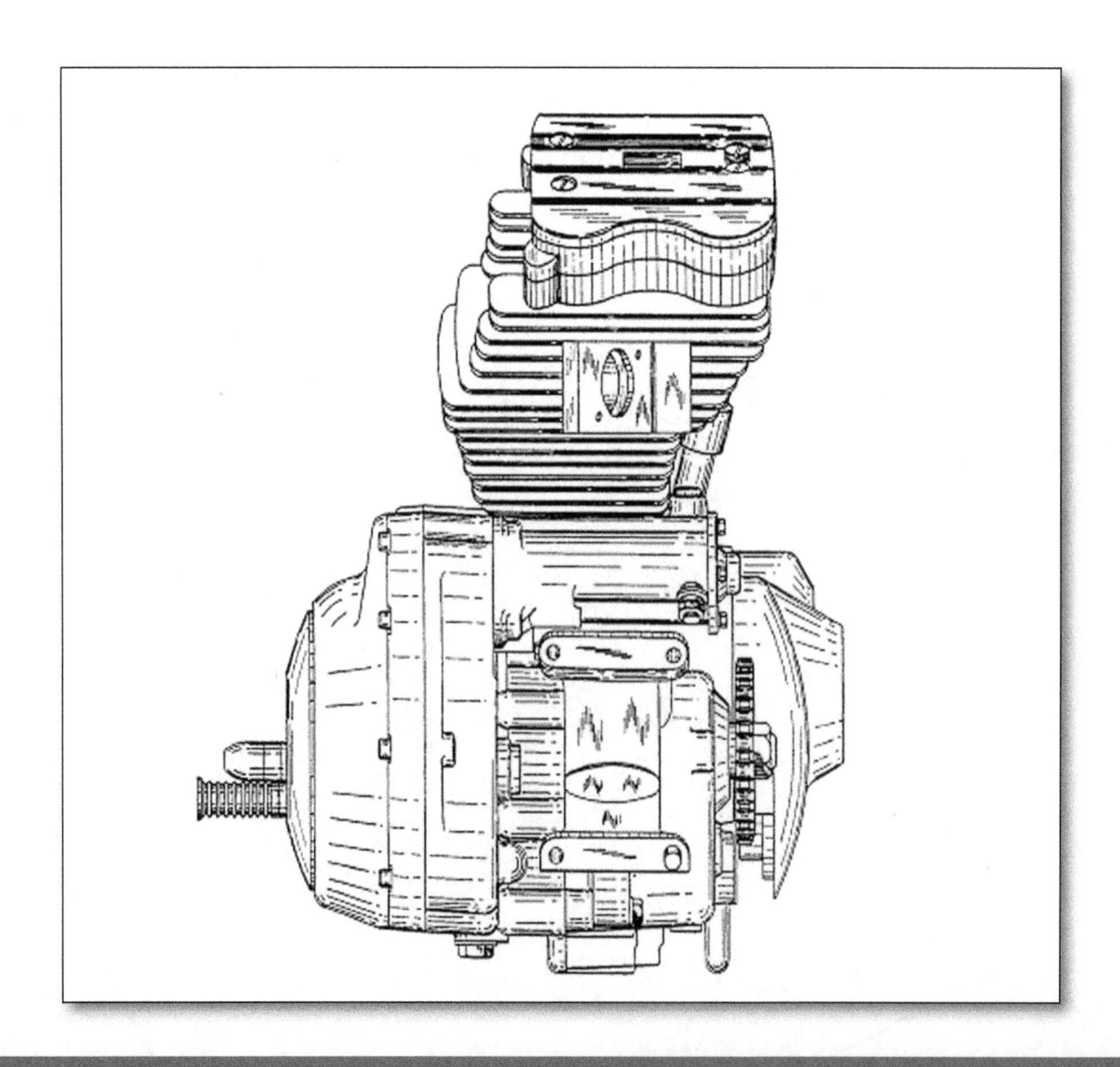

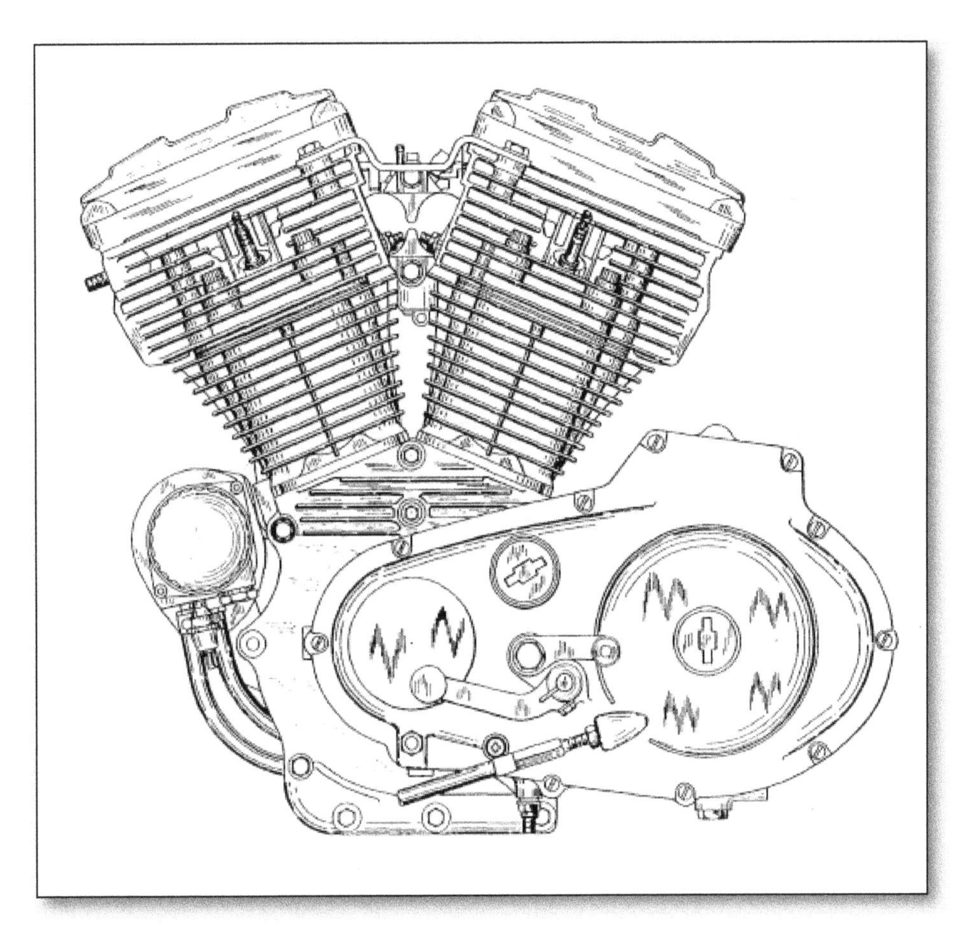

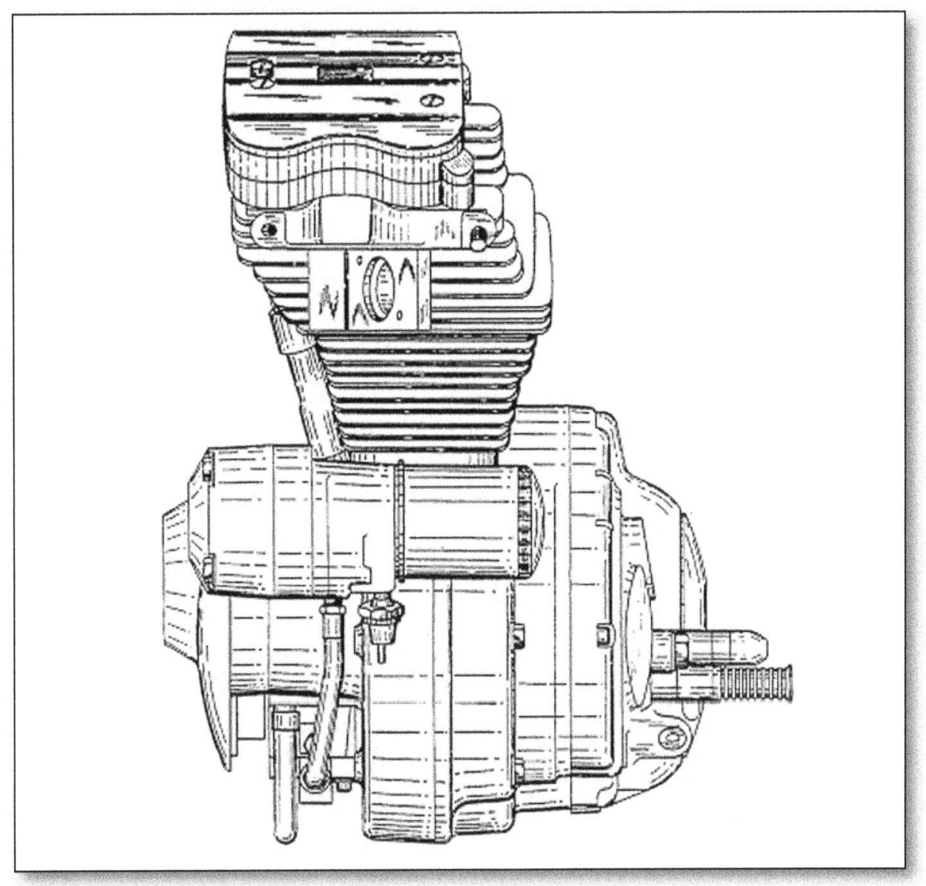

MOTERCYCLE ENGINE

W. G. DAVIDSON Feb. 16, 1988 No. D294,264

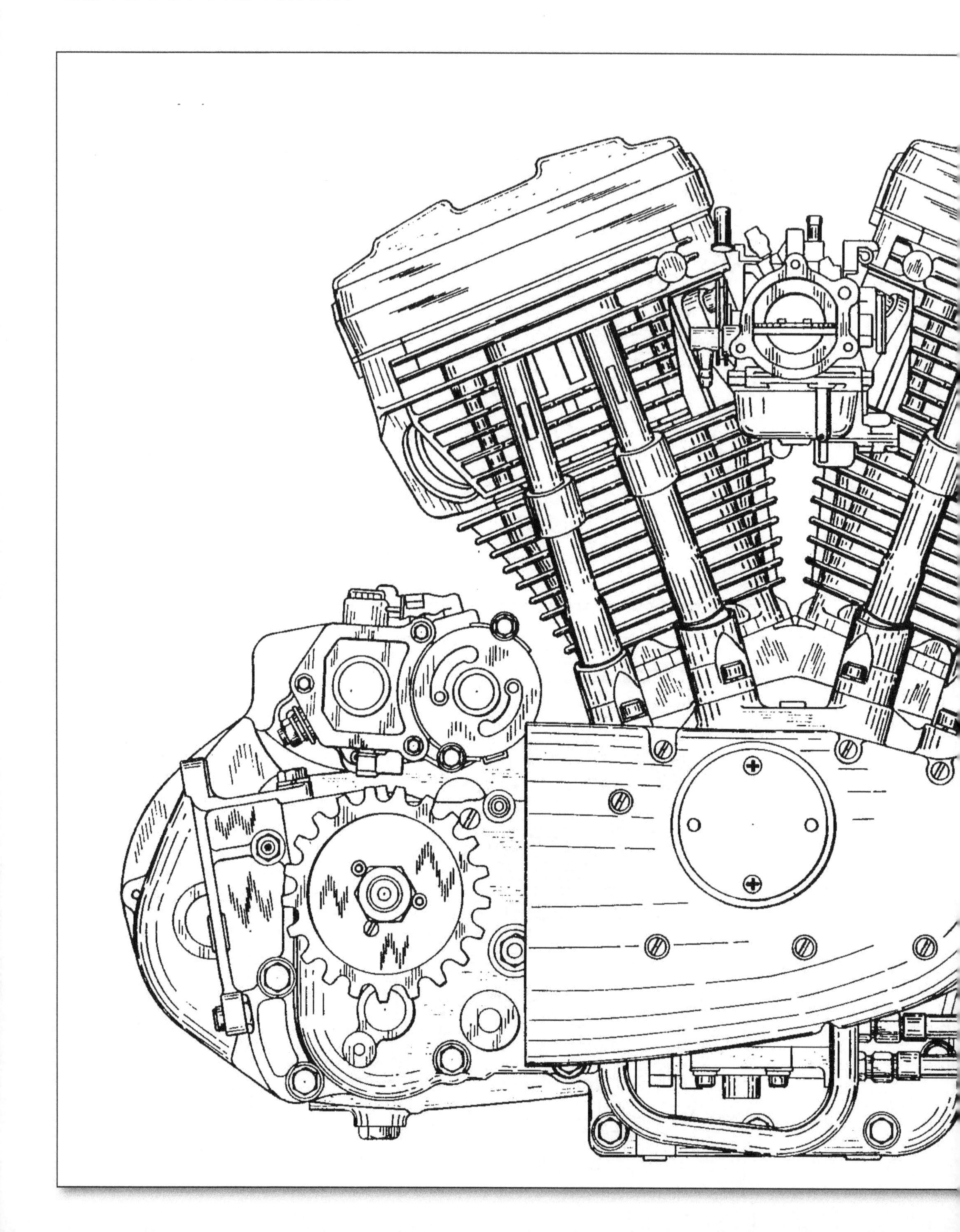

W. G. DAVIDSON

MOTERCYCLE ENGINE
Feb. 16, 1988

No. D294,264

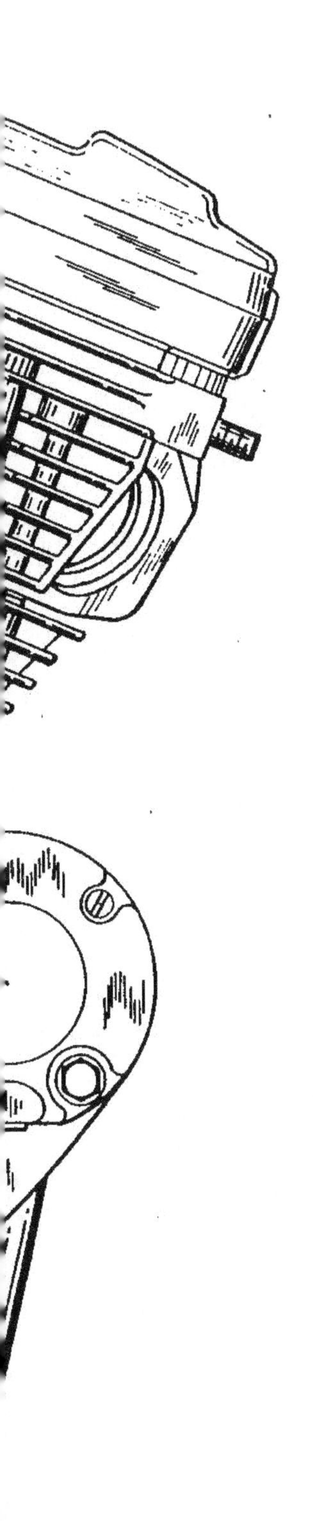

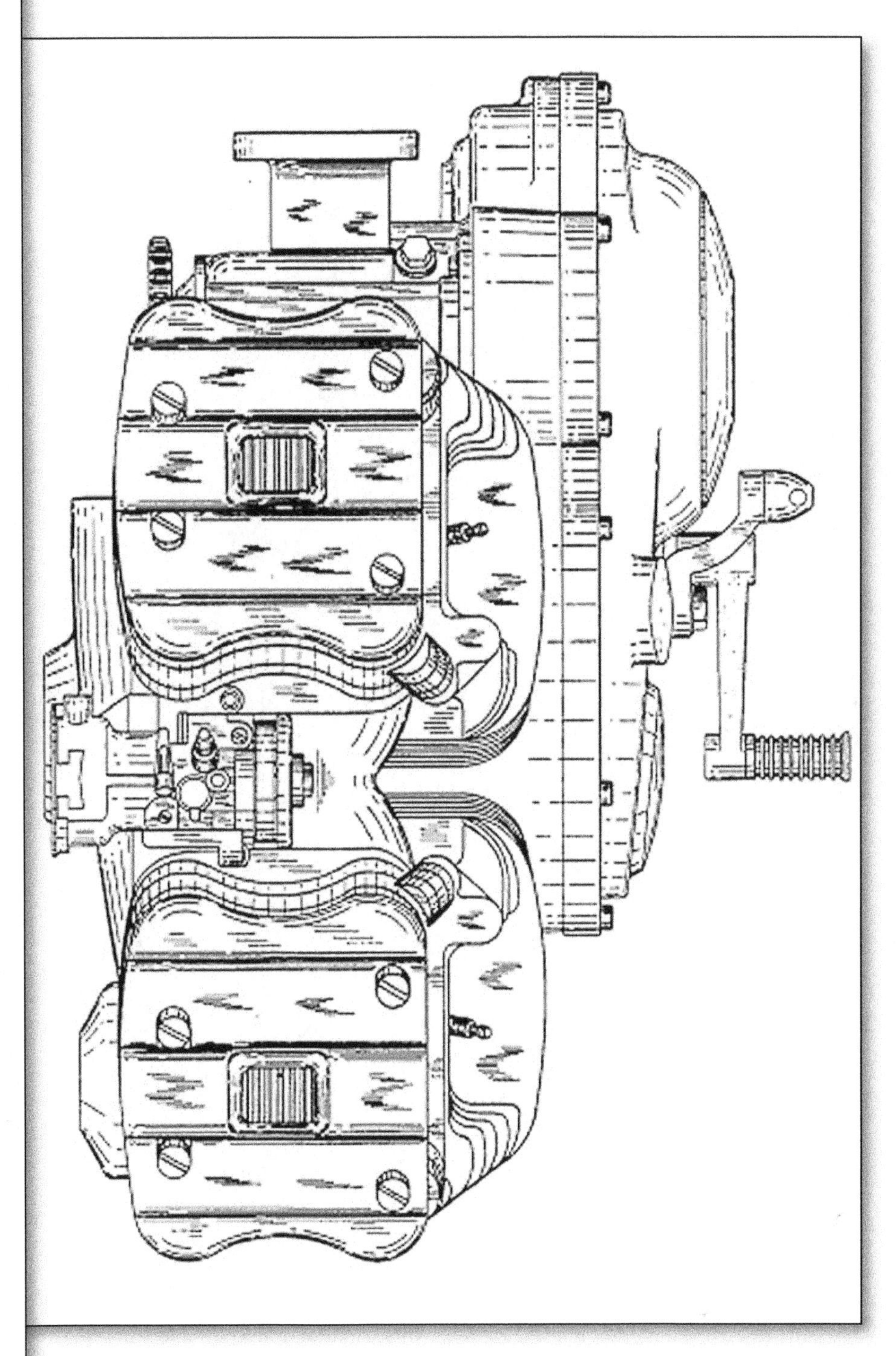

Here is a design patent you might recognize by a man named George Lucas...

Fig. 1.

Fig. 2.

Fig. 3.

Fig. 4.

G.W. LUCAS
TOY FIGURE
Aug. 10, 1982
No. D265,754

Notice how each side of Yoda is displayed to show every feature. FIGS. 1 and 2 show front and rear perspective views. The other views are from each side, and yes, even from the bottom.

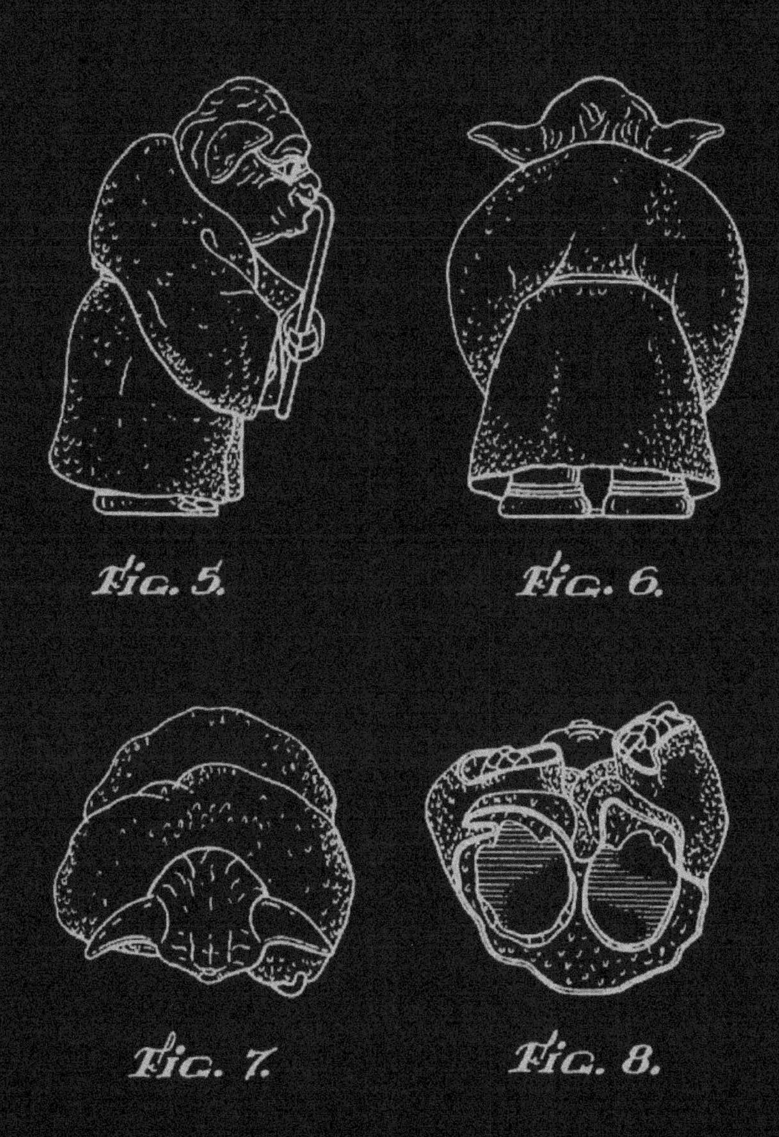

"Meditate on this I will."

~Yoda

Here's a design patent that has become a symbol of America and the freedom for which she stands. This patent, from 1879, was published before the rules were in place requiring all sides of the object to be illustrated.

LIBERTY ENLIGHTENING THE WORLD.

A. BARTHOLDI DESGIN FOR A STATUE Feb. 18, 1879 No. 11,023

Notice the extensive shading in the drawing to depict the folds in Liberty's robe. Even the background has been cared for in excruciating detail. India ink is unforgiving in that a line drawn is a permanent line. These were the days before CTRL-Z. The amount of time and attention involved with this single figure must have been enormous.

The style for design patent drawings has evolved over time, as has the style for everything from hair to cars to…crash helmets. Look at this modern design patent from 2010.

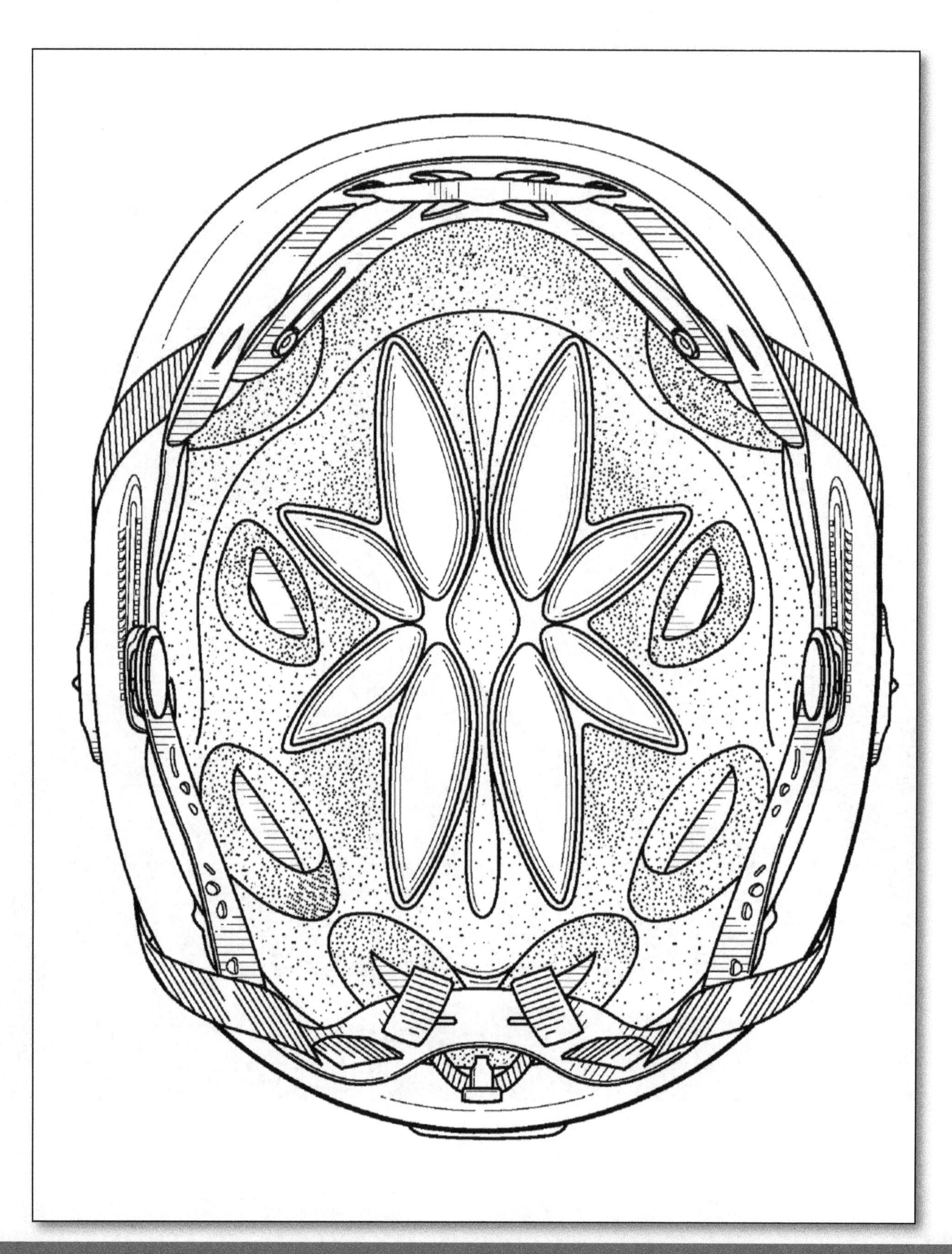

PAUL PETZL
CRASH HELMET
Nov. 30, 2010
No. D628,346

What is truly amazing is that all of these beautiful drawings are done within stale, art-less governmental guidelines. We've all had our eyes glaze-over reading government forms from the Department of Motor Vehicles, the IRS, even on the back of a fishing license from the Department of Fish and Game. The United States Patent and Trademark Office is no different.

Below I've copied a sample paragraph from the PTO's Utility Patent Drawing Guide. This section covers the parameters for a sectional view of an object. The entire manual, by the way, is 135 pages long. Each and every patent drawing must meet the requirements set forth, and this paragraph will give you a clear idea of how exciting the reading is!

> "37 CFR 1.84(h)
>
> (3) Sectional views. The plane upon which a sectional view is taken should be indicated on the view from which the section is cut by a broken line. The ends of the broken line should be designated by Arabic or Roman numerals corresponding to the view number of the sectional view, and should have arrows to indicate the direction of sight. Hatching must be used to indicate section portions of an object, and must be made by regularly spaced oblique parallel lines spaced sufficiently apart to enable the lines to be distinguished without difficulty. Hatching should not impede the clear reading of the reference characters and lead lines. If it is not possible to place reference characters outside the hatched area, the hatching may be broken off wherever reference characters are inserted. Hatching must be at a substantial angle to the surrounding axes or principal lines, preferably 45°. A cross section must be set out and drawn to show all of the materials as they are shown in the view from which the cross section was taken. The parts in cross section must show proper material(s) by hatching with regularly spaced parallel oblique strokes, the space between strokes being chosen on the basis of the total area to be hatched. The various parts of a cross section of the same item should be hatched in the same manner and should accurately and graphically indicate the nature of the material(s) that is illustrated in cross section. The hatching of juxtaposed different elements must be angled in a different way. In the case of large areas, hatching may be confined to an edging drawn around the entire inside of the outline of the area to be hatched. Different types of hatching should have different conventional meanings as regards the nature of a material seen in cross section."

As if this isn't punishment enough, look at this comments section meant to clarify the above...

> 37 CFR 1.84(h) [COMMENTS]
>
> With respect to 37 CFR 1.84(h)(3), section lines should be designated by numbers corresponding to the view number and not by letters.
>
> Hatching as described in 37 CFR 1.84(h)(3) and shading as described in 37 CFR 1.84(m) are not the same technique:
>
> Hatching is used in cross-sectional views to show "section portions of an object" and consists of "regularly spaced oblique parallel lines." Sometimes a particular form of hatching (see Appendix 3) denotes the material of which a section portion is made.
>
> Shading (see Page 28) is used in perspective views to indicate the "surface or shape of spherical, cylindrical, and conical elements of an object," although "Flat parts may also be lightly shaded." Spaced lines are preferred for shading, although stippling and other techniques may be used.
>
> Example 6 in Appendix 4 shows a use of hatching that is an exception to 37 CFR 1.84(h)(3).

It's within this desert environment that the world of patent art somehow blossoms. The rules are necessary because the system is designed to protect each invention by requiring a consistent and well-defined disclosure. If a clear process of exactly how to go about explaining the invention doesn't exist, how could it ever be protected? And if inventions aren't protectable, the spirit of entrepreneurship and the American Dream is undermined. It's this same spirit that is expressed in patent art.

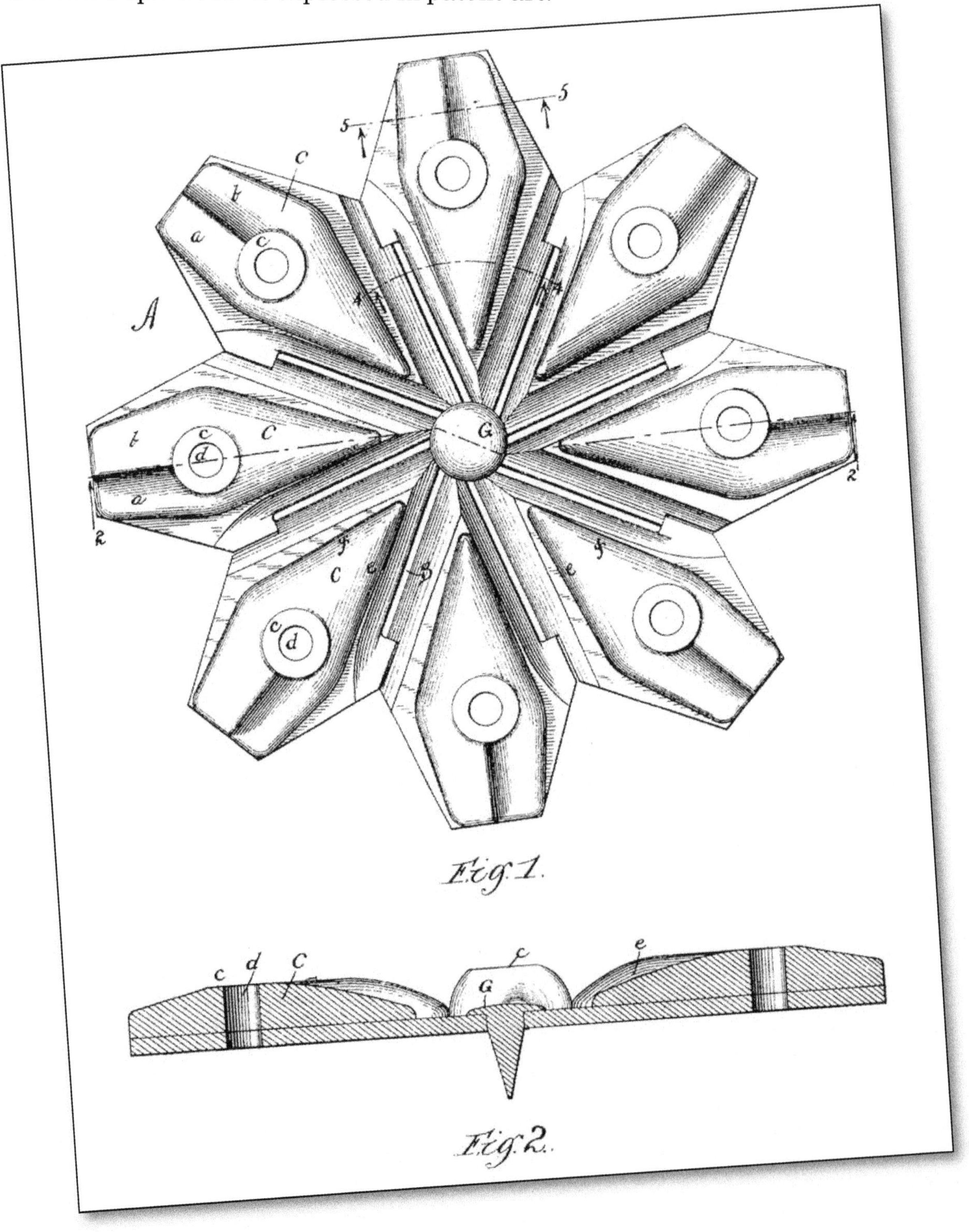

G.A. LOWRY — HEAD PLATE FOR COTTON PRESSES — Feb. 6, 1900 — No. 32,195

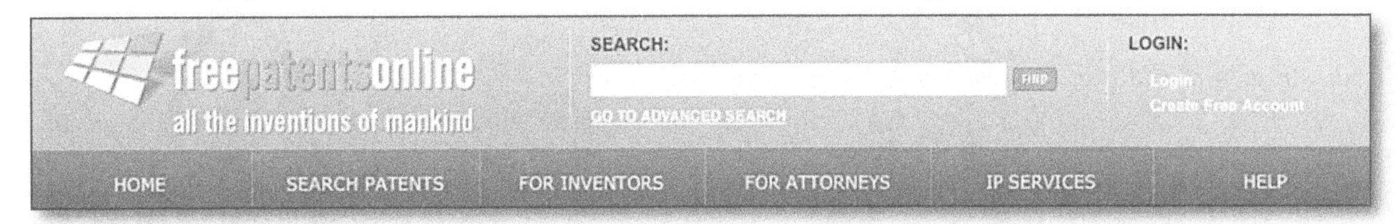

How can you find patent drawings today? As with so much else in the world, it's become simple: freepatentsonline.com or google.com/patents. Both have powerful search and viewing tools. Type in the keyword or patent number and off you go!

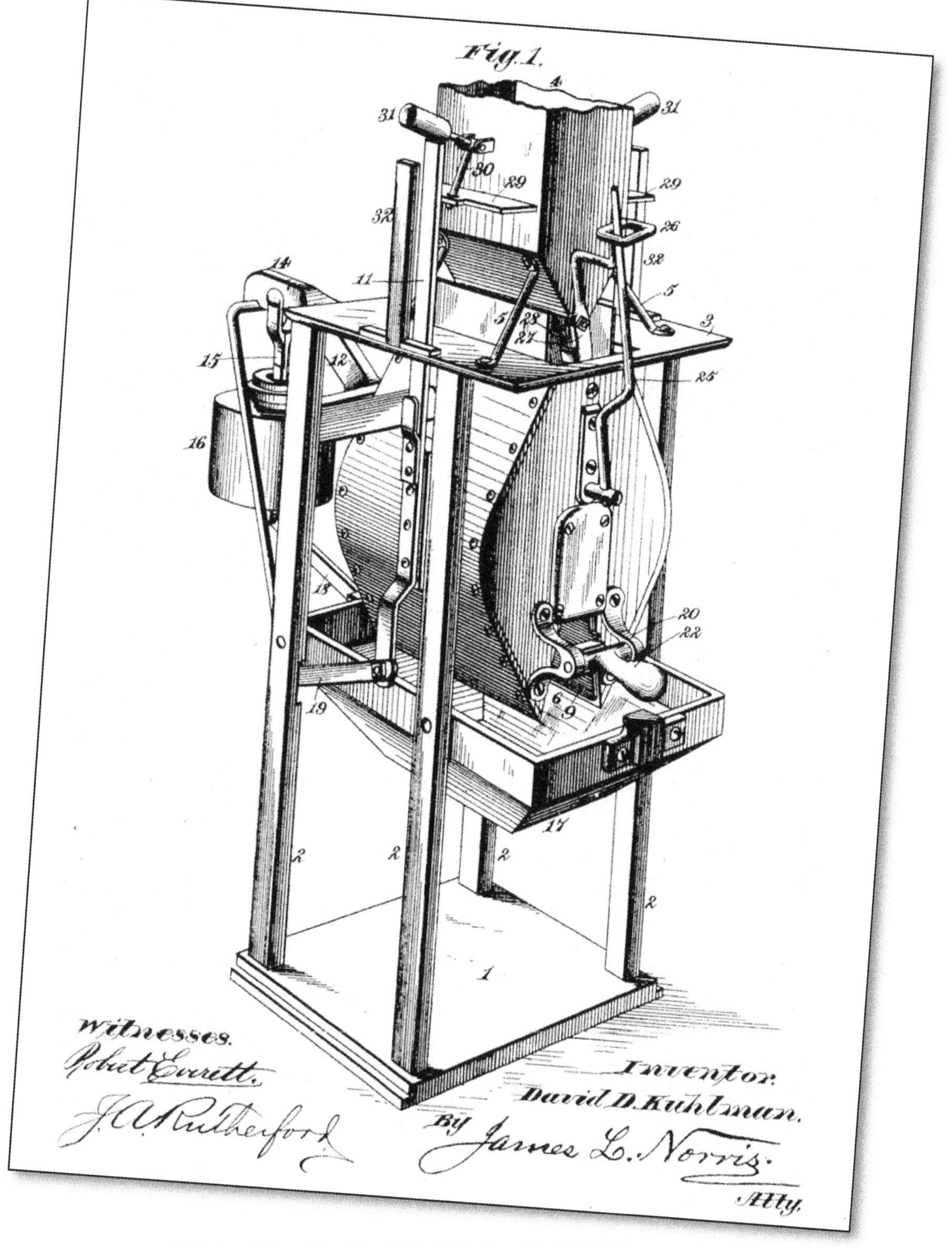

D. D. KUHLMAN AUTOMATIC GRAIN WEIGHING APPARATUS Oct. 16, 1883 No. 286,934

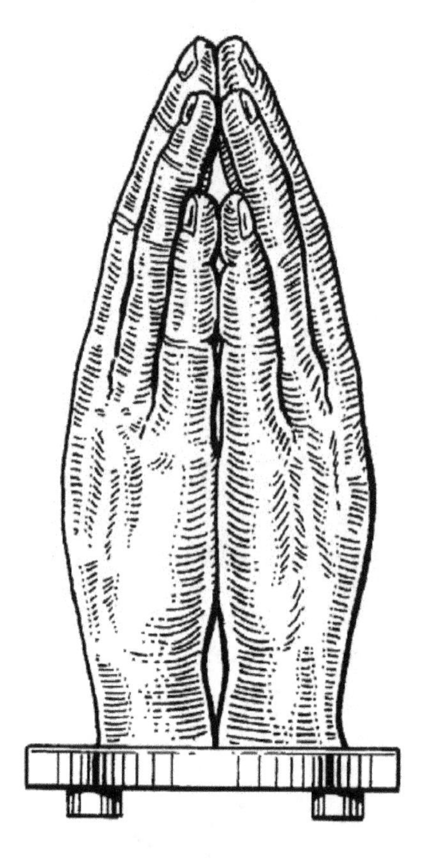

FIG. 3.

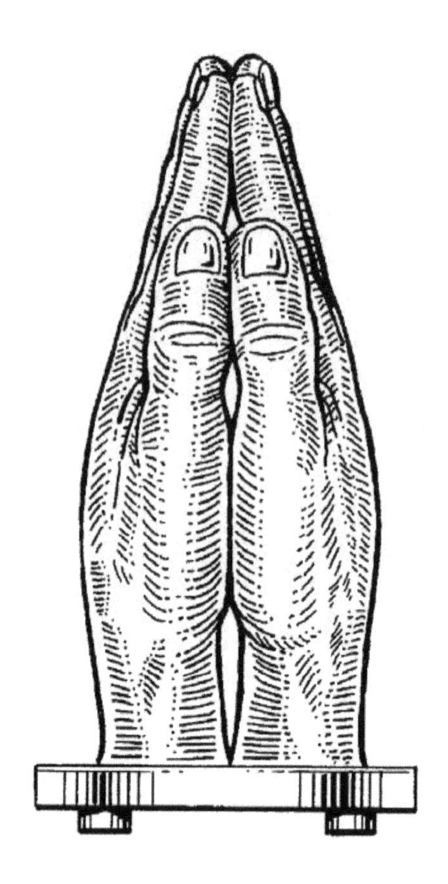

FIG. 5.

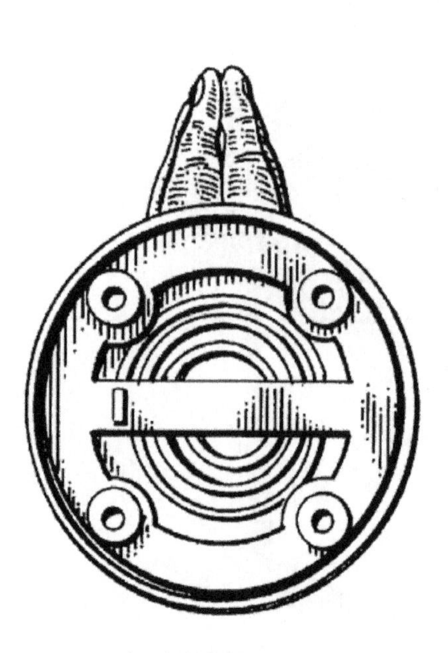

FIG. 4.

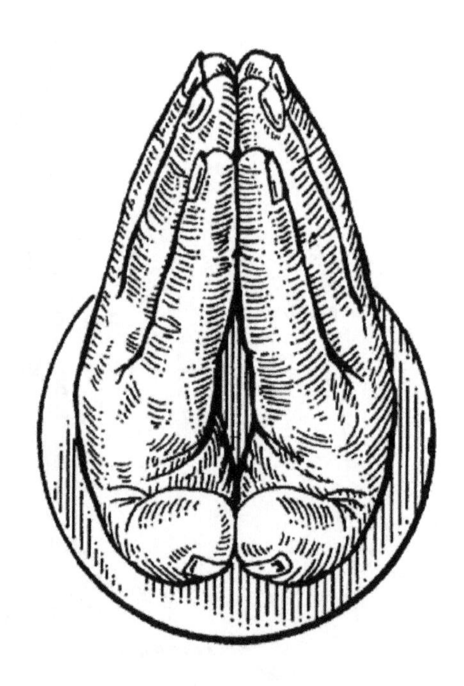

FIG. 6.

Chapter 2

Tools of the Art

As we dig more deeply into the subtleties of patent art and what makes it special, it's essential to understand the rules the artist must follow. To provide a structured environment where the legal rights of an idea can be established without question, regulations have been defined and are strictly upheld.

Let's look at a few of these rules in order to develop a more robust appreciation for patent art.

Shading - Two primary forms of shading exist; one is called straight lined or spaced lined shading, and the other is called stippling. This drawing of a hood ornament is an excellent example of straight lined shading. Note how, other than the outline of the hands, the entire drawing is depicted using short, straight lines.

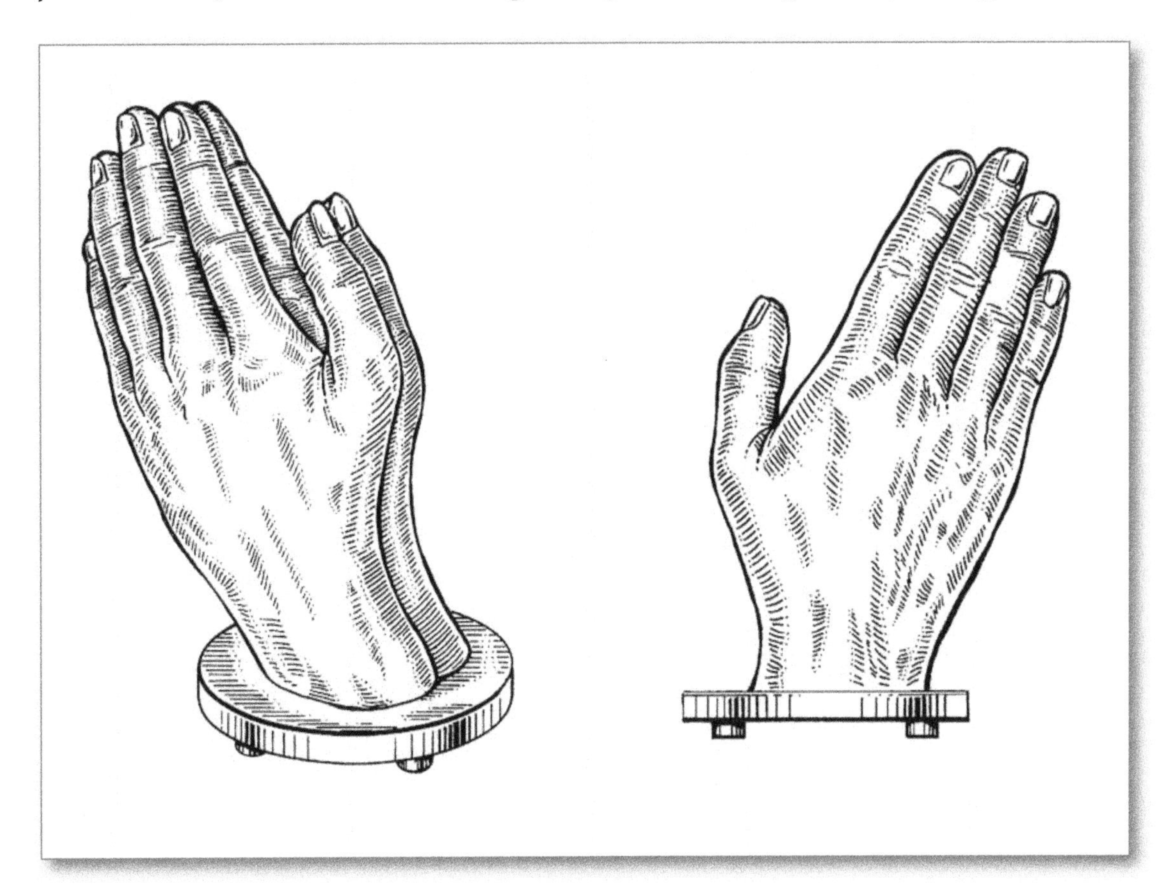

THOMAS T. WASHINGTON SR. HOOD ORNAMENT Nov. 17, 1998 No. D401,202

Another example of straight line shading is this beautiful wristwatch. Note how the lines across the face of the watch (called oblique shading lines) represent a transparent glass surface. The viewer has no doubt as to which elements are transparent and which are opaque; all done with straight line shading. The beveled levels of the frame are also elegantly depicted.

WRIST WATCH
NOBUHIKO NAKANISHI Mar. 7, 1995 No. D356,042

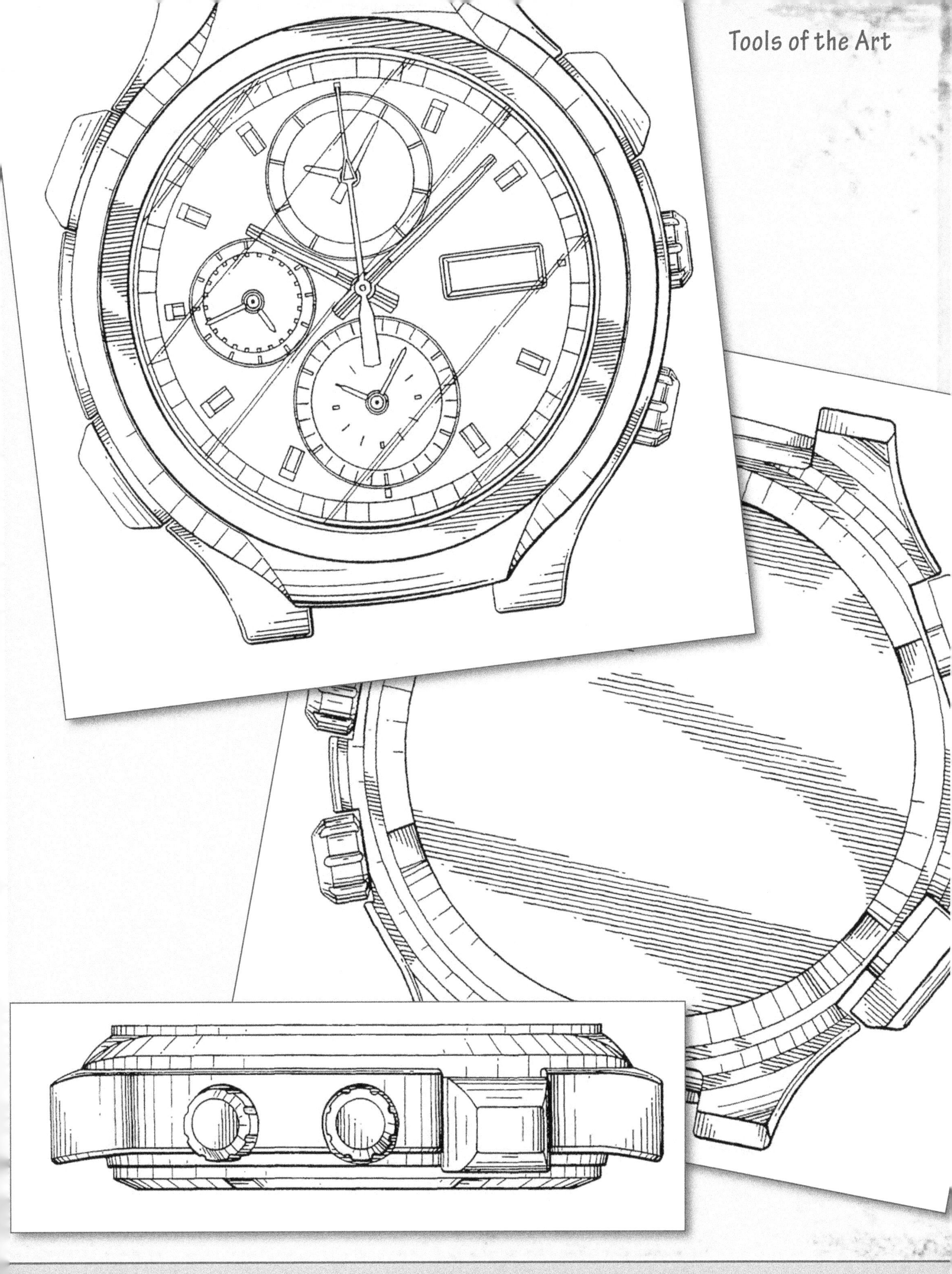

WRIST WATCH
NOBUHIKO NAKANISHI Mar. 7, 1995 No. D356,042

Stippling refers to an alternative shading technique using dots. The drawing below is a superb example of this. Note how beneath the shoelace eyes the straight line method is also used. On the tongue of the shoe and beneath the ankle, checkered lines are the standard symbol for a type of woven fabric. Stippling has traditionally been done by... you guessed it... repeatedly dropping one's pen onto the paper in a painstaking and laborious process.

These tools all abide by the rules and regulations of the PTO. Yet the drawings have been crafted with a life of their own.

SHOE UPPER
JOHNATHAN H. WERMAN Sep. 29, 1998 No. D398,751

GOLF CART
W. B. BUCHECKER OCT. 21, 1997 No. D385,219

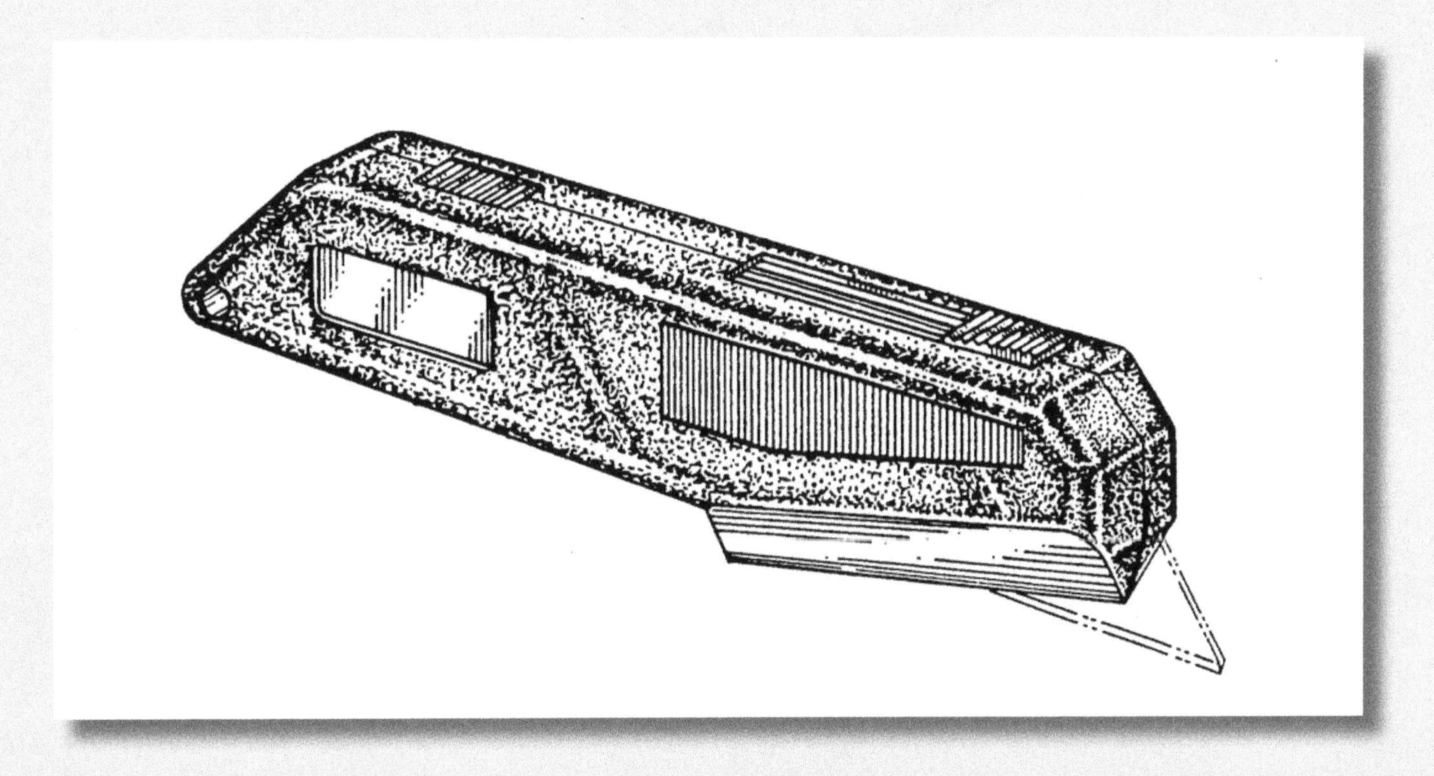

CUTTING TOOL
J. H. PERKINS JULY 5, 1994 No. D348,383

The fun design below for a pacifier shows the artistic advantages of using stippling. In theory the straight line method of shading would suffice, but stippling allows for more subtle work.

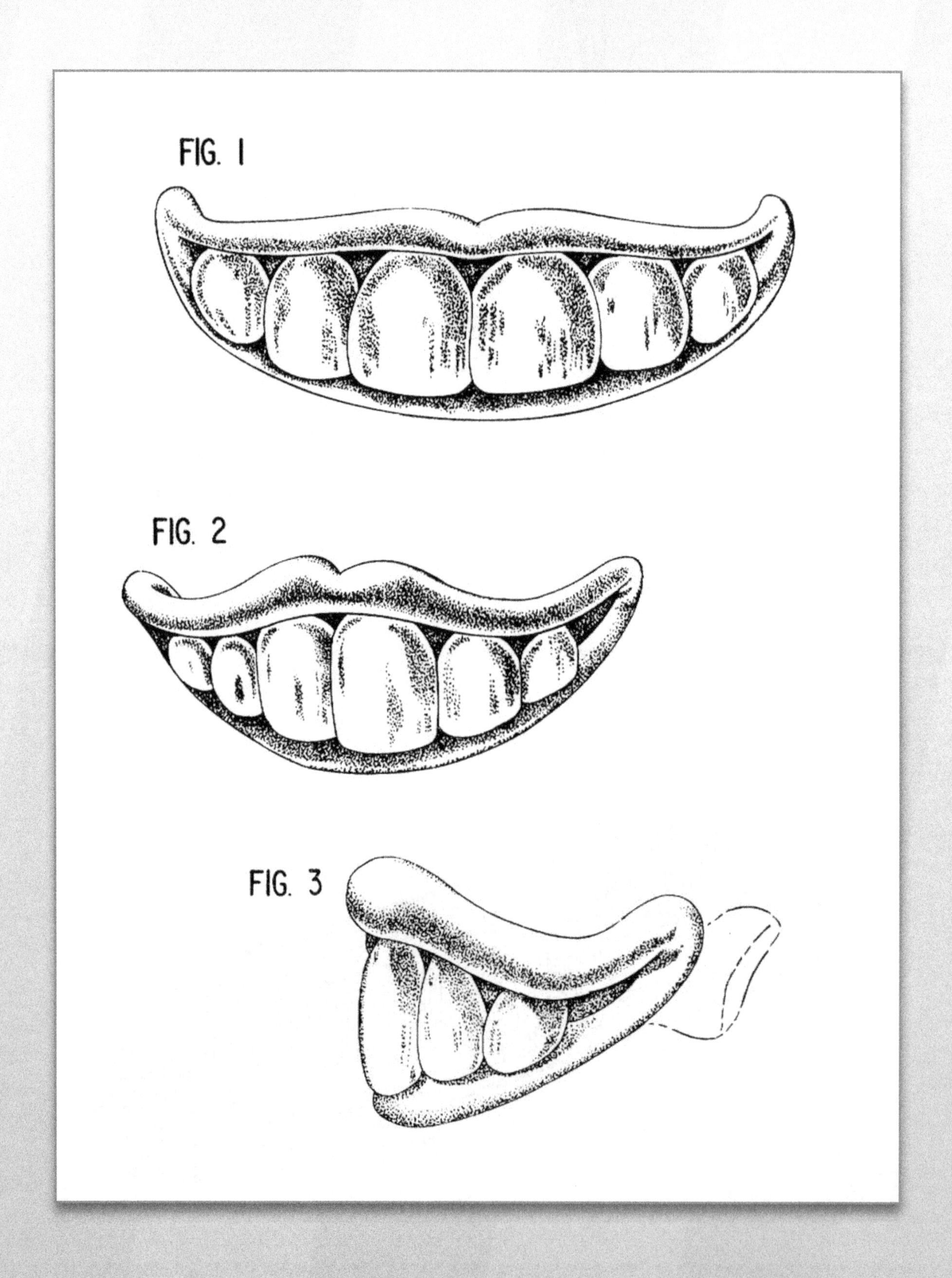

PACIFIER
ROBERT L. QUALLY Oct. 18, 1983 No. D271,052

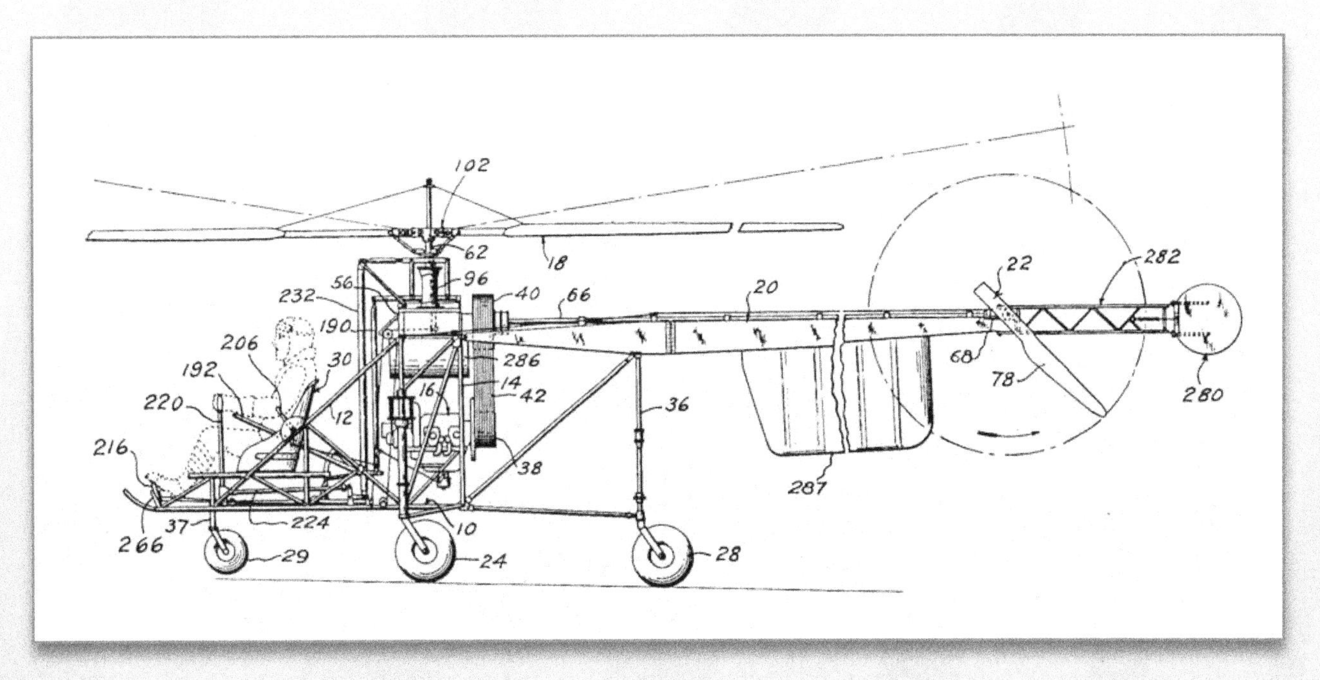

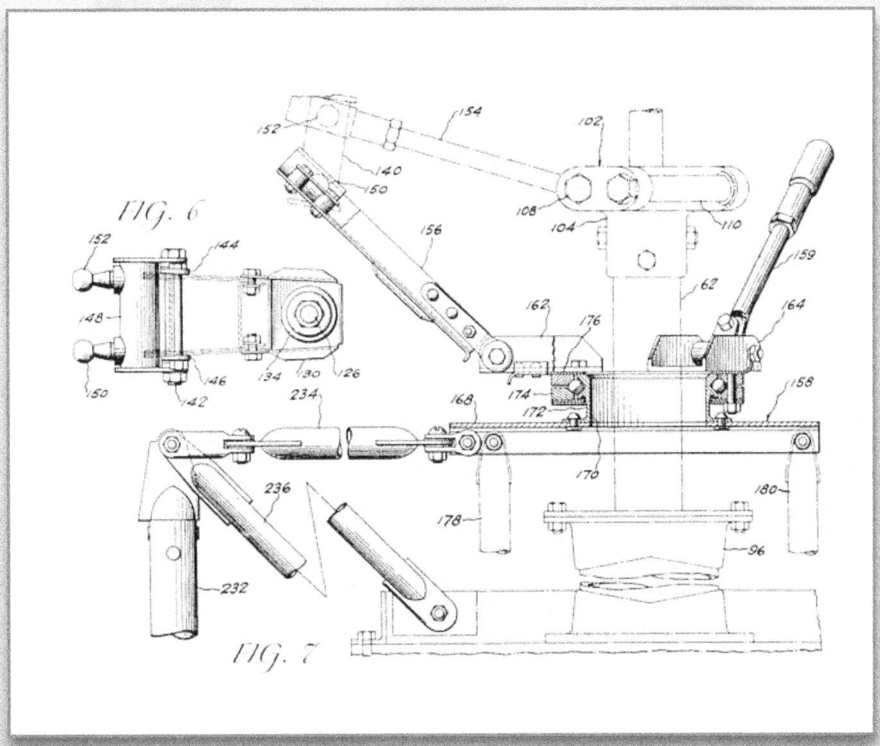

Broken lines are used to show aspects of the environment that aren't part of the patented information, but yet help to place the object in context. For example, in this patent application for a direct-lift airplane, i.e., an early helicopter, the pilot isn't part of the patent. However, showing where the pilot sits is integral to a full understanding the idea.

Additionally, the break-lines shown above the number 287 on the tail piece communicates to the viewer that the exact length of the tail is not depicted. The circle in broken lines depicts the span of the rotation of the tail rotor.

DIRECT-LIFT AIRCRAFT
IGOR I. SIKORSKY Apr. 6. 1940 No. 2,318,259

The following device for the raising and buoying up of ships also beautifully illustrates the benefits of using broken lines to place the context of the patented mechanism. When we're able to see exactly how the ship appears within the device we have an immediate and powerful dose of visual information. This is another example of how with a few strokes of an artist's pen, a thousand words are depicted.

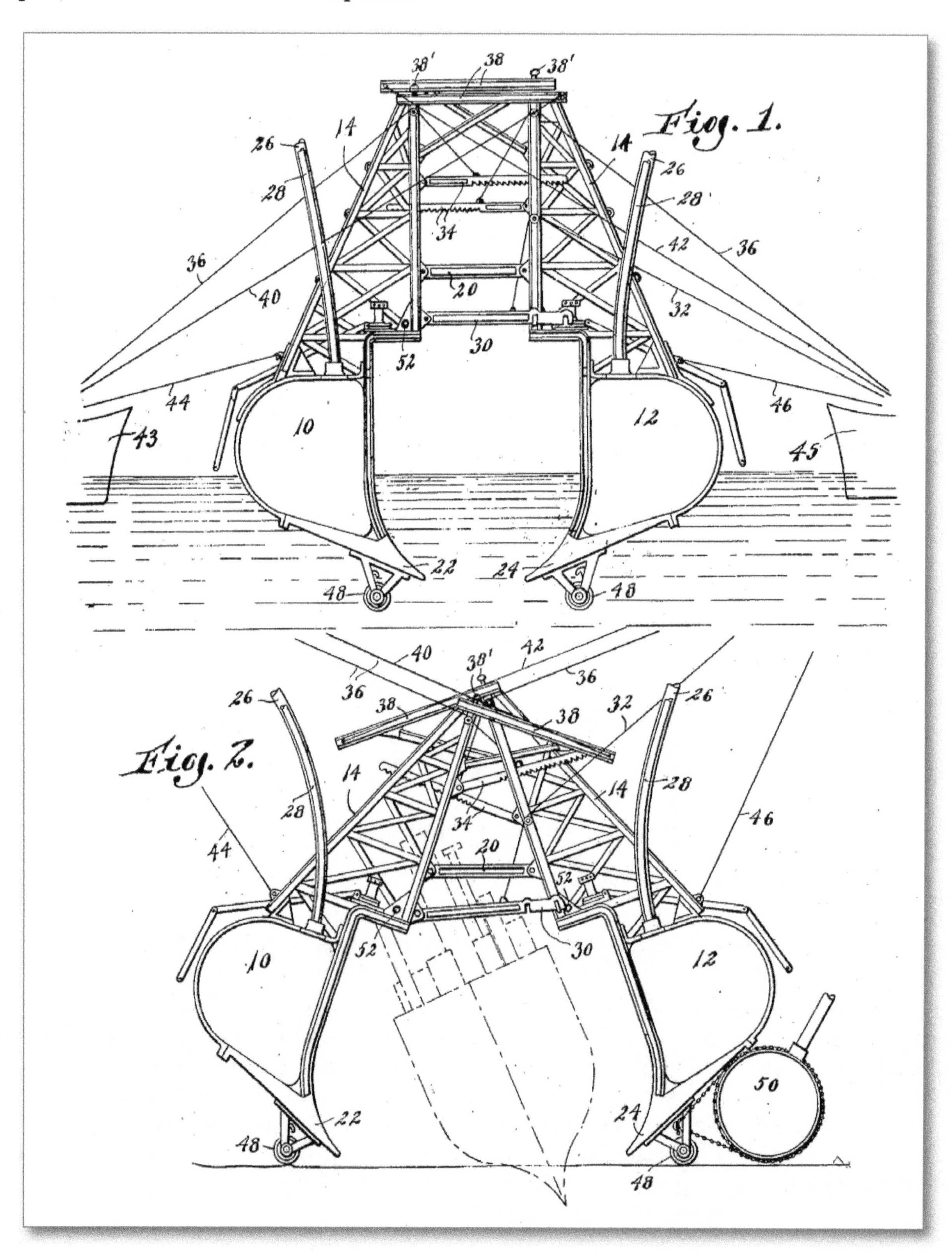

DEVICE FOR RAISING AND FOR BUOYING UP SHIPS
JOHN C. HILLS June 24, 1930 No. 1,767,672

Broken lines are also used to show how an object might move and what the subsequent positions would be. For an excellent example of this, look at the 1882 patent for opera glasses. In Figure 2, the movement of the lens encasing is clearly laid out for the viewer. An arrow is used to show the rotational direction, and a separate image of the size and rings of the lens holder is placed to the side.

Note also how straight line shading is used in combination with stippling such that the texture of the object can almost be felt. Even the ridged metal of the focus knob in the center is such that you can almost feel it beneath your fingers.

OPERA-GLASS
B.H. BLANK Sept. 12, 1882 No. 264,130

This apparatus for facilitating walking, running, and jumping from 1890 is an interesting example of how different perspectives and the use of broken lines depict the function of the object.

Figures 1 and 2 are side and back elevational views showing how the apparatus fits the man's body. Note his clothing and mustache which, although unnecessary to explain the patented device, add to the era and artistic impulse. Even the font of the figure numbers is stylish, in a day well before fonts could be downloaded to one's computer! This latter aspect is one area where there are no rules, and therefore the illustrator's personal touch can and often does shine through.

The three subsequent drawings reveal how the apparatus works for walking, running, and jumping. They not only demonstrate the use of the invention but are beautiful to behold.

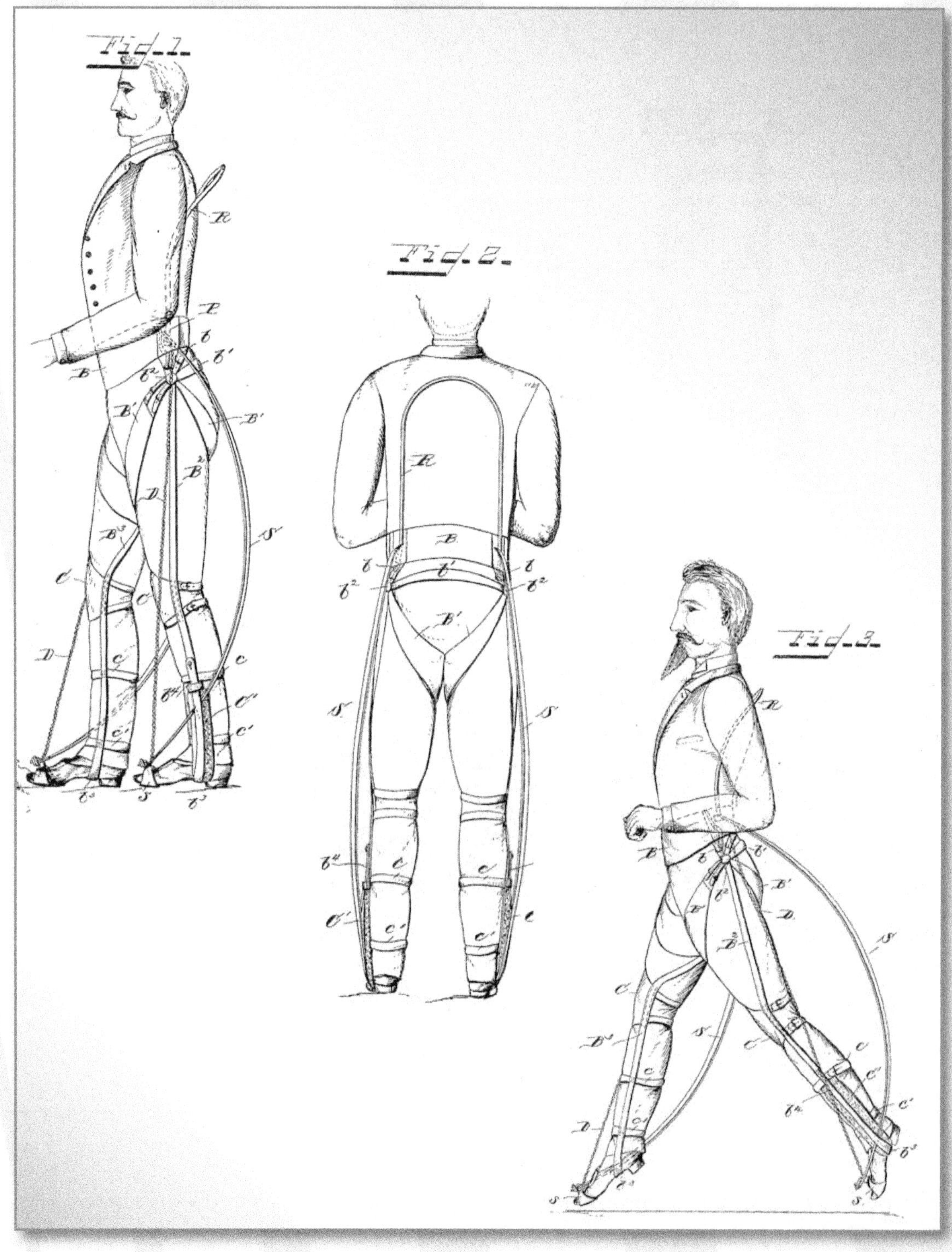

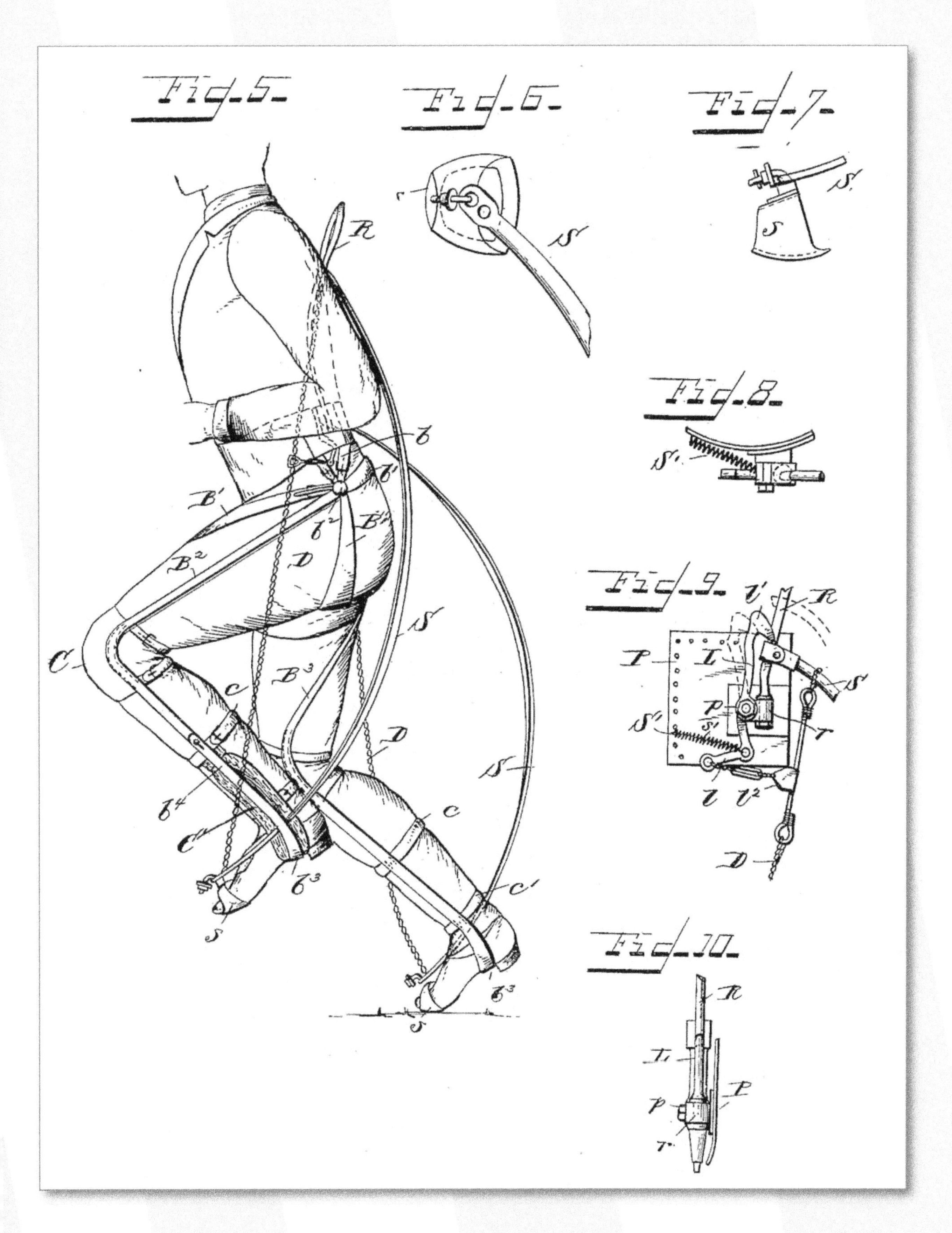

APPARATUS FOR FACILITATING WALKING, RUNNING, AND JUMPING
N. YAGN. JAN. 28, 1890 No. 420,179

Arrows are also used to show a sequence of events that take place upon use of the invention. This 1963 patent of a space capsule demonstrates this perfectly. The first figure is of the capsule itself, including a cutaway view of the interior. Drawings 6a through 6h illustrate the rocket's ascent and ensuing capsule descent with parachute.

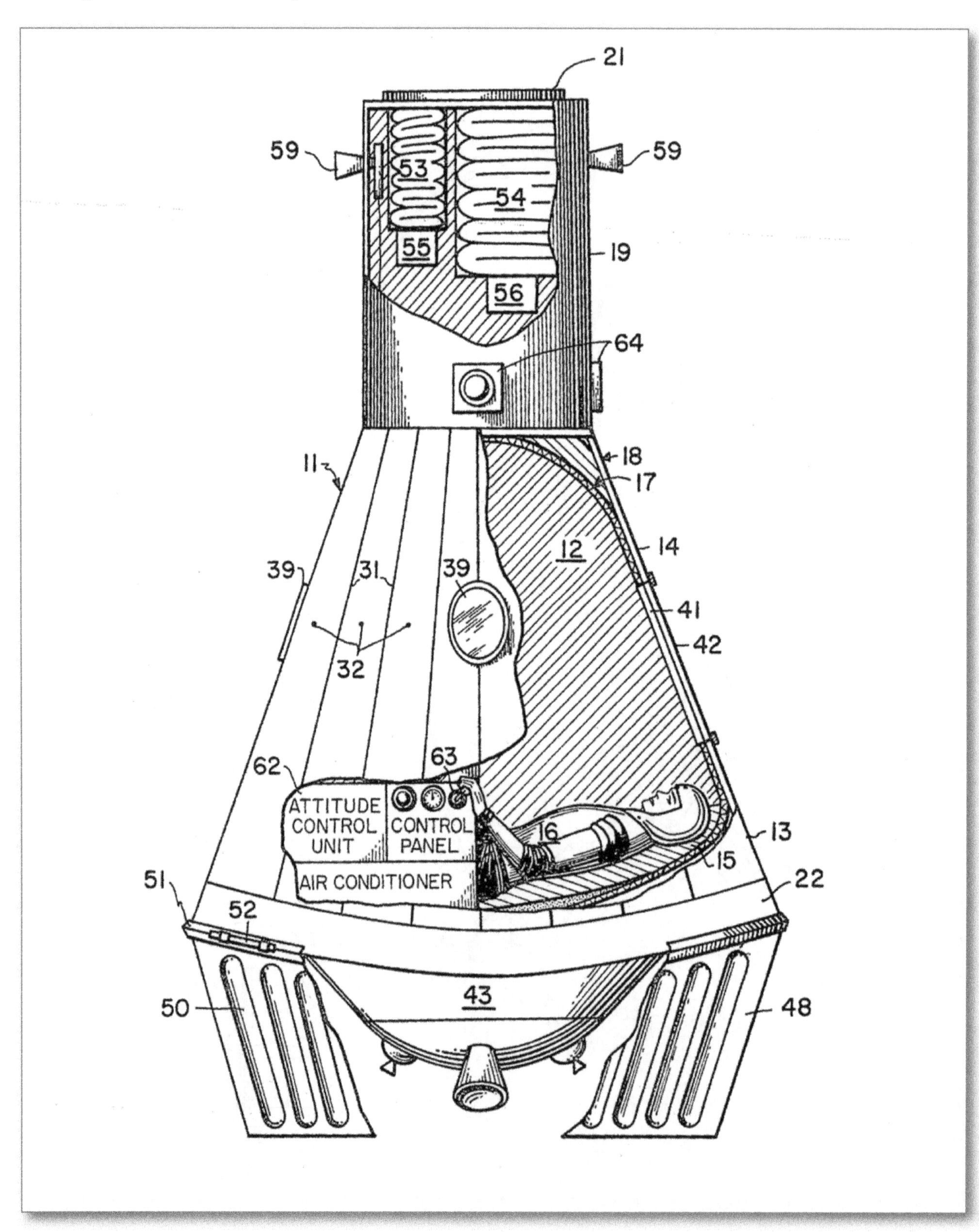

M.A. FAGET SPACE CAPSULE June 11, 1963 No. 3,093,346

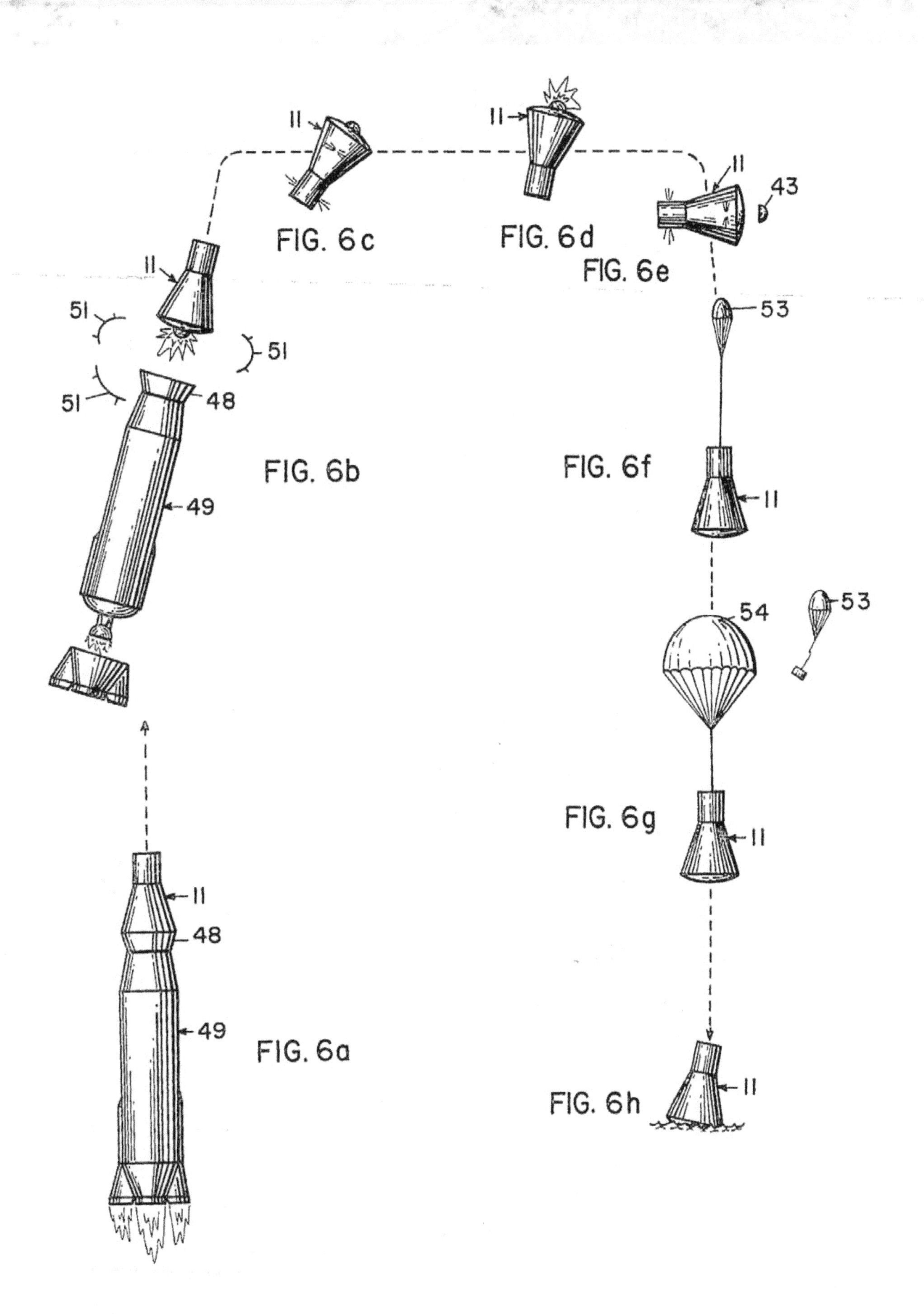

11
FIG. 6c
11
FIG. 6d
11
43
FIG. 6e
11
51
51
51
48
FIG. 6b
49
53
FIG. 6f
11
54
53
FIG. 6g
11
11
48
49
FIG. 6a
FIG. 6h
11

Crucial to the full disclosure of an invention is showing it from as many angles as are necessary to explain what it is and how it works. The drawings need to completely illustrate the invention and, if a utility patent, the text must back this up with written details.

This drawing of a velocipede from 1869 shows two basic views: side and front elevational views. A broken line (labeled **x** below) is used to depict a vertical section line, showing the details of the device as if it were sliced straight through. Broken lines are also used to depict motion in the man's legs and in the two small wheels along the circumference of the main wheel. While apparently not a market success, this whimsical invention can still be enjoyed today as "prior art" art, as it were.

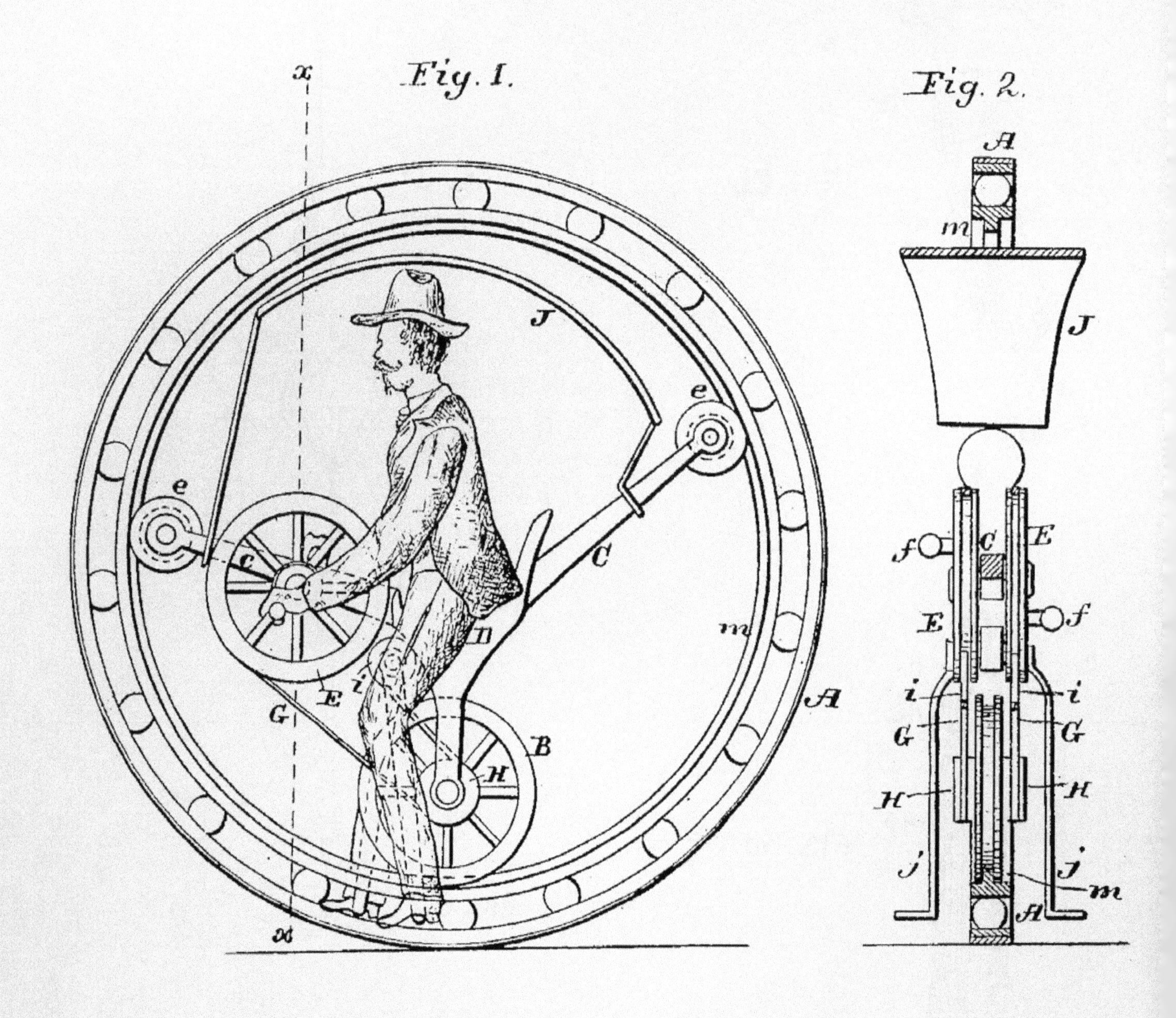

IMPROVEMENT IN VELOCIPEDES
R.C. HEMMINGS July 13, 1869 No. 92,528

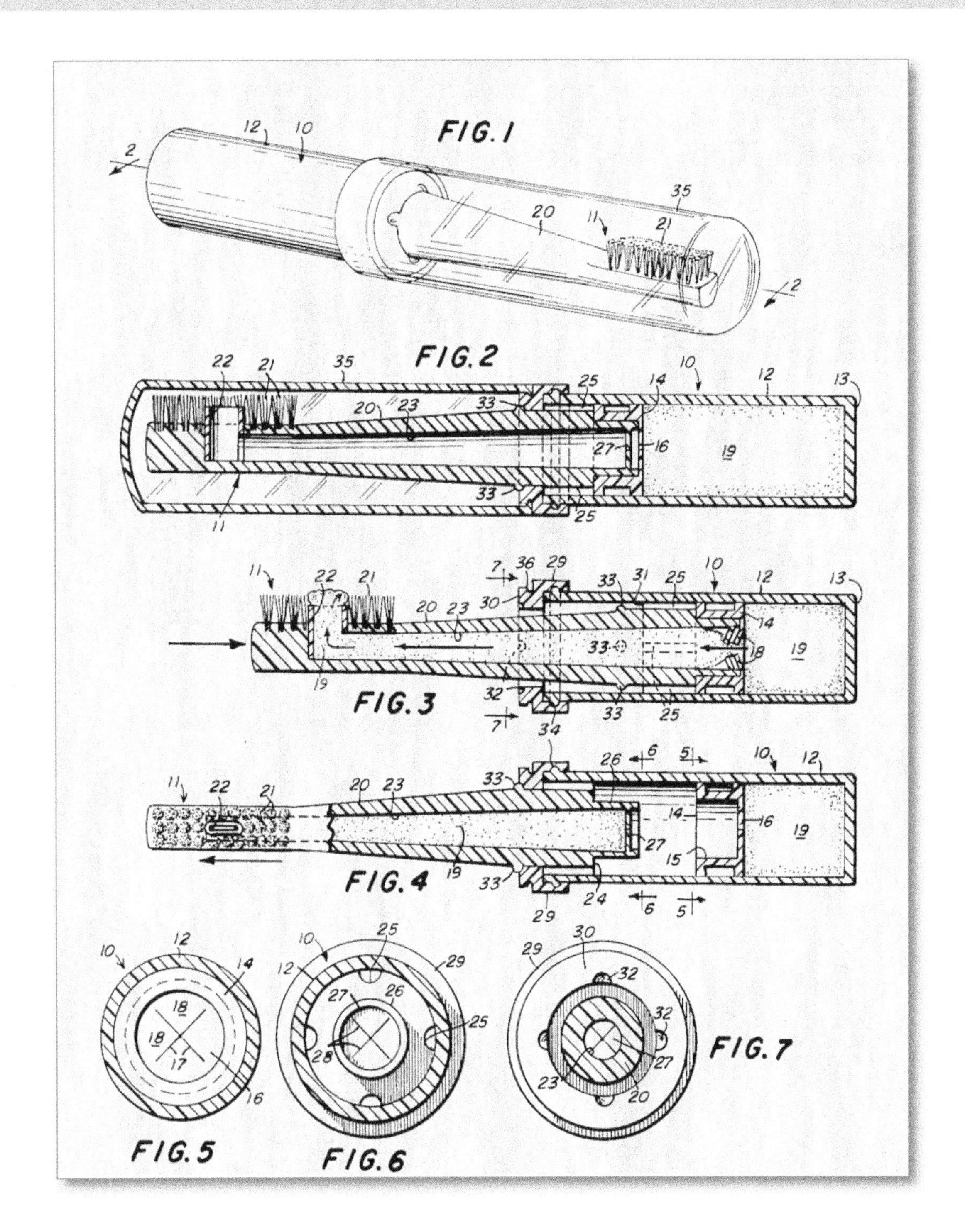

The combined dispensing toothpaste holder and brush is a wonderful example of the usage of different materials. Figure 1 shows the invention in whole. Note the oblique lines that reveal the transparency of the cap. The toothpaste is represented by a gritty substance you can almost taste as it gets pressed upward through tufts of bristles in Figure 3. The balance is opaque plastic material.

Figures 2, 3, and 4 are lengthwise cross-sections that demonstrate the inner workings of the mechanism. Figures 5-7 are perpendicular cross-sections leaving no detail to doubt.

The entire set of drawings fits neatly on one page and is both effective and beautiful.

COMBINED DISPENSING TOOTHPASTE HOLDER AND BRUSH
M. T. COSTANZA JAN. 4, 1966 No. 3,227,165

This is an astounding cross sectional drawing of an aircraft power plant. Although we as viewers may have no idea what the details mean, the intricacy leaps out from the page. Each type of shading represents a different material or element.

Figures 3-6 are further details and are breathtaking in their symmetry.

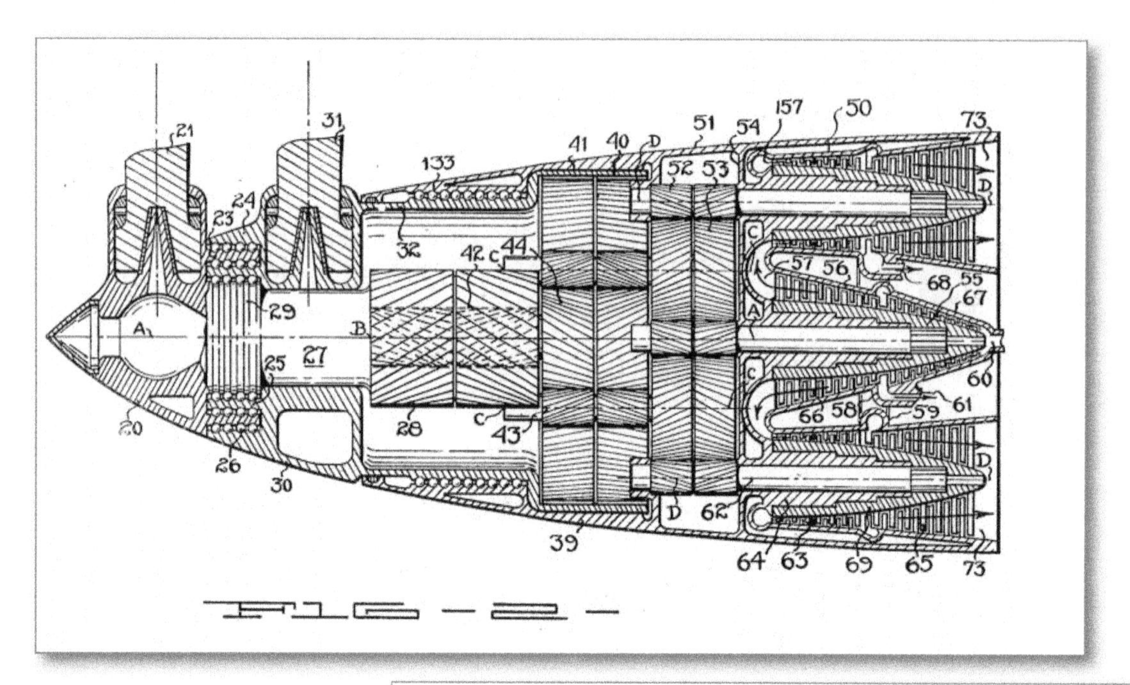

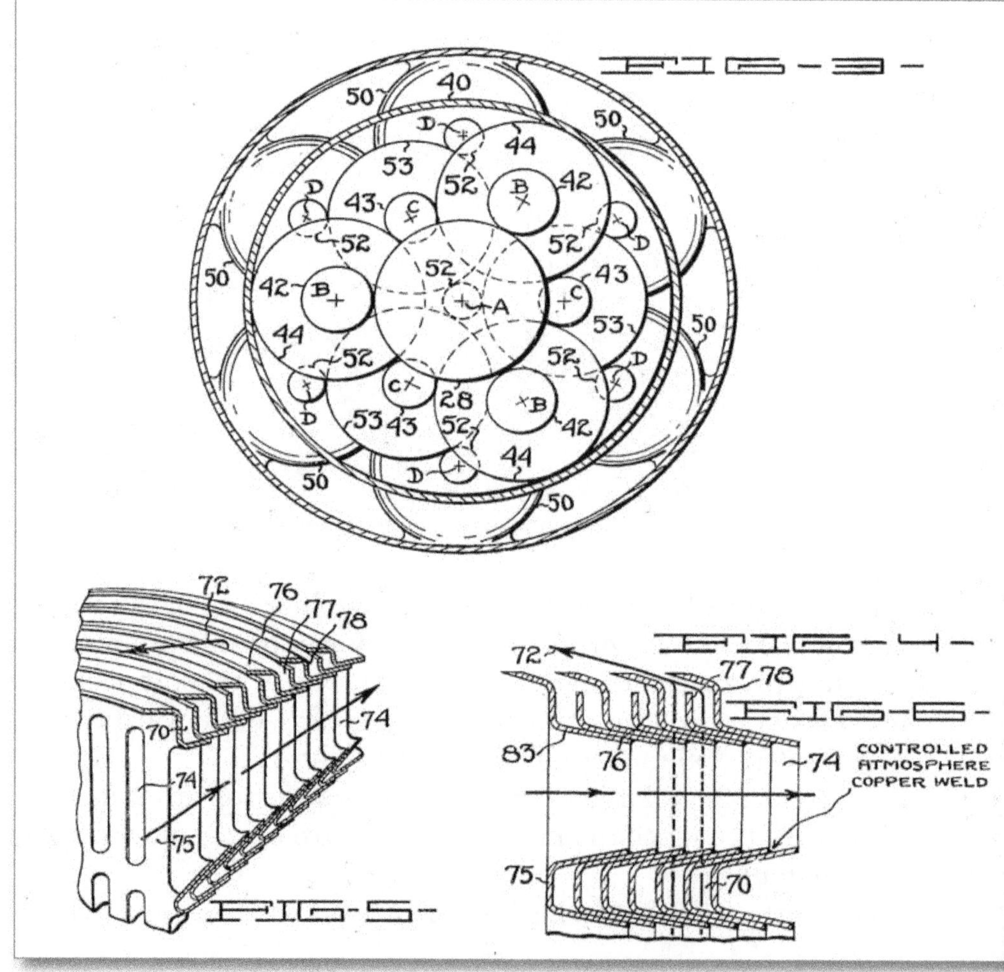

AIRCRAFT POWER PLANT

N.C. PRICE May 30, 1939 2,160,281

Below, the artist has used large-scale cross sectional views to clearly illustrate the functionality of a moving staircase; what we now call an escalator.

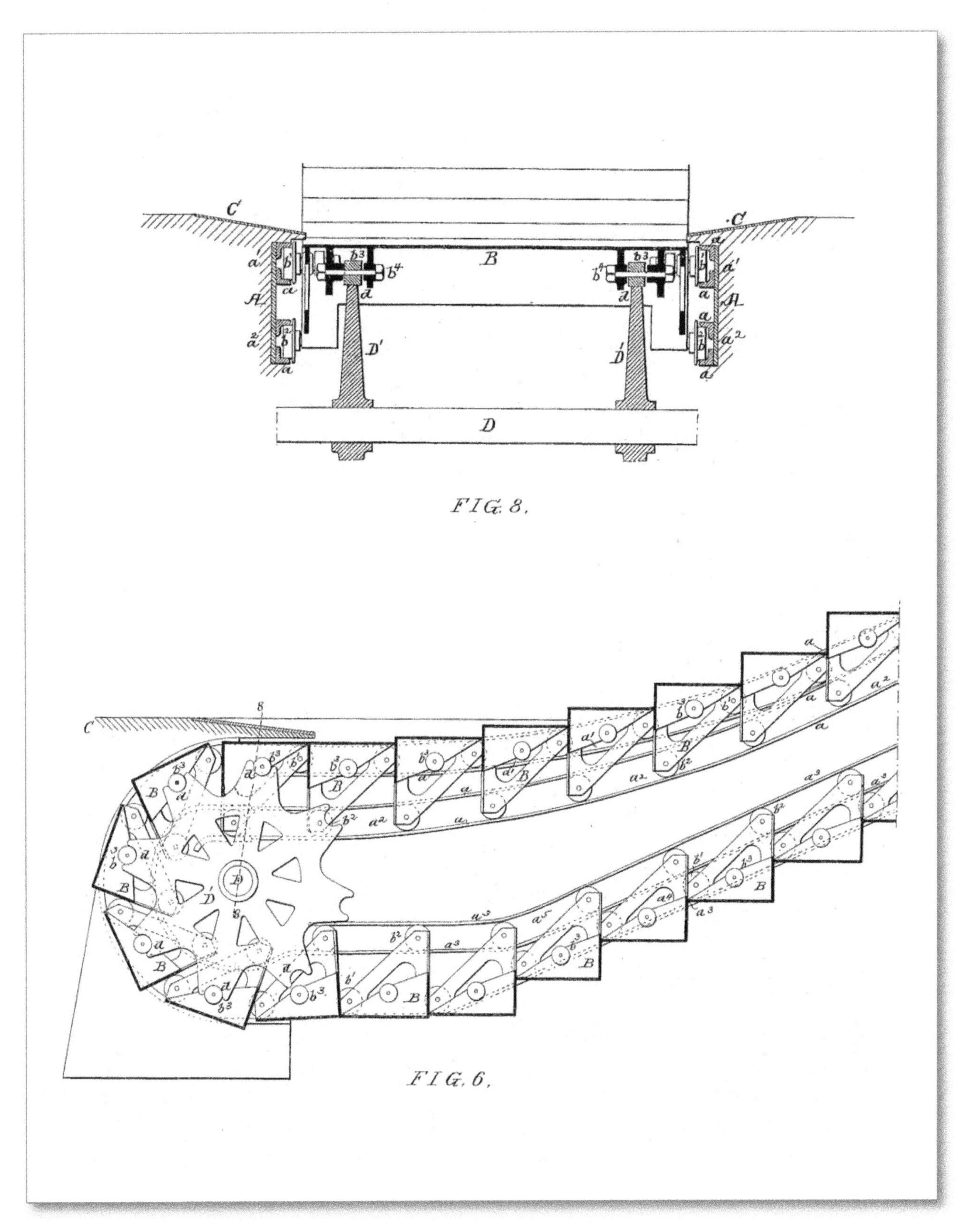

J.M. DODGE MOVING STAIRWAY Feb. 8, 1898 No. 598,772

The state of an invention in time can also be shown, such as with before and after drawings of the action of an invention. The novelty wig patent below illustrates this in such a way that it's difficult not to chuckle.

NOVELTY WIG
H.M. TATE Oct. 19, 1926 No. 1,604,087

An "exploded" view allows the artist to detail each piece of an invention and how they are put together as a whole. This technique is enormously useful and seen often in utility patents. The illustration below of an electric guitar vibrato device illustrates this concept perfectly. Figure 7 is of the device as whole, and Figure 6 is the exploded view.

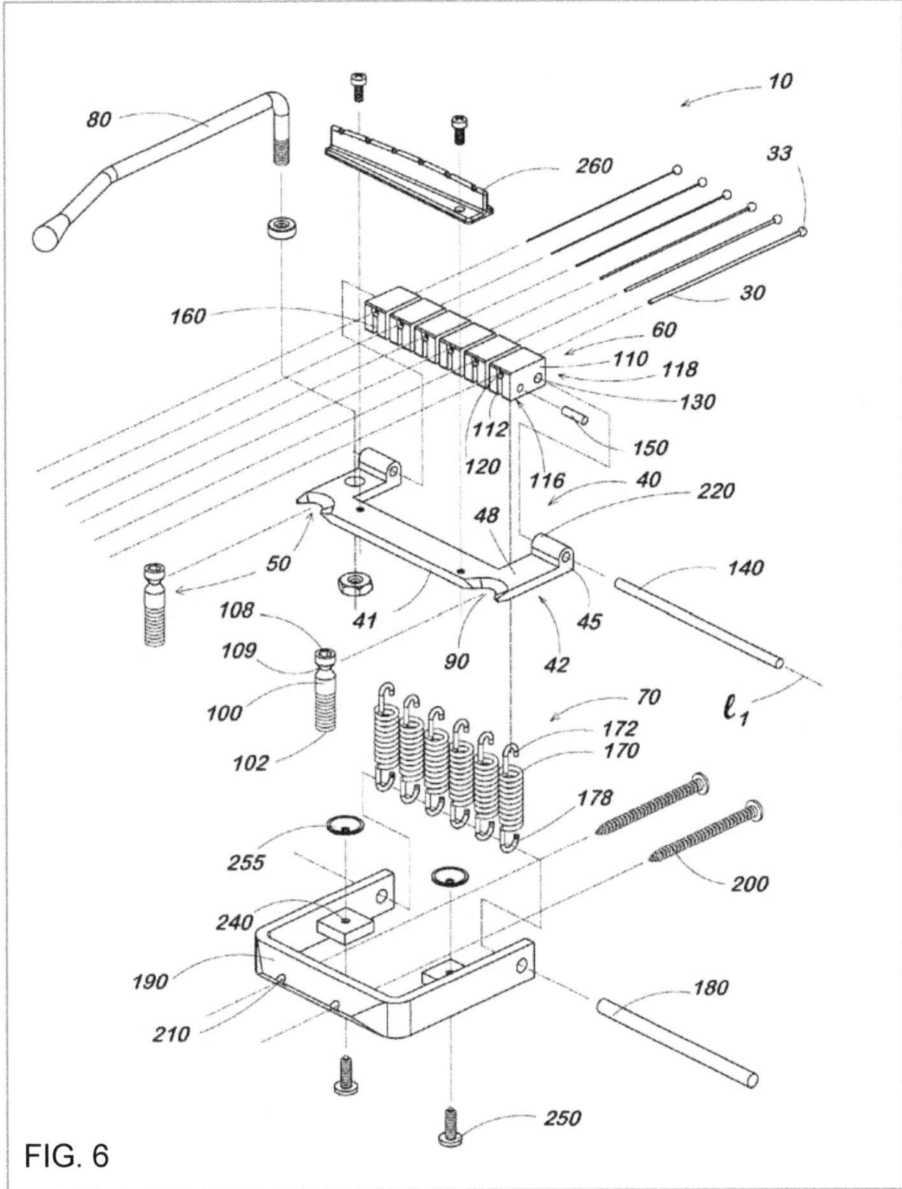

FIG. 6

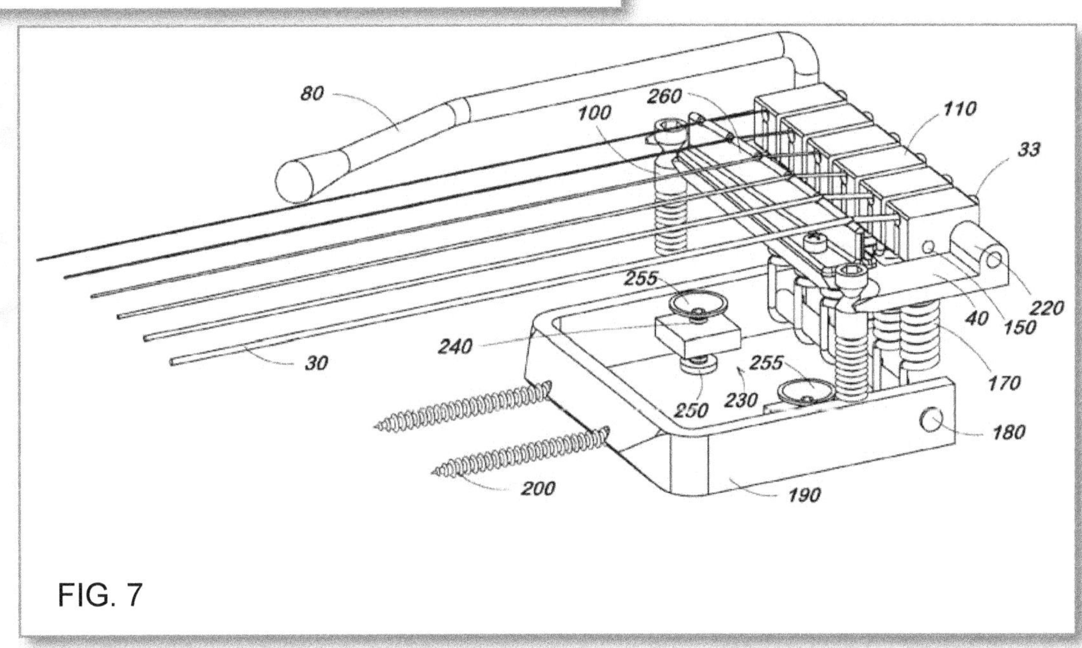

FIG. 7

STRINGED INSTRUMENT VIBRATO DEVICE
R.L. SLAVIK May 18, 2010 NO. 7,718,873

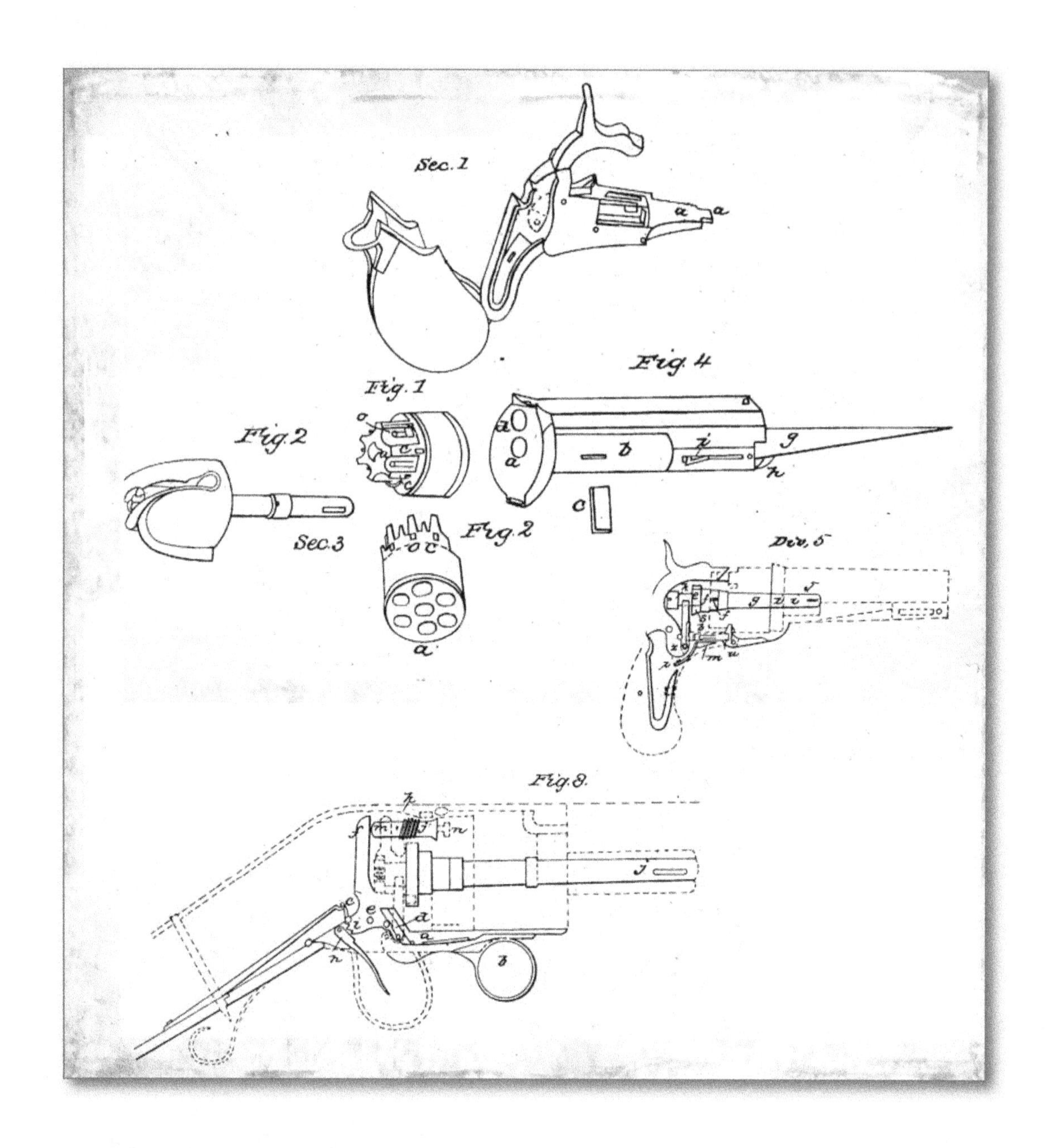

As you've probably noticed, many patent drawings incorporate several tools of patent art we've seen, all in the same figure. Interestingly, these tools have been used for centuries; our progressing technologies haven't changed them... a case of "if it's not broken, don't fix it."

Look at this 1836 patent for the Colt revolver. Even as far back as 1836, the exploded view was used to explain an assembly in the same way we do today. Broken lines are used to set context for the discussion of Figs. 5 and 8. Nearly all of the elements are shown in a perspective view to provide hints as to the depths of each nook and cranny, and each individual piece is illustrated in its own small figure to the left.

S. COLT — IMPROVEMENT IN FIREARMS — Feb. 25, 1836 — No. 9430X

Differing materials and textures have their own designated patterns, as set by the PTO. Above you've seen many drawings with specific types of hash marks and shade lines. Each represents a material or type of area designated by the US Patent and Trademark Office's manual on utility and design patent drawings. Below is a page from the manual.

Symbols for Draftsmen

Graphical symbols for conventional elements may be used on the drawing when appropriate, subject to approval by the Office. The symbols that follow have been approved for such use. This collection does not purport to be exhaustive; other standard and commonly used symbols will also be acceptable provided they are clearly understood, are adequately identified in the specification as filed, and do not create confusion with other symbols used in patent drawings.

NOTES: In general, in lieu of a symbol, a conventional element, combination or circuit may be shown by an appropriately labeled rectangle, square or circle; abbreviations should not be used unless their meaning is evident and not confusing with the abbreviations used in the suggested symbols.

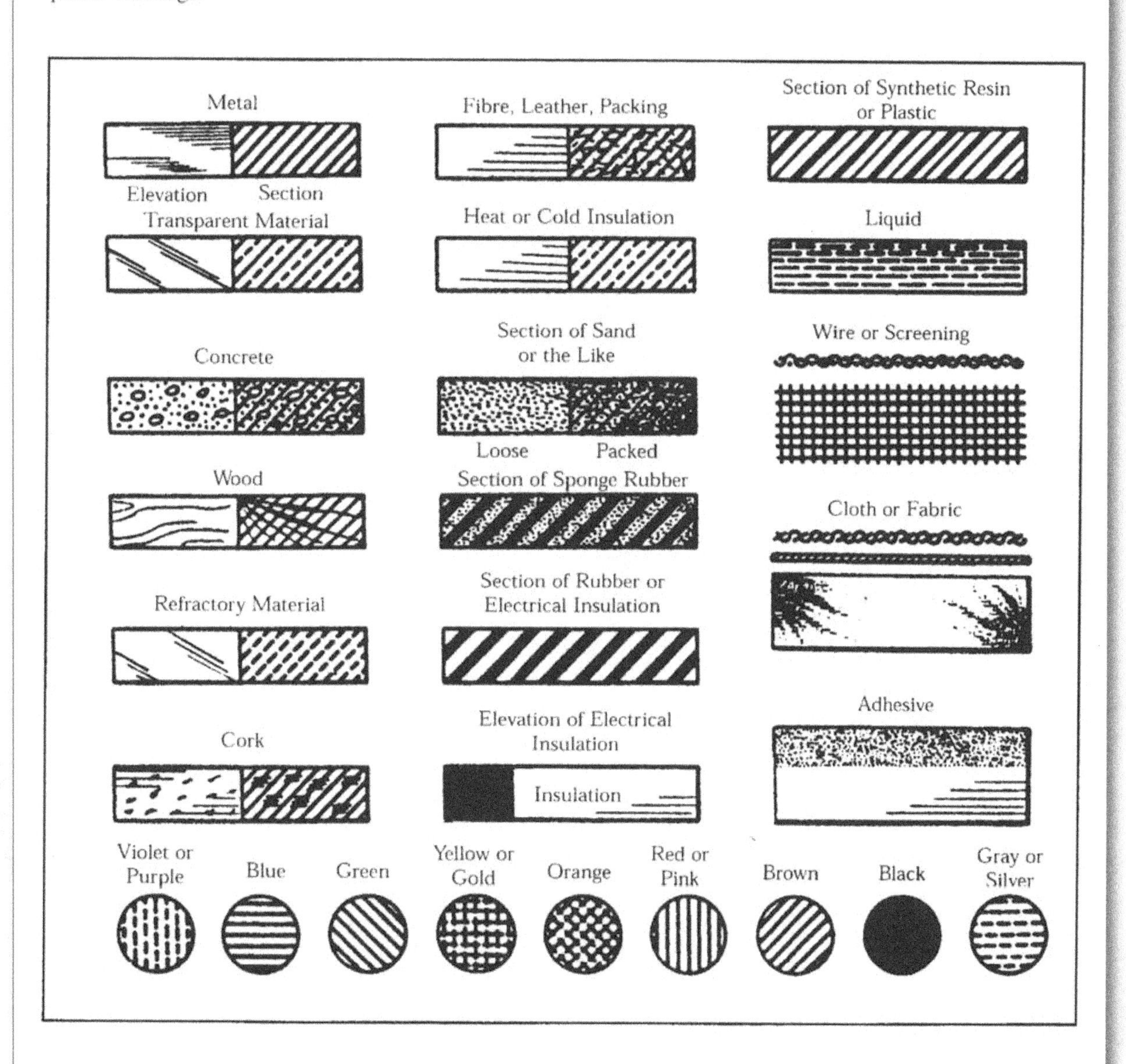

Why so many different patterns? The drawing below of a composite surfboard internal structure clearly exhibits the need for and usage of different drawing designations for materials.

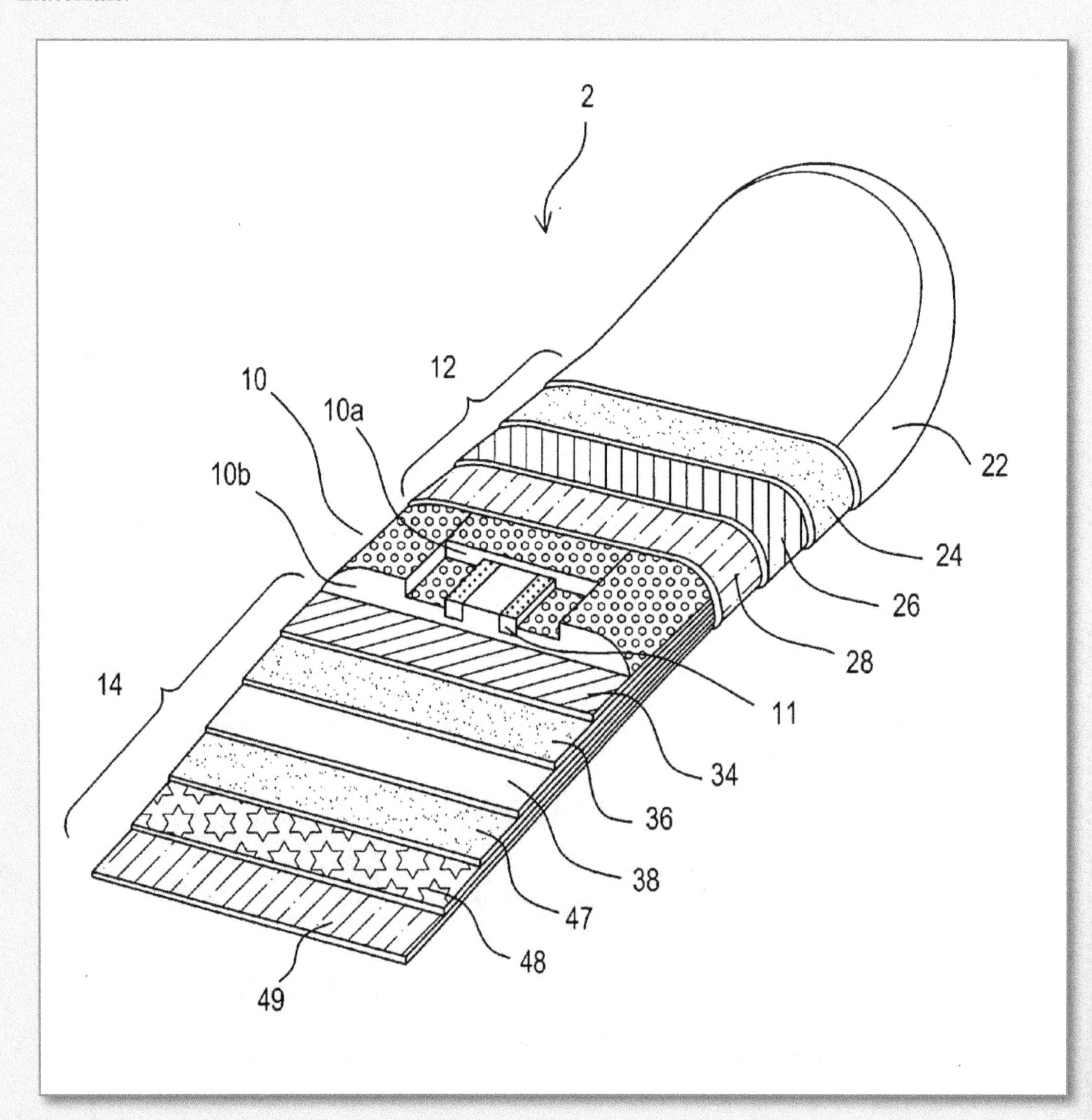

FOAM DECK COMPOSITE SURFBOARD
W.K. CHEUNG July. 5, 2007 NO. 7,507,133

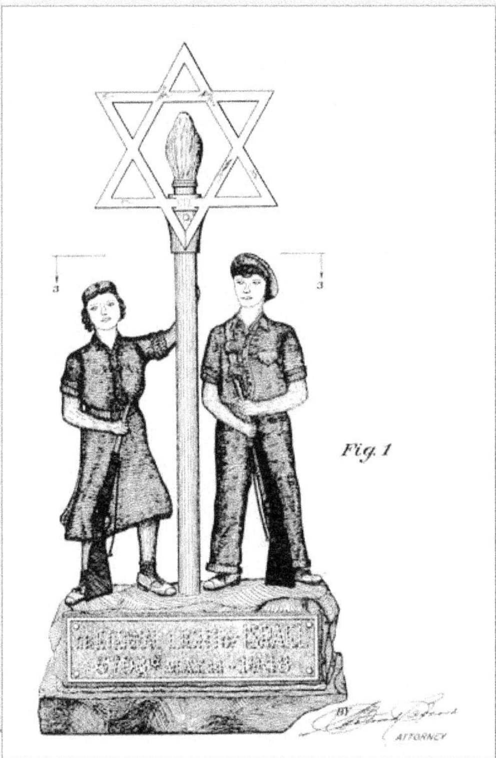

This drawing not only utilizes the required lines to designate wood, but also shows an interesting perspective from above, a "top plan view." The patent is a design for a combination statue and lamp.

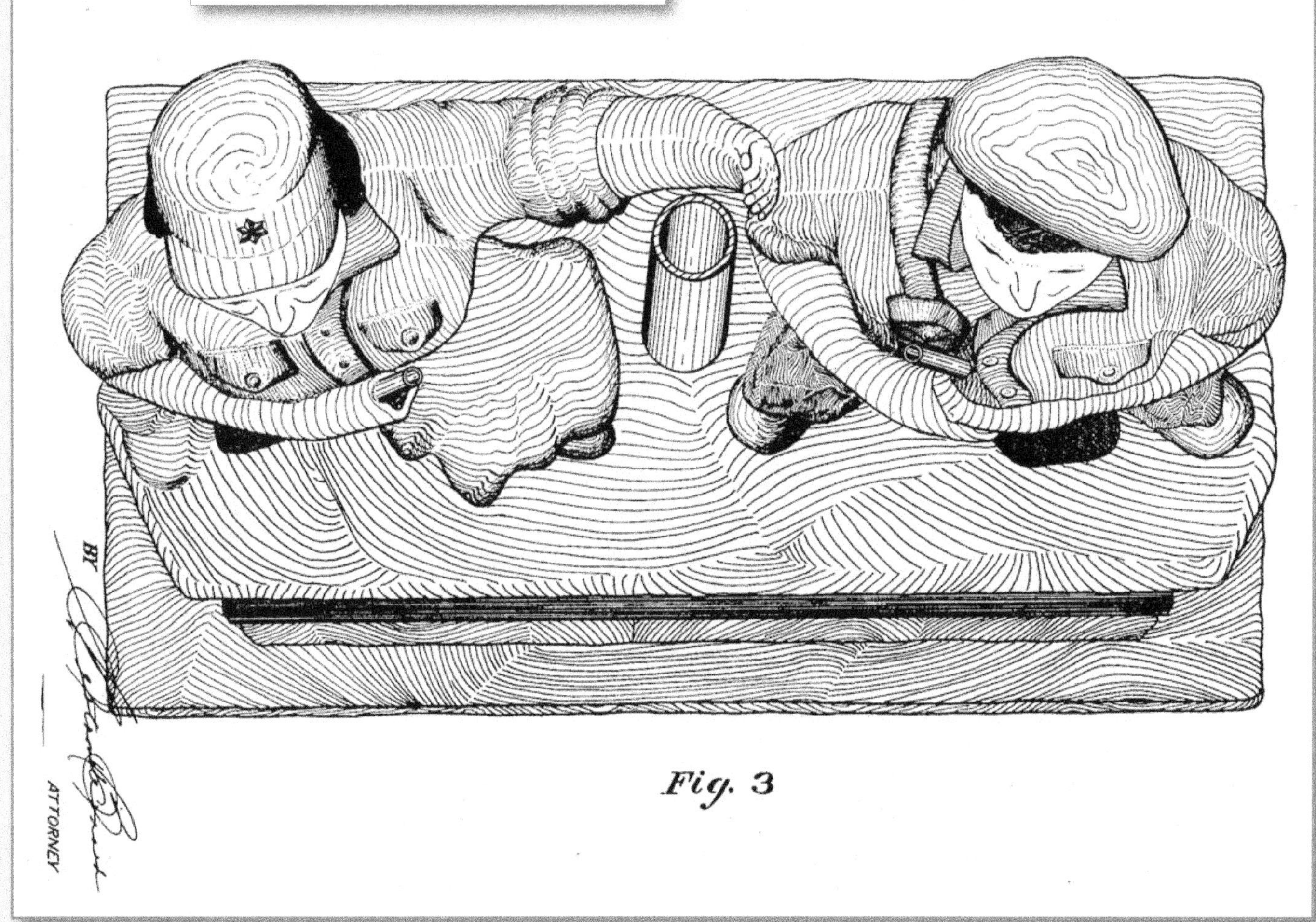

COMBINATION STATUE AND LAMP
N. LICHTENSTEIN May 22, 1951 No. 163,397

Given the enormous variety of fabrics and materials that exist, the PTO rules and regulations cannot define a pattern for each. In these cases the artist must represent the material to the best of his or her ability. The following patents spanning over one hundred years show how beautifully this can be done.

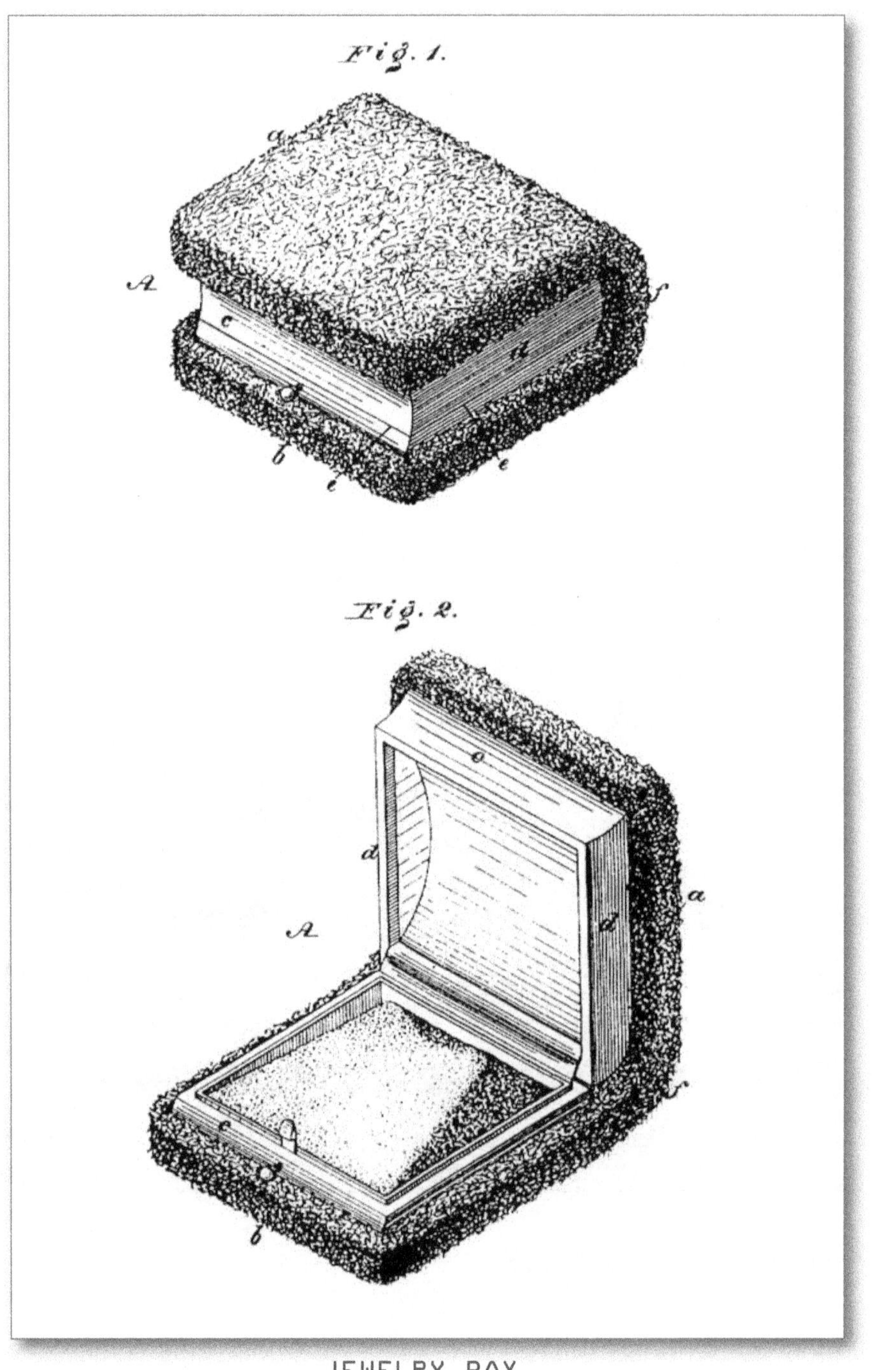

JEWELRY BOX
H.B. SOMMER Sept. 15, 1885 No. 16,254

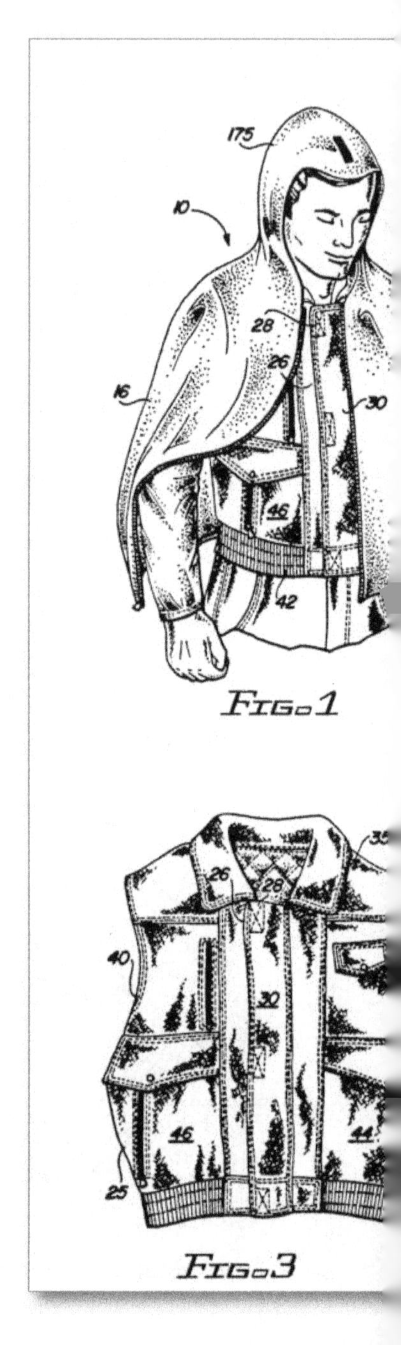

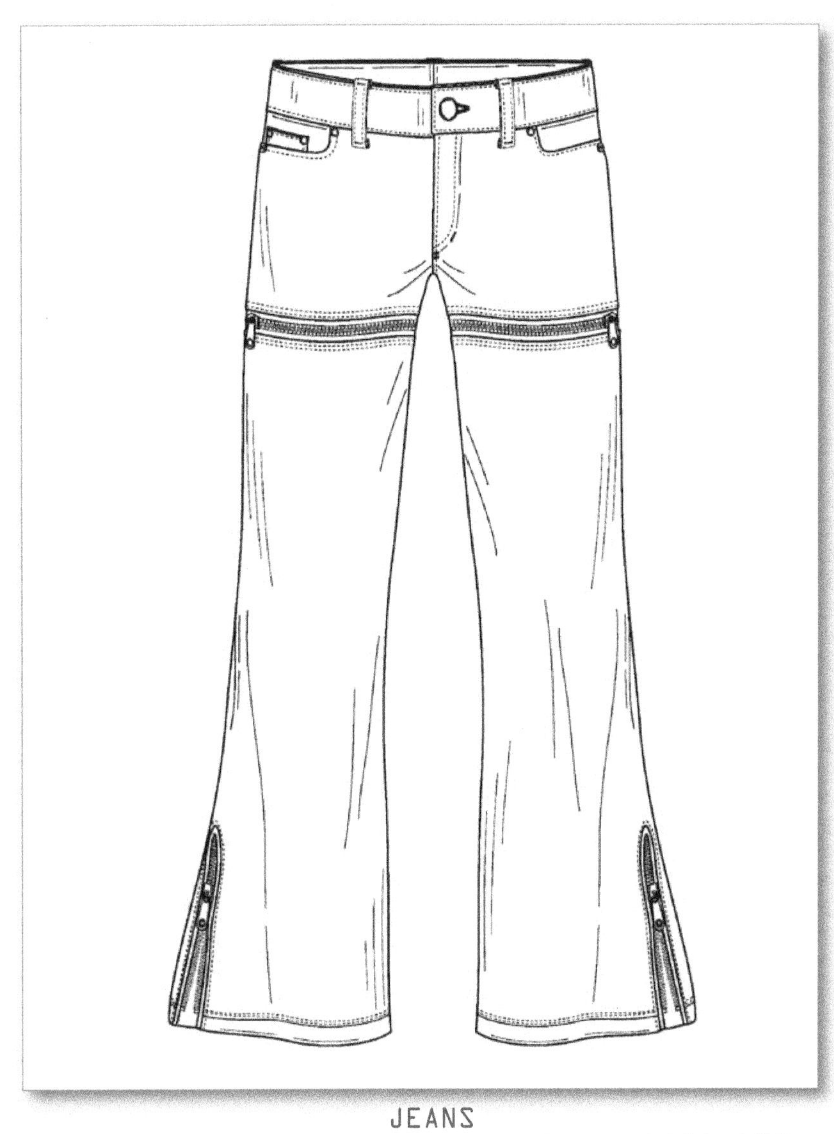

JEANS
KEN CHRISTIANSEN Jun. 1, 2010 No. D616,630

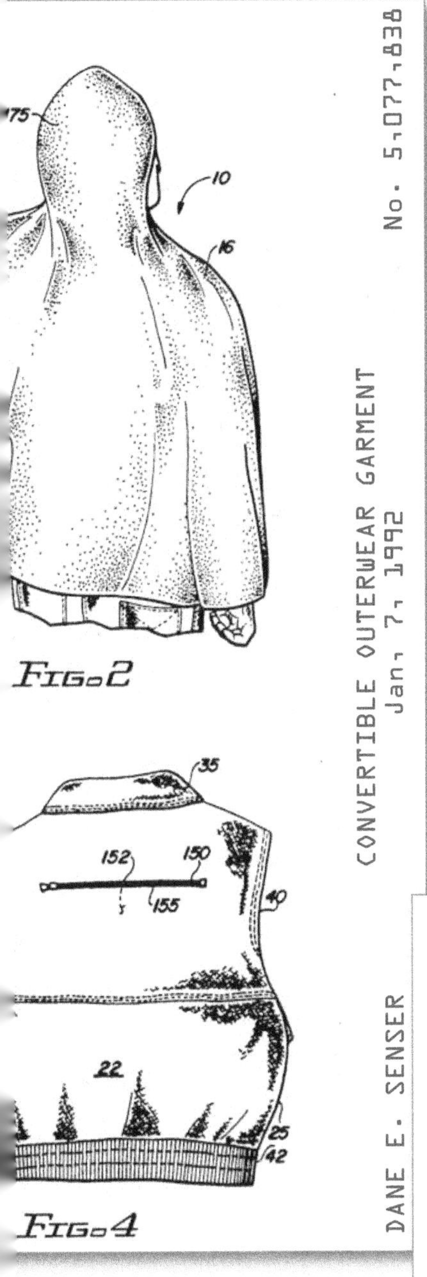

CONVERTIBLE OUTERWEAR GARMENT
Jan. 7, 1992 No. 5,077,838
DANE E. SENSER

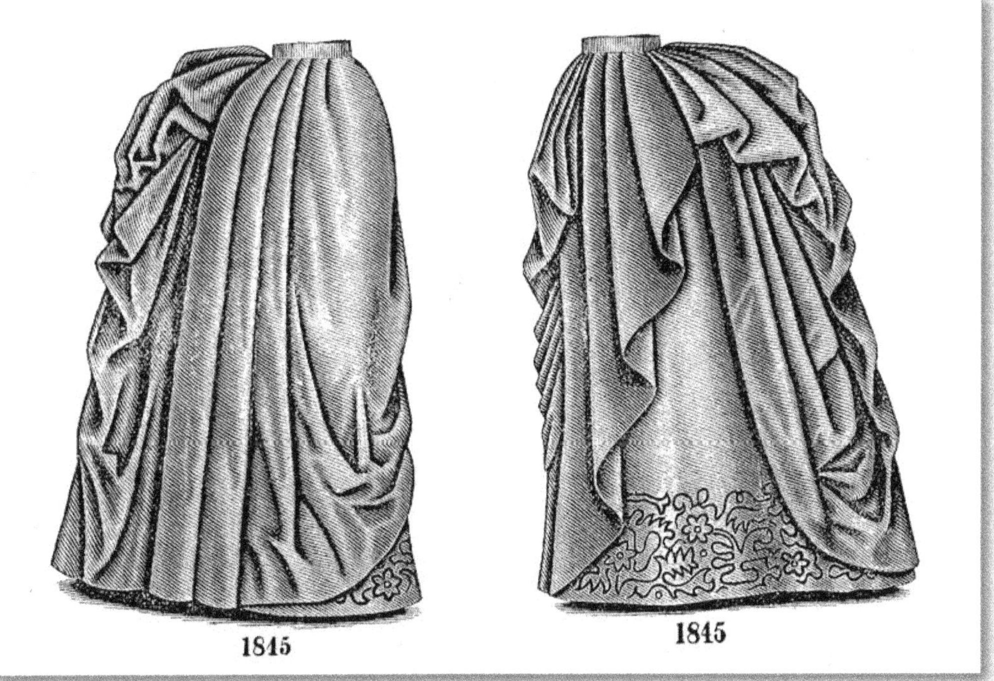

LADY'S WALKING-SKIRT
MARY TURNER Nov. 15, 1887 No. 17,886

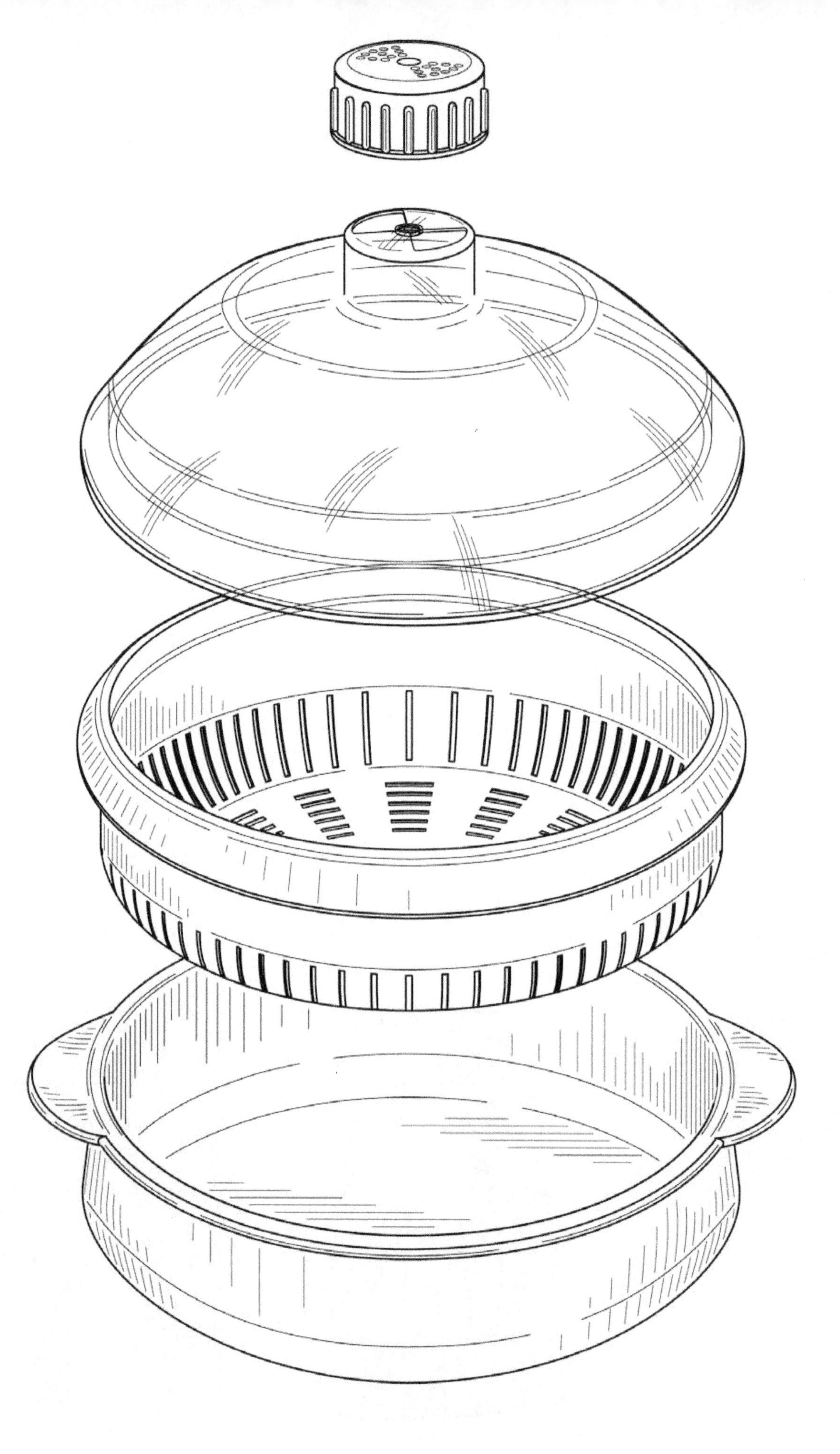

MICROWAVE STEAMER

T.T. HOANG MAI Feb. 9, 2010 No. D609,523

Chapter 3

Patent Art Evolution

The art of the patent, as with any art, is not static but rather an evolving process of expressing creativity within set parameters. Over the almost two hundred years of patent art, not only have styles changed, but so have the inventive subjects. We've seen the horse and buggy go out and spaceships come in. The telegraph has morphed into an iPhone with GPS, and the medical field is virtually unrecognizable from its forbearers.

Patent art has evolved accordingly. Artist's styles have changed in some important ways, just as has what's being dreamed up in the mind of the inventor.

In this chapter I'll walk you through the amazing evolution of patent art. Let's begin with the 1913 drawing below for a food and dish warmer, which is both elegant and detailed. Figure 1 uses straight line shading in an excellent top view of the invention with a cut away section showing the heating apparatus beneath. Figure 2 is a side view with a partial cross section showing the workings in minute detail.

Compare this with the modern day microwave steamer at left. Straight line shading is used again but the lines are bolder and the feel is sharper. Each is beautiful in its own way, yet they are strikingly different. Needless to say, the technology depicted is light years apart.

Equally important, both drawings served their purpose to legally claim the inventive concept. The job gets done and the art swirls amongst it.

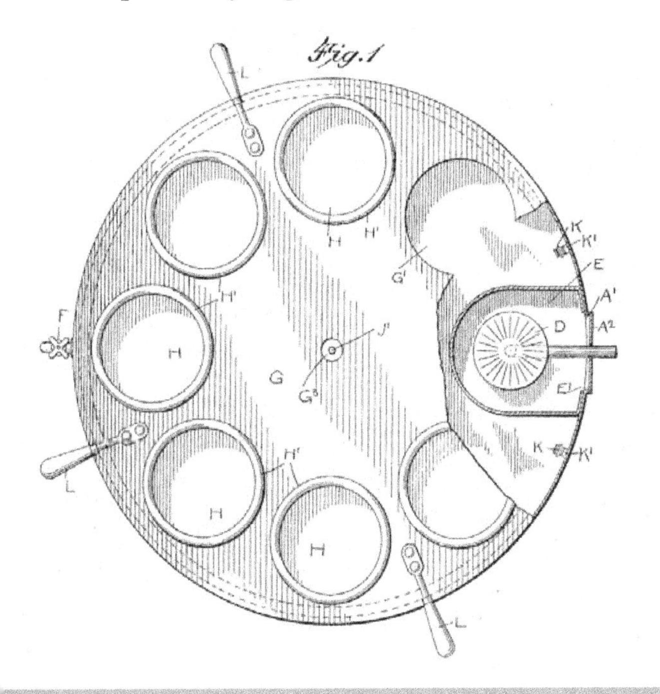

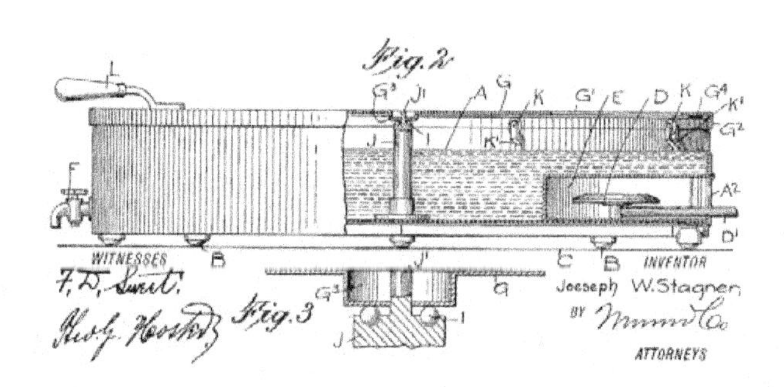

FOOD AND DISH WARMER
J.W. STAGNER July 8, 1913 No. 1,067,152

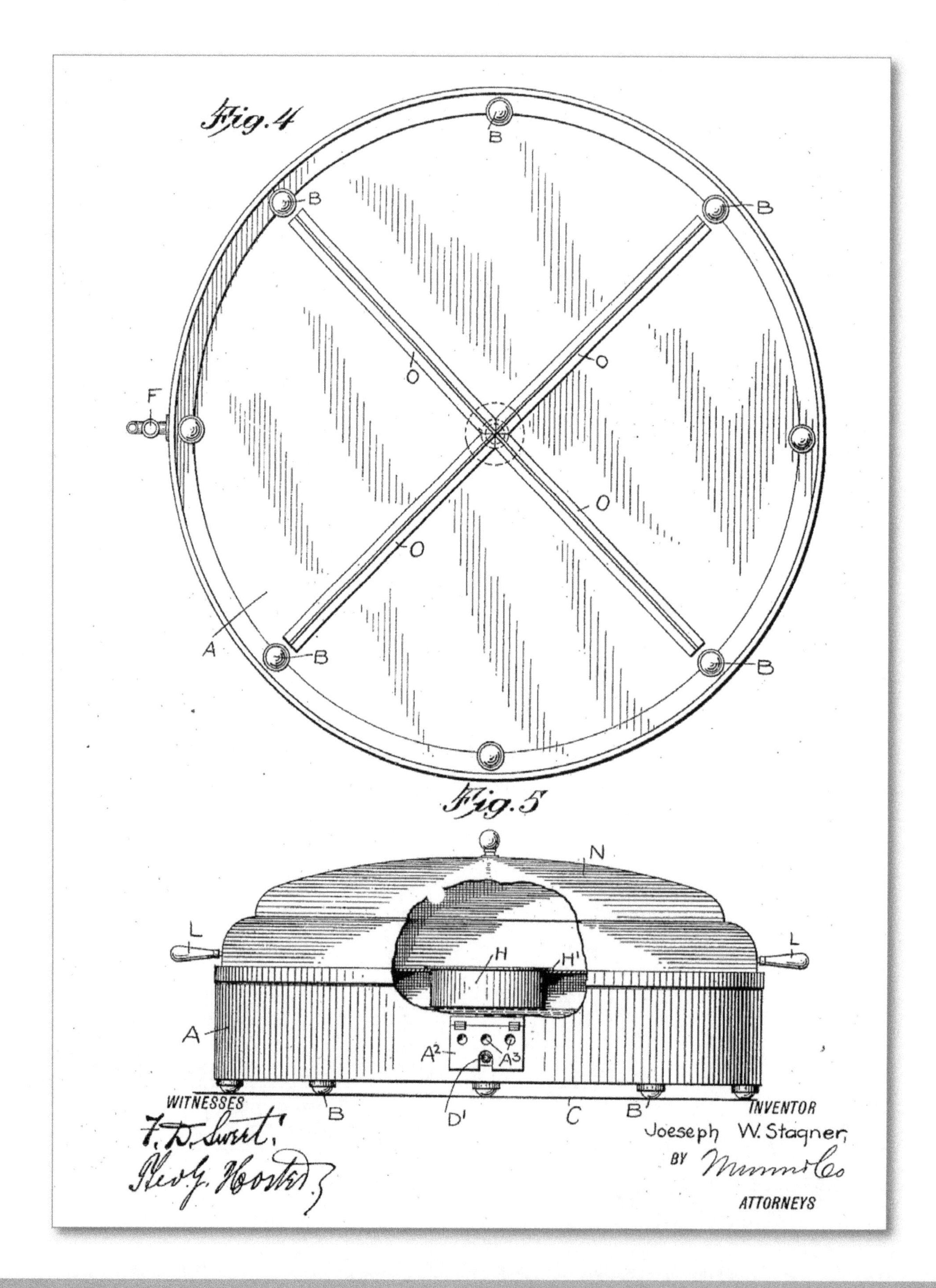

J.W. STAGNER FOOD AND DISH WARMER July 8, 1913 No. 1,067,152

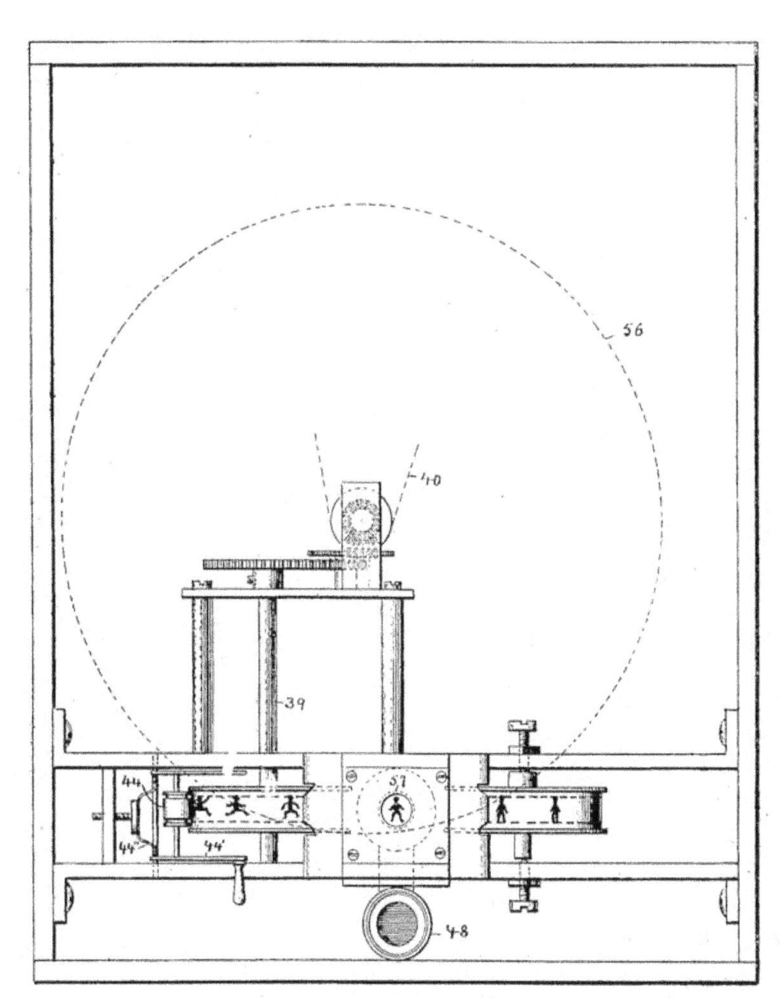

The enormous transformation in technology over the last one hundred years is illustrated with flare in the next four drawings. The first two are Thomas Edison's groundbreaking patent for a movie projector. Each of the patent drawing rules discussed earlier is followed. One of the main features is the broken lined circles illustrating the image projected outwards. Note how the man is shown running through the film. Figures 4 and 5 demonstrate how the physics work in an eerily satisfying geometric design.

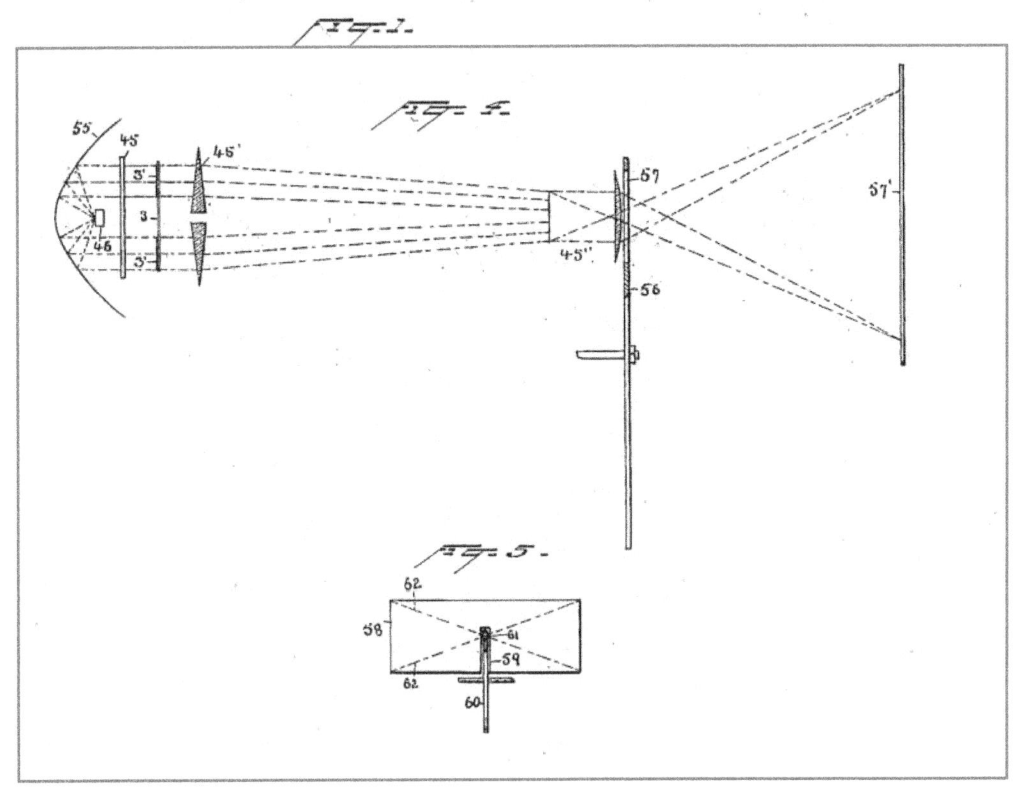

APPARATUS FOR EXHIBITING PHOTOGRAPHS OF MOVING OBJECTS
T.A. EDISON. Mar. 14, 1893 No. 493,426

Below are two drawings of locks spanning 110 years. The different styles are obvious. The first transports the viewer back in time with the large, looping handwriting and hand drawn figures and letters.

In contrast, the drawing of the bicycle lock has bolder lines, most probably computer generated, with distinct numbering. Separations are used in the u-shaped piece to show indeterminate length while broken lines allow us to visualize the motion of the lock opening.

Clearly, the eras are transported along with the ideas in which the inventions were born.

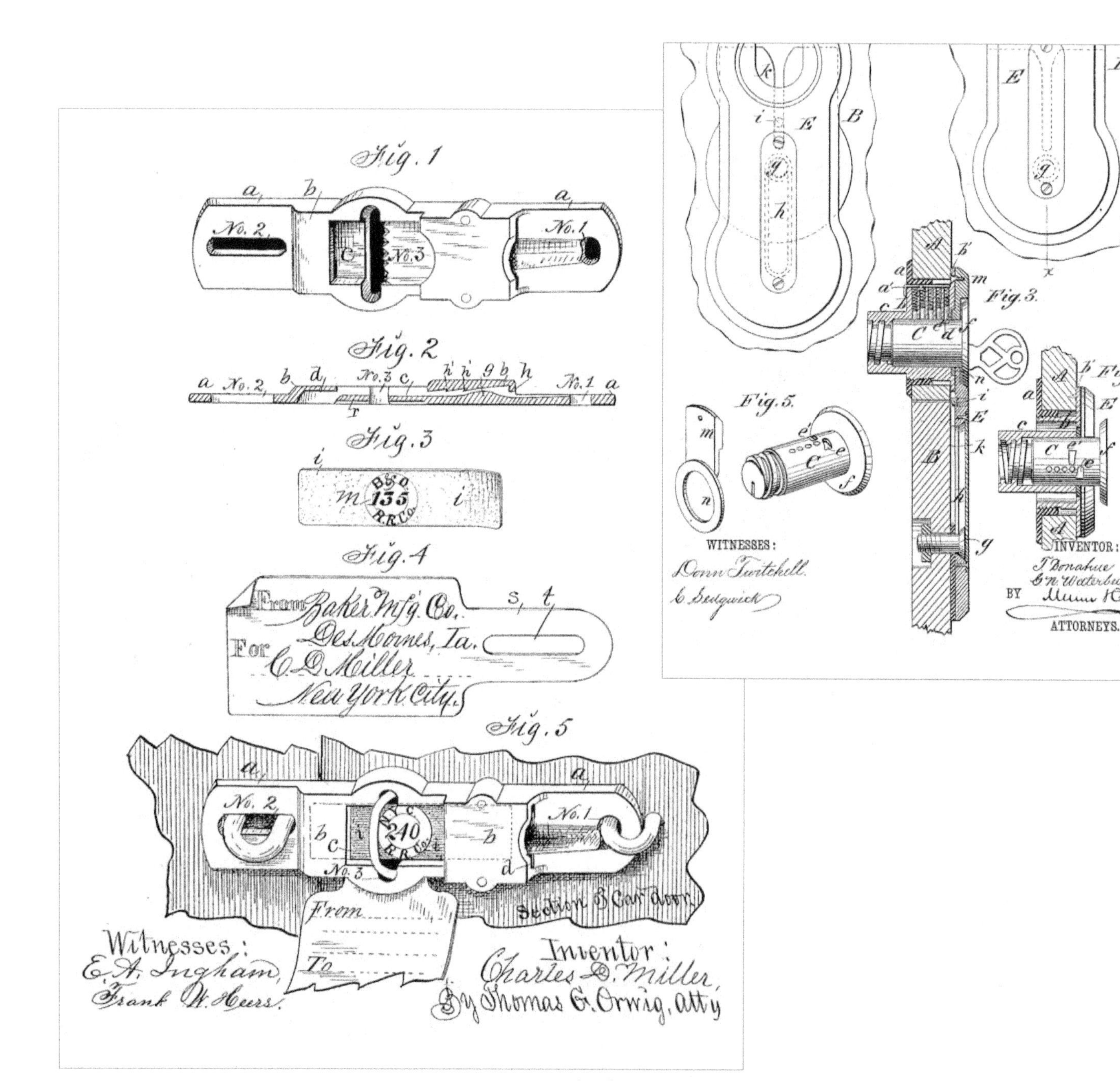

SEAL-LOCK
C.D. MILLER Oct. 31, 1882 No. 266,867

The second set of drawings is of the news feed system used in Facebook. In a completely different artistic style, the method of posting on the Facebook wall is explained.

Is there more art in Edison's patent drawings? Possibly, but Facebook has made a huge impact on modern culture and the patent drawings are certainly an interesting way to see a bit of history in the making.

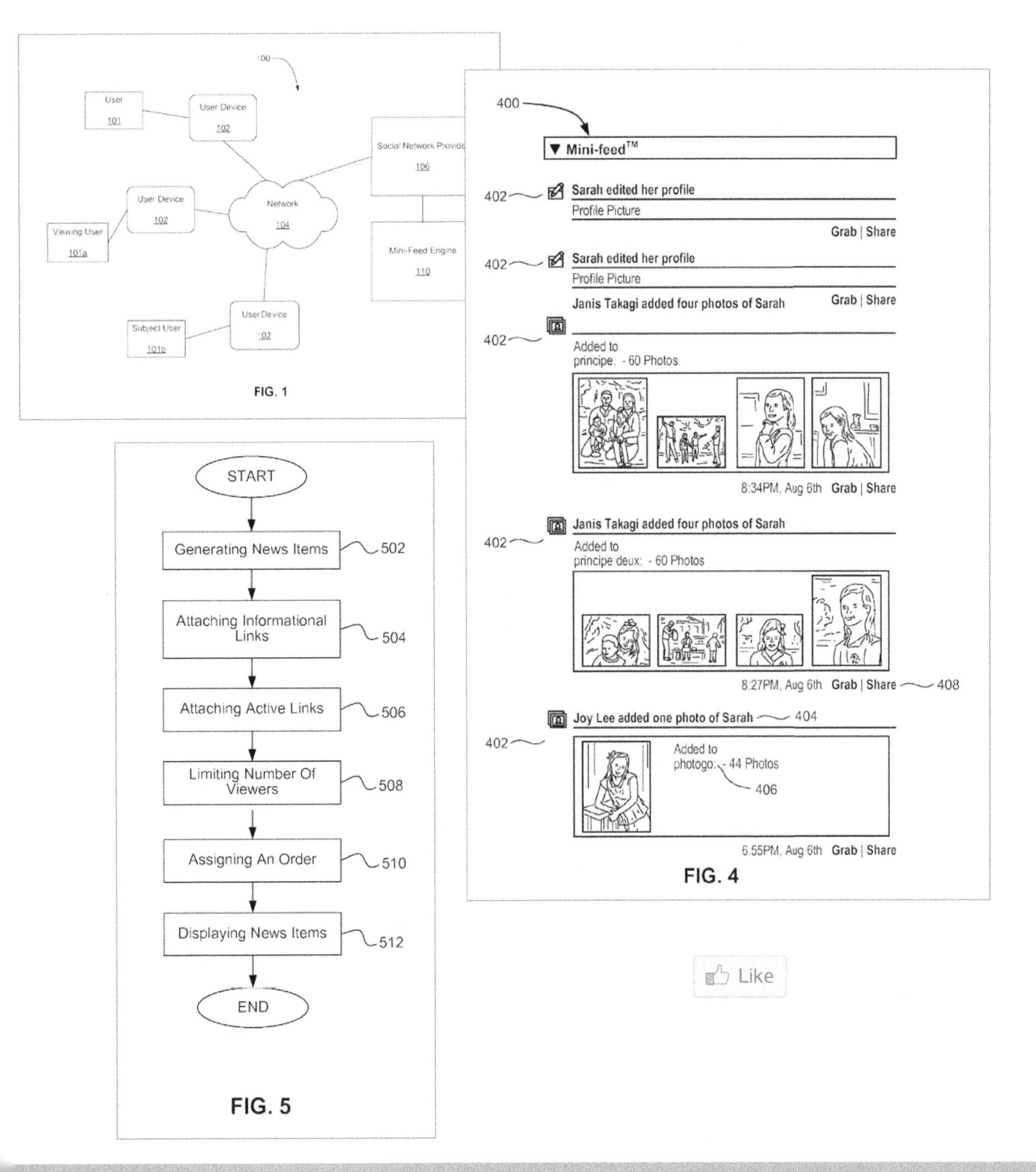

Entertainment for children is wildly different today than from what it was a century ago. The following two patents demonstrate this quite effectively. The drawings on these next two pages show a rag doll. Fine detail is used in her clothing and hair, and it's obvious the artist spent considerable time and effort on the drawing. Figures 2 and 3 disclose how she is assembled.

On the following two pages are two drawings of a far more modern entertainment device: a handheld Nintendo video game system. Figures 1-3 show the device's exterior and how thumbs are used to control it. Figure 4 shows how the device functions. Compare this to how the rag doll "functions." More than sixty years of difference, yet each with its own beauty.

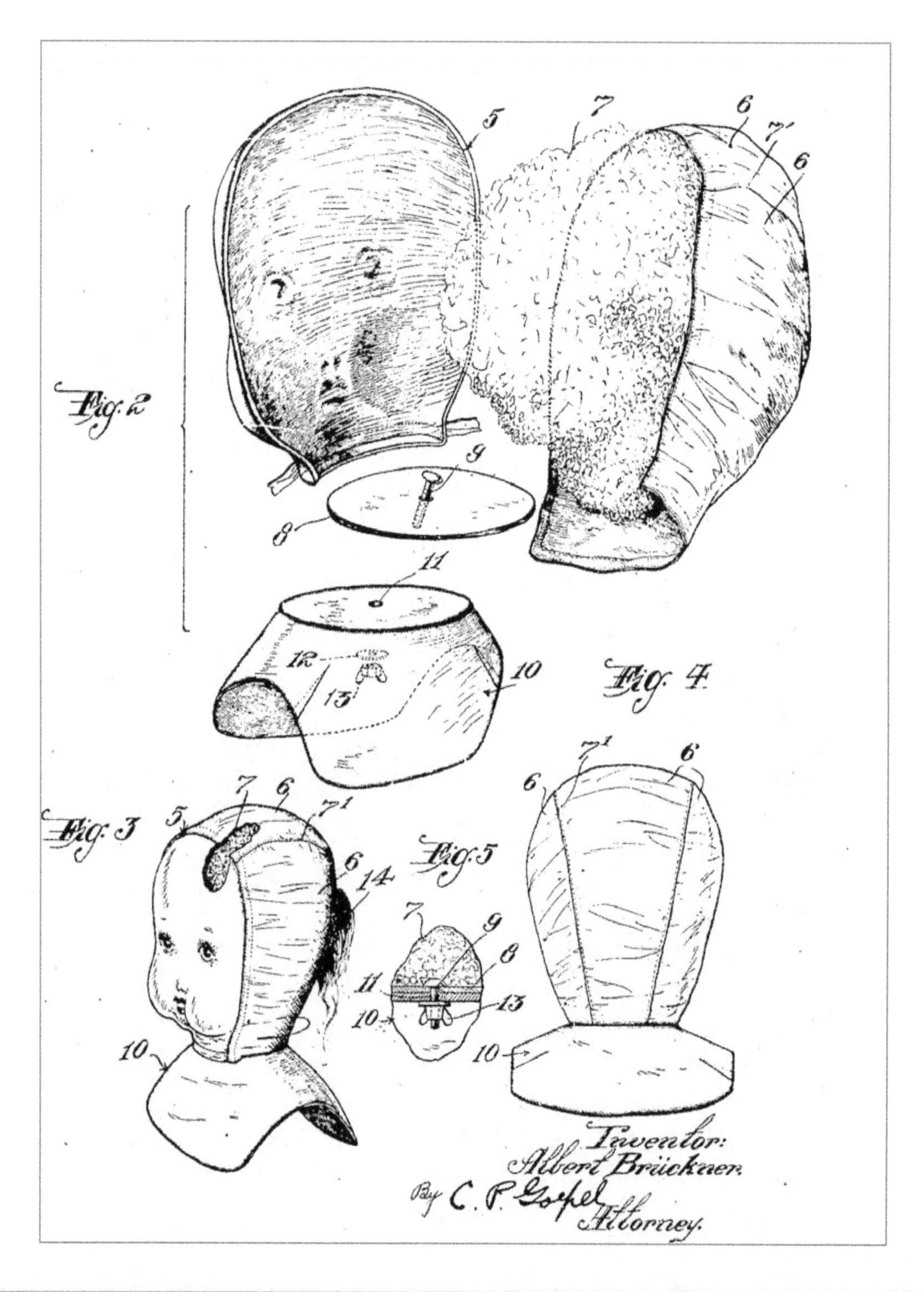

RAG DOLL
A. BRÜCKNER Oct. 20, 1925 No. 1,558,232

RAG DOLL
A. BRÜCKNER Oct. 20, 1925 No. 1,558,232

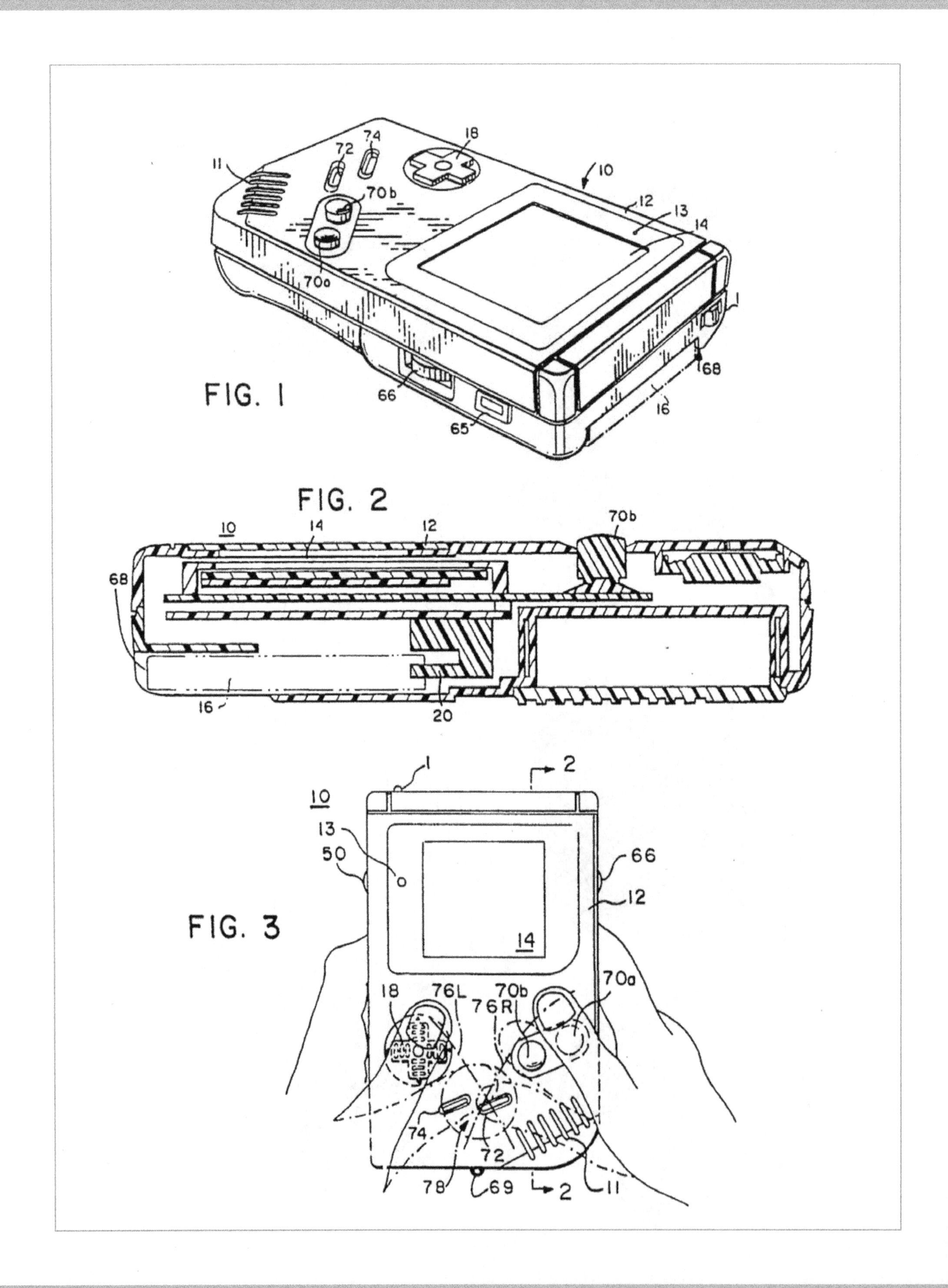

COMPACT HAND-HELD VIDEO GAME SYSEM
SATORU OKADA Feb. 9, 1993 No. 5,184,830

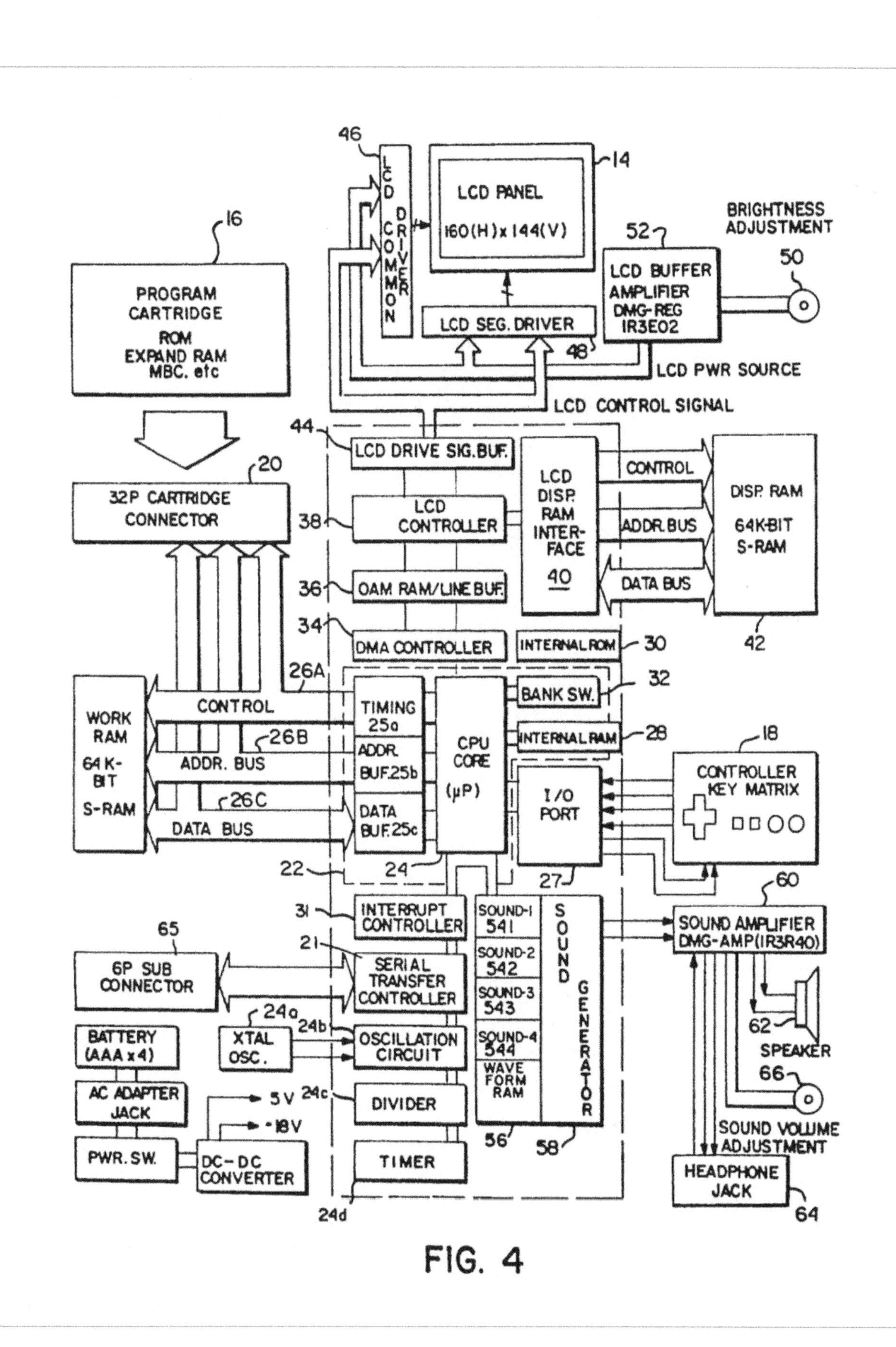

46
LCD COMMON
LCD DRIVER
LCD PANEL
160(H)x144(V)
14
BRIGHTNESS ADJUSTMENT
52
50
LCD BUFFER AMPLIFIER DMG-REG IR3E02
LCD SEG. DRIVER
48
LCD PWR SOURCE
LCD CONTROL SIGNAL
16
PROGRAM CARTRIDGE
ROM
EXPAND RAM
MBC. etc
20
32P CARTRIDGE CONNECTOR
44
LCD DRIVE SIG.BUF.
38
LCD CONTROLLER
LCD DISP. RAM INTER-FACE
40
CONTROL
ADDR.BUS
DATA BUS
DISP. RAM
64K-BIT S-RAM
42
36
OAM RAM/LINE BUF.
34
DMA CONTROLLER
INTERNAL ROM
30
26A
BANK SW.
32
WORK RAM
64K-BIT
S-RAM
CONTROL
TIMING 25a
ADDR. BUF.25b
DATA BUF.25c
CPU CORE
(μP)
INTERNAL RAM
28
26B
ADDR. BUS
26C
DATA BUS
I/O PORT
18
CONTROLLER KEY MATRIX
22
24
27
60
31
INTERRUPT CONTROLLER
SOUND-1 541
SOUND-2 542
SOUND-3 543
SOUND-4 544
WAVE FORM RAM
SOUND GENERATOR
SOUND AMPLIFIER DMG-AMP(IR3R40)
65
6P SUB CONNECTOR
21
SERIAL TRANSFER CONTROLLER
24a
24b
XTAL OSC.
OSCILLATION CIRCUIT
BATTERY (AAA x4)
AC ADAPTER JACK
PWR. SW.
5V
-18V
24c
DIVIDER
DC-DC CONVERTER
TIMER
24d
56
58
62
SPEAKER
66
SOUND VOLUME ADJUSTMENT
HEADPHONE JACK
64

FIG. 4

The following two examples are again of dolls and demonstrate not only the change in artistic style but also in cultural norms. On the first doll from 1895, notice the intricate detail incorporated in her clothing and face. Her body is completely covered giving her a matronly, modest feel.

DOLL
B. WILMSEN June 11, 1895 No. 24,381

Just sixty years later, the patent for a doll stand shows a completely different young woman. Long legs and a slender female figure clad in what might be a swimsuit reveal not just more body, but a seismic cultural shift. The past one hundred years have seen more changes than we often realize, and this is one example of such.

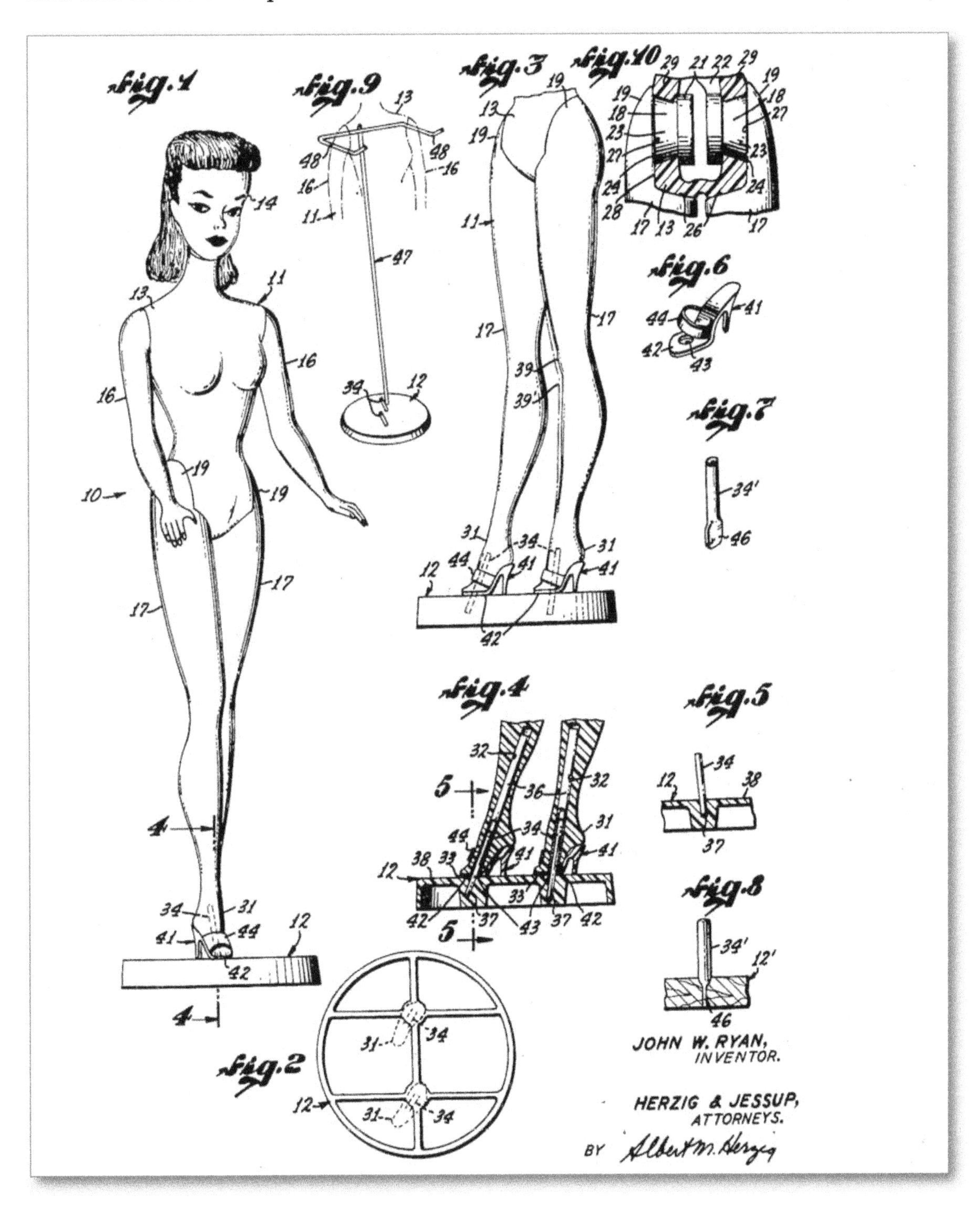

DOLL CONSTRUCTION

J. W. RYAN Nov. 21, 1961 No. 3,009,284

The following examples explore two ideas: the difference between the artistic styles of musical instrument patents, and the representation of a person, such as rock star Eddie Van Halen.

First, this is a classic example of the difference in artistic styles spanning nearly one hundred years. The instrument drawing in the 1899 patent has extensive detail and nuance. Each specific material is clearly depicted such that they almost become tangible.

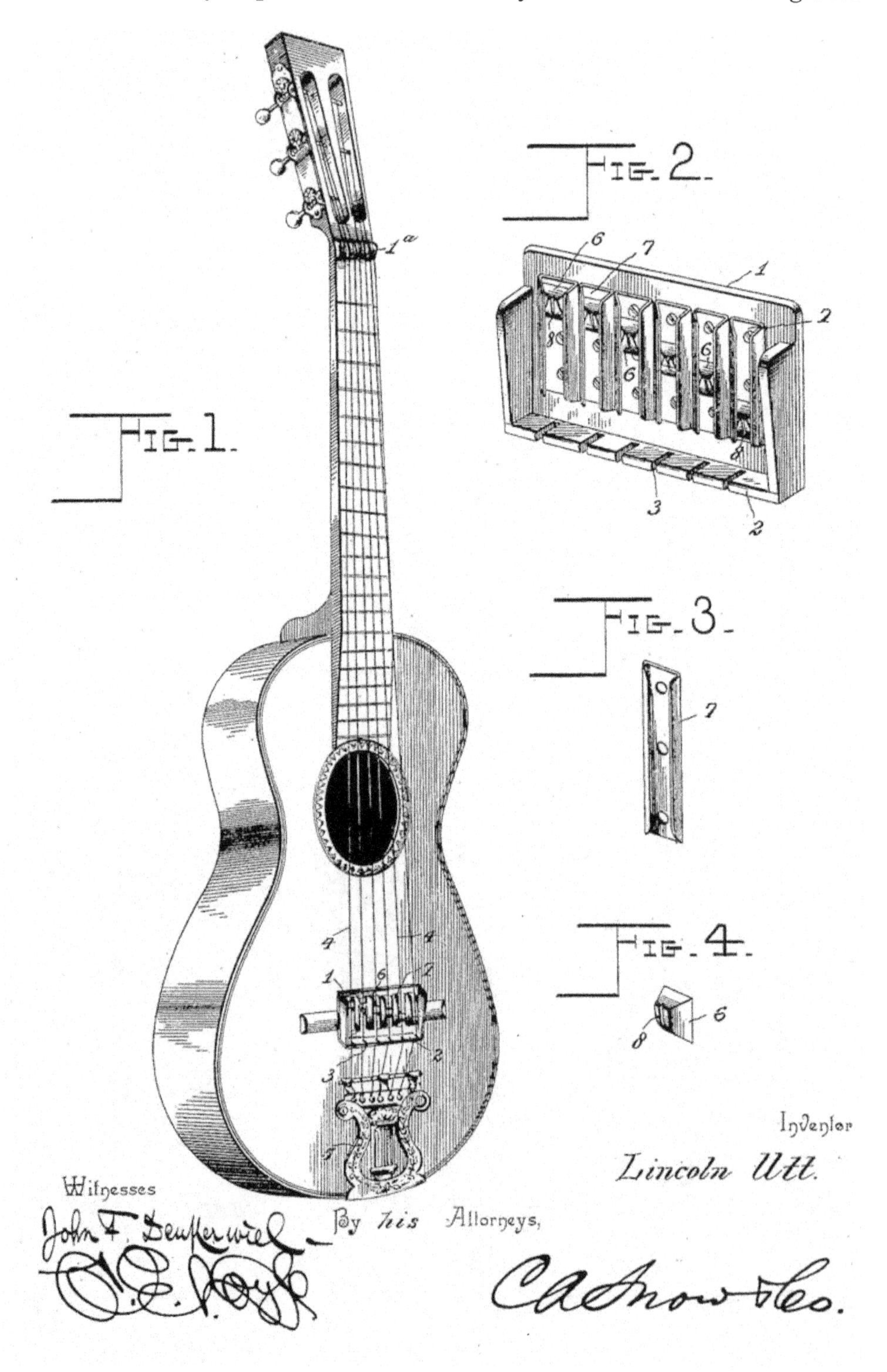

BRIDGE FOR STRINGED INSTRUMENTS
L. UTT. Nov. 29, 1898 No. 615,053

The second set of drawings from 1987, also clearly outlays the invention. However, the detail and artistic impulse is subdued except for the drawing of the musician, assumedly Van Halen himself. From a sterile, legal patent application perspective, there's no need for the caught-in-the-moment quality. However, here, once again, the artistic urge bursts forth and we get a glimpse of how the guitar support is actually used and would be seen when used.

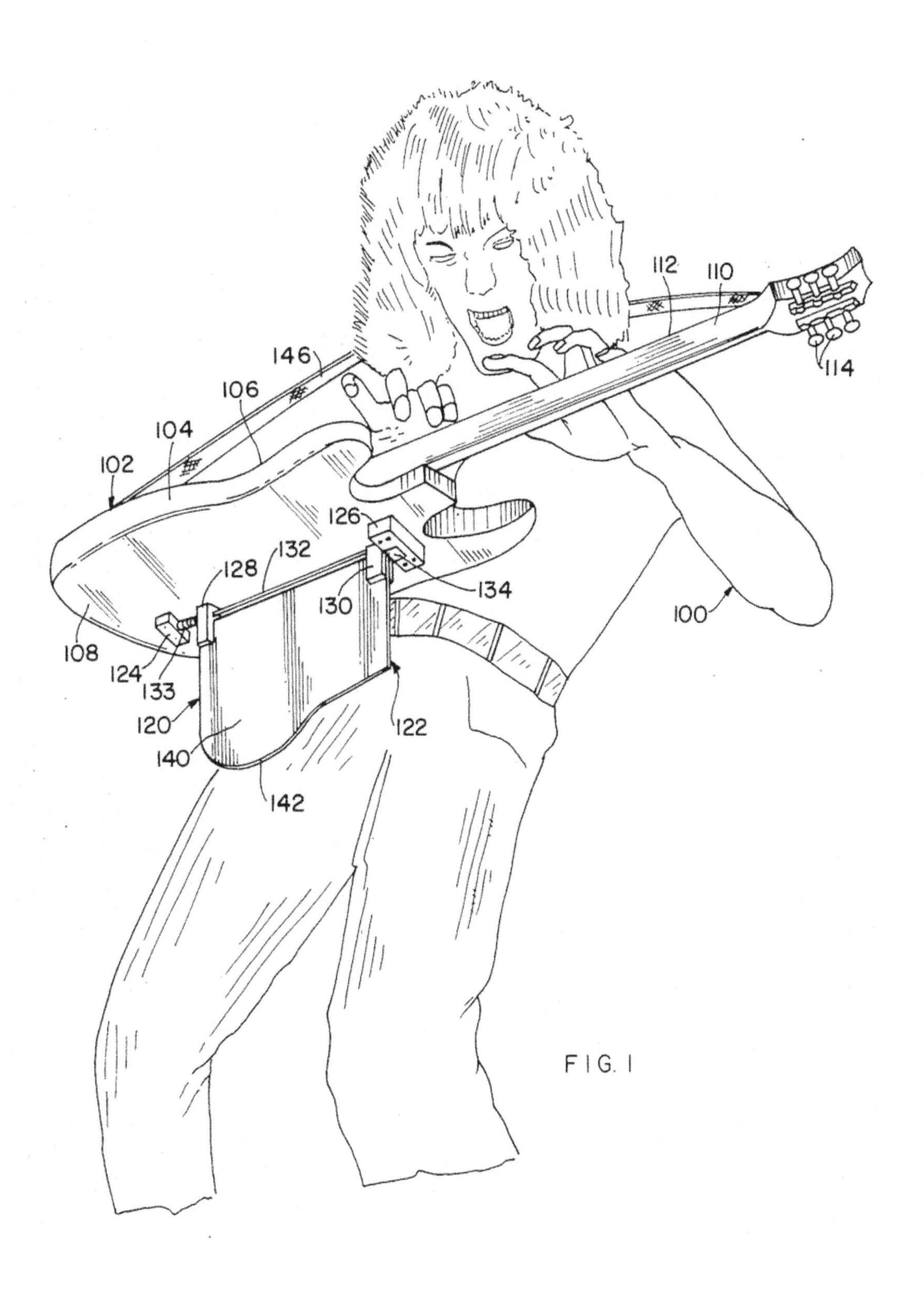

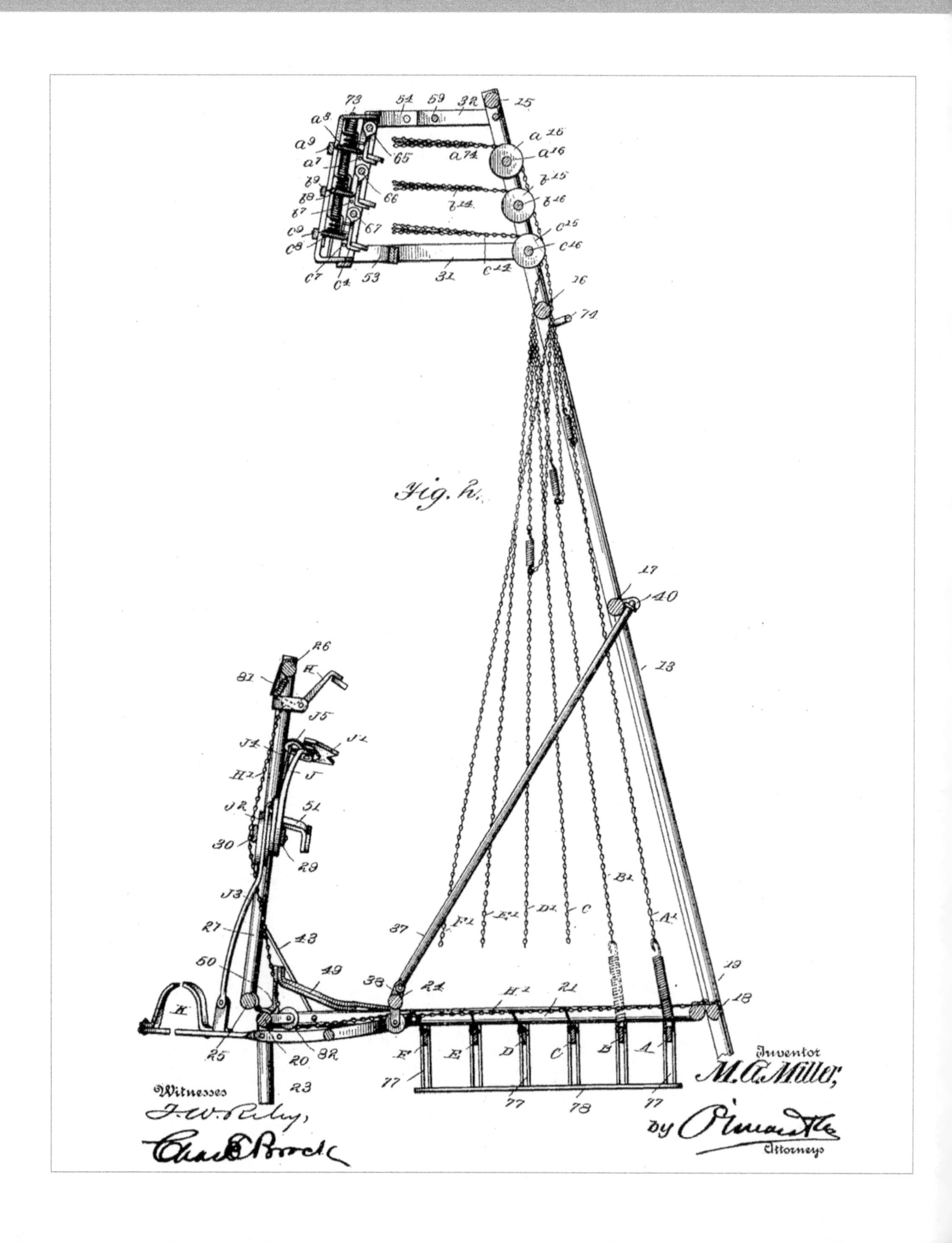

GUITAR SUPPORT AND PLAYER
M.G. MILLER Nov. 21, 1899 No. 637,273

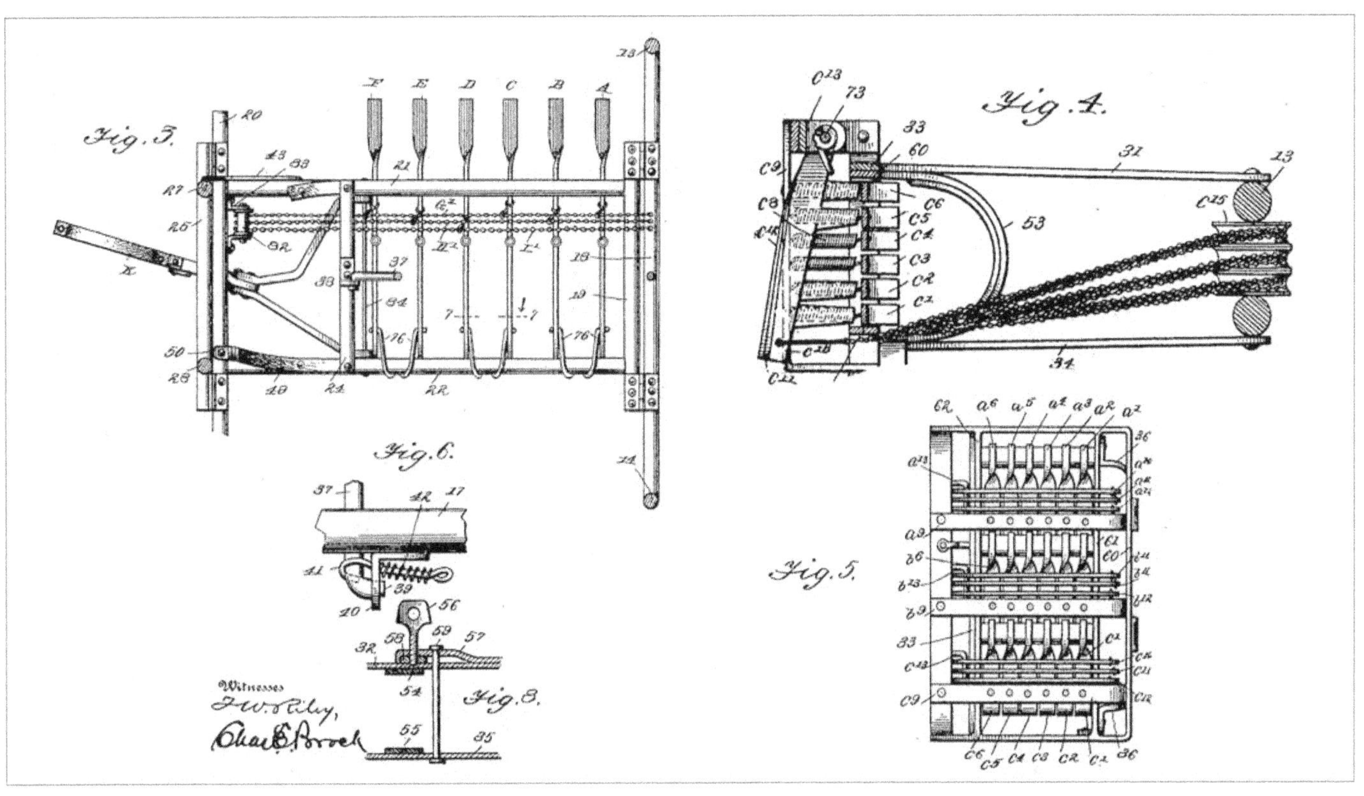

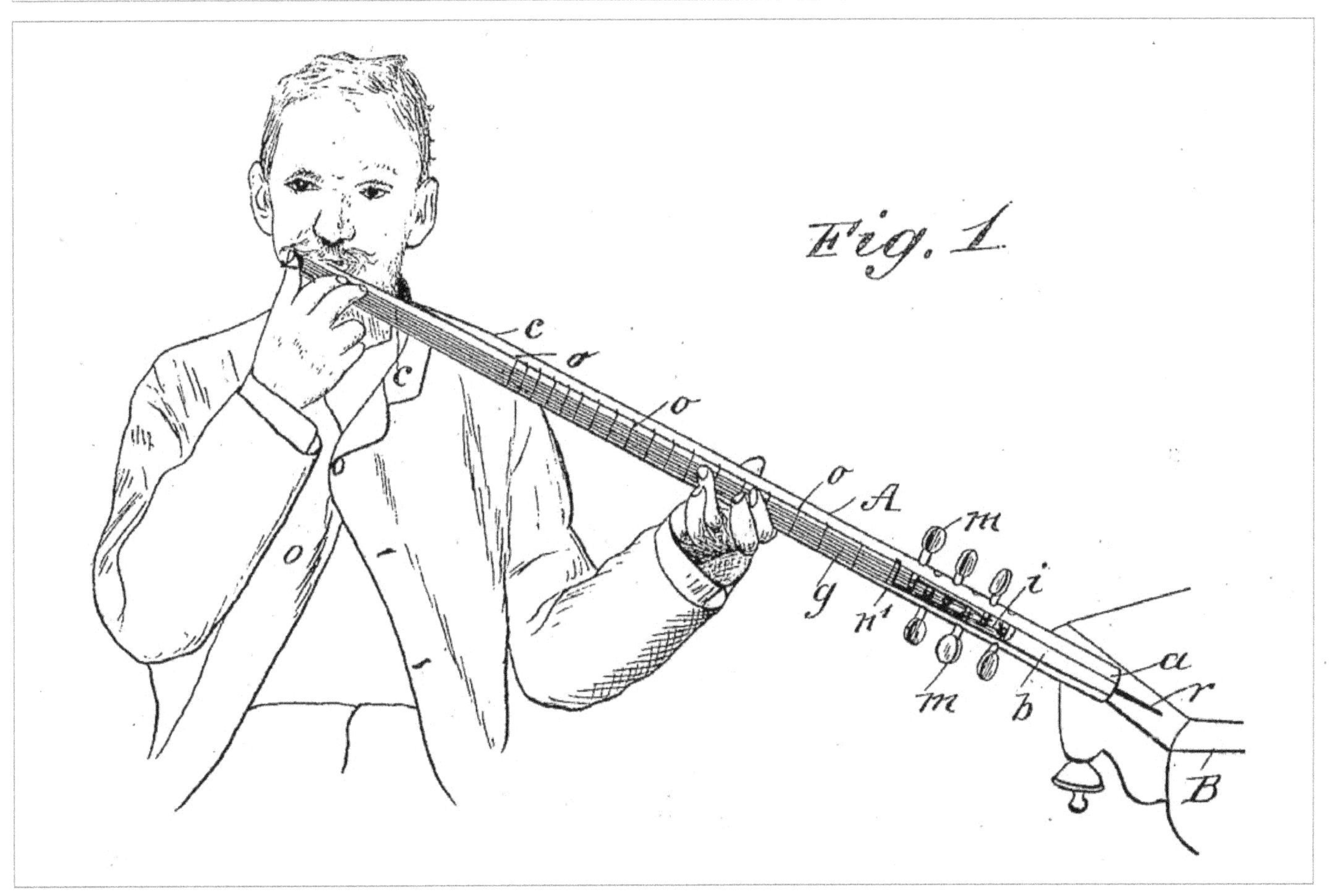

MUSICAL INSTRUMENT
E. ENRIQUEZ Oct. 16, 1894 No. 527,675

One of the most rapidly developing areas of change over the last several decades has been in the field of medicine. The medical treatments our grandparents received were far different from those used today. However, it's not just in the care of patients that changes have occurred. Our understanding of how the body and nature work has increased countless fold.

The following two examples demonstrate just how far we've come. The first is a beautiful drawing of a rather crude dentist's drill; a perspective real enough to strike fear in the bravest hearts. The second is a patent for a molecular model. Gorgeous in both its artistic beauty and in the core of nature it reveals.

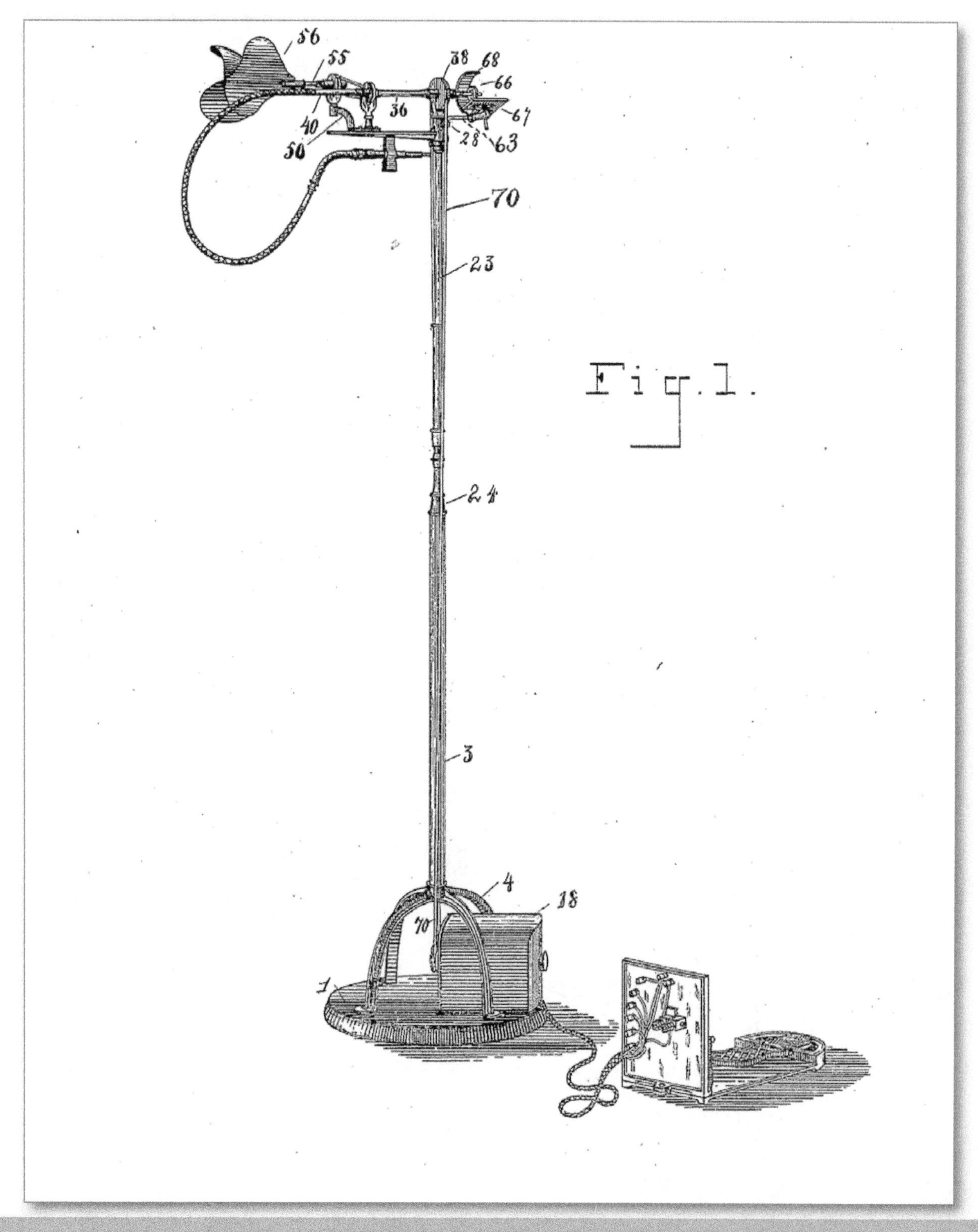

A. RETTER DENTAL DRILL Mar. 11, 1890 No. 423,344

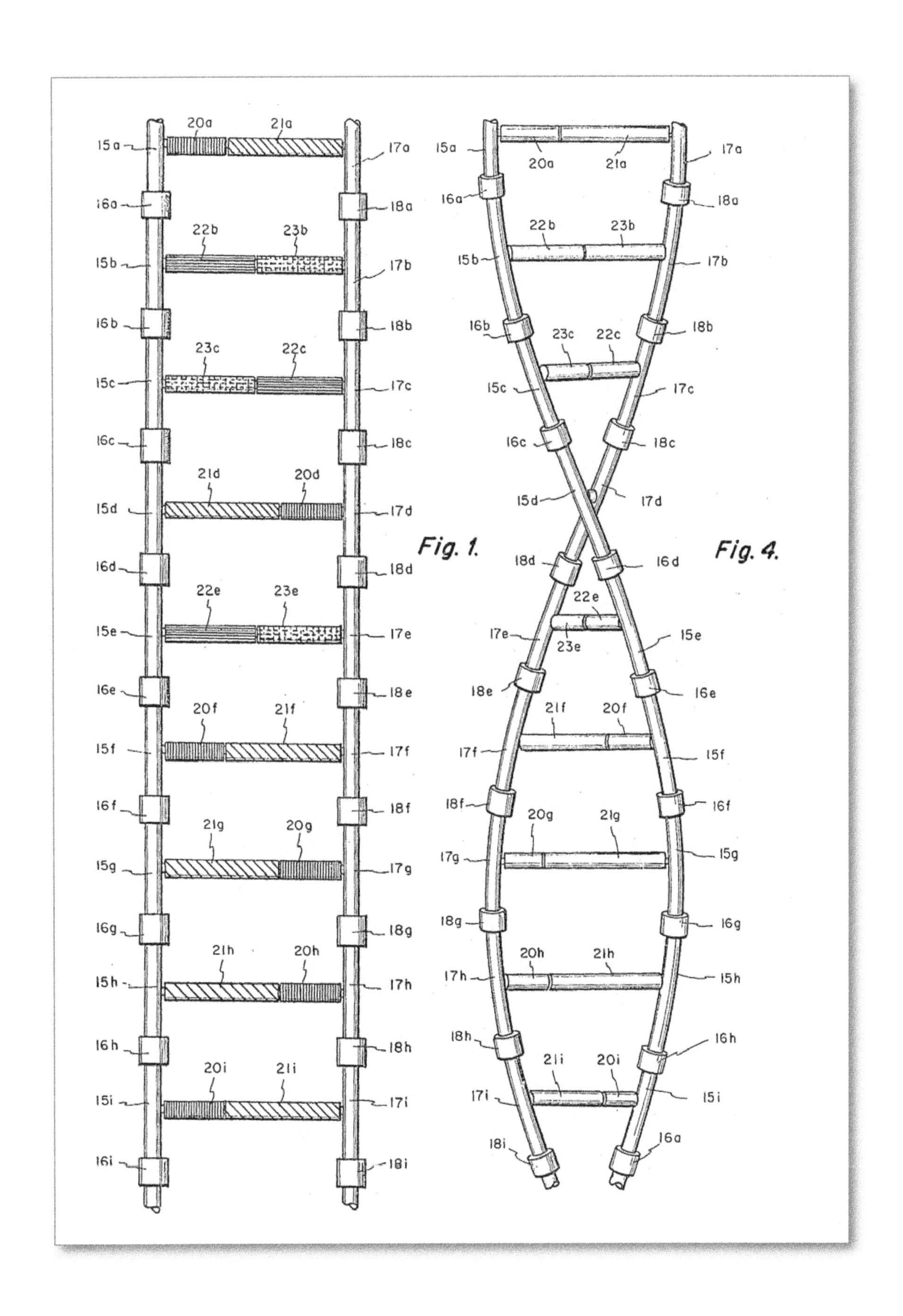

T. KLOTZ — MOLECULAR MODELS — Jan. 10, 1967 — 3,296,714

The next technological advancement really needs no introduction. Take a look at the road engine from 1895 versus that of 1995.

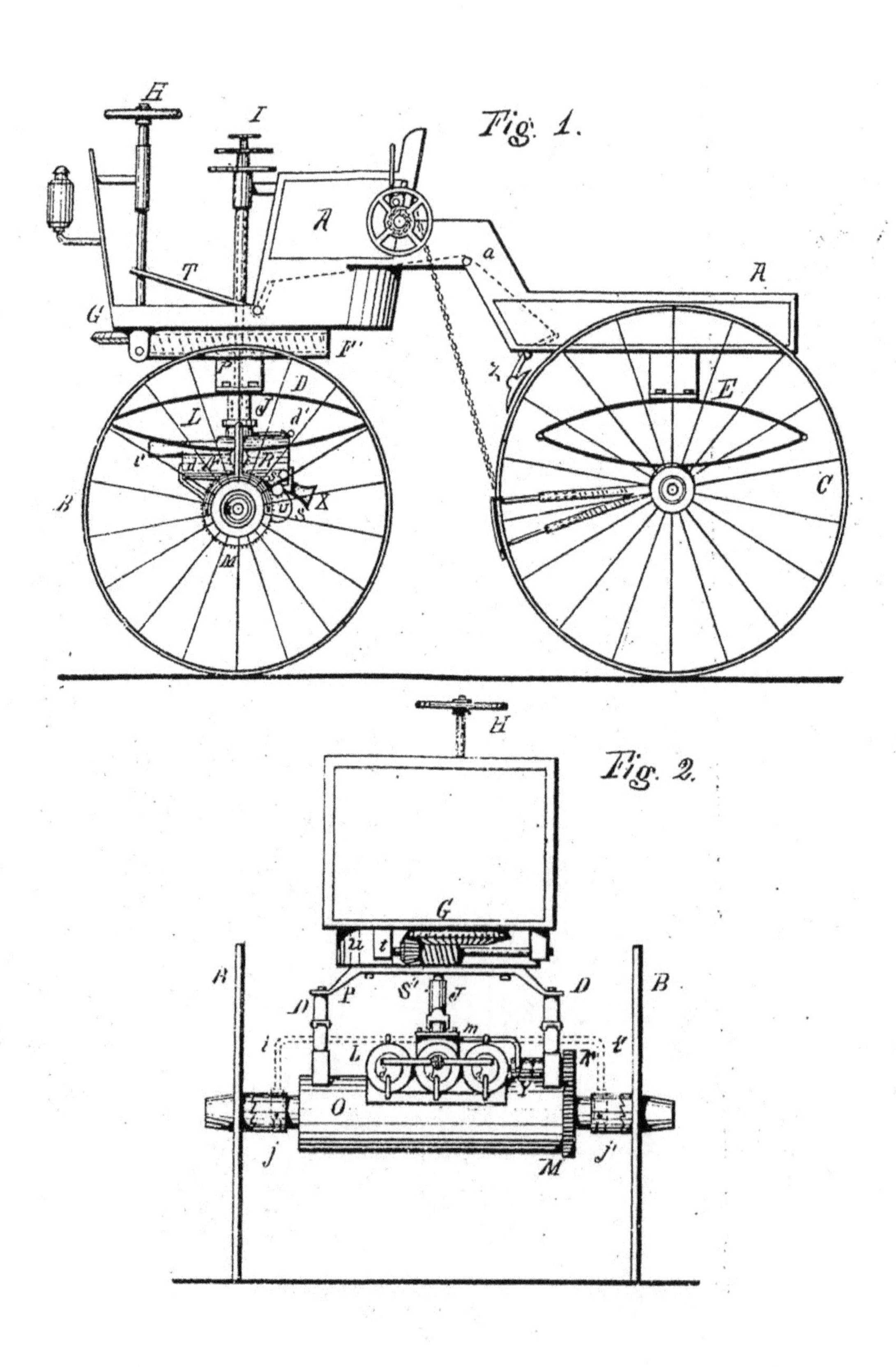

G.B. SELDEN ROAD-ENGINE Nov. 5, 1895 No. 549,160

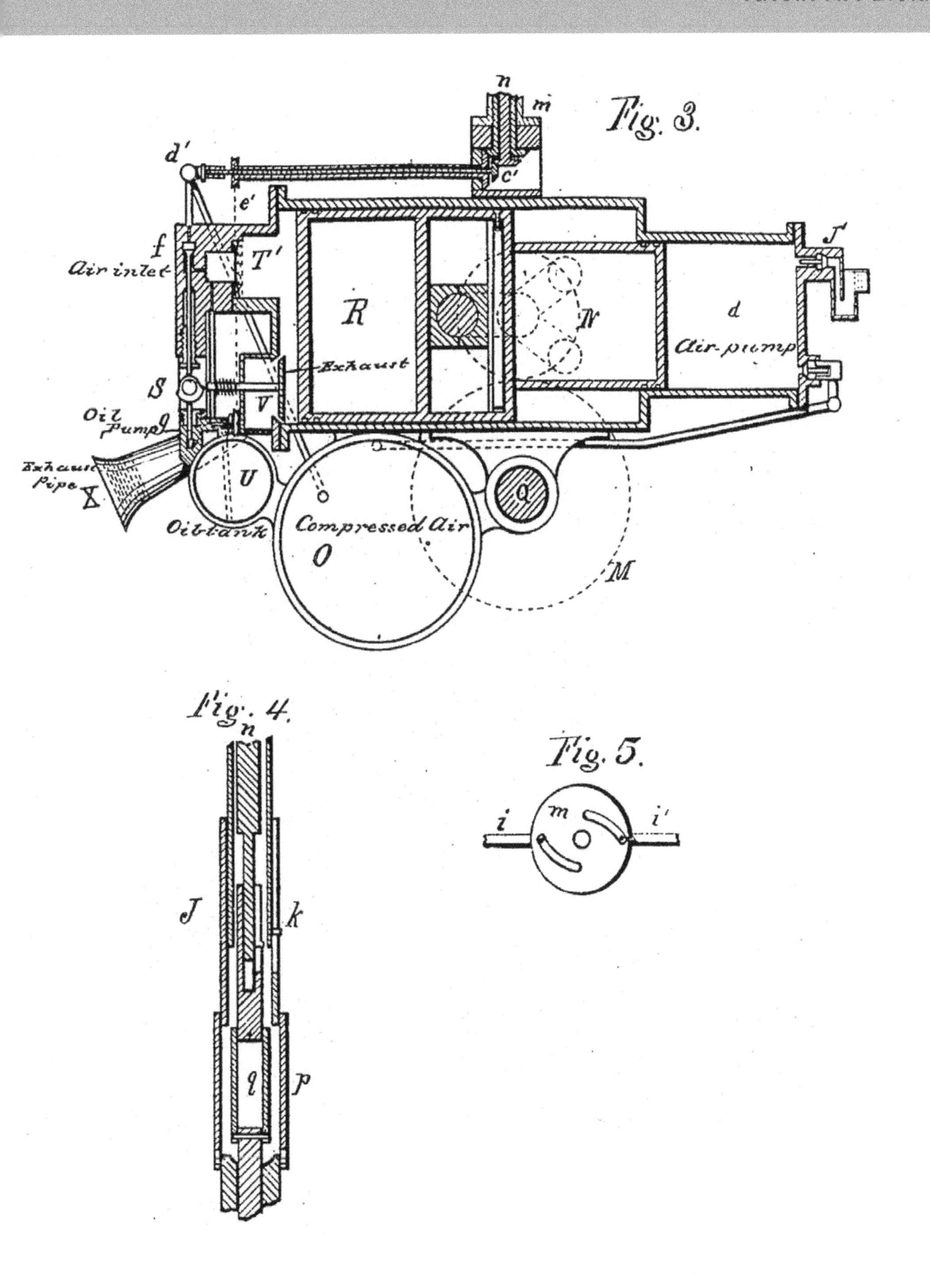
Fig. 3.
n
m
d'
c'
e'
f
Air inlet
T'
R
N
d
Air-pump
J'
Exhaust
S
V
Oil Pump
g
Exhaust Pipe
X
U
Oil tank
Compressed Air
O
Q
M
Fig. 4.
n
J
k
q
p
Fig. 5.
i
m
i'

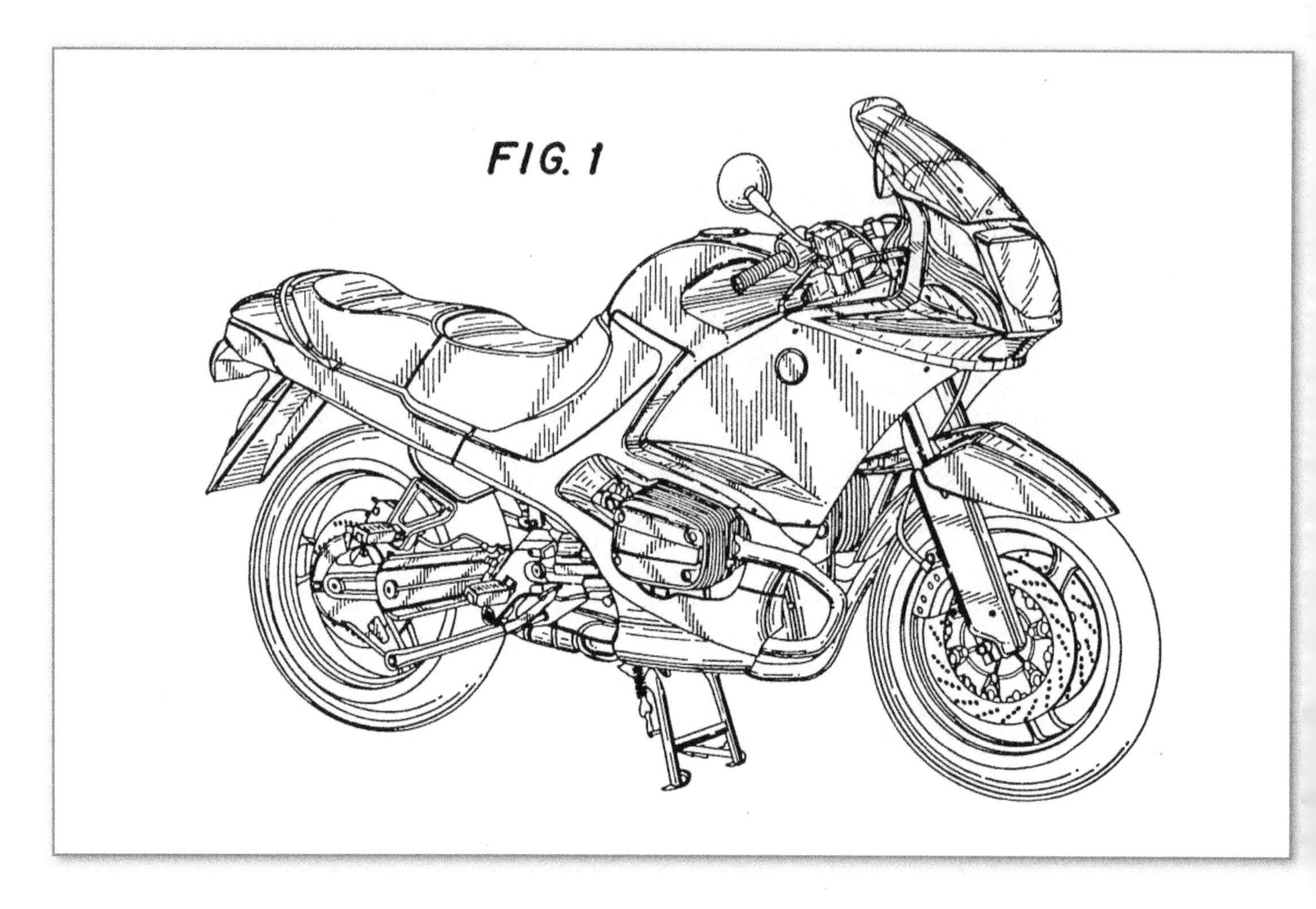

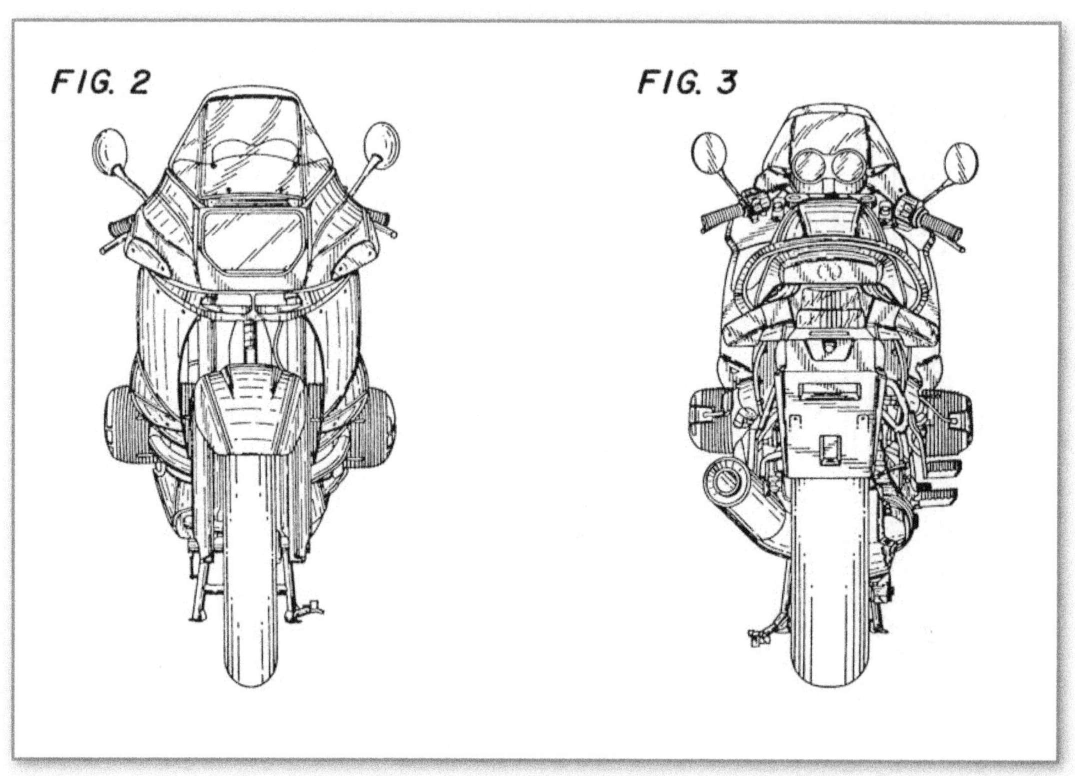

HEINRICH ET AL.

MOTORCYCLE
JUNE 14, 1994

No. D347,808

FIG. 1

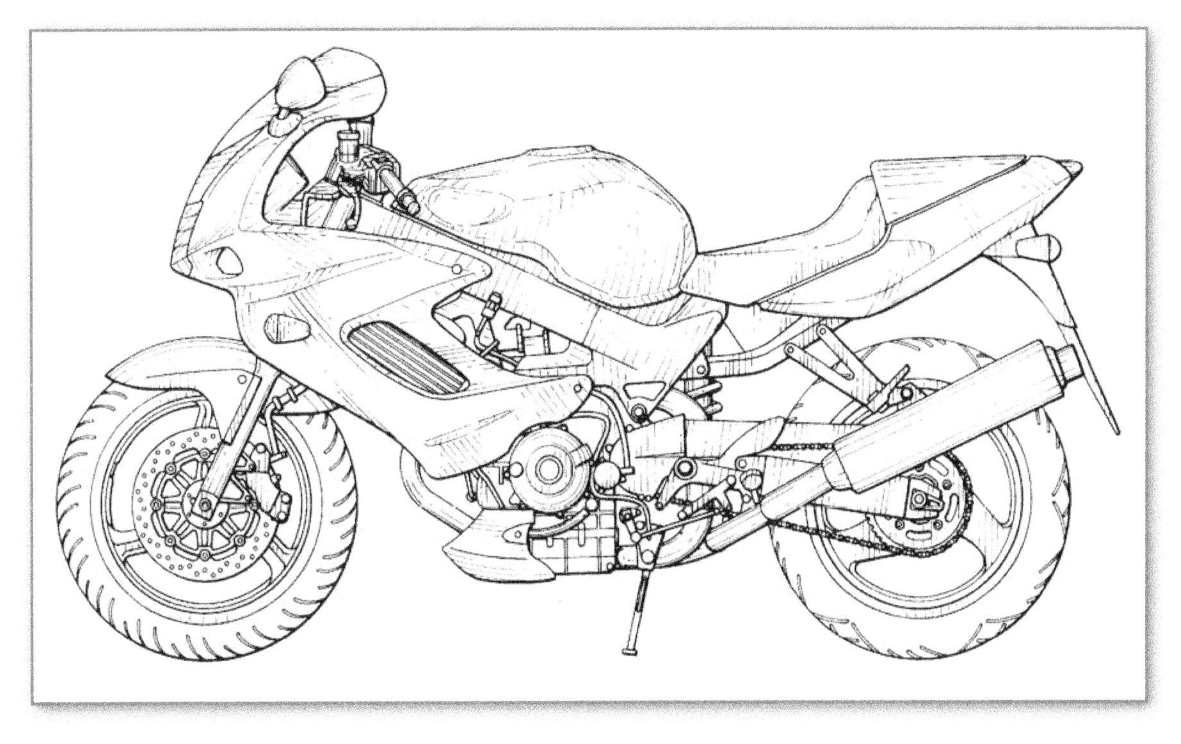

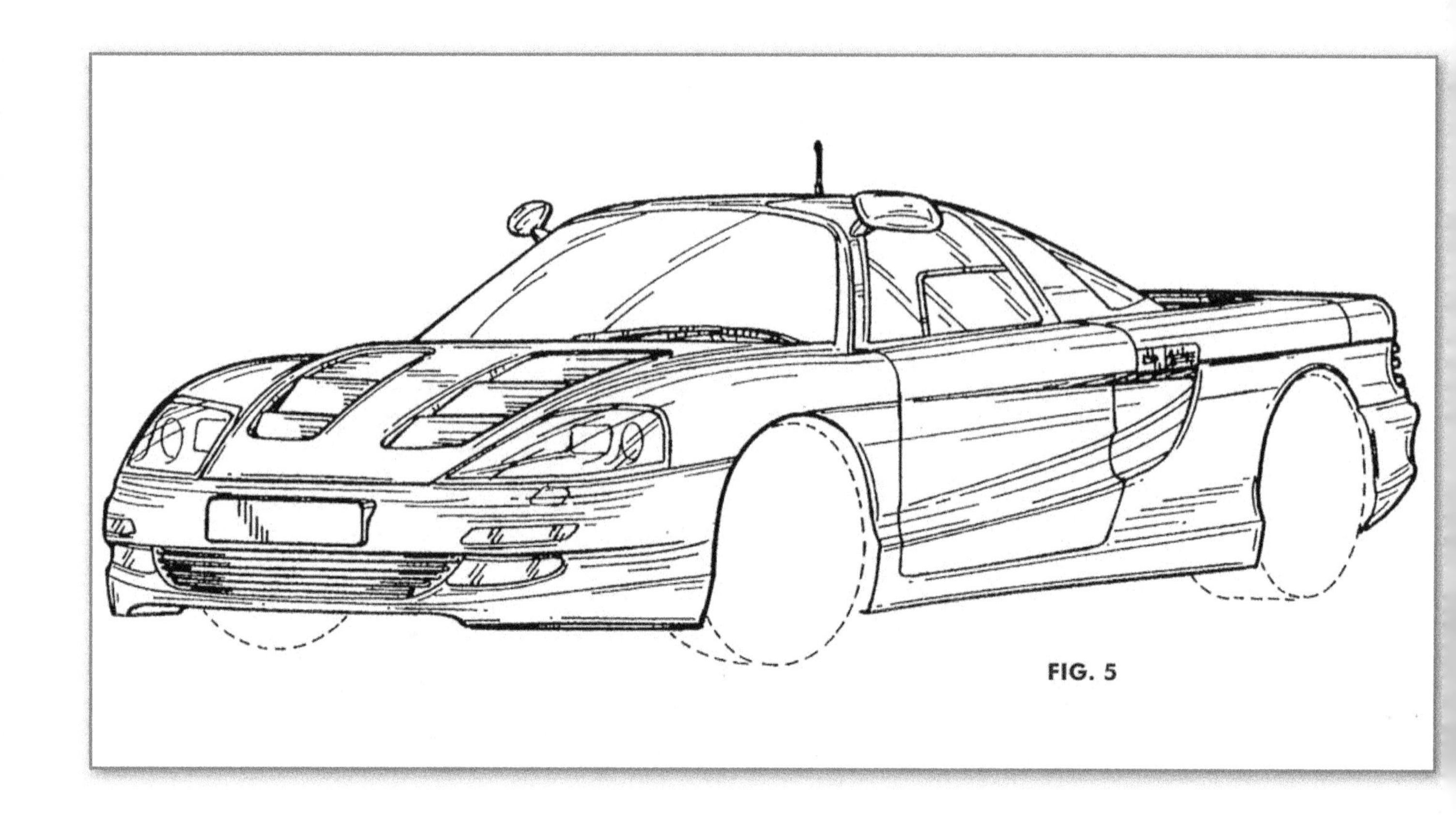

FIG. 5

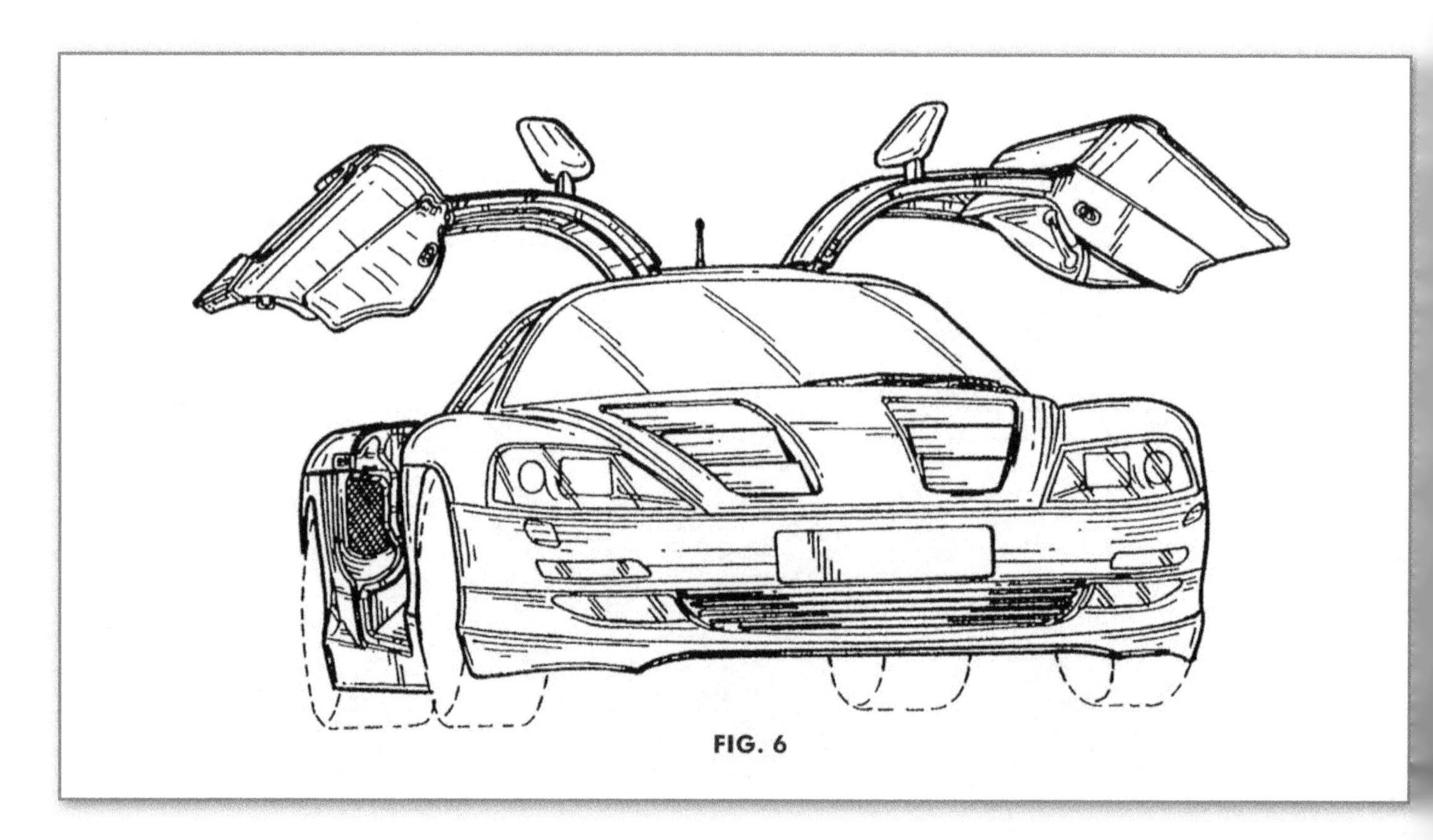

FIG. 6

BRUNO SACCO

SPORTS CAR BODY
May 2, 1995

No. D357,887

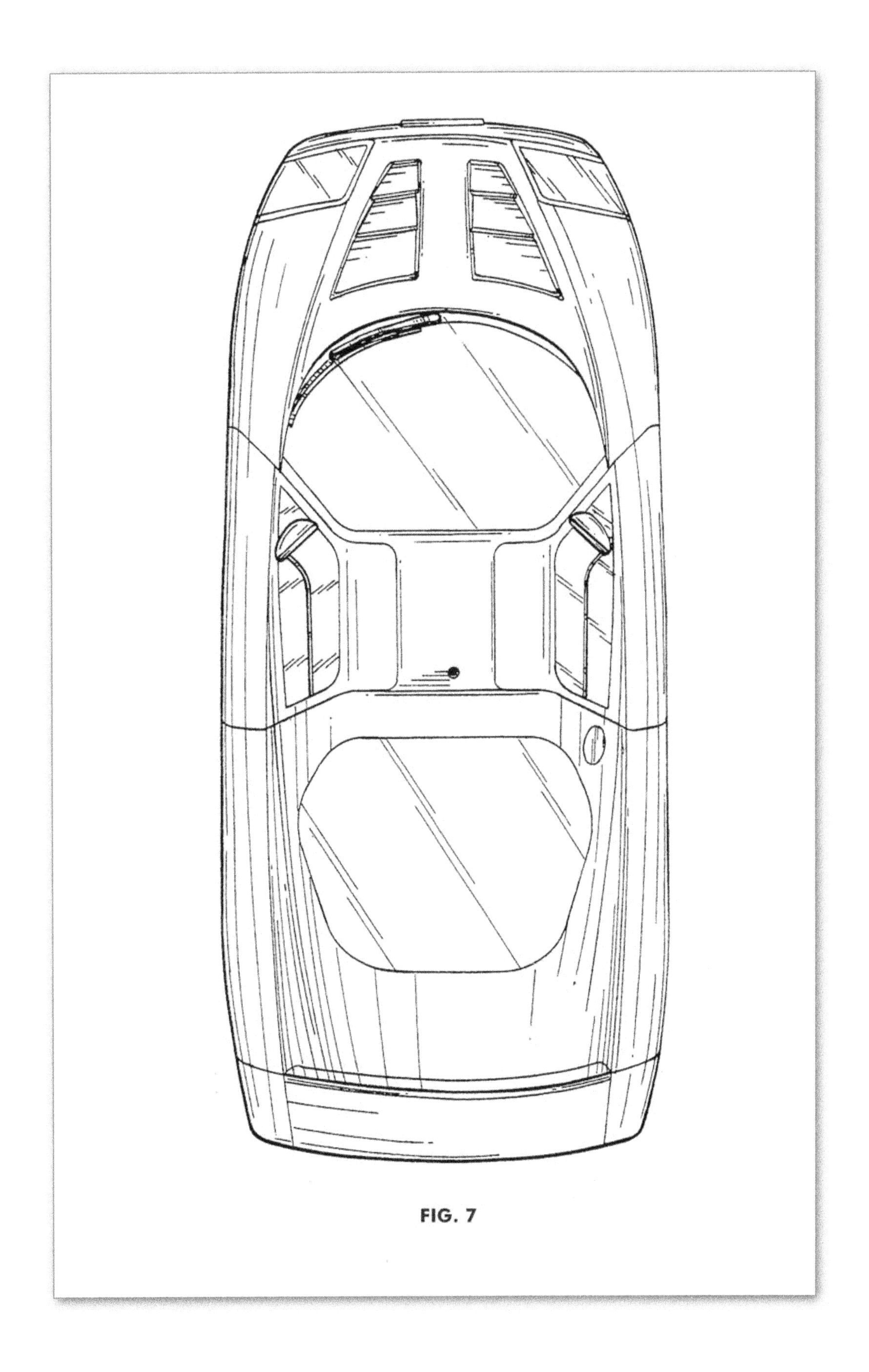

FIG. 7

Patent art examples of progress in technology could go on indefinitely. There are very few areas of our lives that modern science hasn't completely changed. Within it all, the art of the patent thrives. The following drawings of garden tools couldn't show this more clearly. The first illustrates an invention in intricate hand-drawn detail. The second example of the garden hose attachment is bold, confident, beautiful and undoubtedly drawn with the aid of a computer. Each drawing does its job in disclosing the invention, and both reveal the artistic nature of humankind itself.

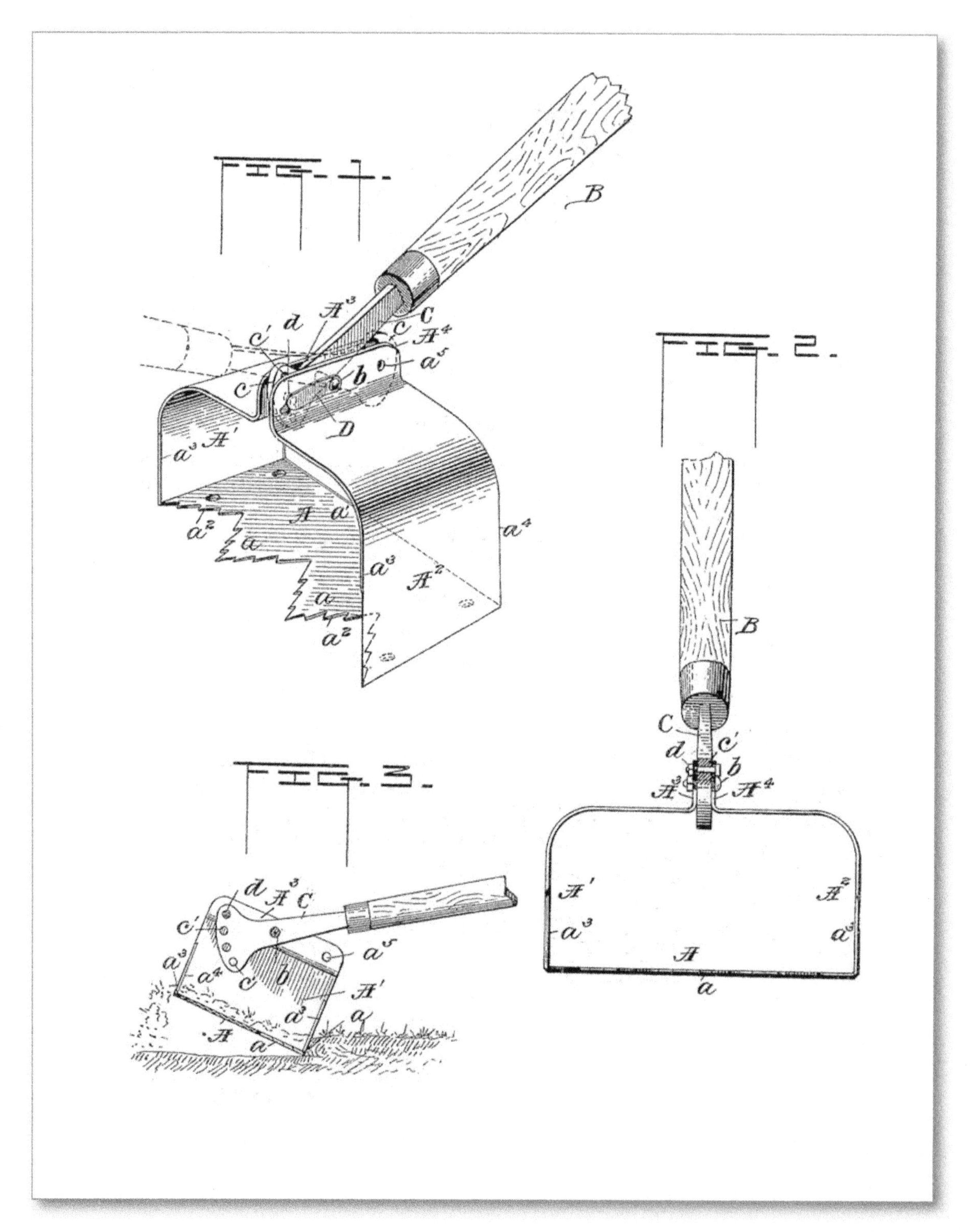

M. POWERS GARDEN TOOL Feb. 21, 1893 No. 492,364

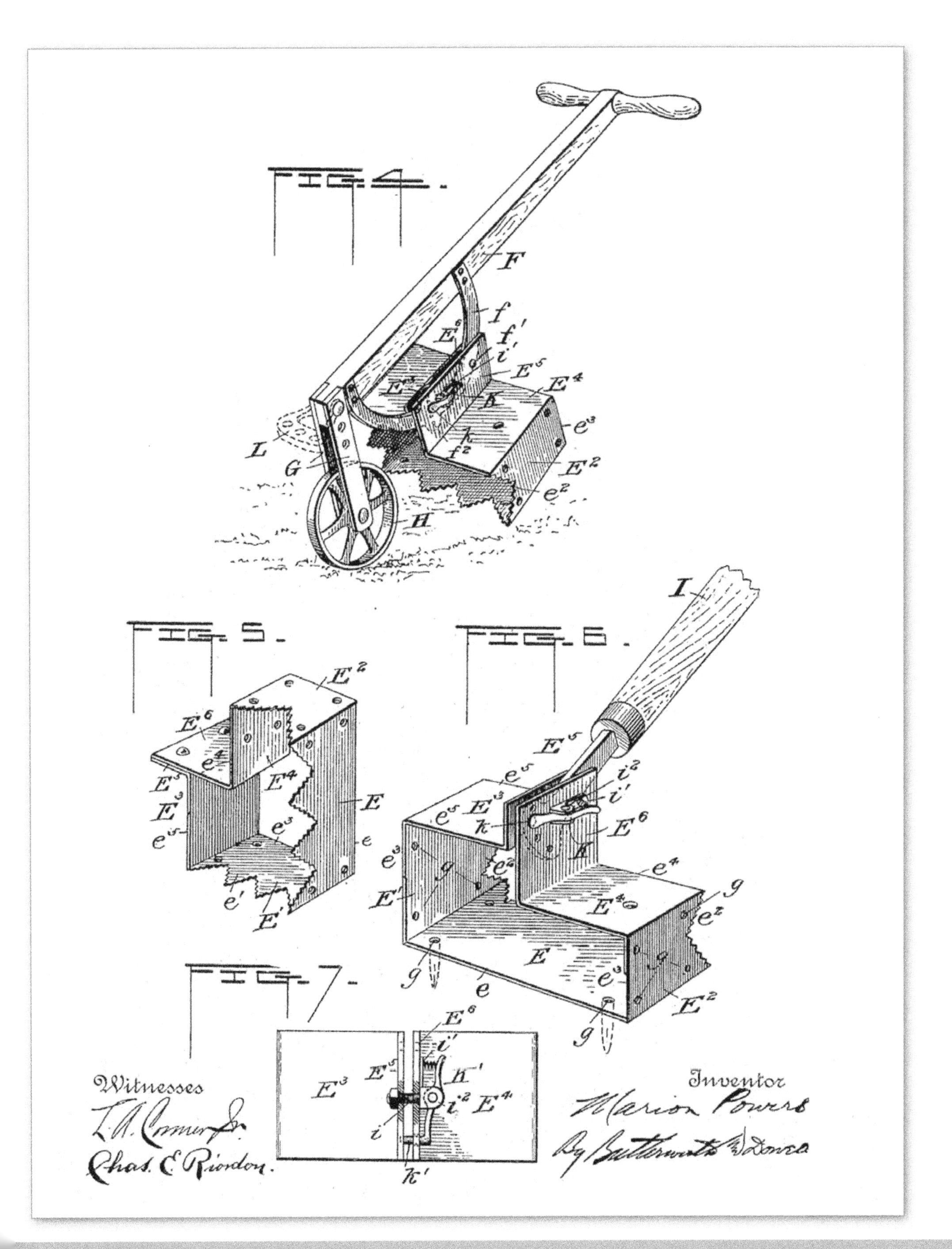

M. POWERS

GARDEN TOOL
Feb. 21, 1893

No. 492,364

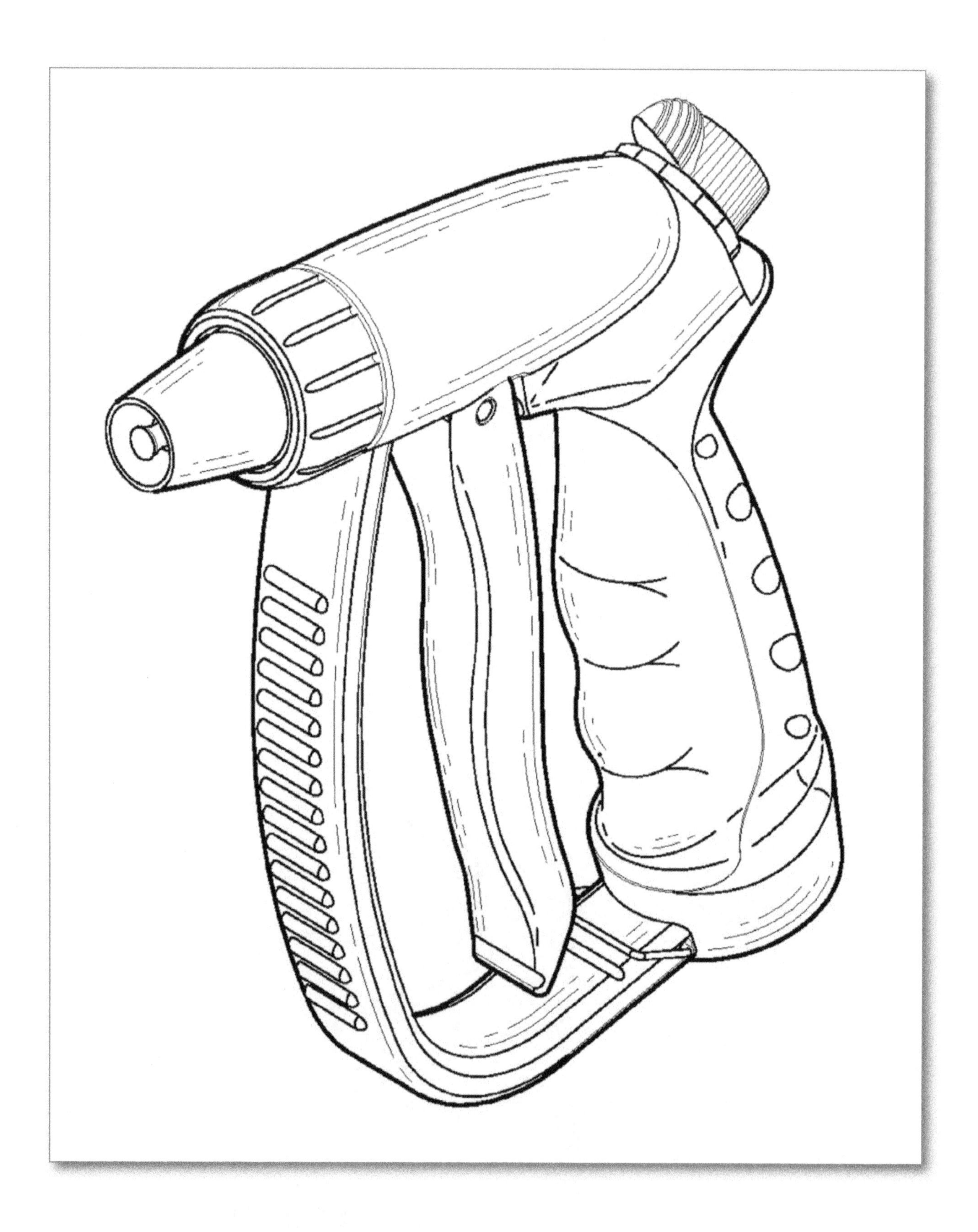

CHIN-YUAN CHEN

WATER SPRAY GUN
May 4, 2010

No. D615,157

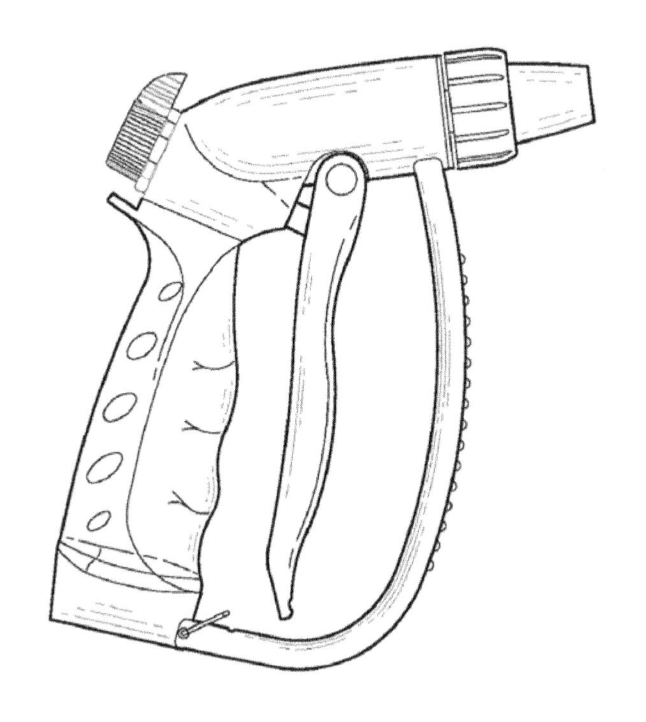

FIG. 4

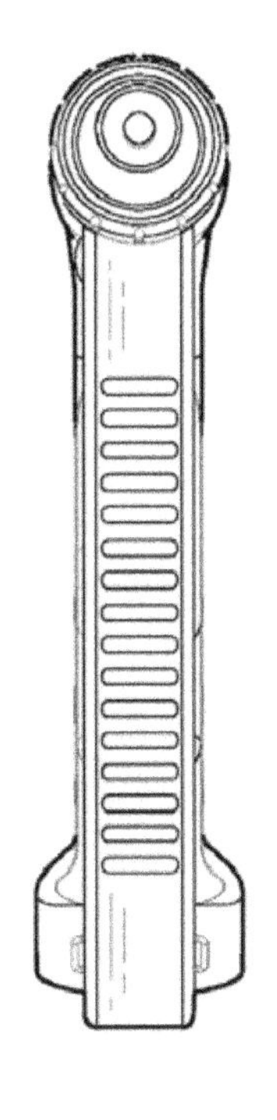

FIG. 2

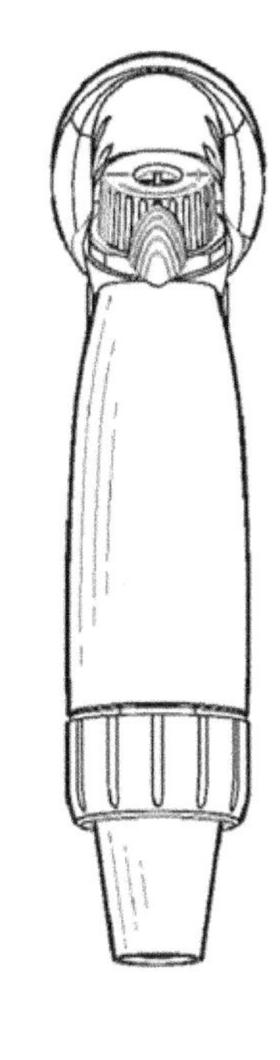

FIG. 6

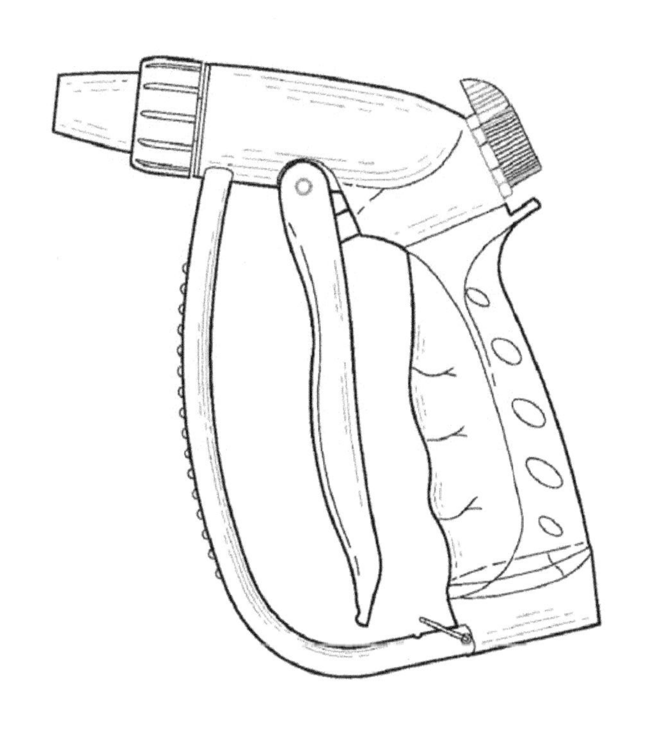

FIG. 5

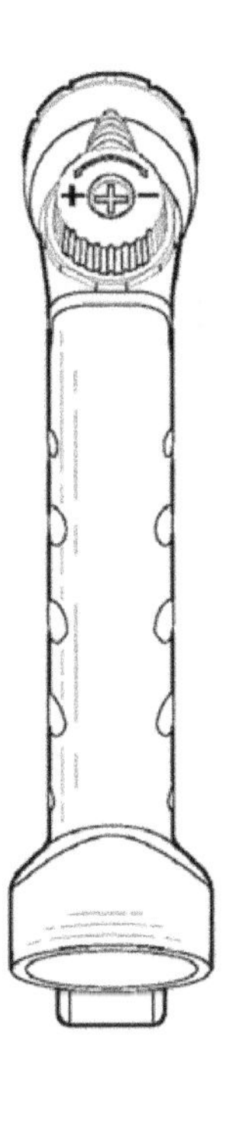

FIG. 3

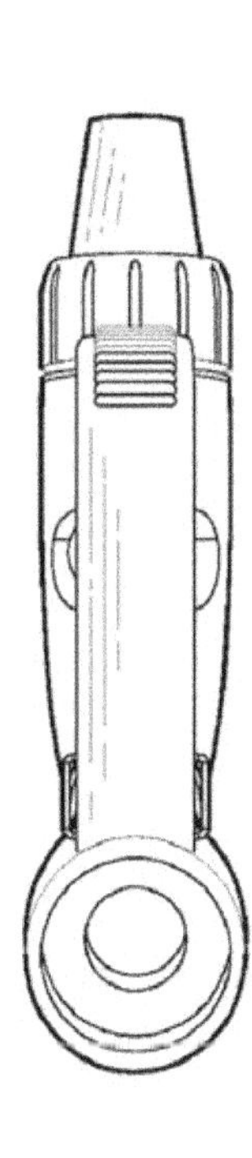

FIG. 7

The final four patent drawings in this chapter reiterate the central theme: patent art reflects what has changed in both inventions and the cultural style of the times. No individual era is better or worse. The beauty of art thrives within them all and begs the question, what will patent art look like in another hundred years?

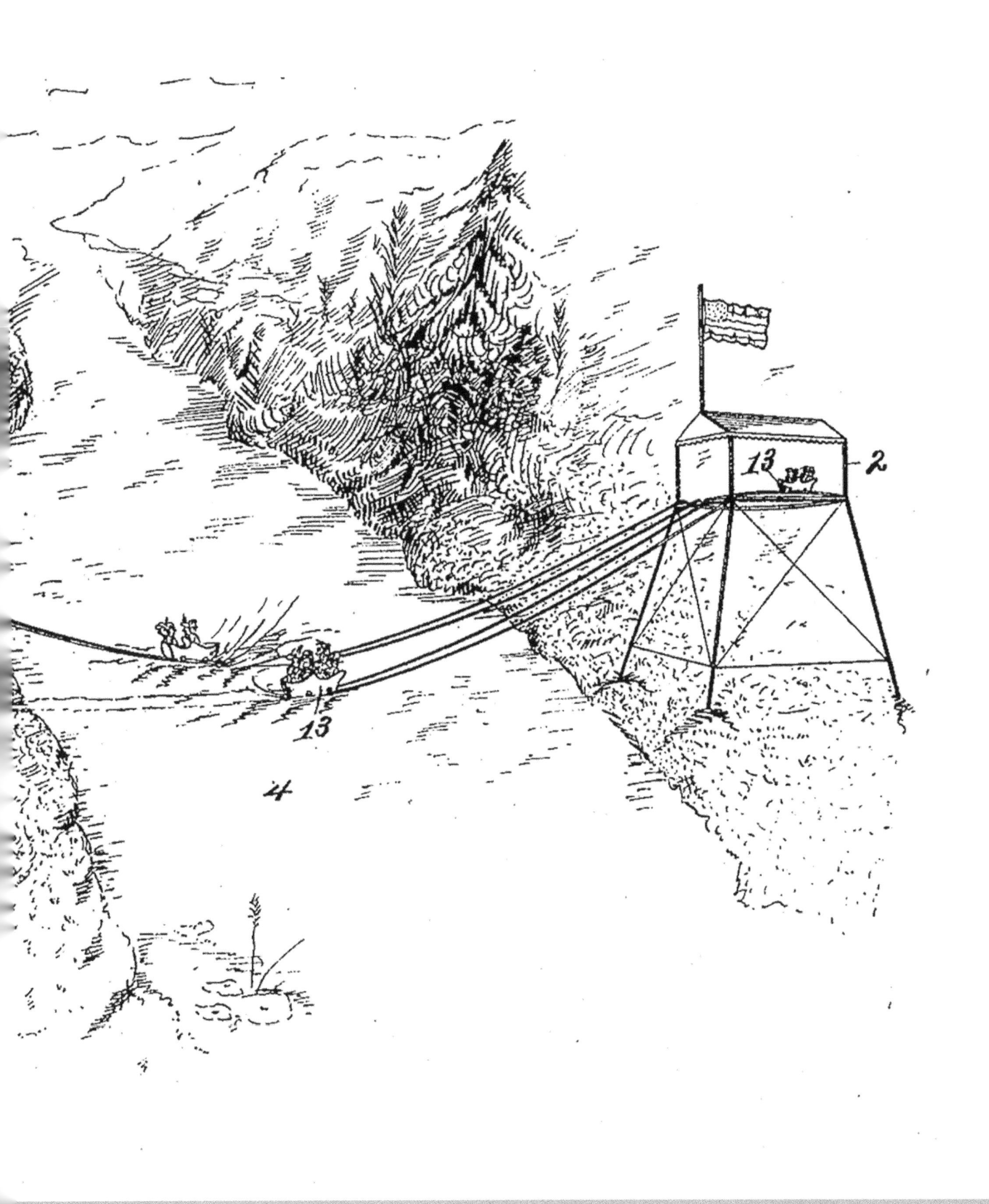

AMUSEMENT APPARATUS
D.M. HARMAN Oct. 27, 1896 No. 570,016

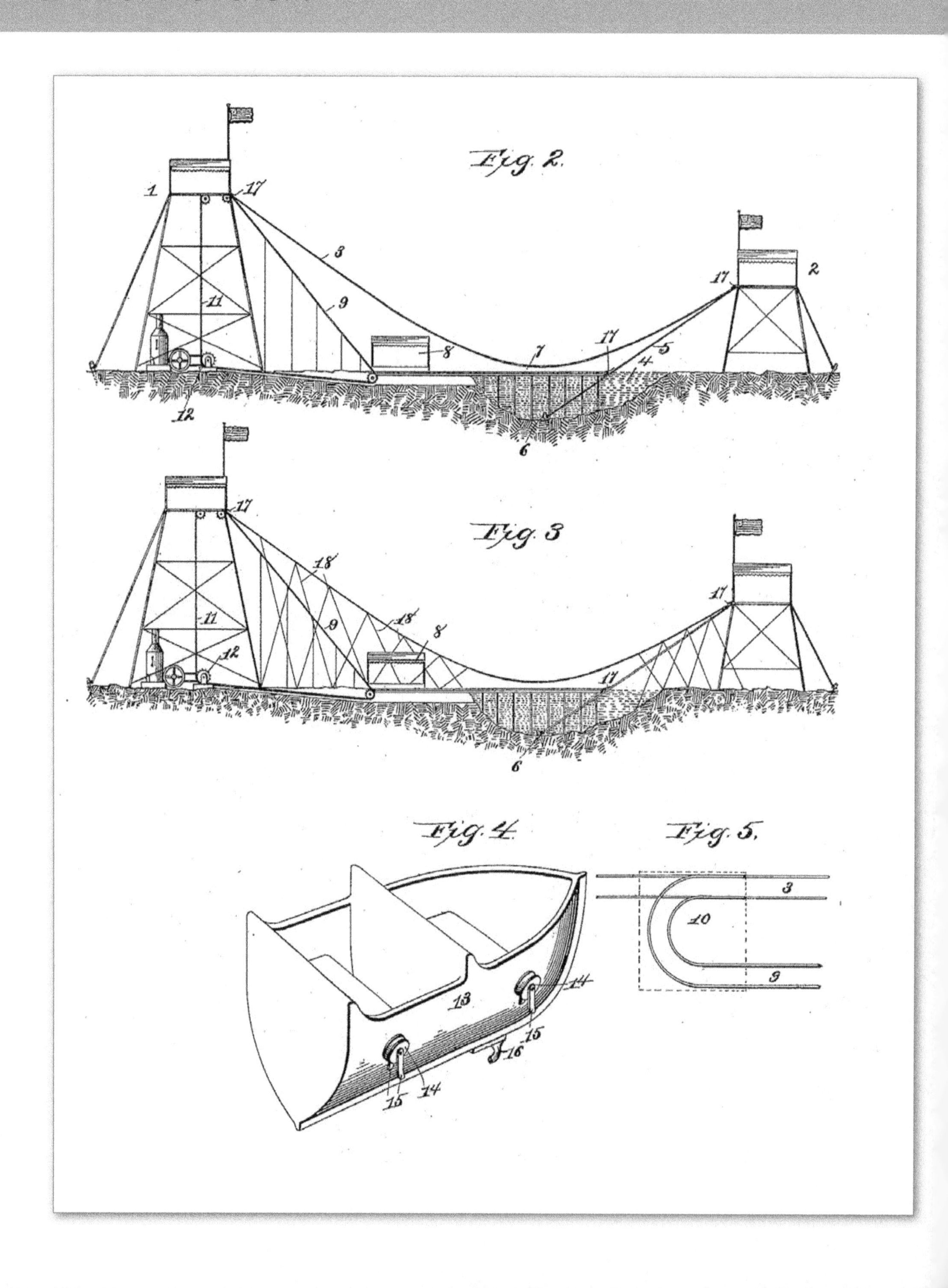

D.M. HARMAN

AMUSEMENT APPARATUS
Oct. 27, 1896

No. 570,016

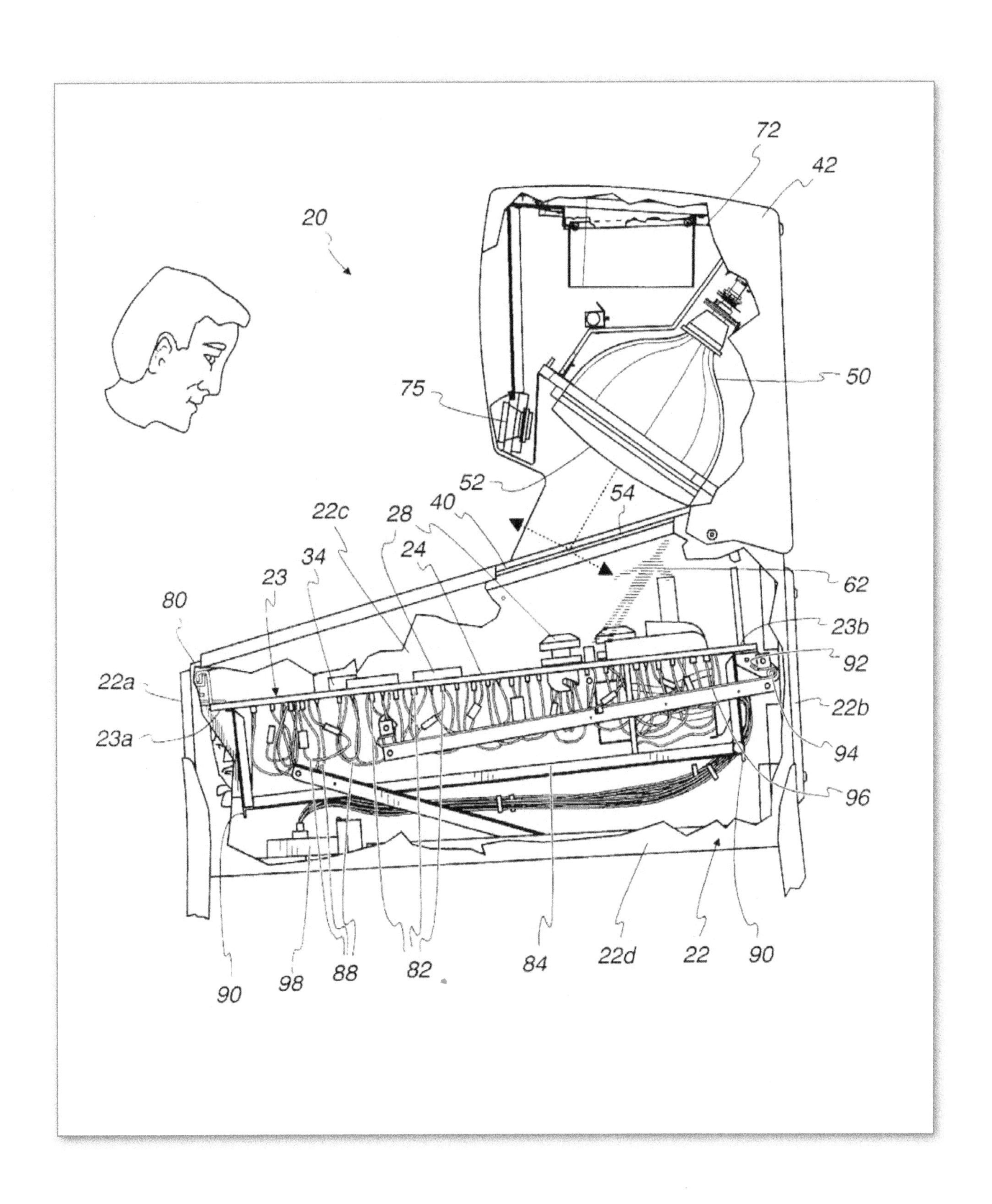
72
42
20
50
75
52
54
22c
28
40
24
34
23
62
80
23b
92
22a
22b
23a
94
96
90
98
88
82
84
22d
22
90

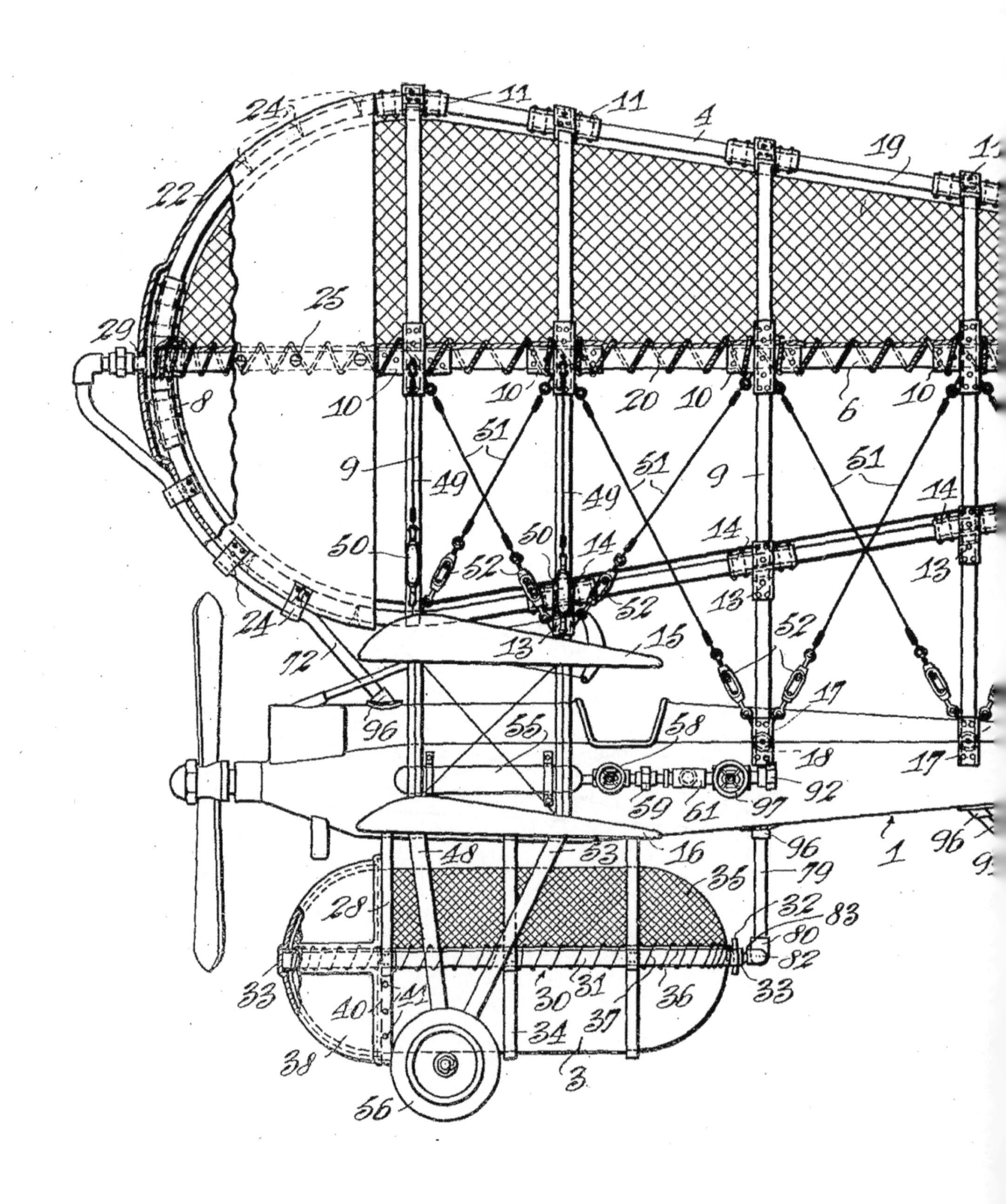

H.L. KUHN DIRIGIBLE AIRPLANE Mar. 14, 1933 1,901,173

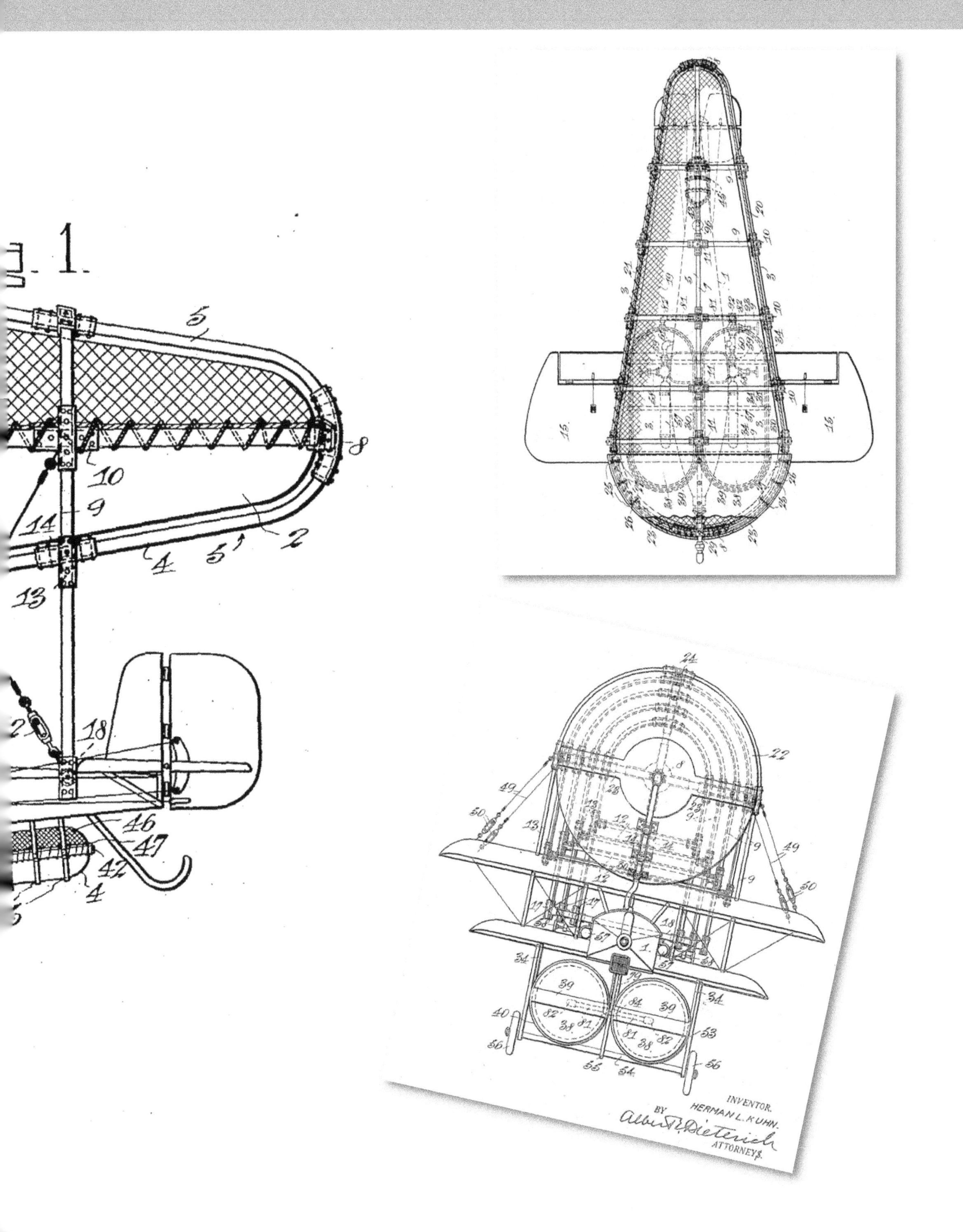
INVENTOR.
HERMAN L. KUHN.
BY
Albert R. Dieterich
ATTORNEYS.

Eli Whitney.

To all to whom these presents shall come, Greeting:

I Certify, That the annexed Writings and Drawings are True Copies of Original papers deposited in this Office by Eli Whitney and still remaining therein:

In faith whereof, I James Madison Secretary for the Department of State of the United States of America, have signed these presents, and caused the Seal of my Office to be affixed hereto, at the City of Washington, this Twenty fifth day of November, A.D. 1803, and in the Twenty eighth year of the Independence of the said States.

James Madison

Description of a New Invented Cotton Gin; or Machine for cleaning and separating Cotton from its Seeds.

This Machine may be described under five divisions, corresponding to its five principal parts: viz. 1st The frame; 2, the cylinder; 3, the breastwork; 4, the clearer; and 5, the hopper.

1st. The frame, by which the whole work is supported and kept together, ought to be made of well seasoned timber, so that it may be firm and steady, and never become loose in the joints. Scantling four inches by three, will perhaps be stuff, of as suitable size as any. The frame should be of a square or parallelogramic form, the width must answer to the length of the cylinder and the height and length may be proportioned as circumstances shall render convenient.

In the Drawing annexed, Fig. 1, is a section of the machine. A represents the cylinder, B, the breastwork, C the clearer, and D, the hopper.

II. The cylinder is of wood; its form is perfectly described by its name, and its dimensions may be from six to nine inches diameter, and from two to five feet in length. This cylinder is placed horizontally across the frame, in such manner as to give room for the clearer on one side of it, and the hopper on the other, as in Fig. 1.

Its height, if the machine is worked by hand should be about three feet four inches; otherwise it may be regulated by convenience. In the cylinder is fixed and Iron axis, so large as to turn in the lathe without quivering. The axis may

CHAPTER 4

Time Travel

As we've seen in previous chapters, the art of the patent has tracked along with the last two hundred years of human history. Sifting through patent drawings is like taking a trip in a time machine. Pivotal moments in world history are revealed, and sometimes we see our own childhood.

Patent art is our own history, collectively and individually. Sit back and enjoy the following drawings. Let the memories triggered in your mind and heart catapult you into visions of your life; memories too seldom stirred, people long forgotten, and eras only faintly remembered. Many of the patents came to life decades before we were born, yet influenced how we have lived and will live for many generations to come. These historic patents speak for themselves. Time travel is possible and the art of the patent is the vehicle.

Eli Whitney and the cotton gin are as American as apple pie and ice cream. Not only are the drawings elegant but the claim text is handwritten in the flowing style of the era.

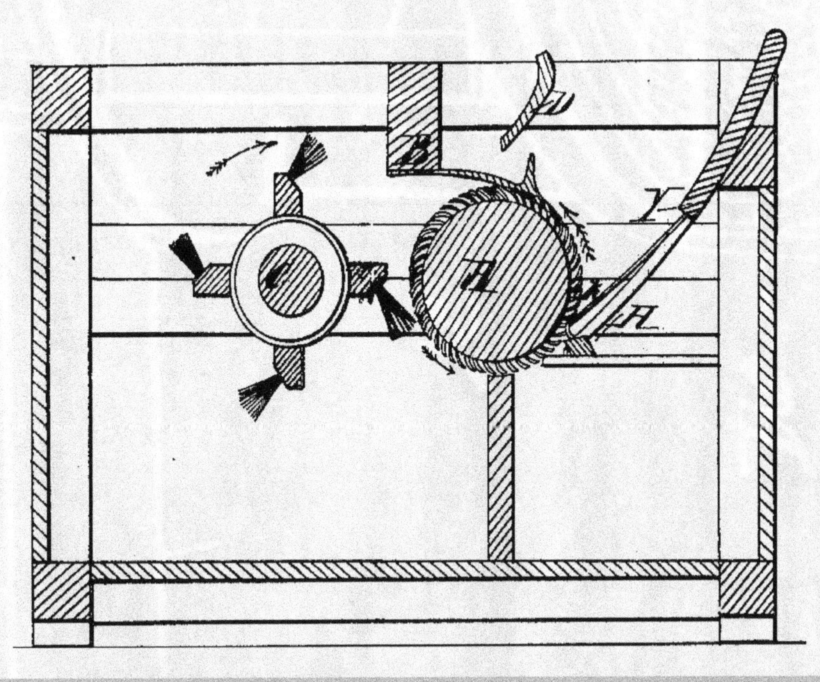

E. WHITNEY

COTTON GIN
MAR. 14, 1794

No. X72

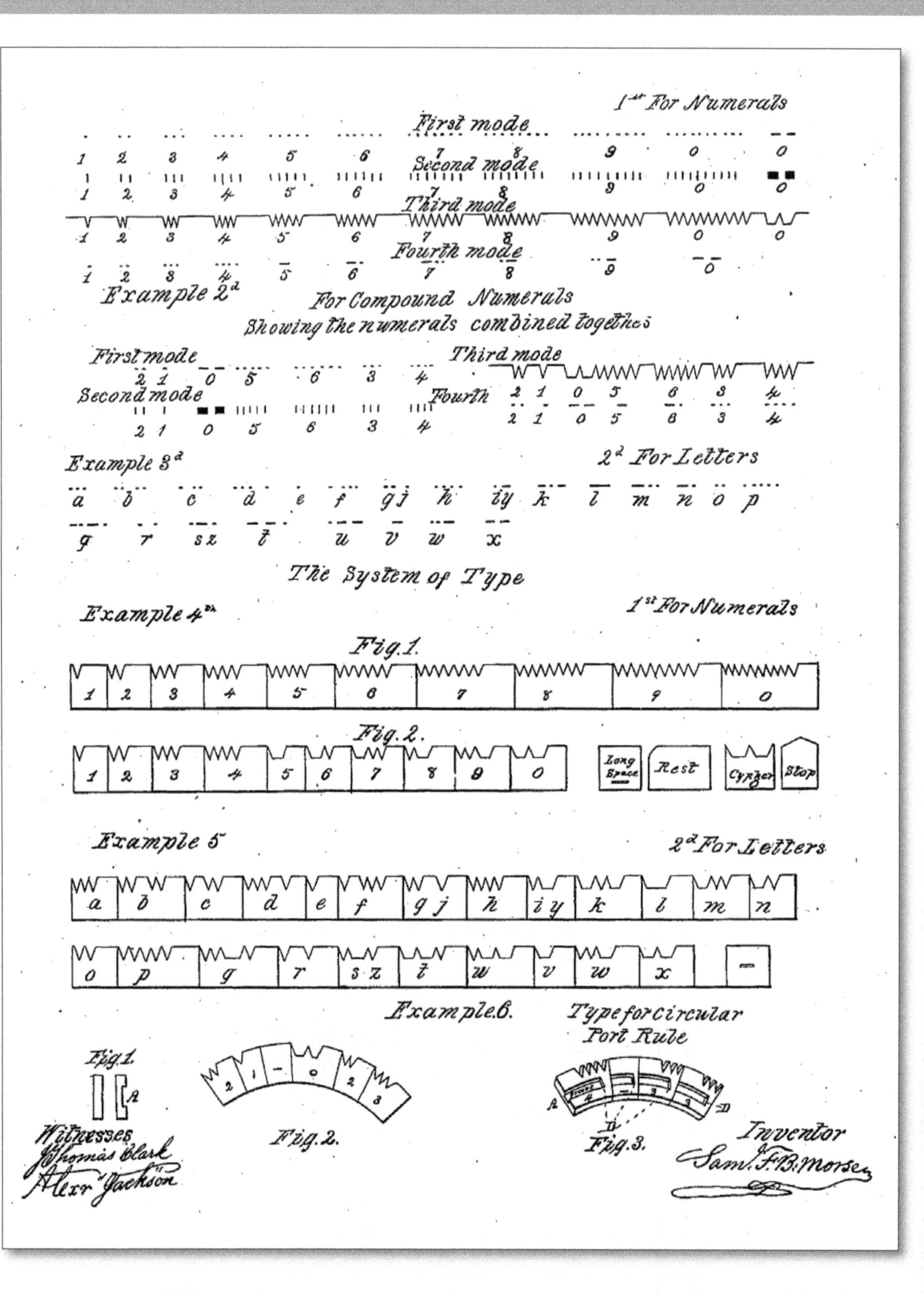

TELEGRAPH SIGNS

S.F.B. MORSE Jun. 20, 1840 No. 1,670

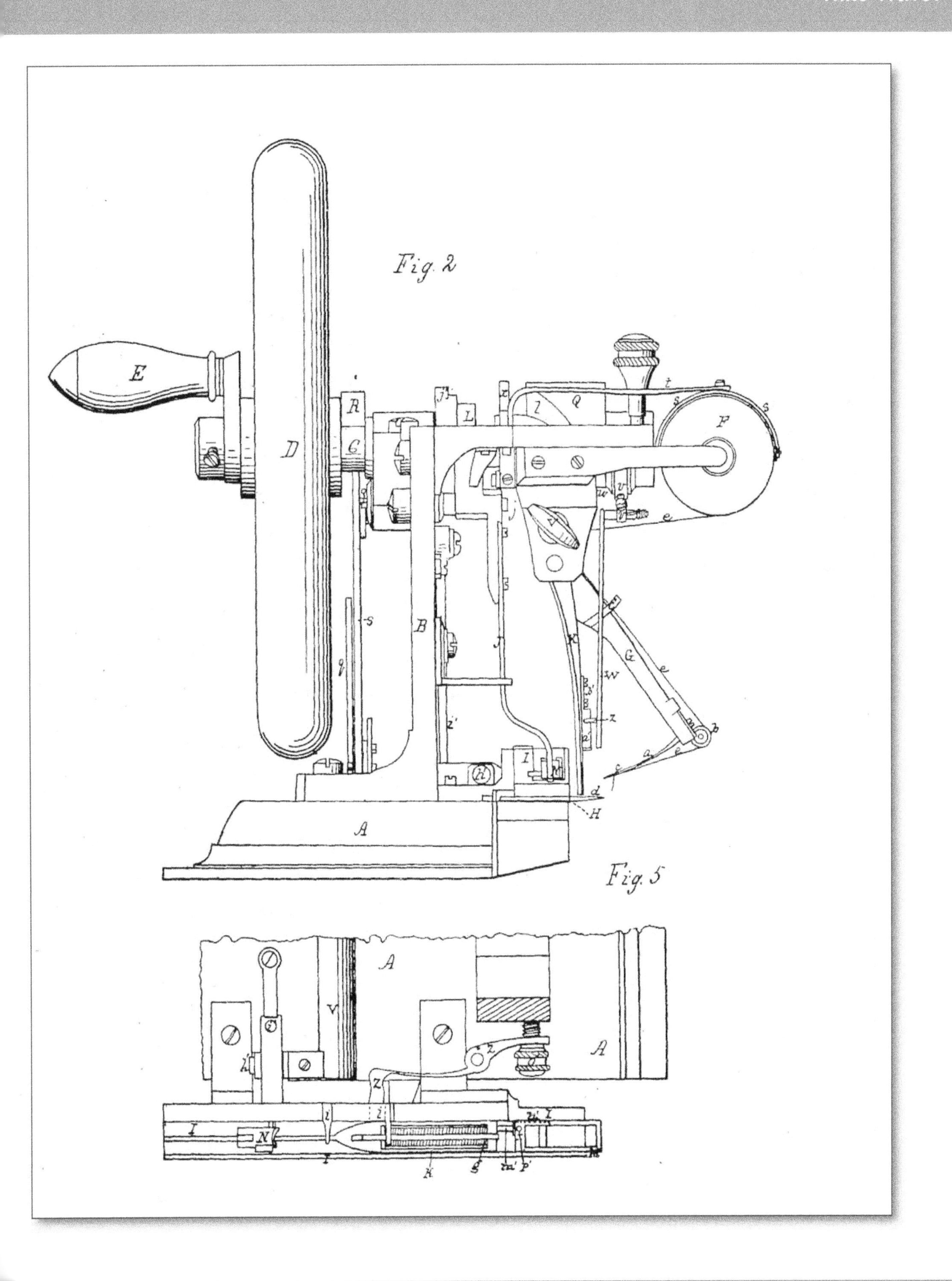
Fig. 2
Fig. 5

Who would've thought you could patent something as simple as the safety pin?

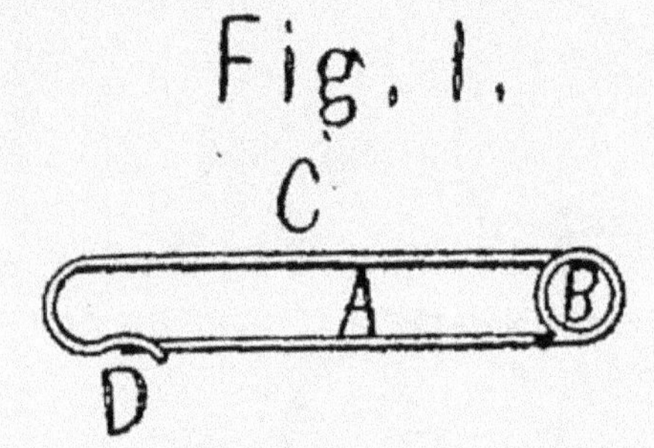

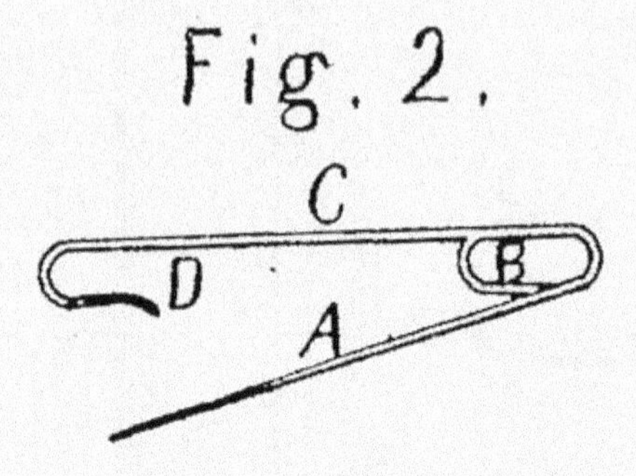

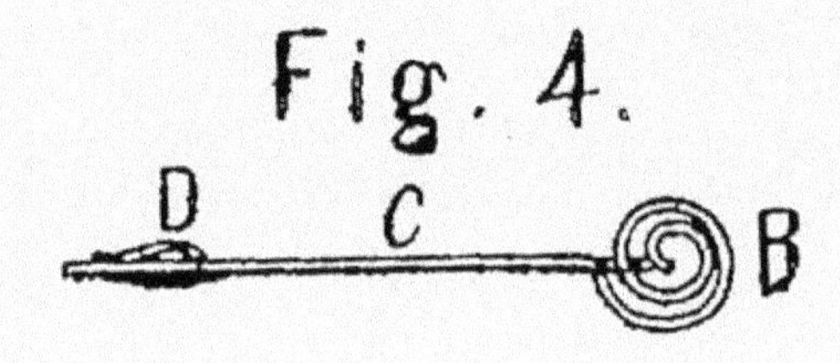

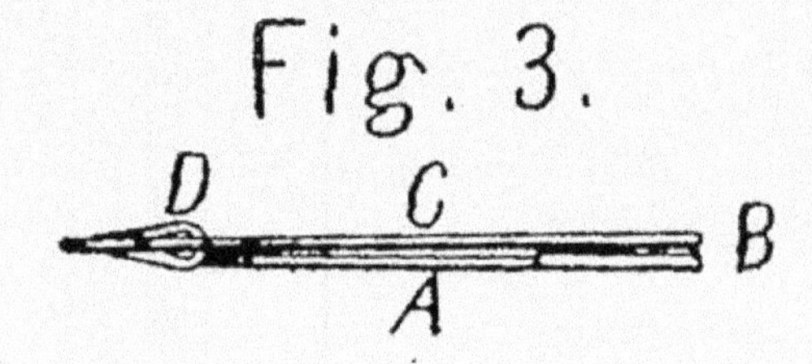

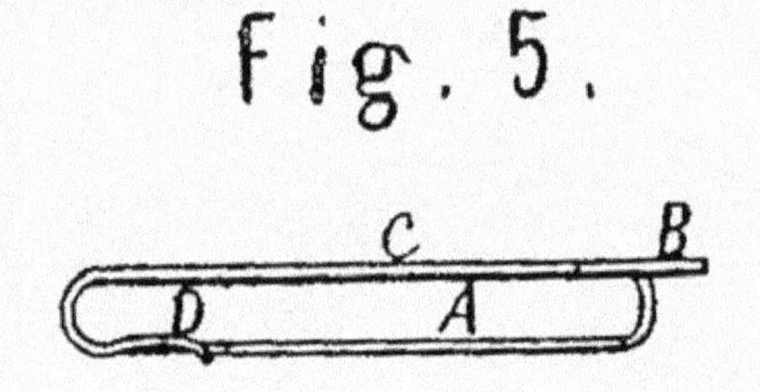

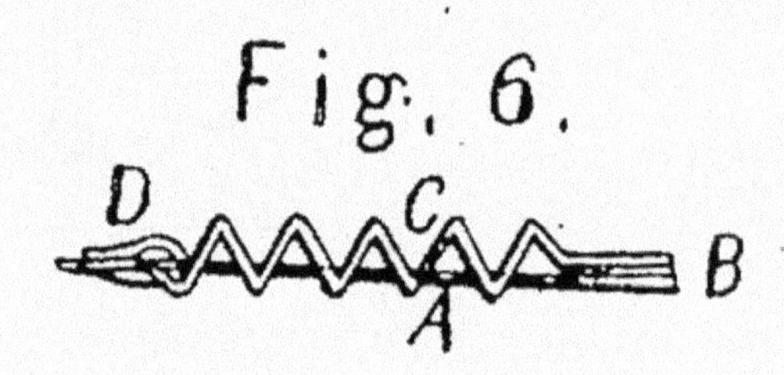

Fig. 7.

W. HUNT

DRESS-PIN
Apr. 10, 1849

No. 6,281

The next time you're in an elevator have a look at the brand name. Chances are it's Otis. The following drawing shows an early version of his elevator, simply called a hoisting apparatus.

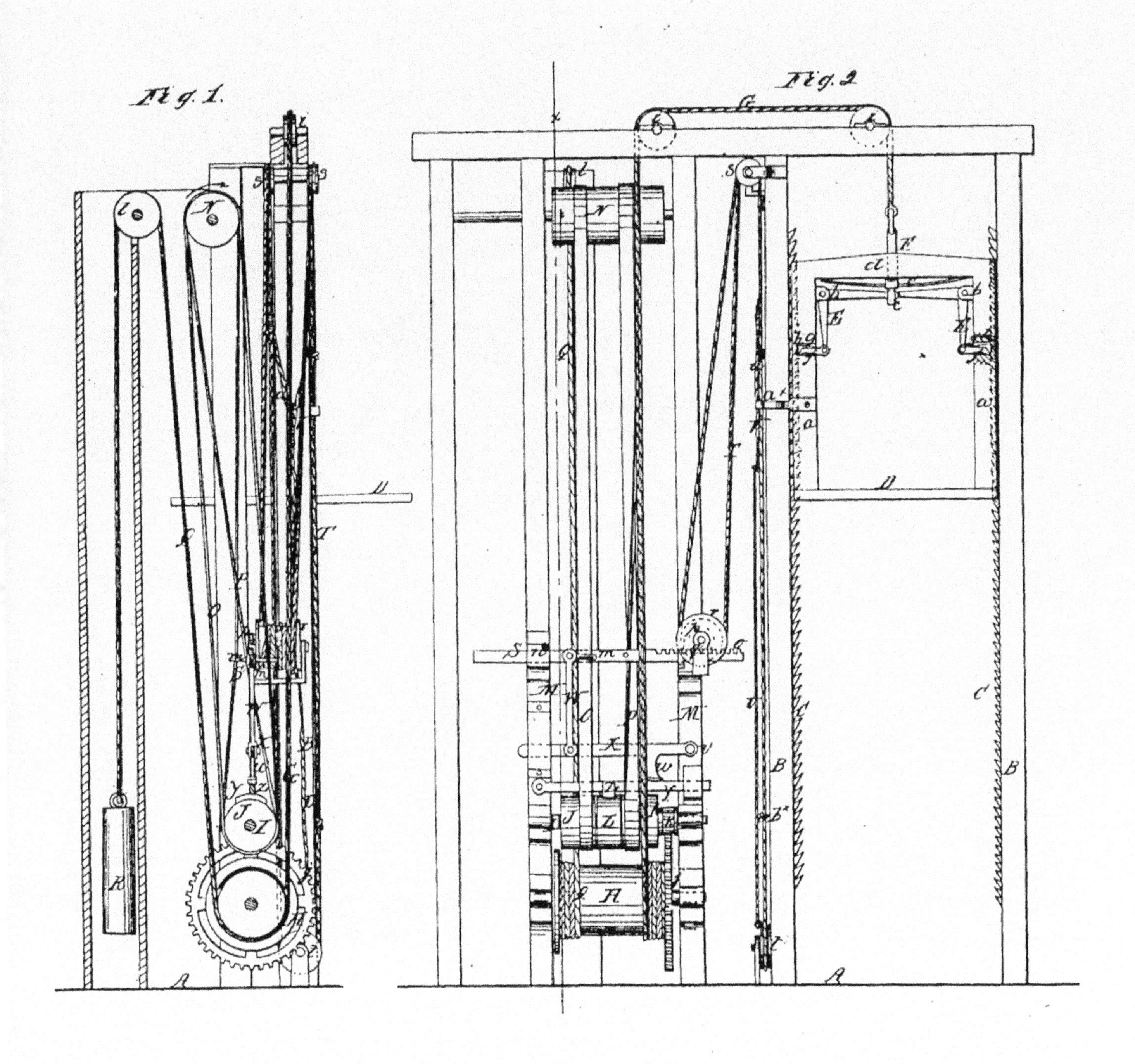

HOISTING APPARATUS
E.G. OTIS Jan. 15, 1861 No. 31,128

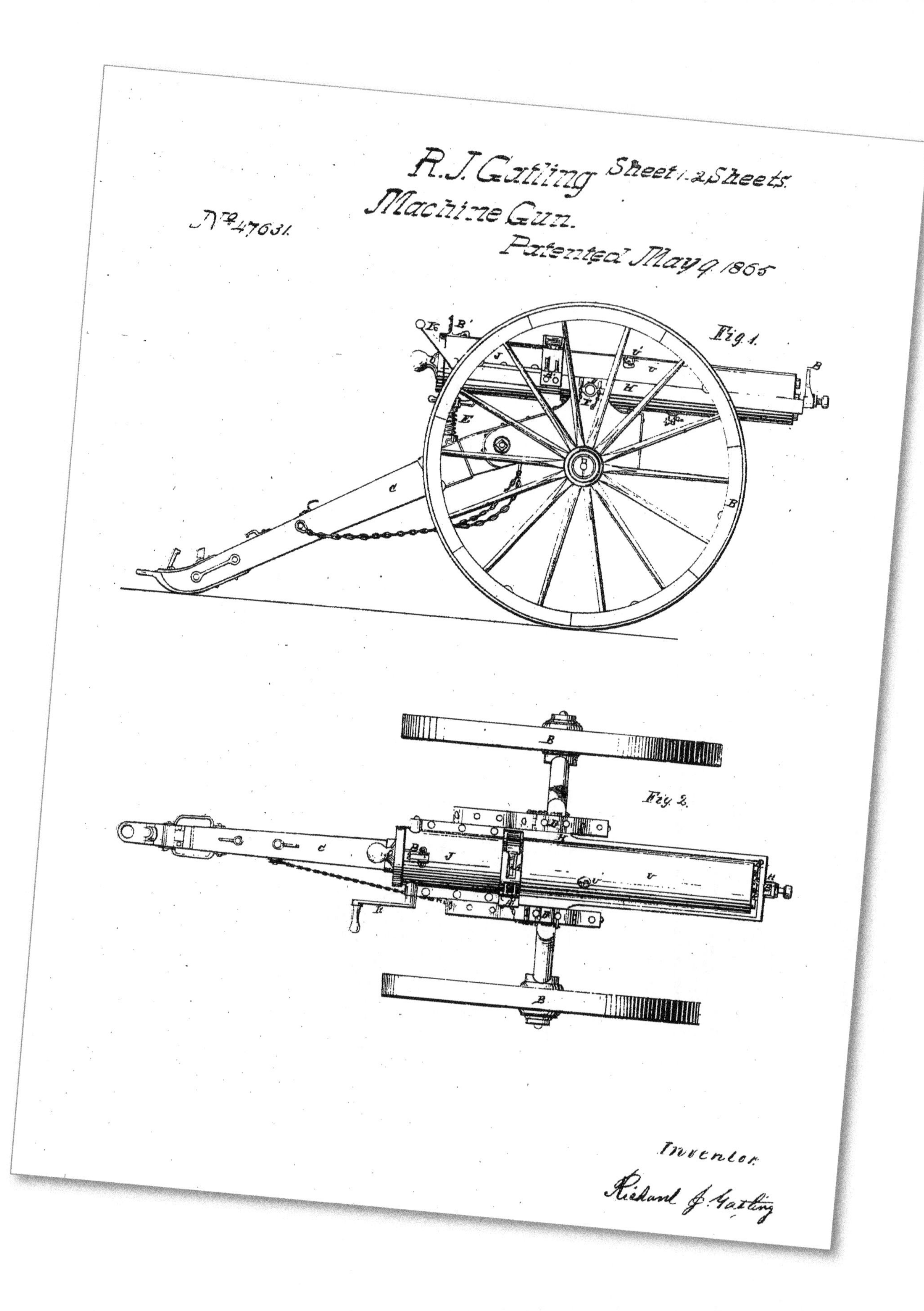

R. J. GATLING — MACHINE GUN — MAY 9, 1865 — No. 47,631

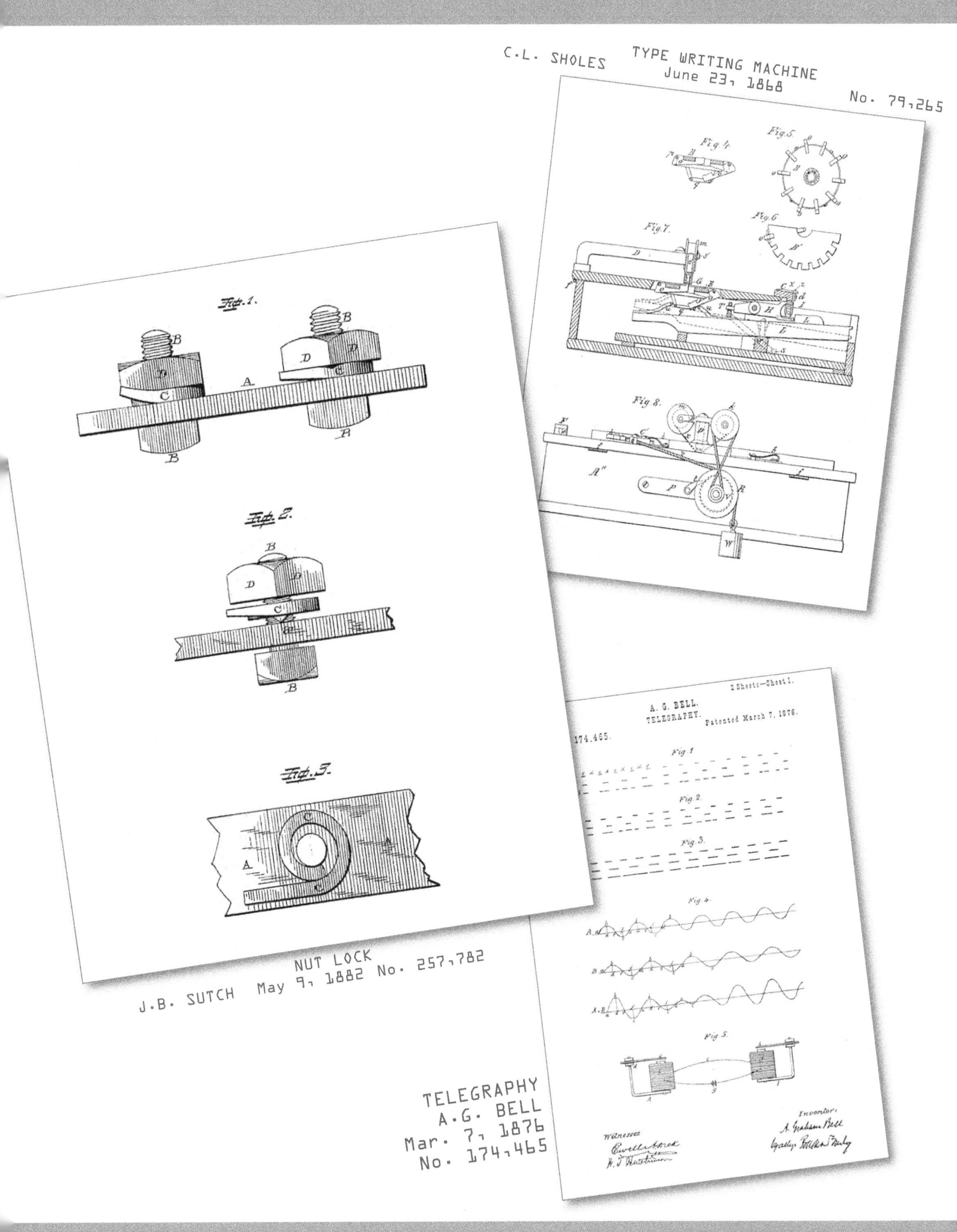
C.L. SHOLES
TYPE WRITING MACHINE
June 23, 1868
No. 79,265
Fig. 4.
Fig. 5.
Fig. 6
Fig. 7.
Fig 8.
Fig. 1.
Fig. 2.
Fig. 3.
NUT LOCK
J.B. SUTCH May 9, 1882 No. 257,782
2 Sheets—Sheet 1.
A. G. BELL.
TELEGRAPHY.
Patented March 7, 1876.
174,465.
Fig 1
Fig 2
Fig 3
Fig 4
Fig 5
Witnesses
Inventor:
TELEGRAPHY
A.G. BELL
Mar. 7, 1876
No. 174,465

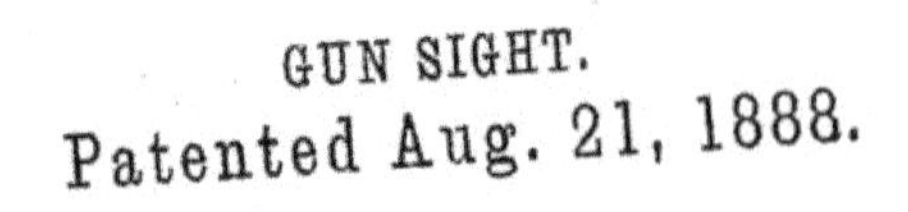

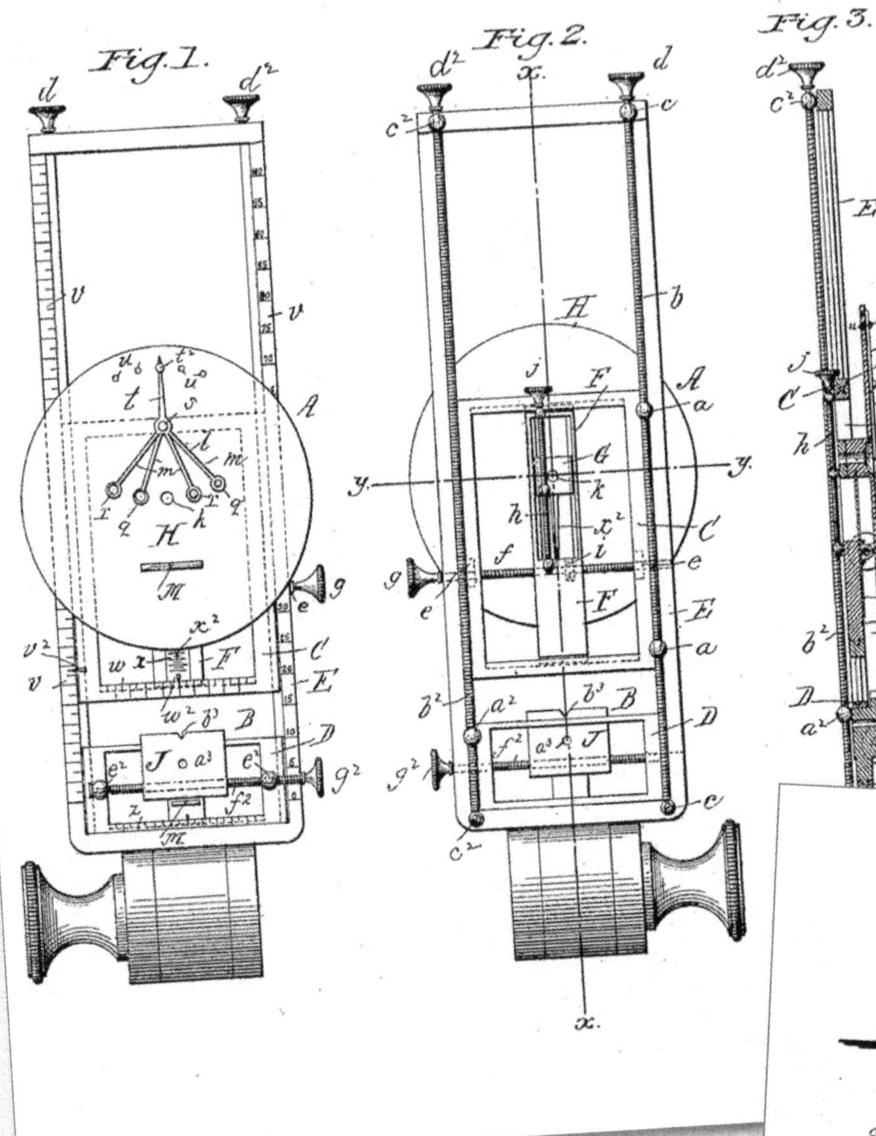

G.W. WOOD & J.W. CARVER
Aug. 21, 1888
No. 388,166

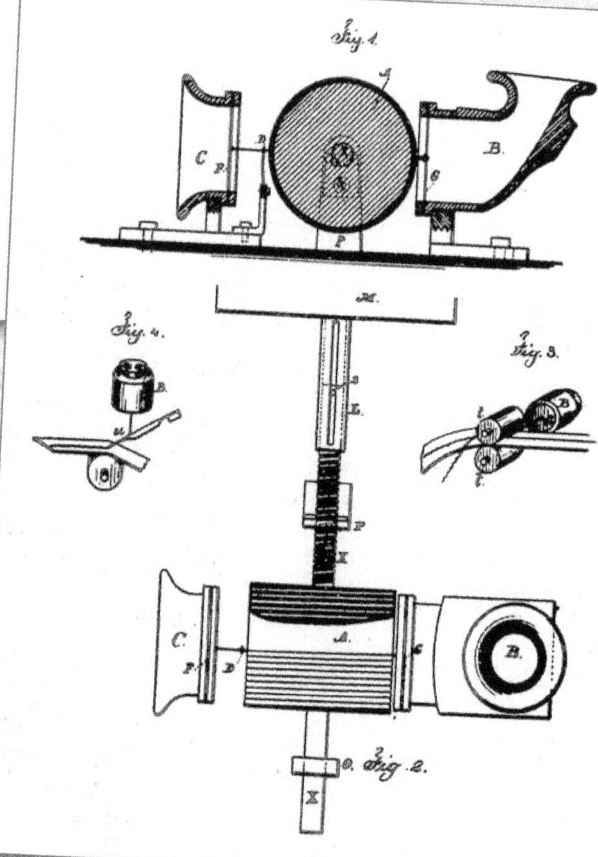

PHONOGREAPH OR SPEAKING MACHINE
T.A. EDISON Feb. 19, 1878 No. 200,521

RANGE
G.G. WOLFE & F. RITCHIE Nov. 2, 1875 No. 8,767

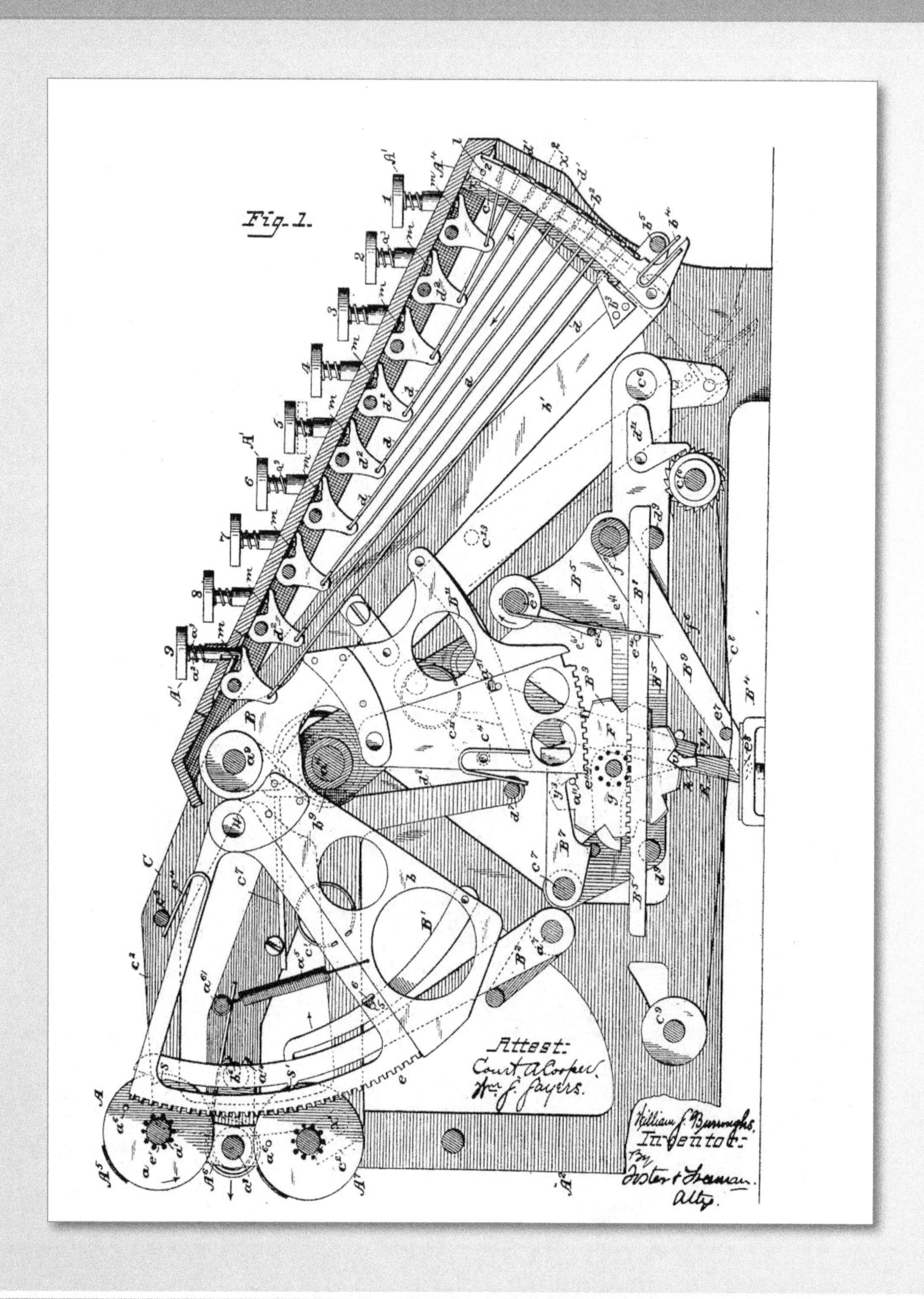

W.S. BURROUGHS CALCULATING MACHINE Aug. 21, 1888 No. 388,116

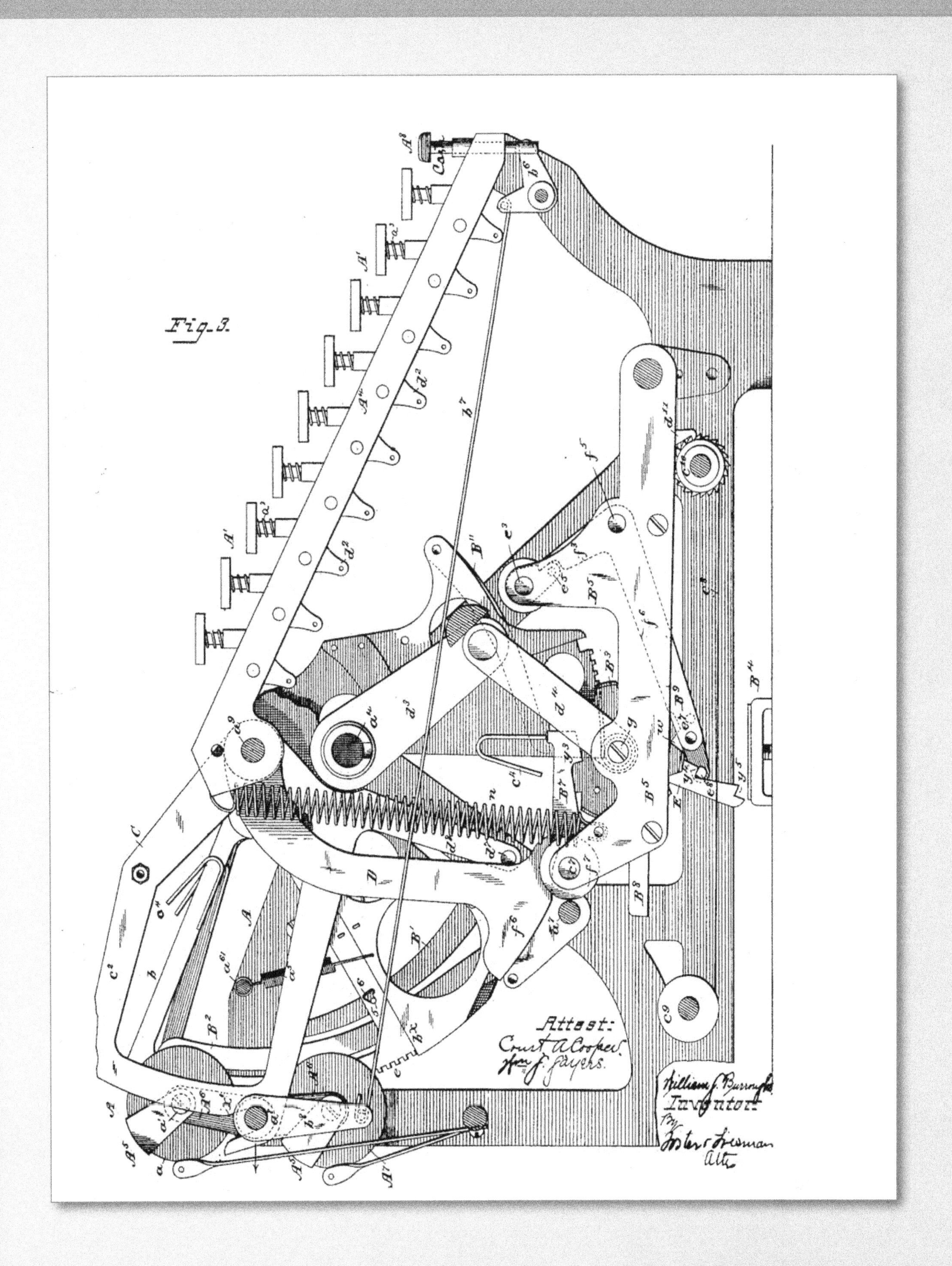

W.S. BURROUGHS — CALCULATING MACHINE — Aug. 21, 1888 — No. 388,116

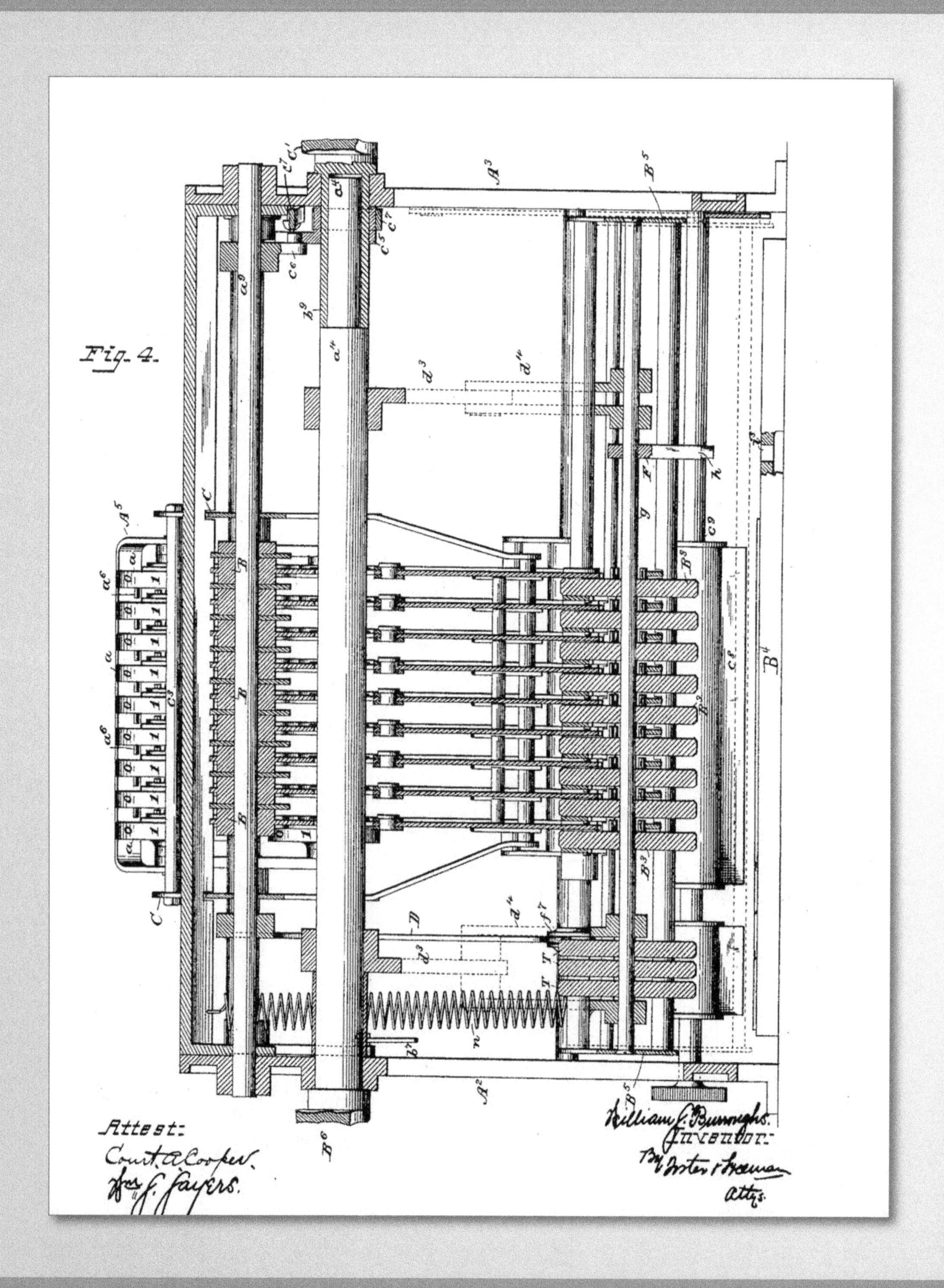

CALCULATING MACHINE
W.S. BURROUGHS Aug. 21, 1888 No. 388,116

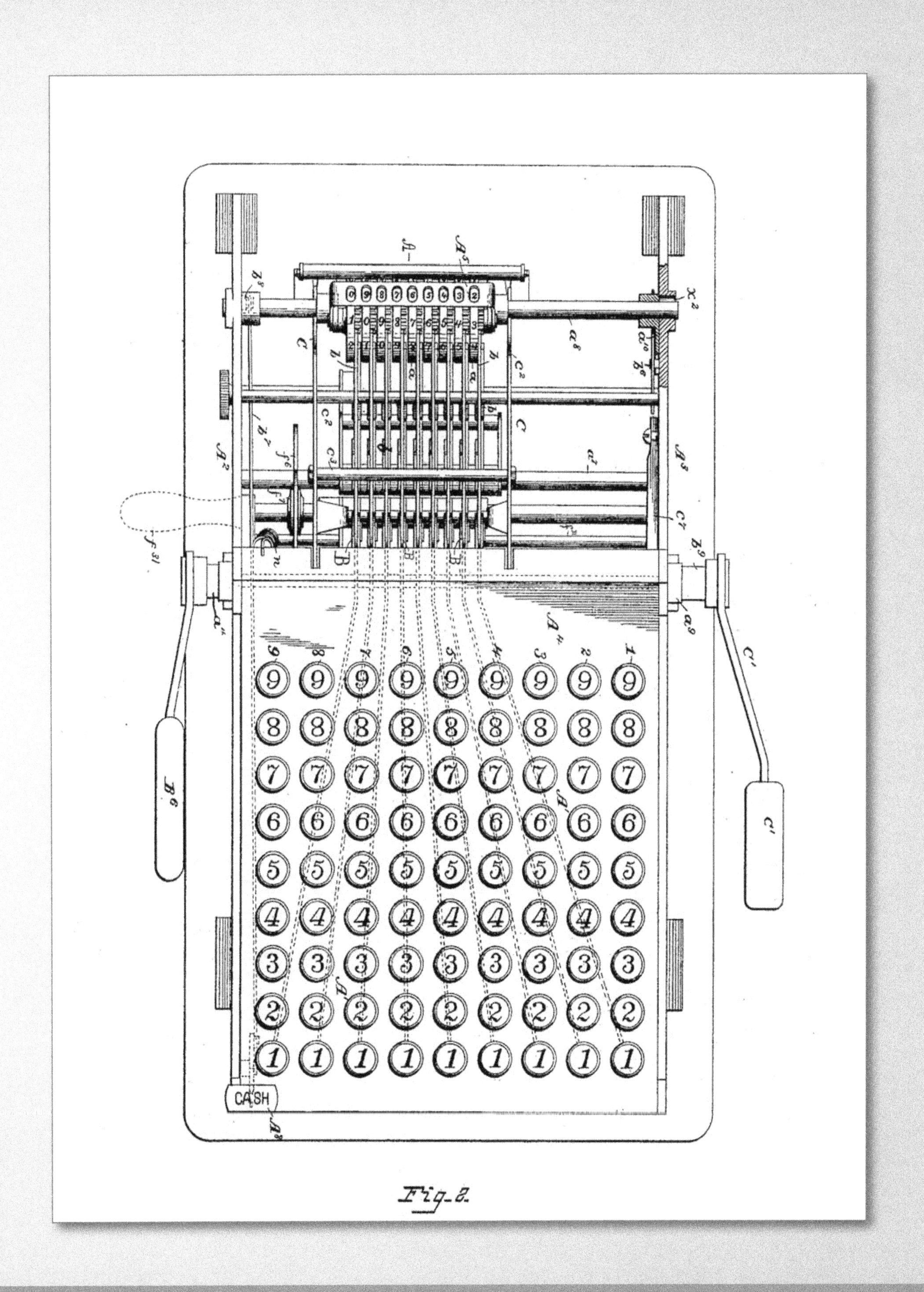

Fig. 2.

CALCULATING MACHINE
W.S. BURROUGHS Aug. 21, 1888 No. 388,116

IN THE FOLLOWING DRAWING, CAN'T YOU HEAR THE PIANO PLAYING AND THE HUSKY VOICES OF COWBOYS TALKING? EVEN THE STALE SMELL OF CIGAR SMOKE WAFTS OUT FROM THE DETAILED DESIGN.

SALOON FIXTURE
D. ROTHSCHILD Feb. 14, 1893 No. 22,222

What an advance this early dish washing machine was, and how fortunate that we don't still use it!

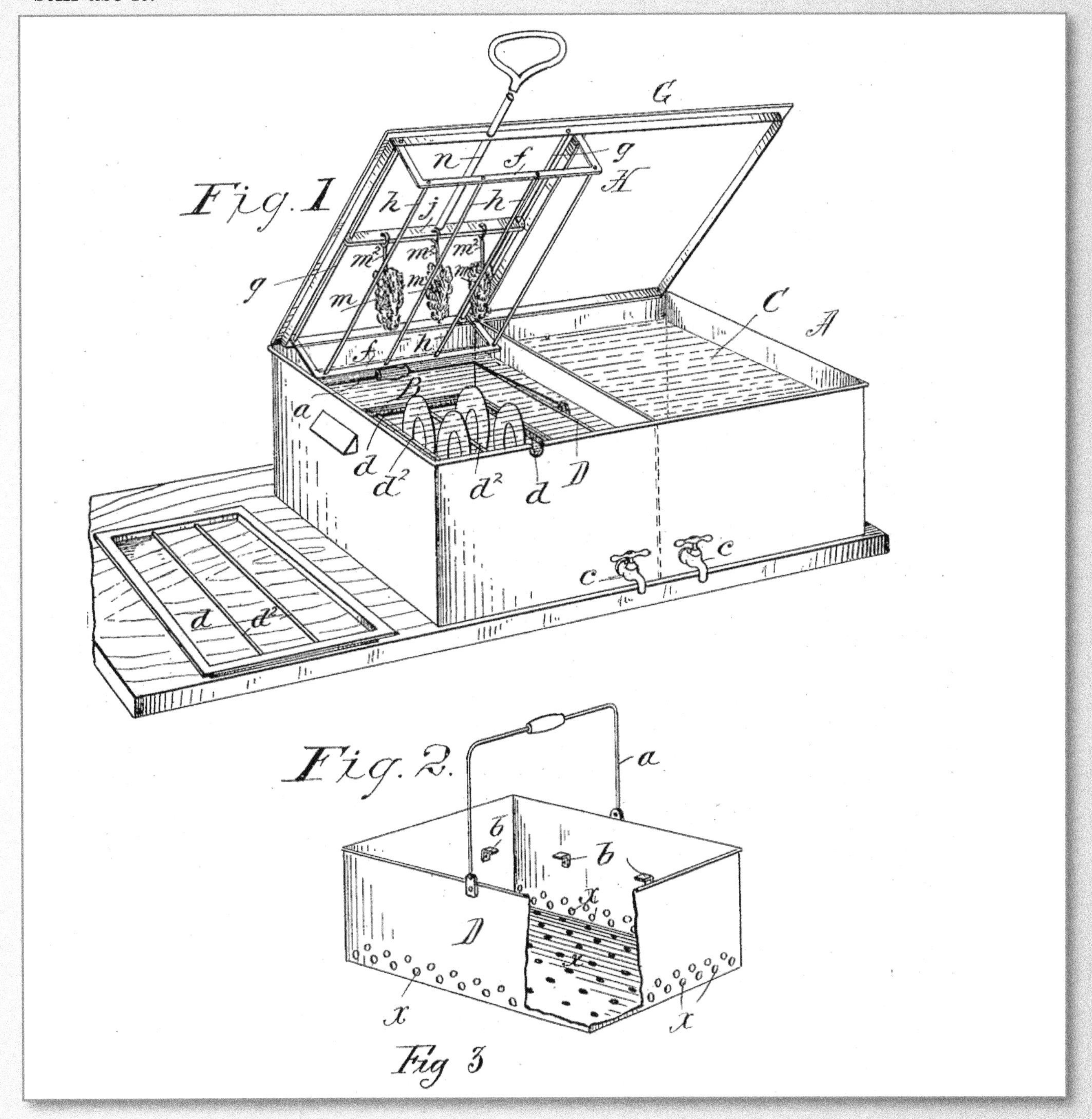

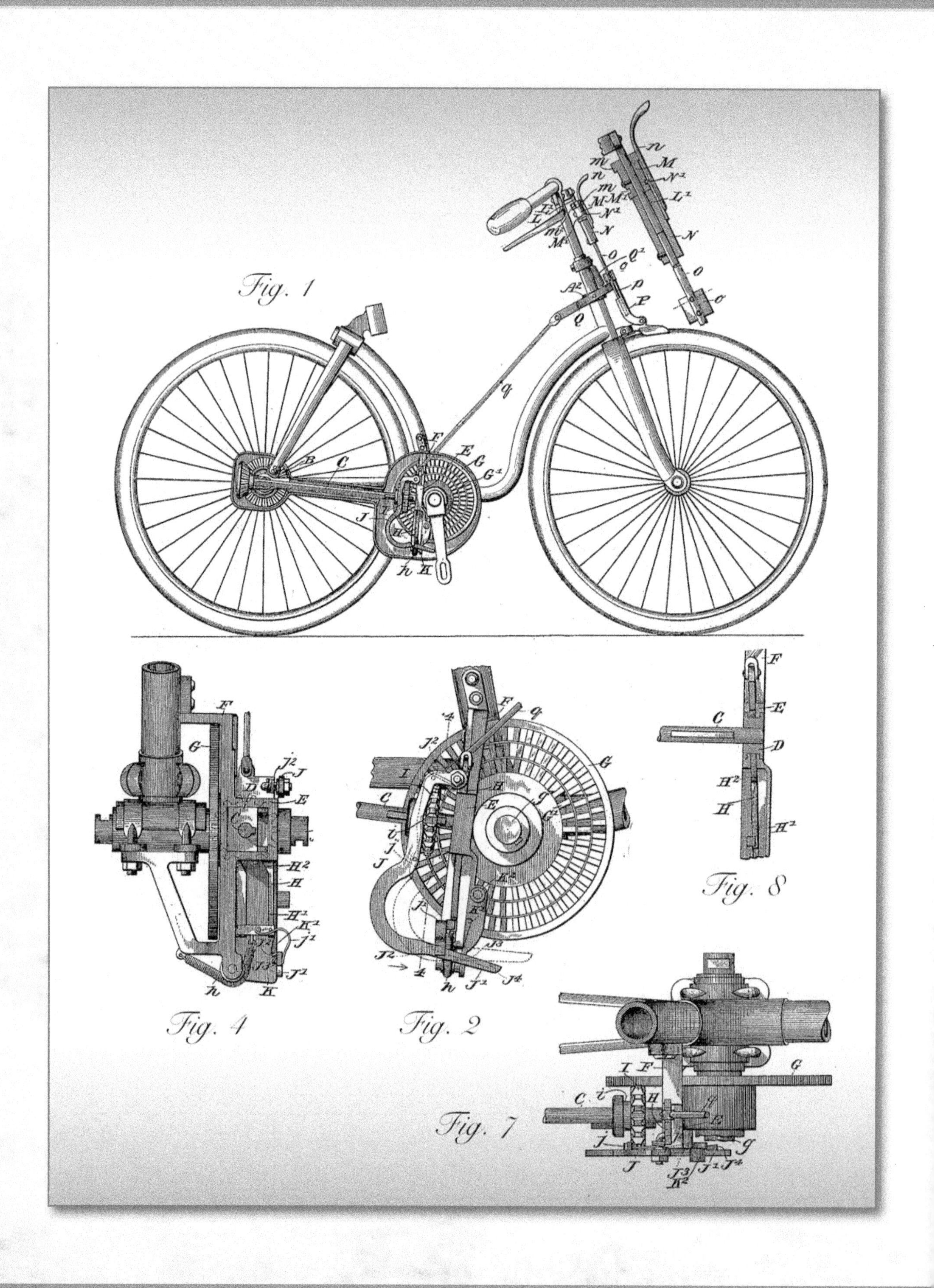

BICYCLE DRIVING GEAR
T.B. SNYDER
Mar. 26, 1895
No. 536,550

How many times has the following invention been used and at the same time cursed: the electric alarm clock.

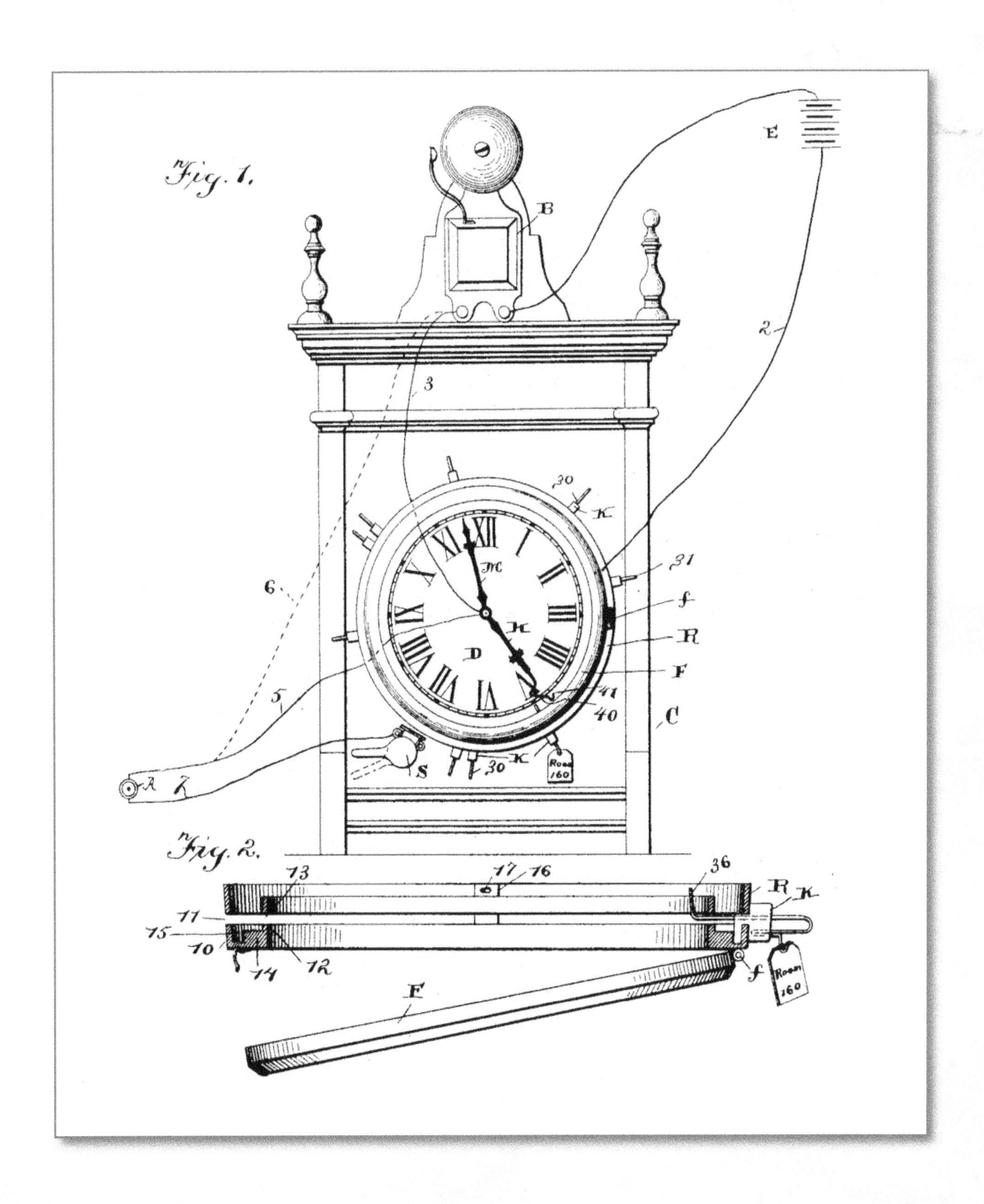

ELECTRIC TIME ALARM CLOCK
M. LEIBECKE May 7, 1895 No. 538,686

Here's a series of drawings that include woderful treatment of just about every shape of surface and type on a single page, except perhaps "fuzzy."

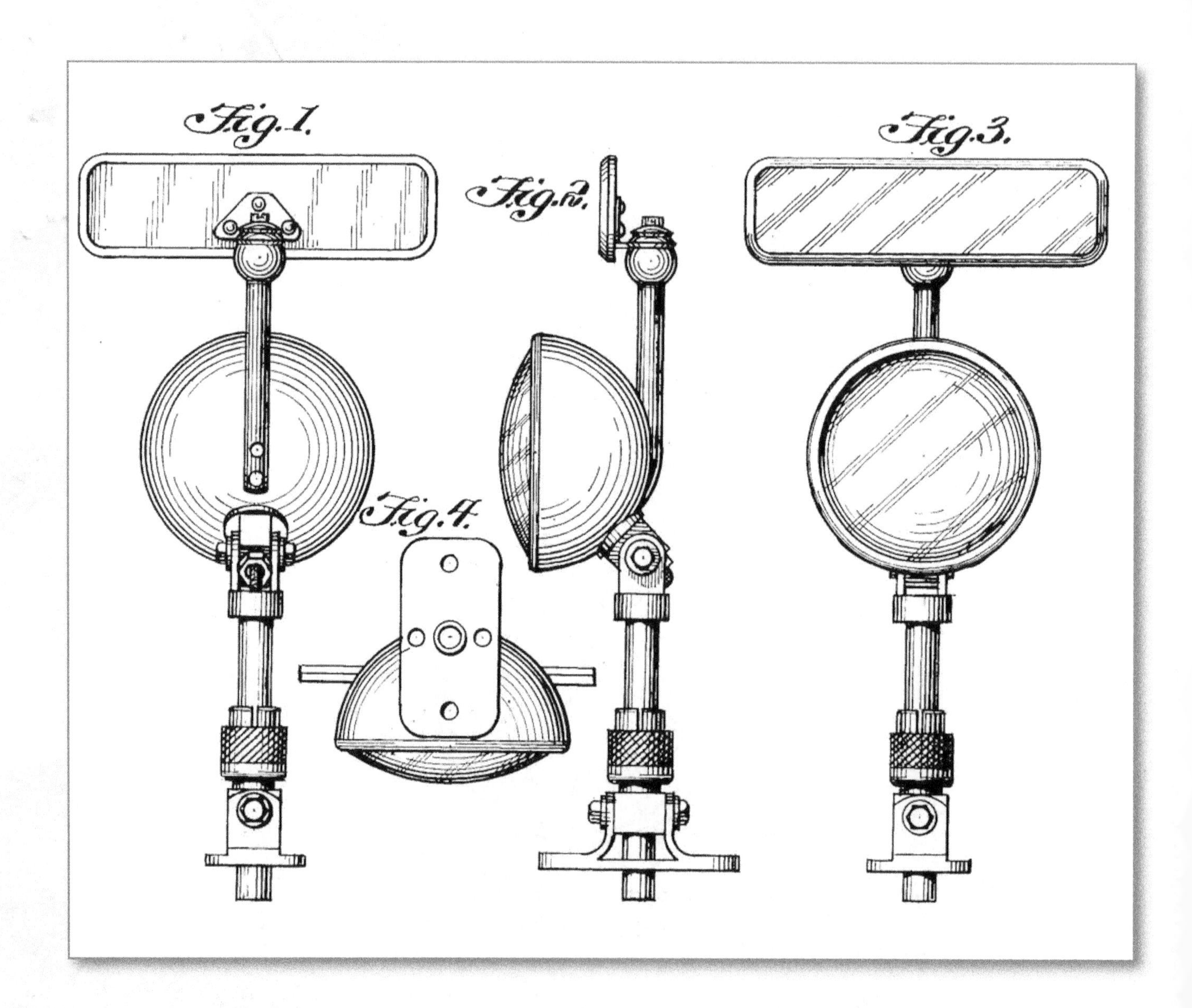

INVENTOR.
Herman Paine,
BY Victor J. Evans & Co.
ATTORNEYS

Another example of how to beautifully show a variety of contours...

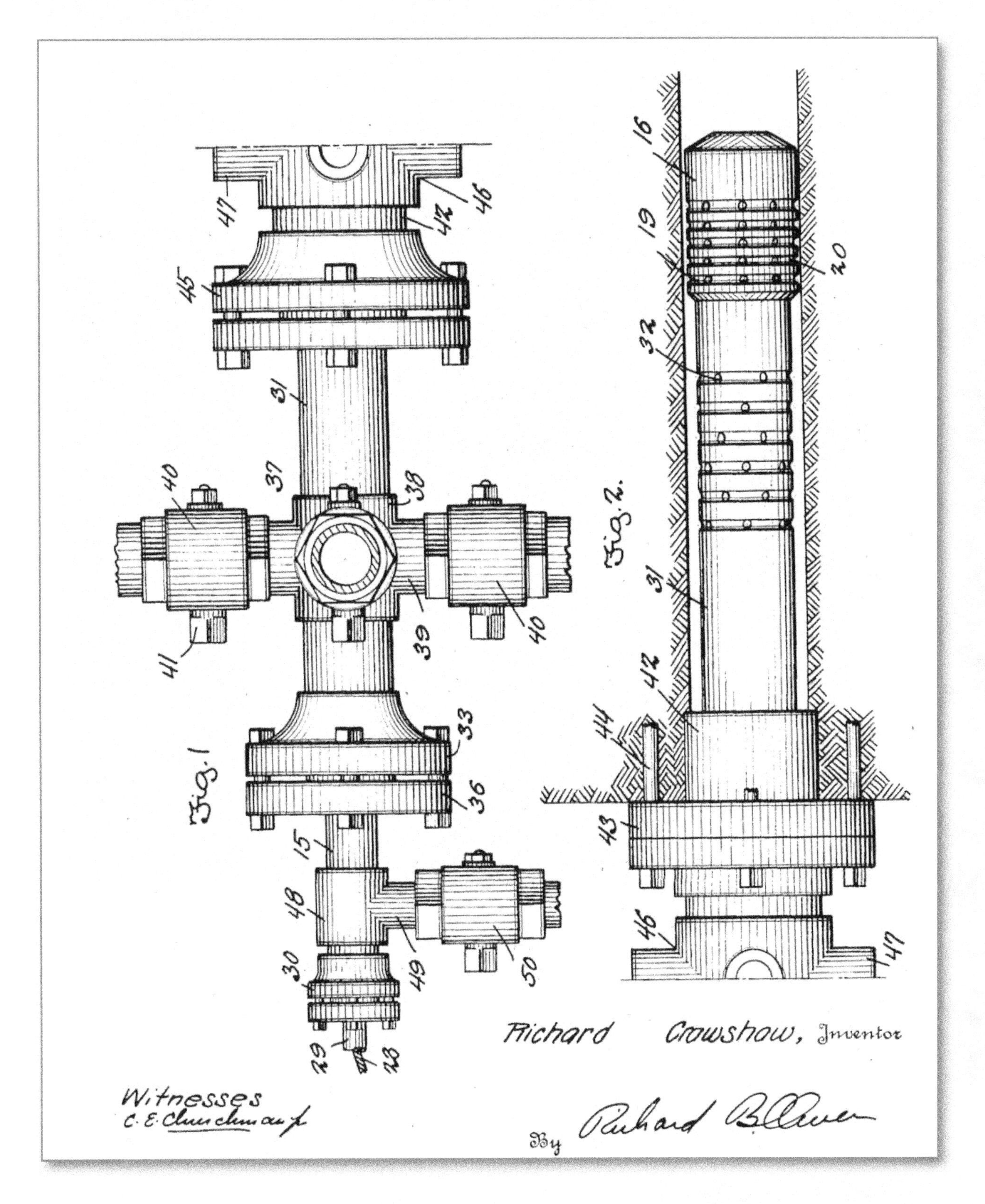

APPARATUS FOR EXTRACTING OIL FROM SHALE
R. CRAWSHAW April 17, 1928 No. 1,666,488

Patents eventually expire, which is why a flood of Monopoly-type games are now available. But the original patent matches quite well to the classic game.

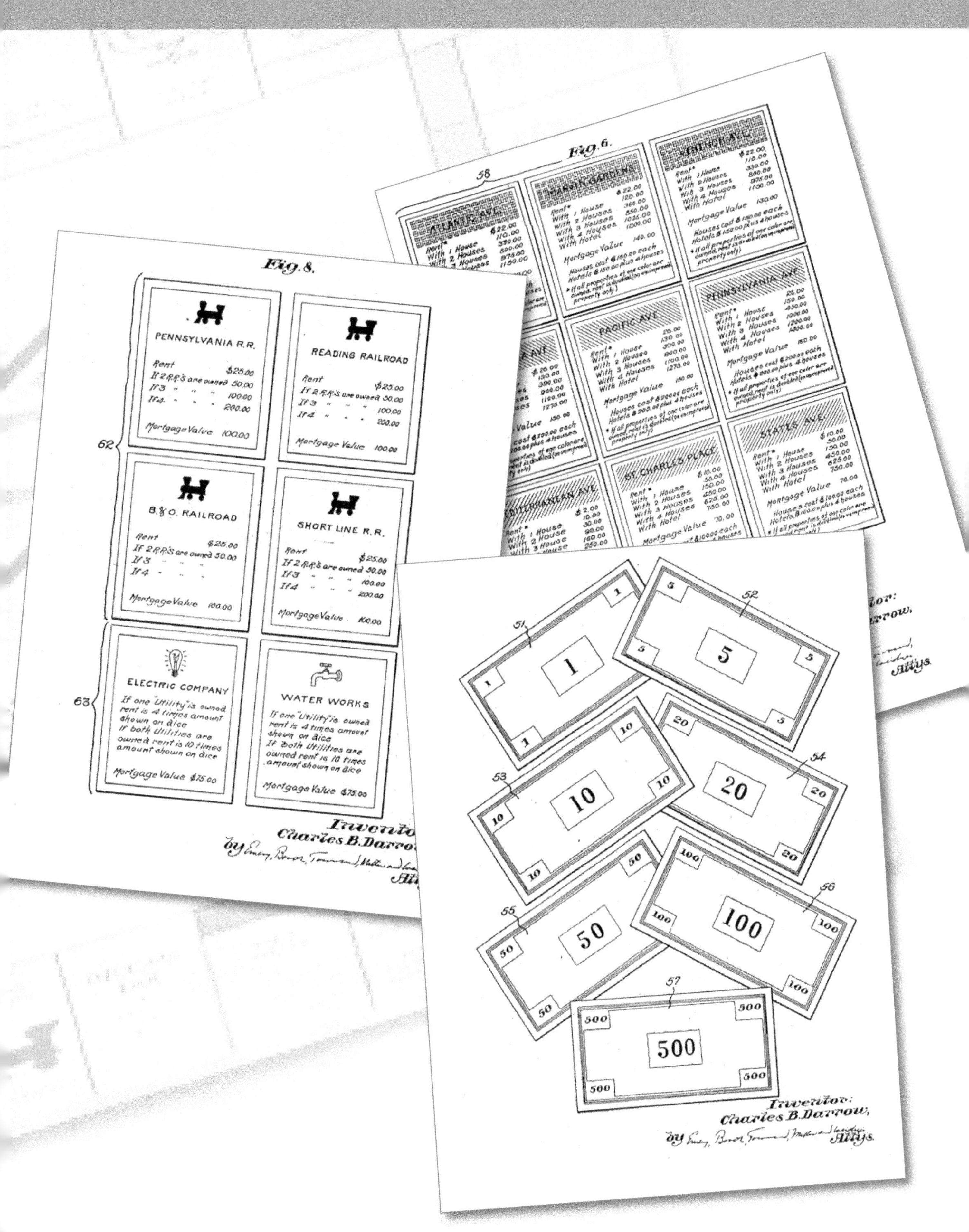
Fig. 8.
PENNSYLVANIA R.R.
Rent $25.00
If 2 R.R.'s are owned 50.00
If 3 " " " 100.00
If 4 " " " 200.00
Mortgage Value 100.00
READING RAILROAD
Rent $25.00
If 2 R.R.'s are owned 50.00
If 3 " " " 100.00
If 4 " " " 200.00
Mortgage Value 100.00
B.& O. RAILROAD
Rent $25.00
If 2 R.R.'s are owned 50.00
Mortgage Value 100.00
SHORT LINE R.R.
Rent $25.00
If 2 R.R.'s are owned 50.00
If 3 " " " 100.00
If 4 " " " 200.00
Mortgage Value 100.00
ELECTRIC COMPANY
If one "Utility" is owned rent is 4 times amount shown on dice
If both Utilities are owned rent is 10 times amount shown on dice
Mortgage Value $75.00
WATER WORKS
If one "Utility" is owned rent is 4 times amount shown on dice
If both Utilities are owned rent is 10 times amount shown on dice
Mortgage Value $75.00
62
63
Inventor
Charles B. Darrow
Fig. 6.
58
ATLANTIC AVE.
MARVIN GARDENS
PACIFIC AVE.
PENNSYLVANIA AVE.
ST. CHARLES PLACE
STATES AVE.
51
52
53
54
55
56
57
1
5
10
20
50
100
500
Inventor:
Charles B. Darrow,
Attys.

An early version of the Ferris wheel.

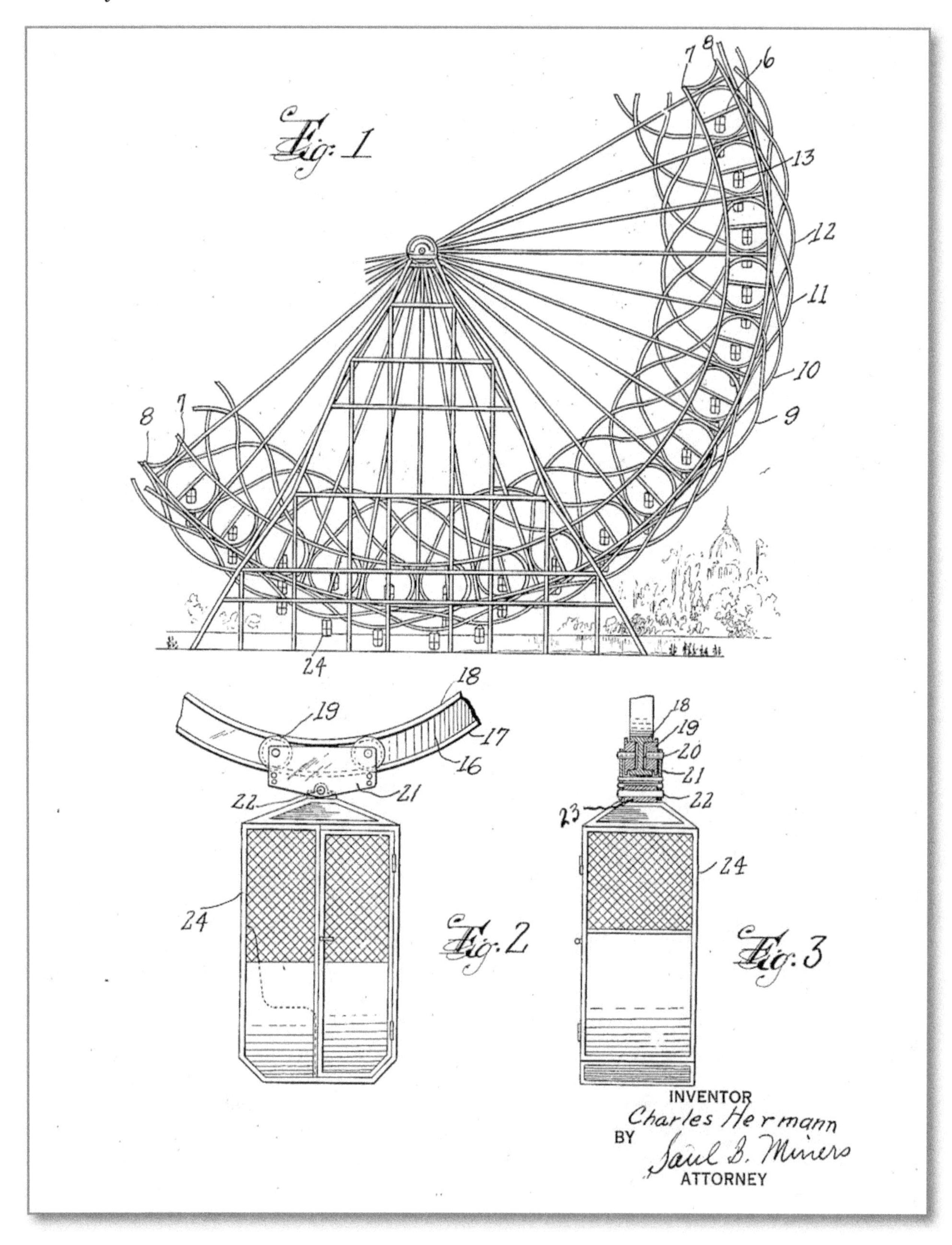

AMUSEMENT DEVICE
C. HERMANN June 1, 1937 No. 2,082,287

The Lego block...

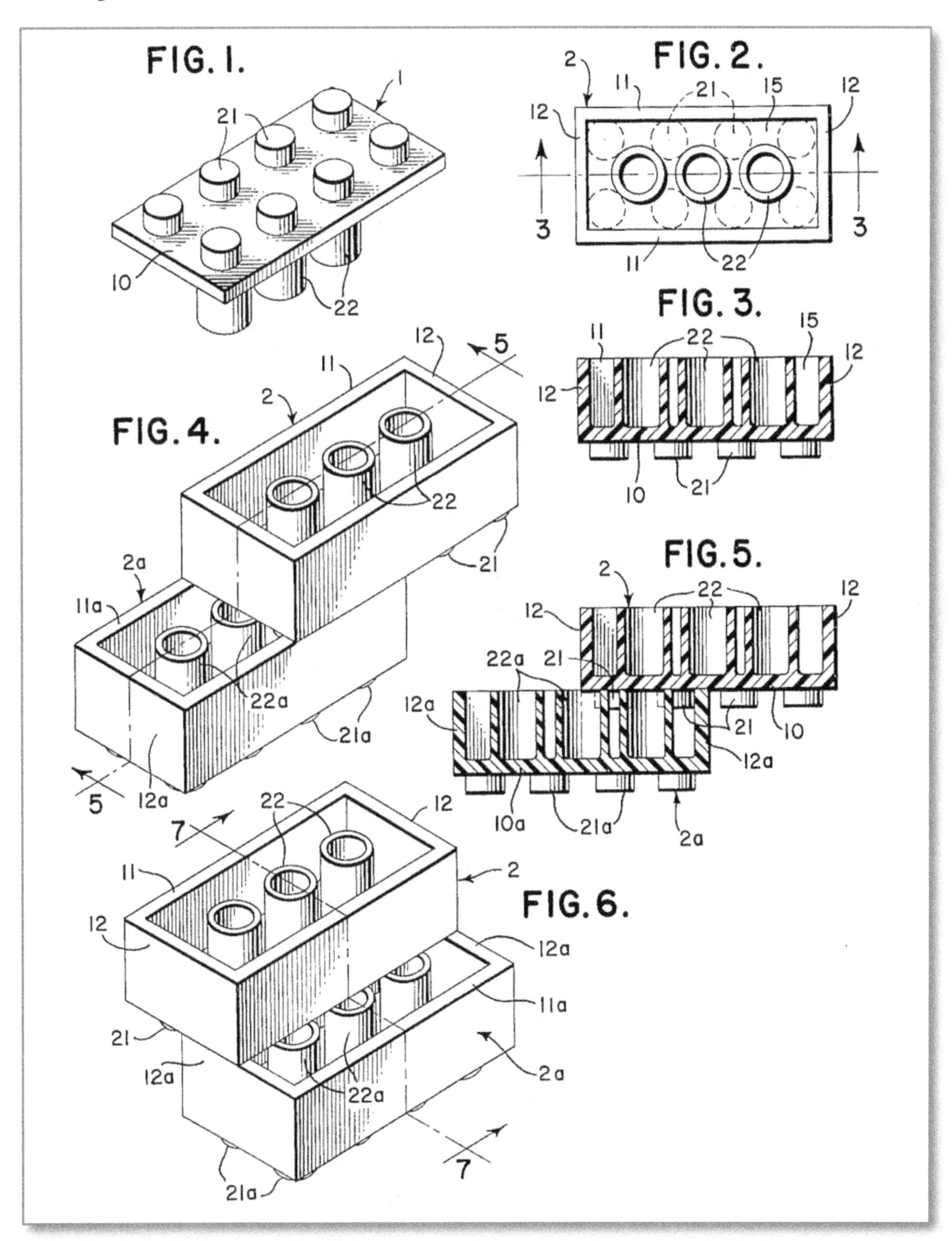

The beginning of animation...

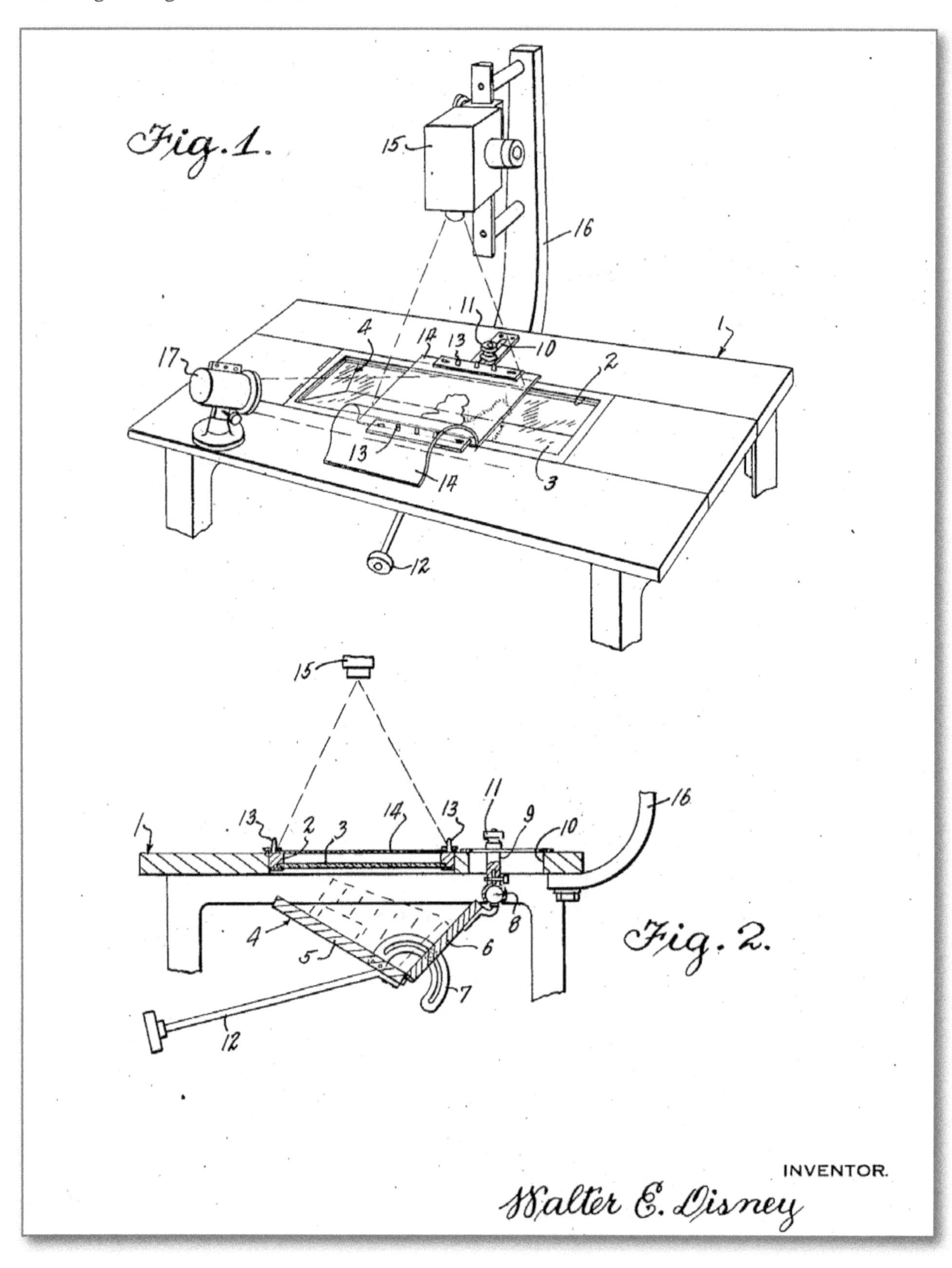

... to a nuclear reactor.

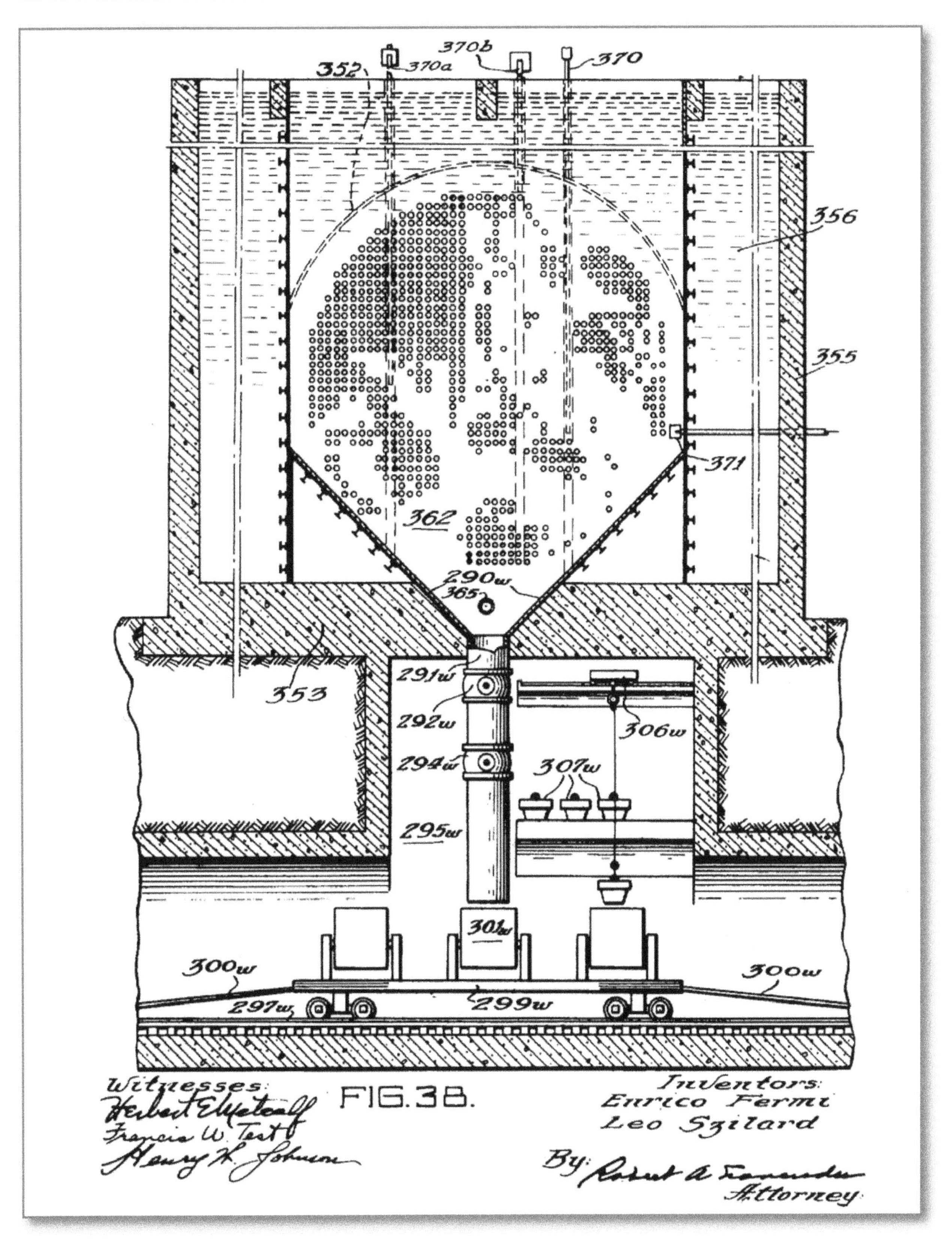

NEUTRONIC REACTOR
E. FERMI May 17, 1955 No. 2,708,656

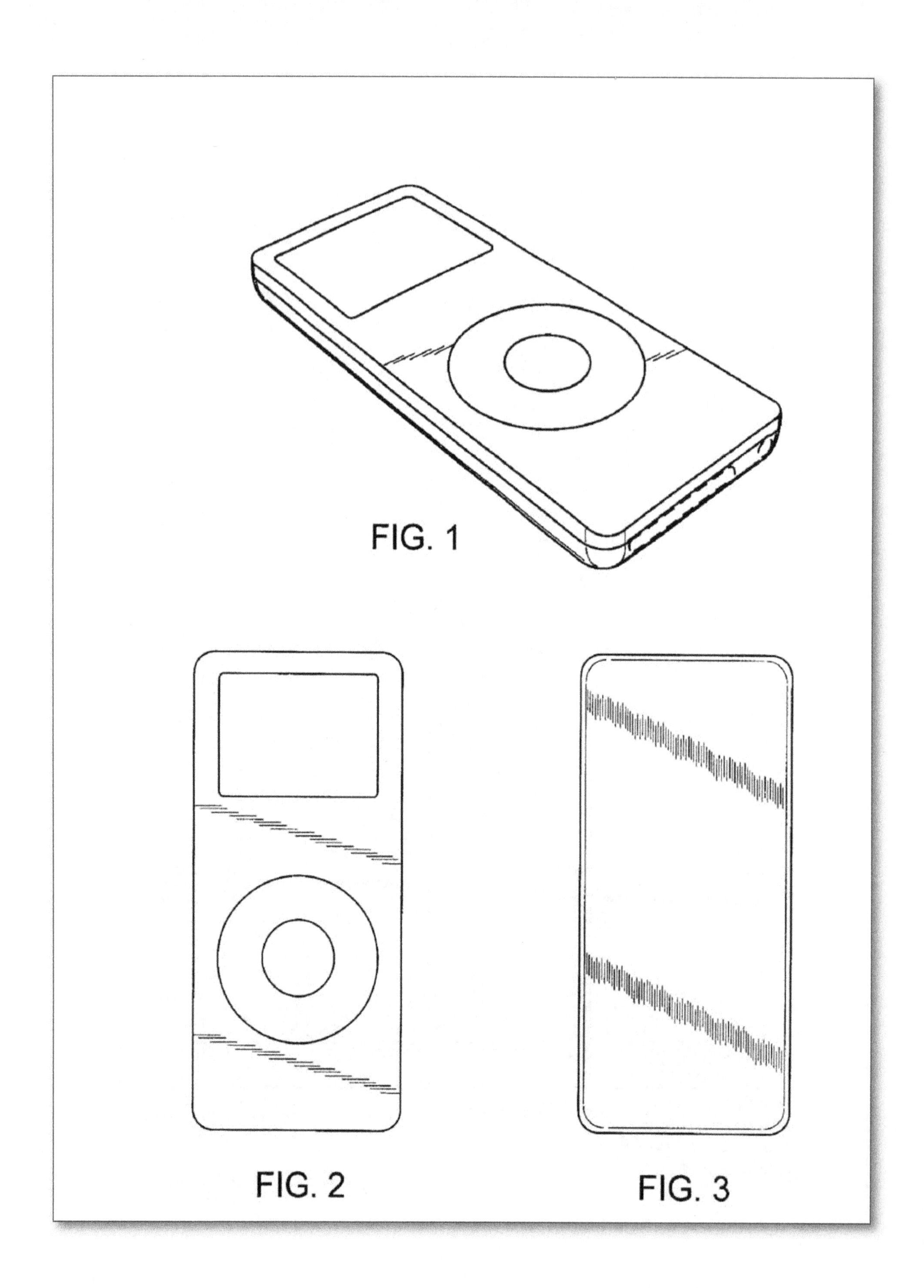

MEDIA DEVICE
ANDRE ET AL (including STEVE JOBS) Mar. 20, 2007 No. D538,820

CHAPTER 5

Modern Patent Art

As we've seen, patent art is a reflection of the technological evolution of humankind. Patent drawings aren't just beautiful, they record the cutting edge of technology, which then itself soon passes into history. Many of today's patent drawings or photographs reflect these quantum developments in technology. Genetically modified organisms, DNA, medicine, hybrid rose bushes, all are patentable and all carry with them new boundaries to the art of the patent.

With the drawings in this chapter we will walk through some of the newest images and ideas at the outer limits of human knowledge. Time travel works both ways in the sense that the future we might not yet understand may have just been patented. Much will be illegible to all but the most scientifically-trained eye; but the beauty still shows through. The images, lines, and photographs have that same eerie attraction that keeps us coming back for more.

Watch now as modern patent art takes us on a bizarre journey to the future.

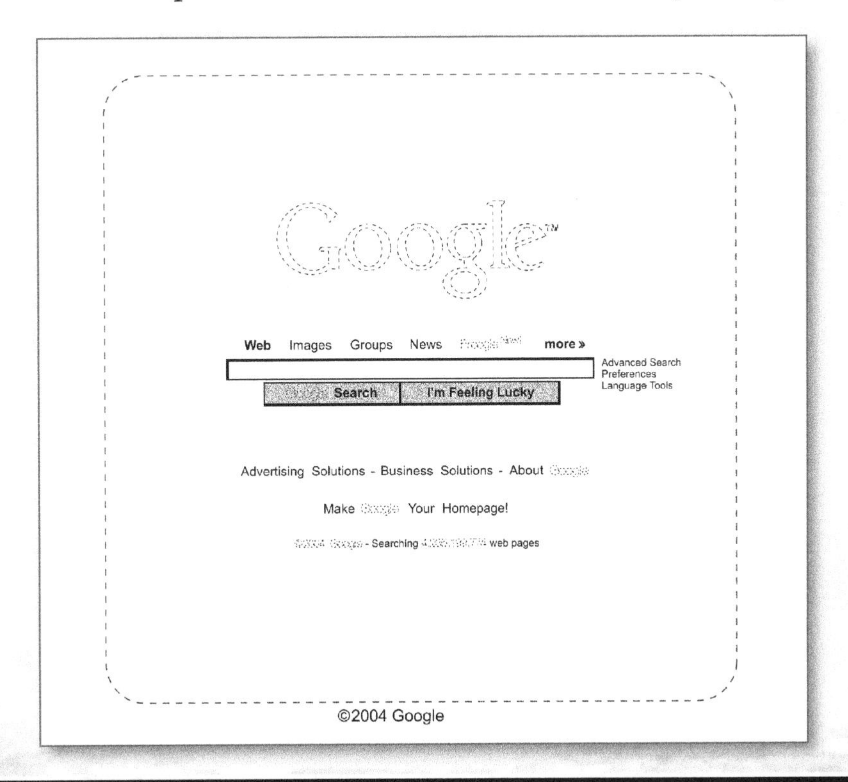

GRAPHICAL USER INTERFACE FOR A DISPLAY SCREEN OF A COMMUNICATIONS TERMINAL
K. C. PELCZARSKI Sep. 1, 2009 No. D599,372

Below is a representation of converting RNA into its complimentary DNA. Really.

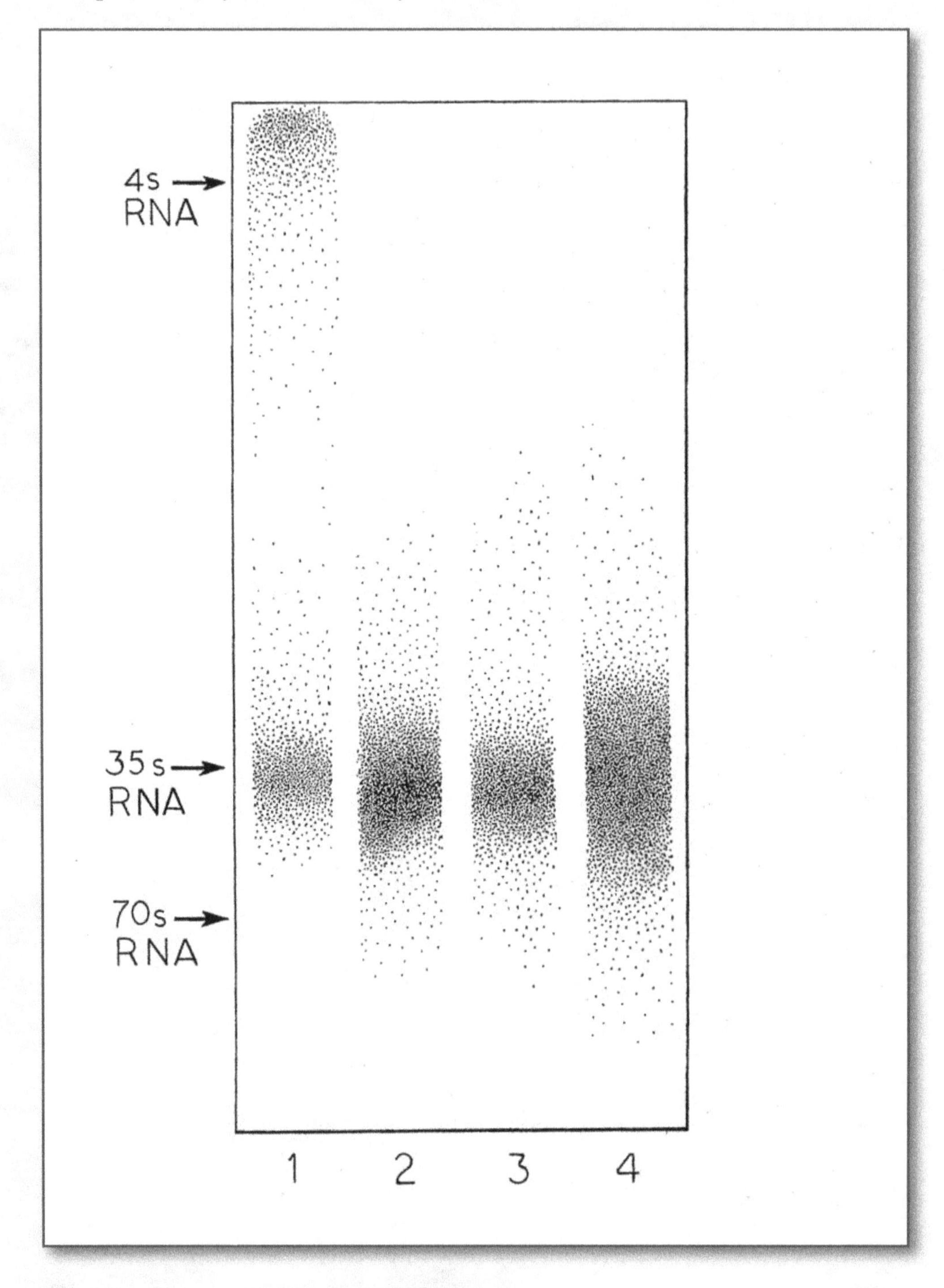

DEOXYRIBOUNUCLEIC ACID SYNTHESIS USING BINDING PROTEIN
PAUL P. HUNG Sep. 23, 1980 No. 4,224,408

The following example is of a cell culture device. Note how the drawing rules put forth by the PTO are still neatly followed, yet we end up with a fantastic drawing fit for the best of our imaginations. Broken lines are used to illustrate interior features, the bottom portion utilizes a cut away, and different materials are designated by the corresponding straight line shading.

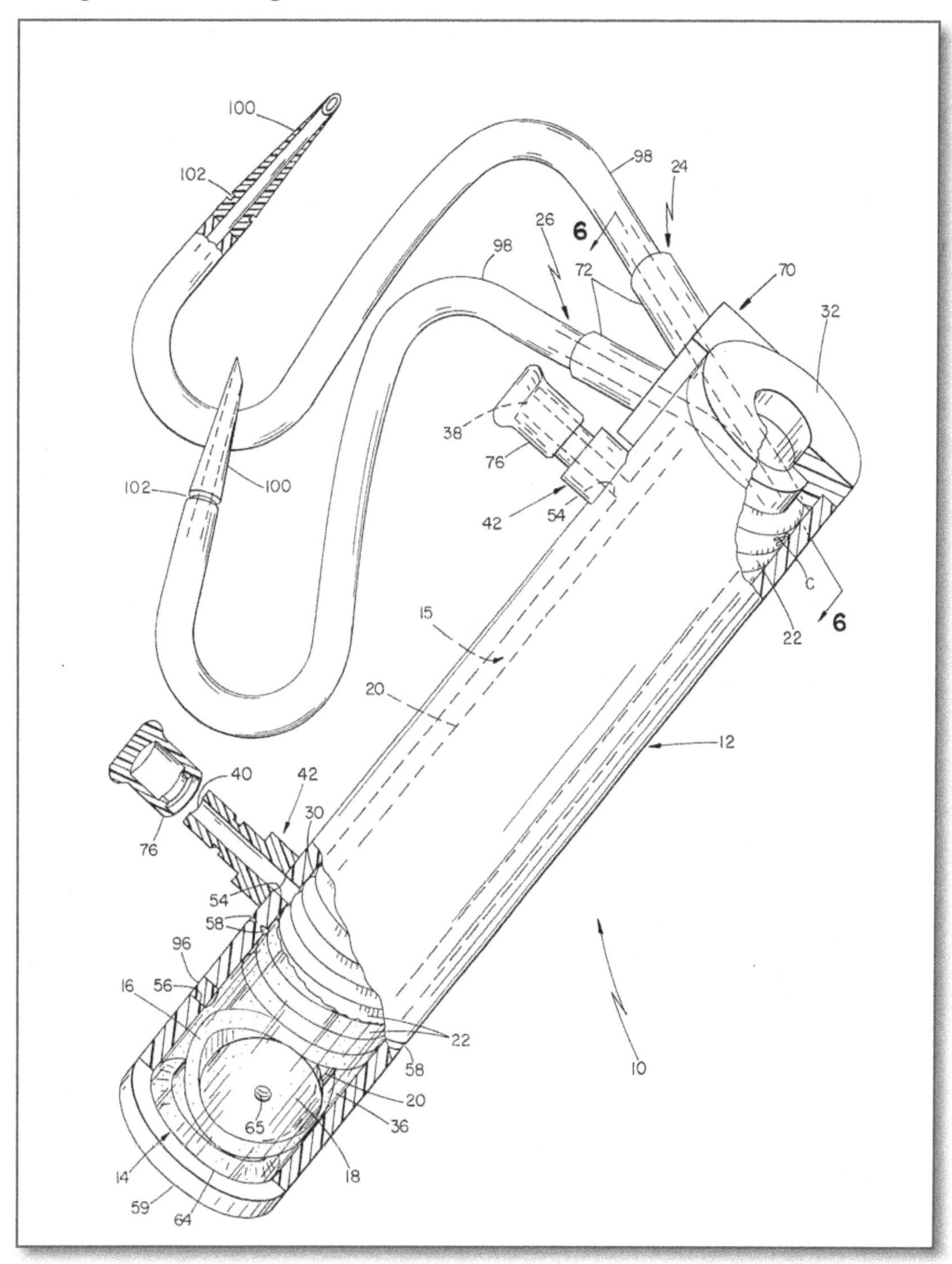

To quote the patent abstract text: "Recombinant microbial cloning vehicles comprising heterologous DNA coding for the expression of mammalian hormone..."

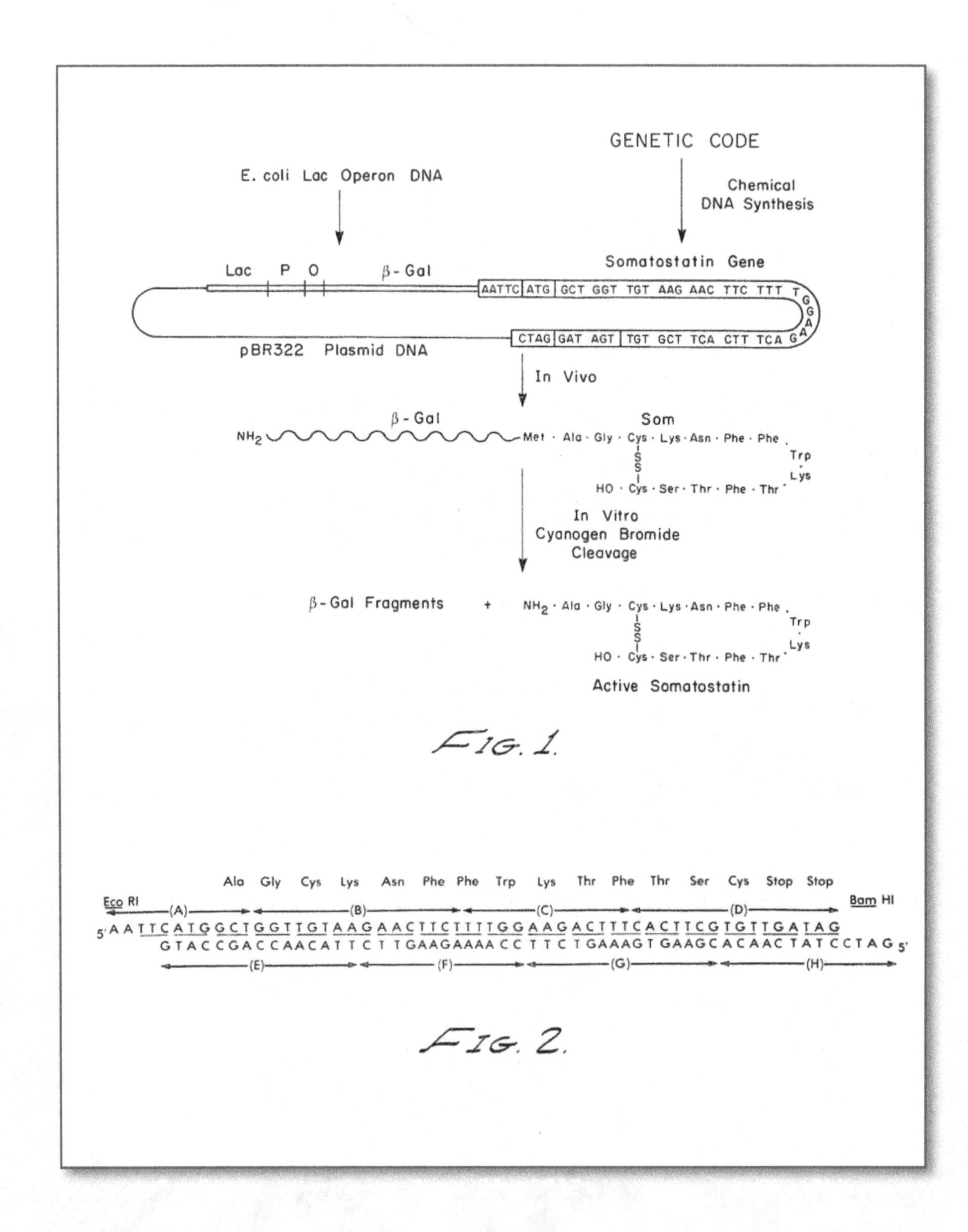

METHOD FOR MICROBIAL POLYPEPTIDE EXPRESSION
ARTHUR D. RIGGS Dec. 28, 1982 No. 4,366,246

Note how the following patent for developing a human epithelium (i.e. tissue) on a mouse depicts the progression of operative events. It also conveys a spooky *Island of Dr. Moreau* feel.

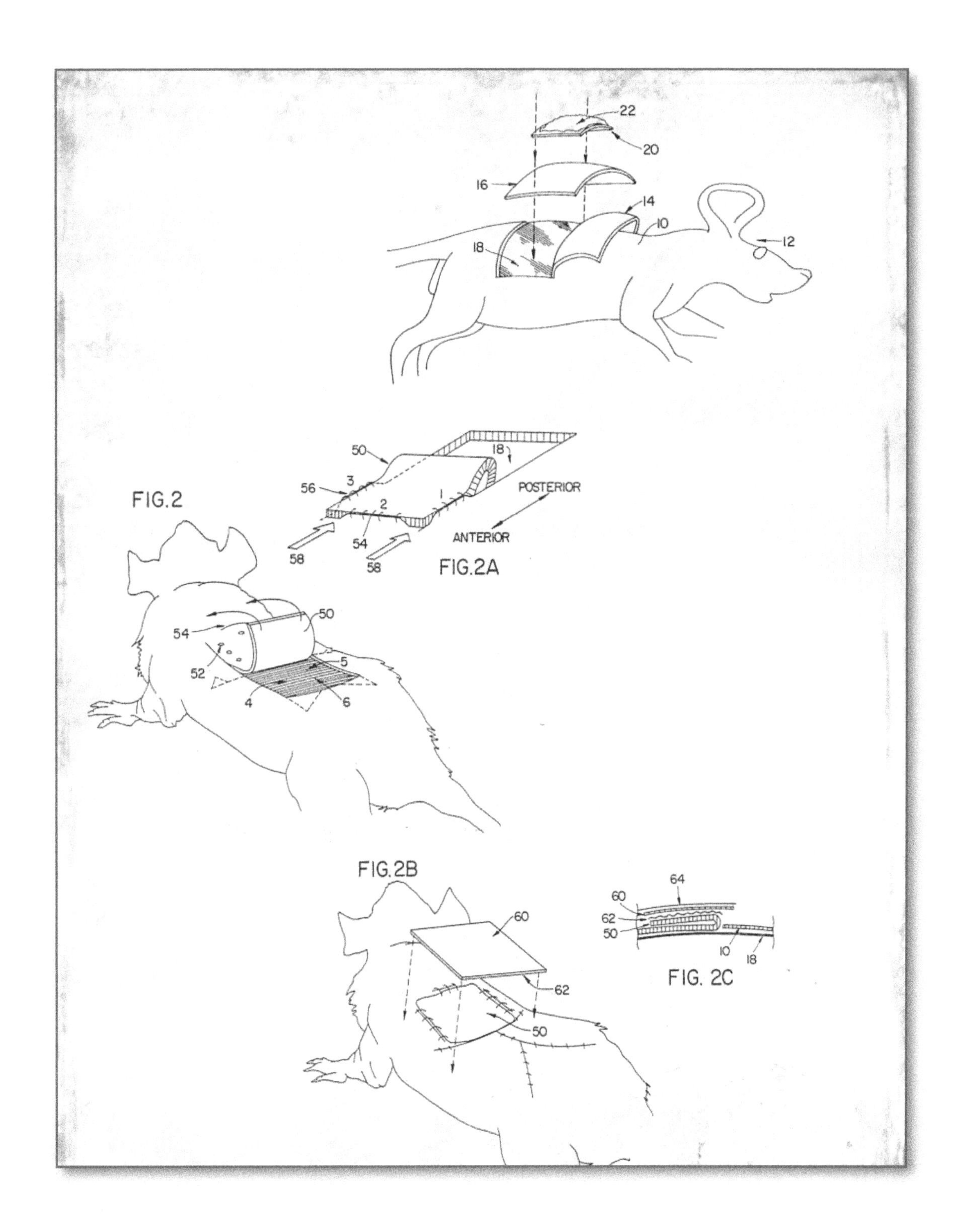

HUMAN EPITHELIUM ORIGINATING FROM CELL CULTURES
YANN BARRANDON Dec. 19, 1989 No. 4,888,291

In the following drawing of a system for exposing a cell culture to a fluid shear force, several interesting patent art tools are used. The straight lined drawing creates a clear, easy to follow image, yet the human hand with the tweezers conveys the delicacy of the apparatus as do the three vertical bent tubes. One can feel movement without understanding the nature of the invention.

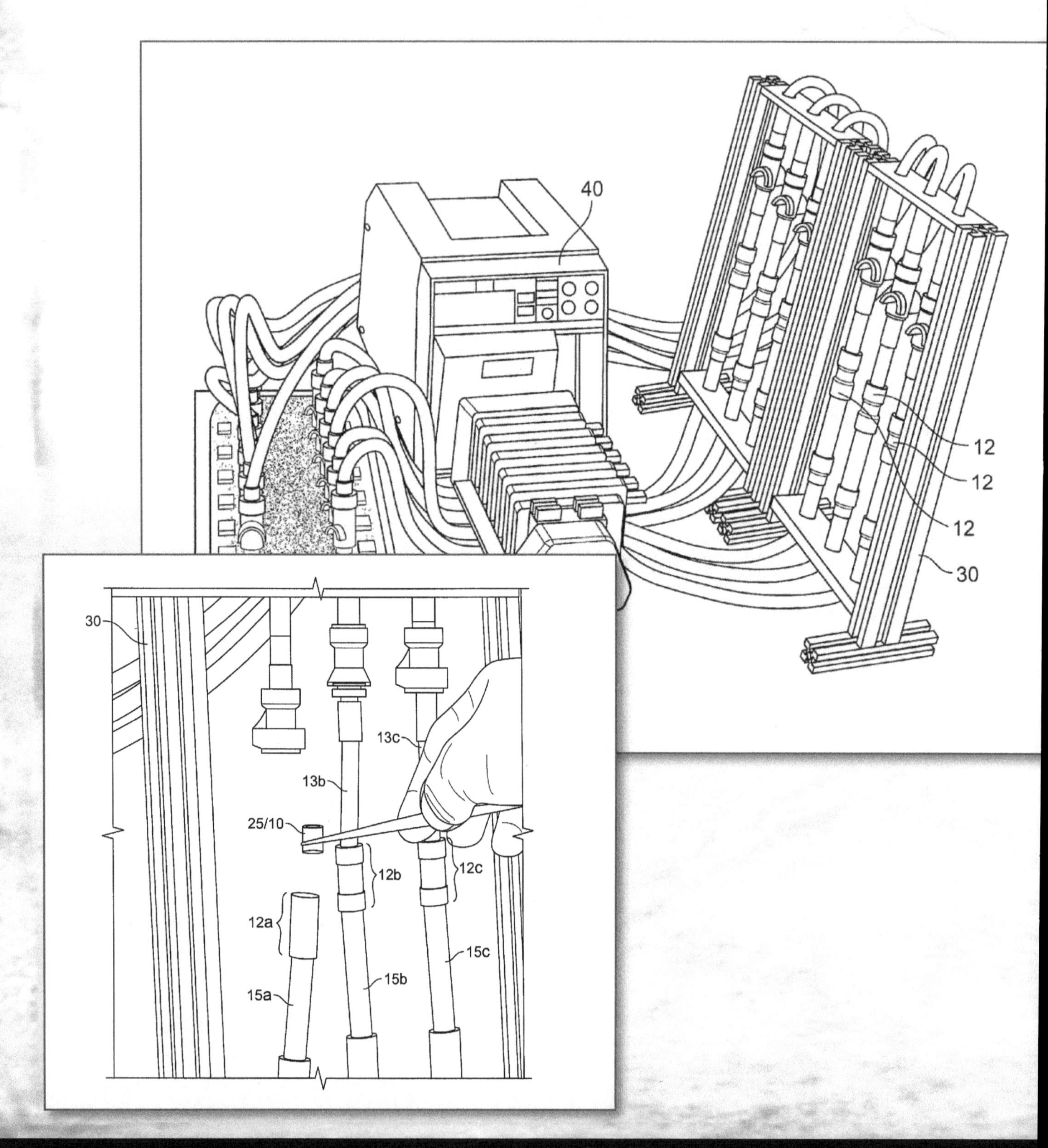

Plant hybrids have been around longer than most of us realize. However, the ability to patent them is relatively new.

HYBRID TEA ROSE PLANT NAMED 'JACSEE'
K.W. ZARY Nov. 30, 1999 No. PP11,138

Plants aren't the only things to be genetically modified. The following patent drawing relates to genetically modified fibroblast cells. (Fibroblast cells are those that help form connective tissue fibers.)

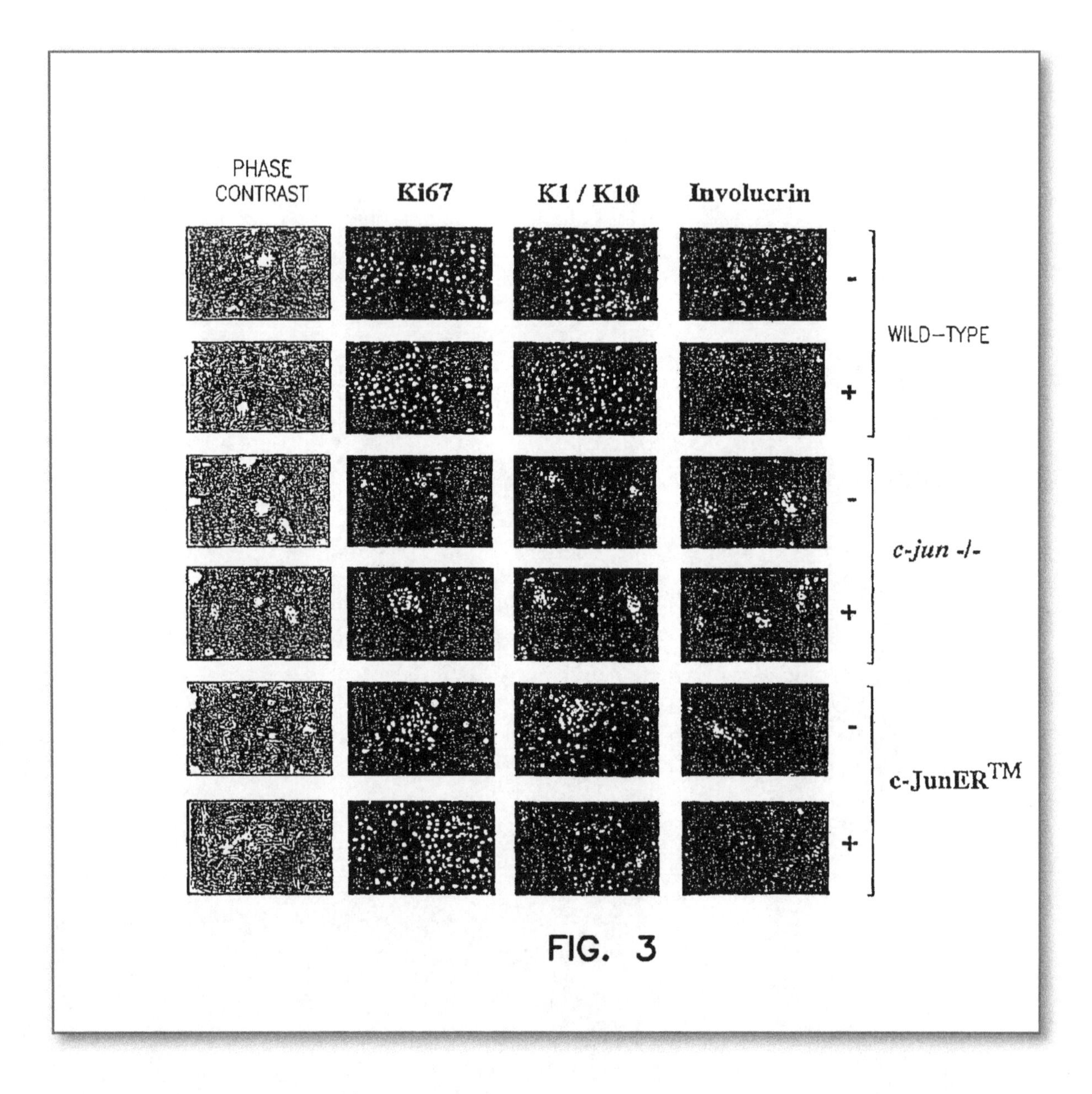

FIG. 3

The following is an example of a drawing that is a pleasure just to sit back and enjoy. Technically it's titled, "Polycrystalline silicon emitter having an accurately controlled critical dimension." A rose by any other name is a funky little drawing.

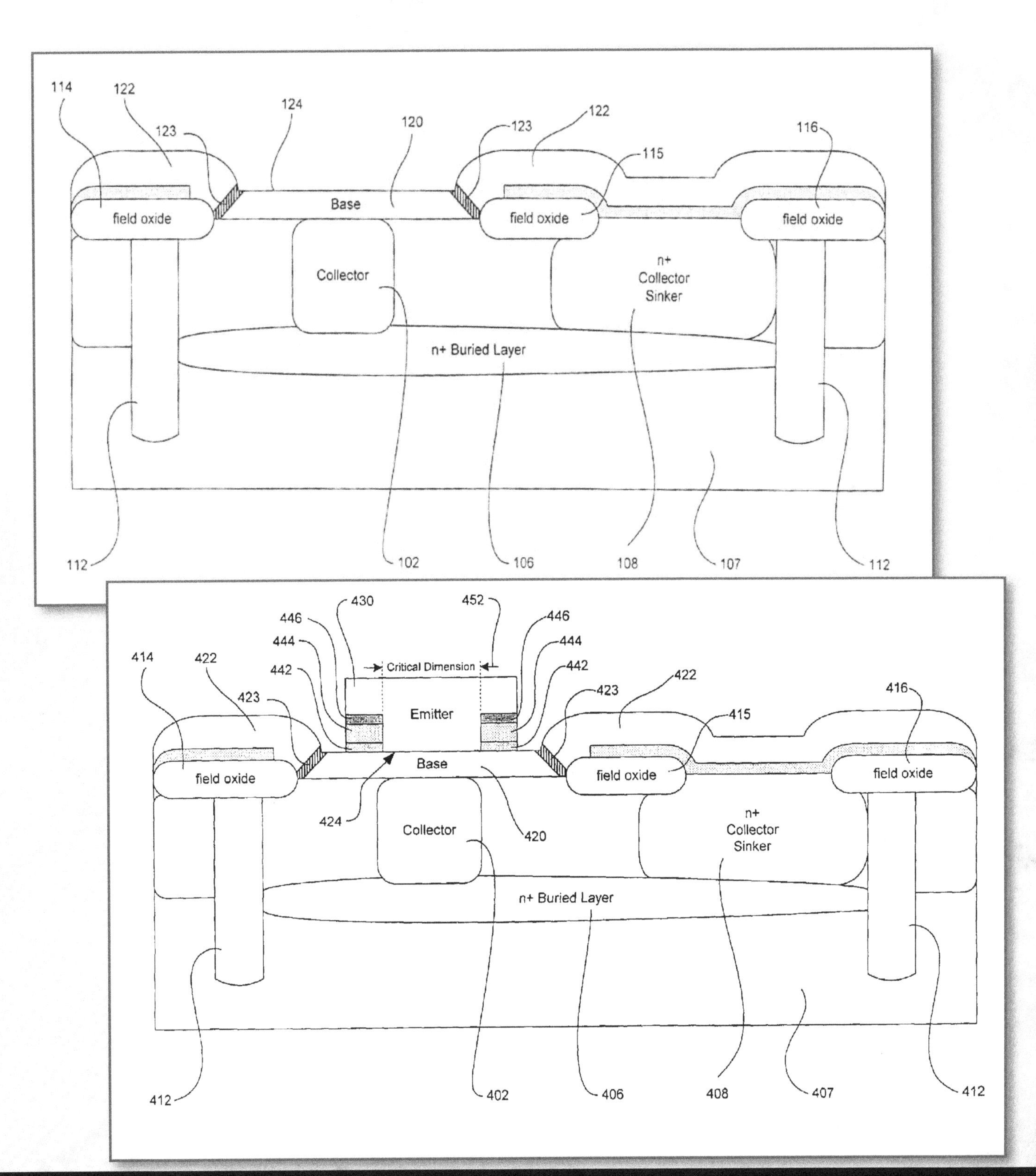

The following are part of a design for a pressurized wound treatment machine.

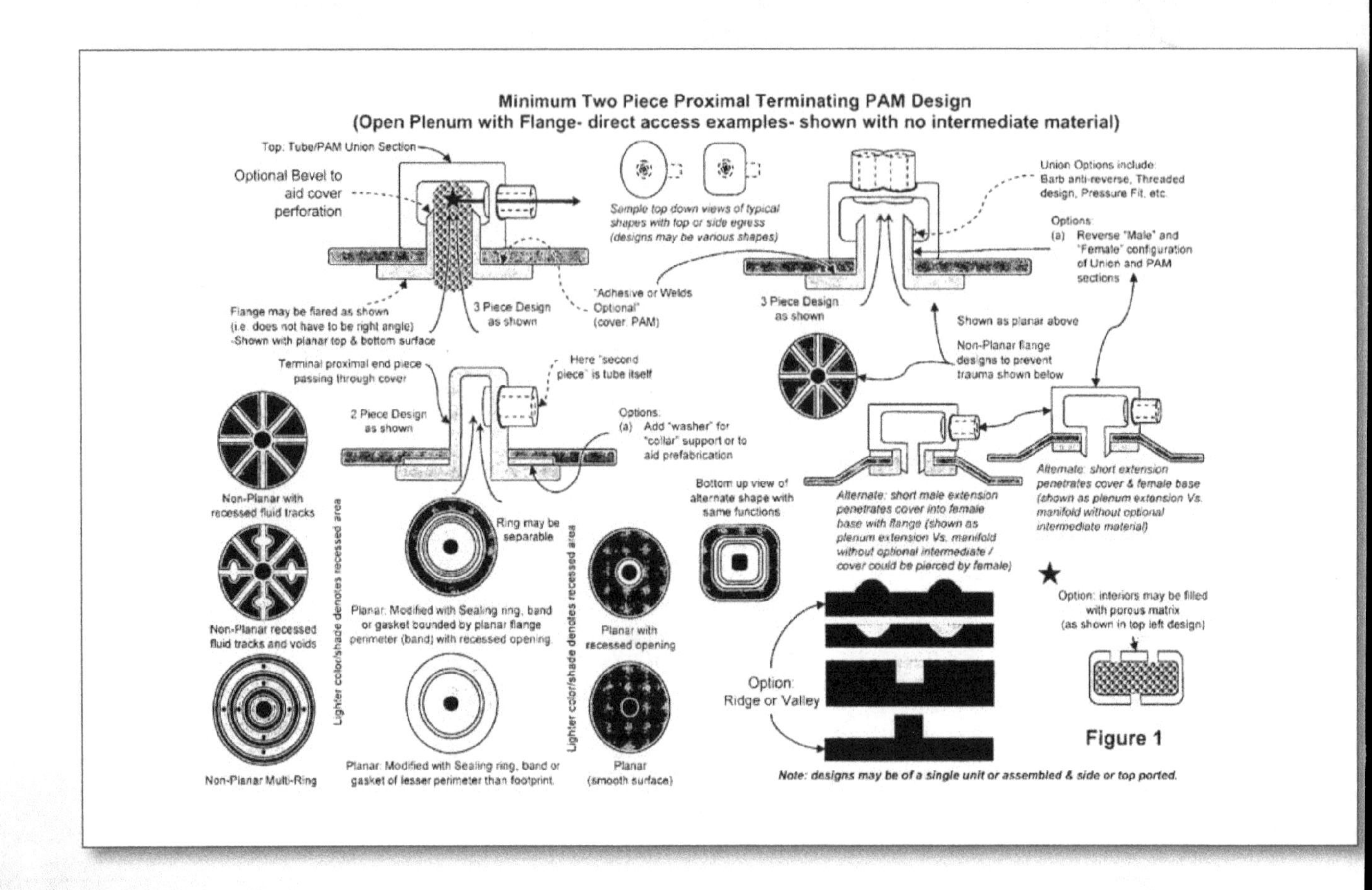

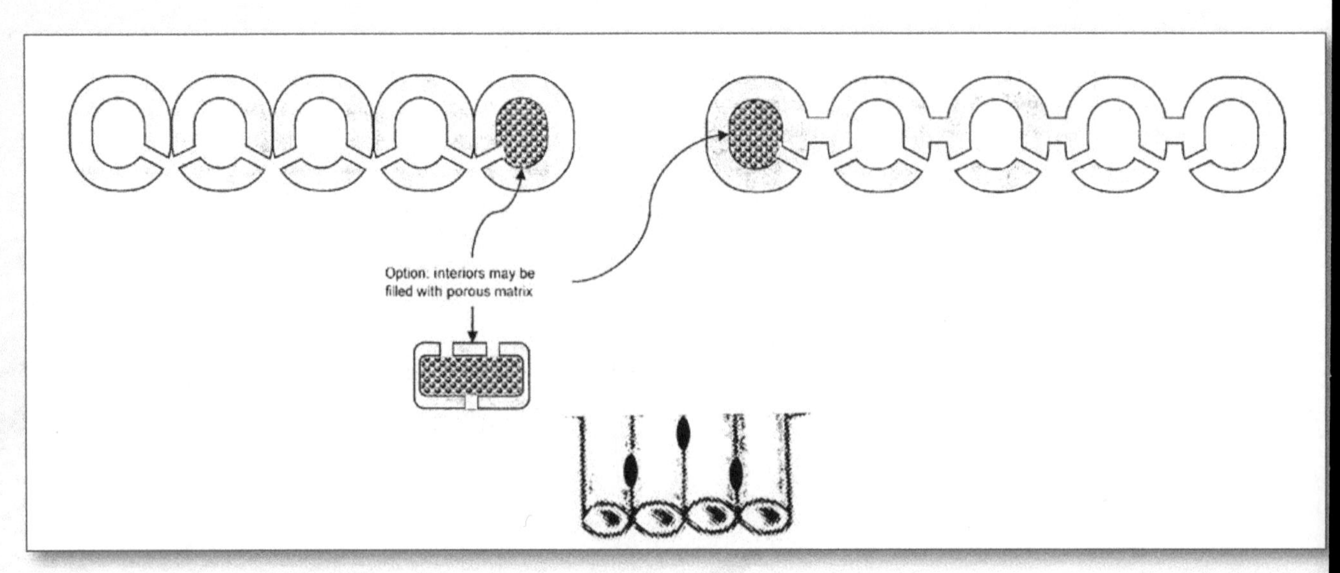

One might wonder how Figure 1 can have so much text... isn't that against the rules? The answe is that this is a patent application that, as of this printing, has not been granted as a patent yet (note that published patent applications start with their year of publication, in this case 2010). This drawing may not survive the examination process... but it's still fun to look at.

METHODS, COMPOSITIONS AND APPARATUSES TO TREAT WOUNDS WITH PRESSURES ALTERED FROM ATMOSPHERIC
CURTIS E. JONES Jan. 21, 2010 No. 2010/0016767

Again in the line of medicine, the following slides are part of the patent application for methods for treating diseases and infections using antibodies.

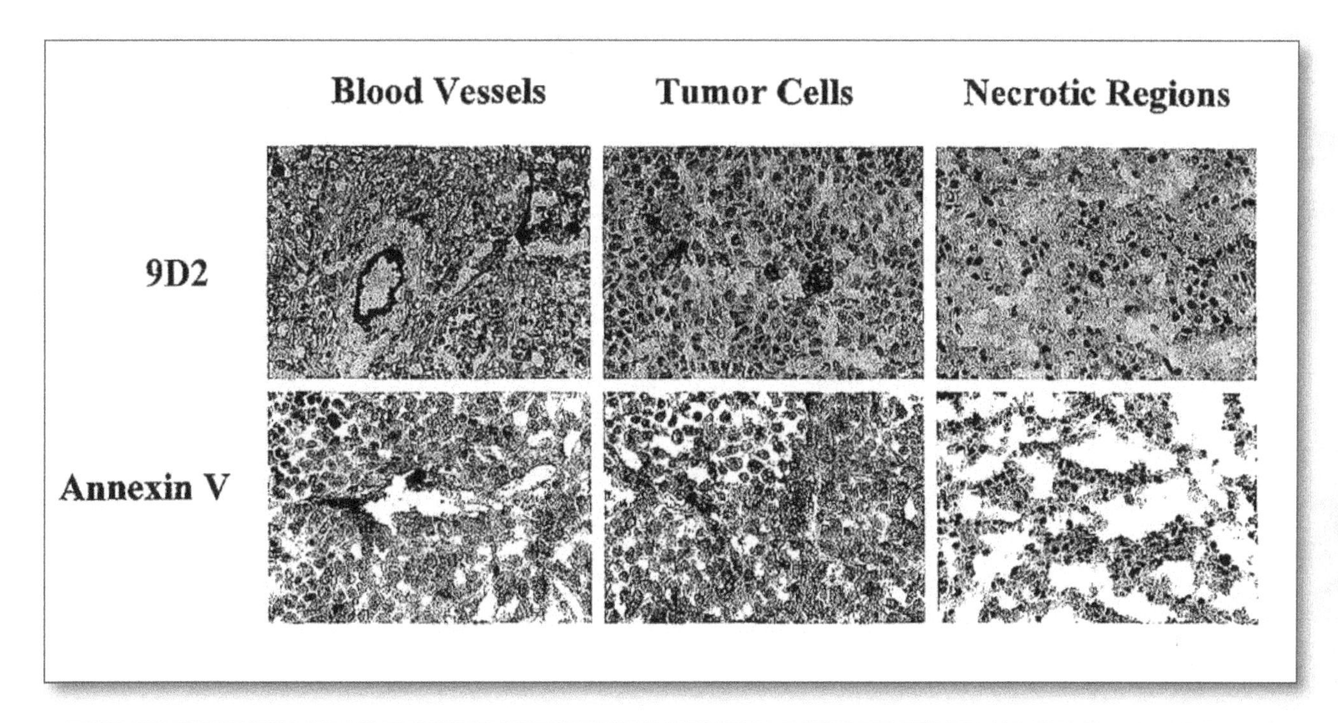

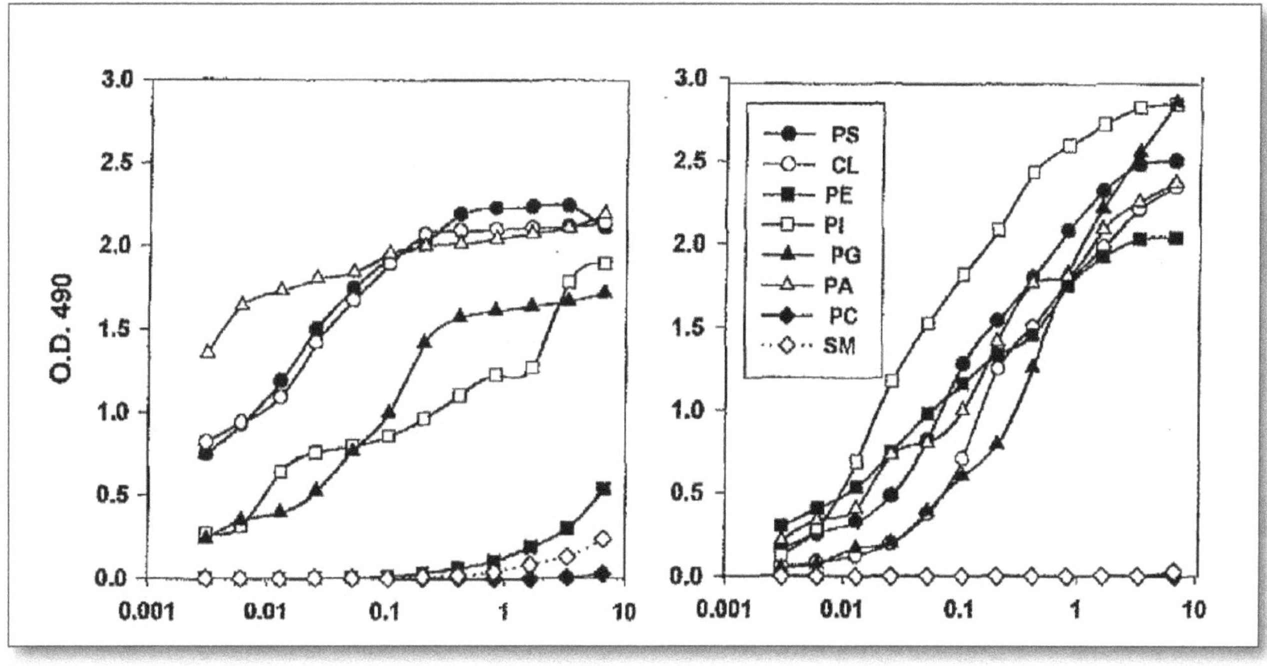

The field of biotechnology is unrecognizable today from what it was twenty years ago and what it will be in another twenty years. Below is the drawing for a gas venting system and, although complex in what it can do, it is elegantly drawn.

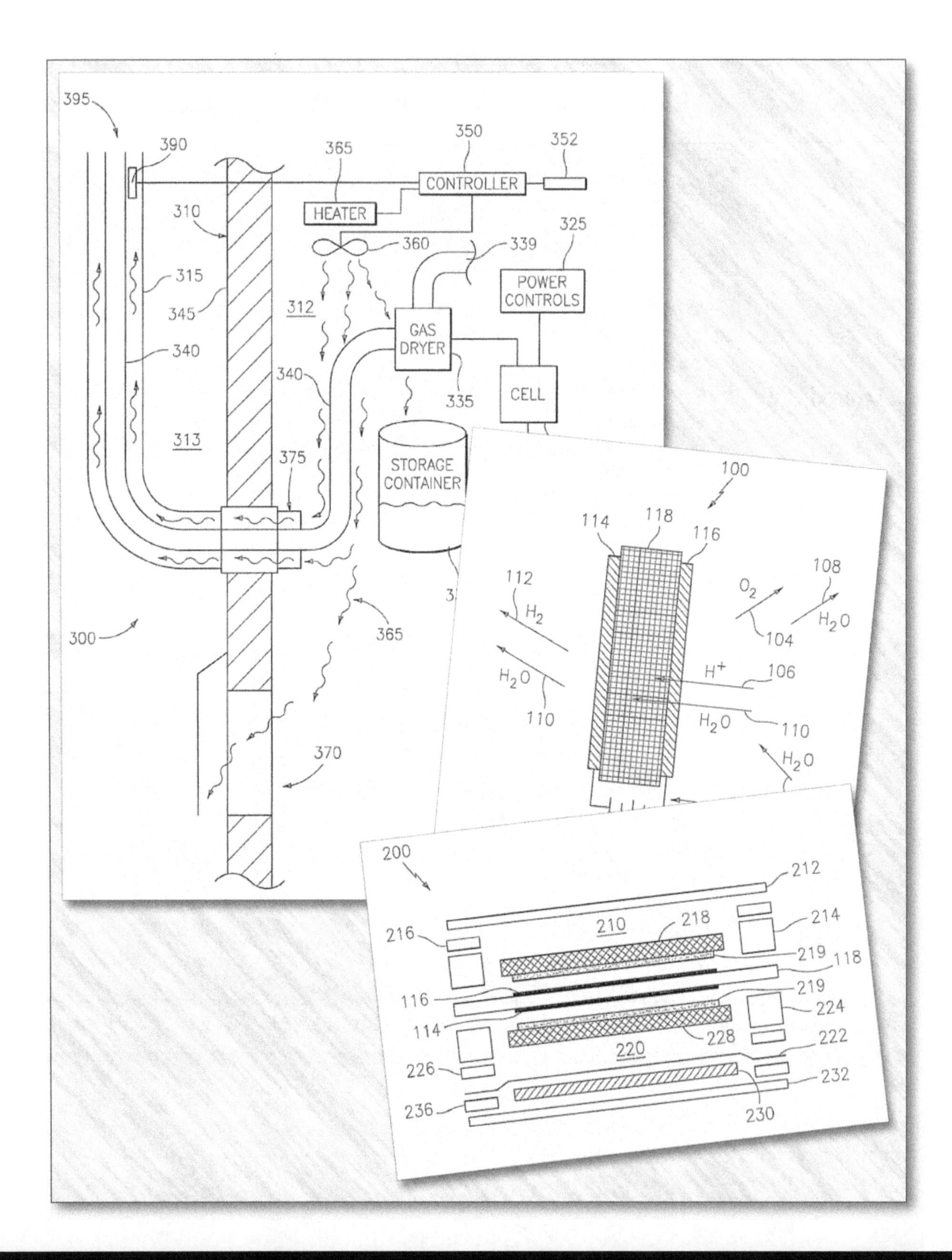

GAS VENTING SYSTEM
AMJAD KHAN Jun. 29, 2010 No. 7,744,733

These drawings addresses the recovery of gas during electrodialysis. Whether you understand them or not, they're fun and full of character.

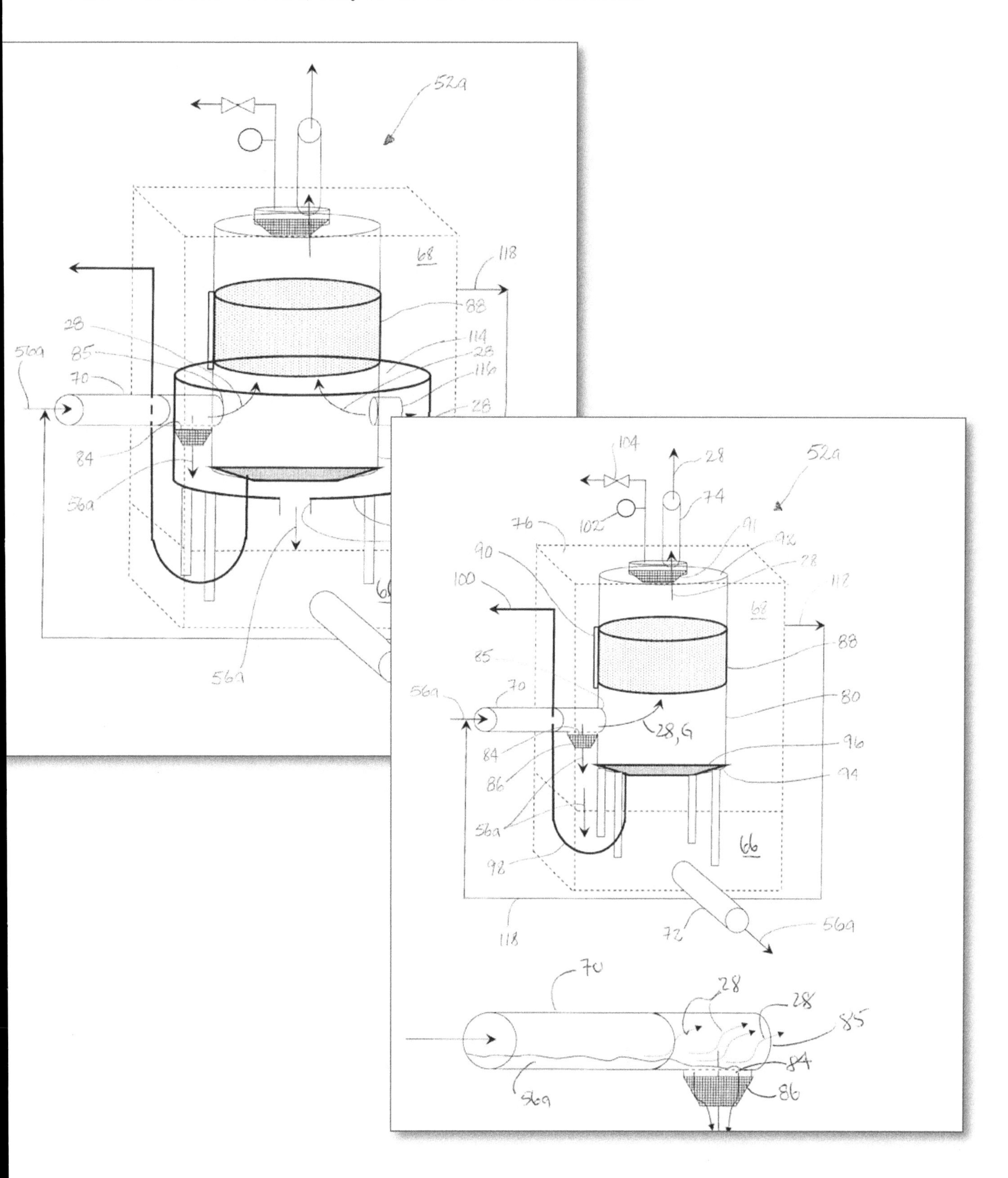

By now we've seen several drawings of the "exploded" view of an invention. The following is another excellent example; this time for an on-site carbon dioxide generator.

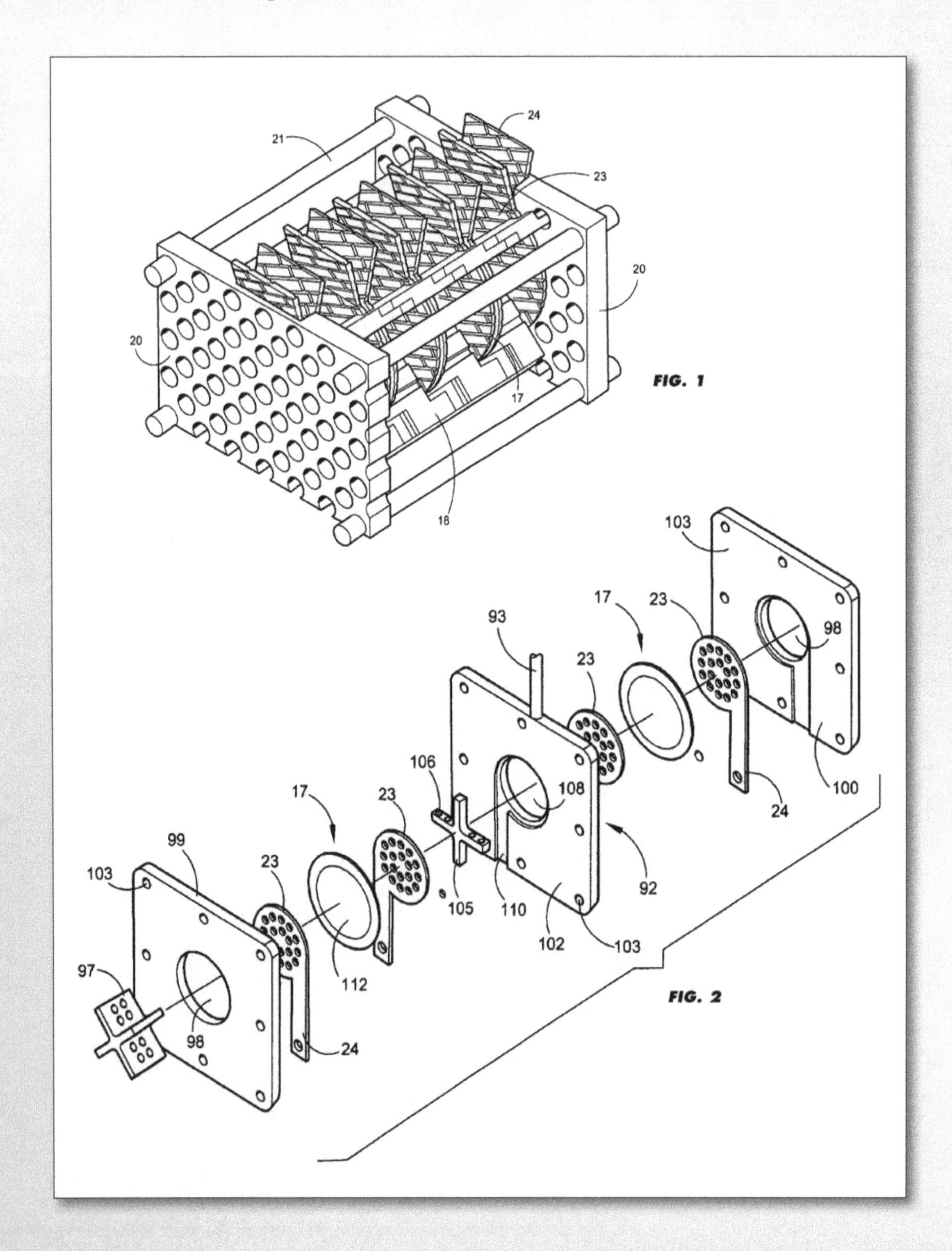

"ON-SITE" CARBON DIOXIDE GENERATOR
HENRI > R. MAGET Aug. 31, 2010 No. US 7,785,450

The title alone of the following image is fun enough to just sit back and imagine what this could be for...

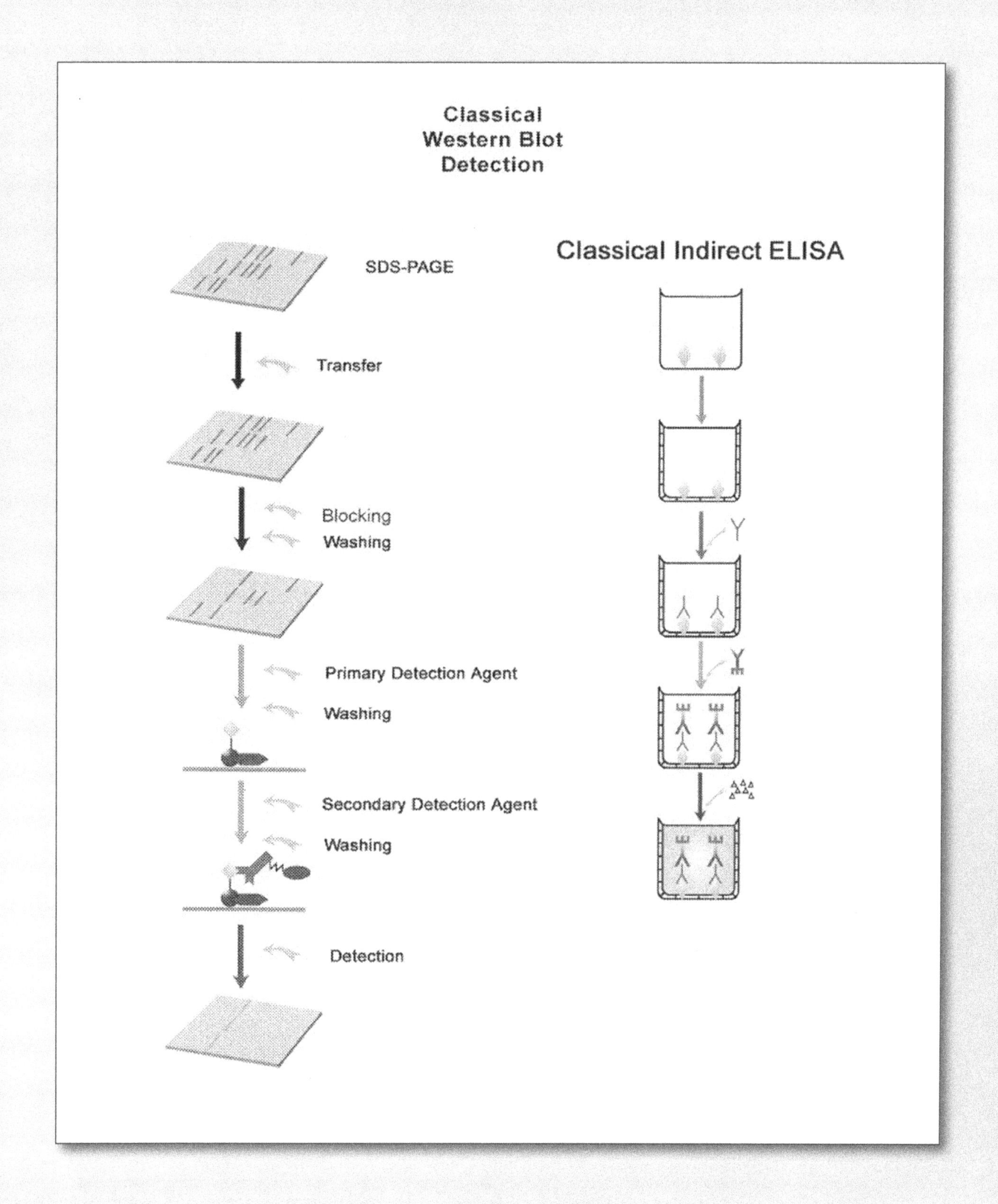

RAPID DETECTION PROCESSES AND RELATED COMPOSITIONS
ZHUYING WANG Apr. 15, 2010 No. 2010/0092991

NASA planet finder? No, a probe for anionic cell surface detection. (Say what?)

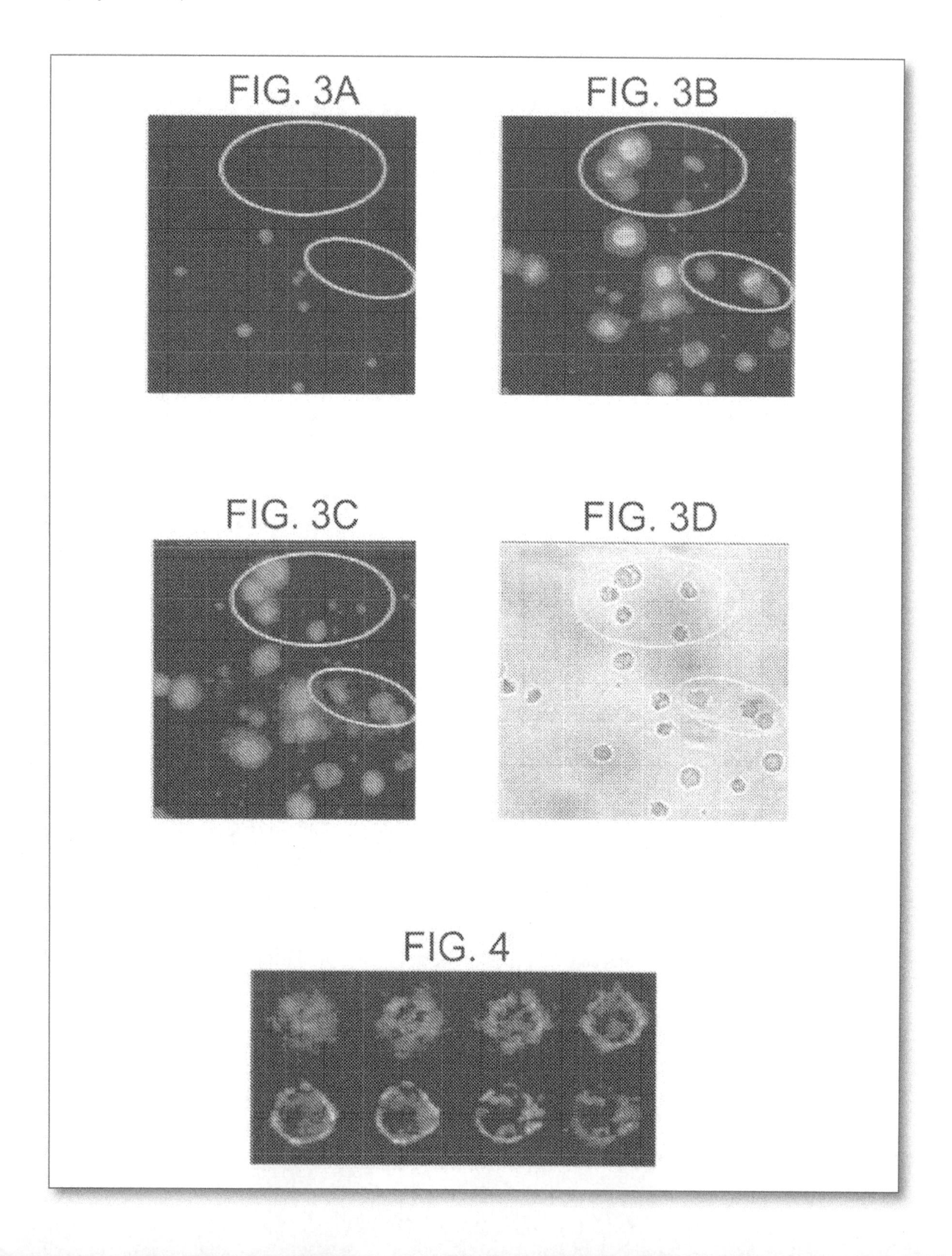

PROBES FOR ANIONIC CELL SURFACE DETECTION
B.D. SMITH Dec. 20, 2010 No. 2010/0331542

Here's something a little more relatable: a method for configuring wireless routers. Makes it look almost easy…doesn't it?

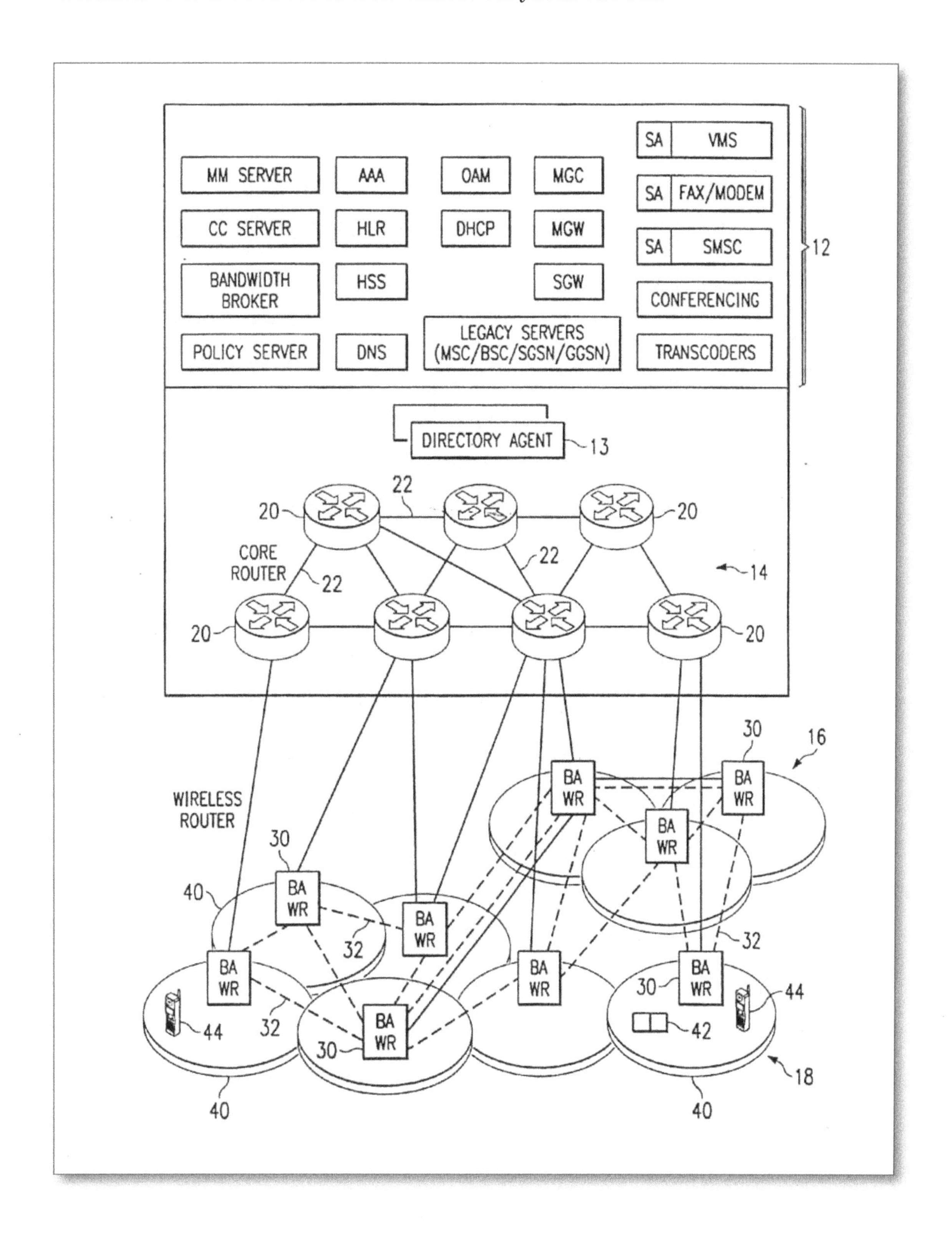

This optical imaging system has a striking resemblance to Edison's movie projector, showing that modern inventors still stand on the shoulders of giants.

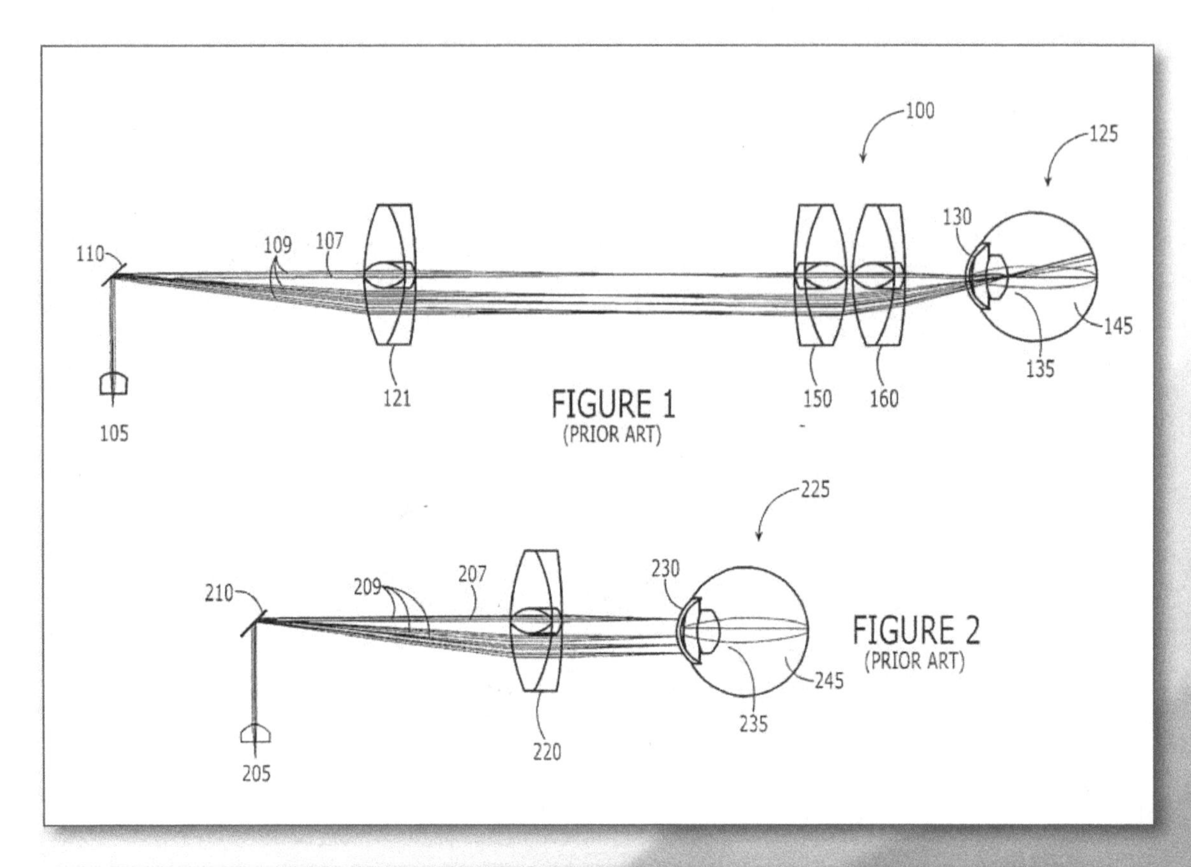

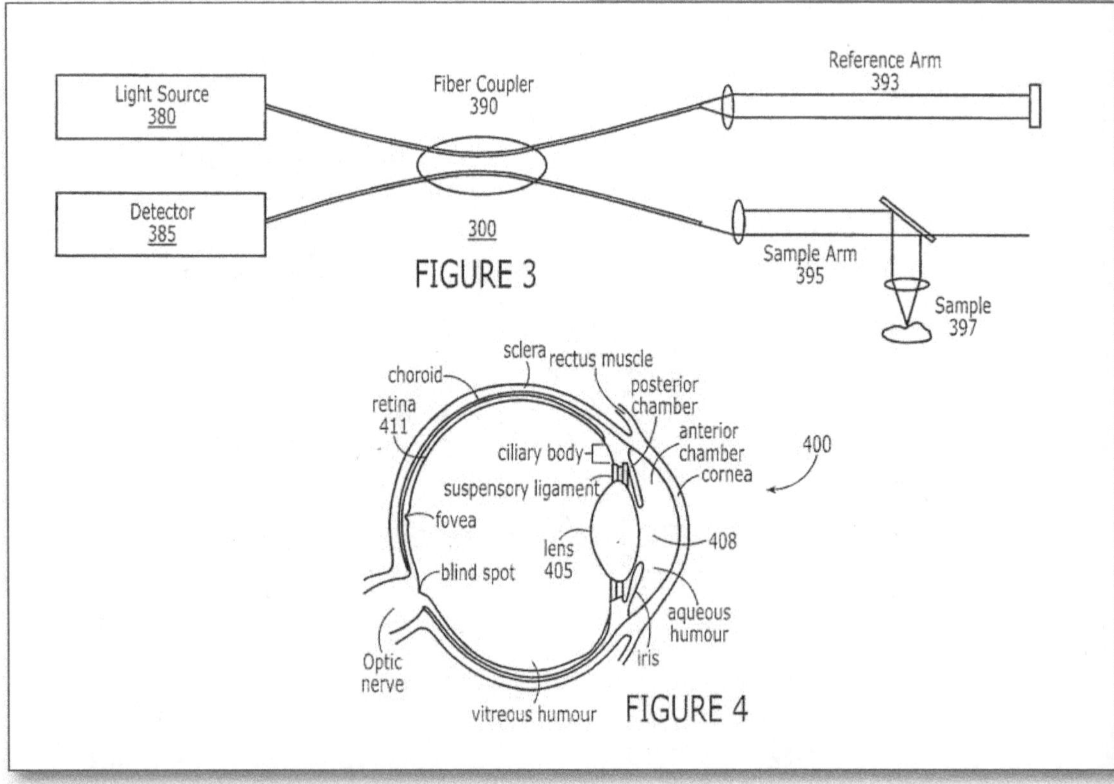

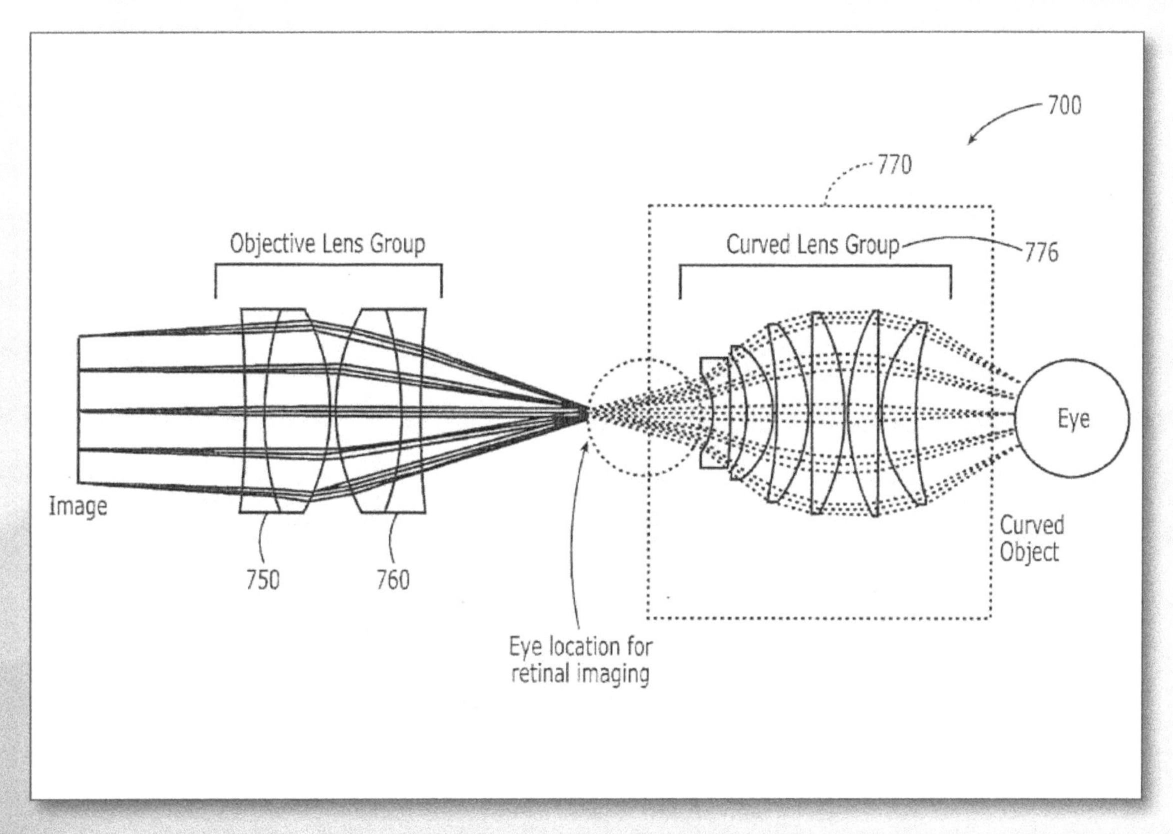
700
770
Objective Lens Group
Curved Lens Group
776
Eye
Image
Curved
Object
750
760
Eye location for
retinal imaging

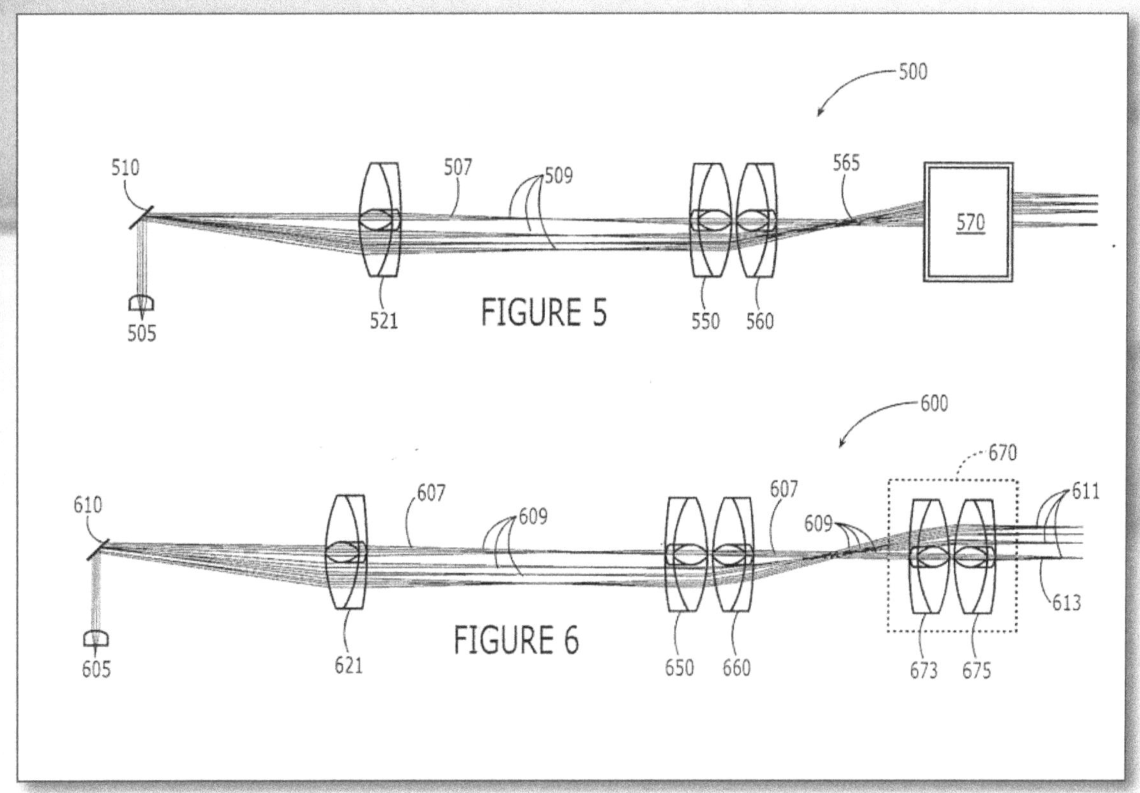
500
510
507
509
565
570
505
521
FIGURE 5
550
560
600
670
610
607
609
607
609
611
613
605
621
FIGURE 6
650
660
673
675

The semiconductor device in the following drawings brings up incongruous architectural images.

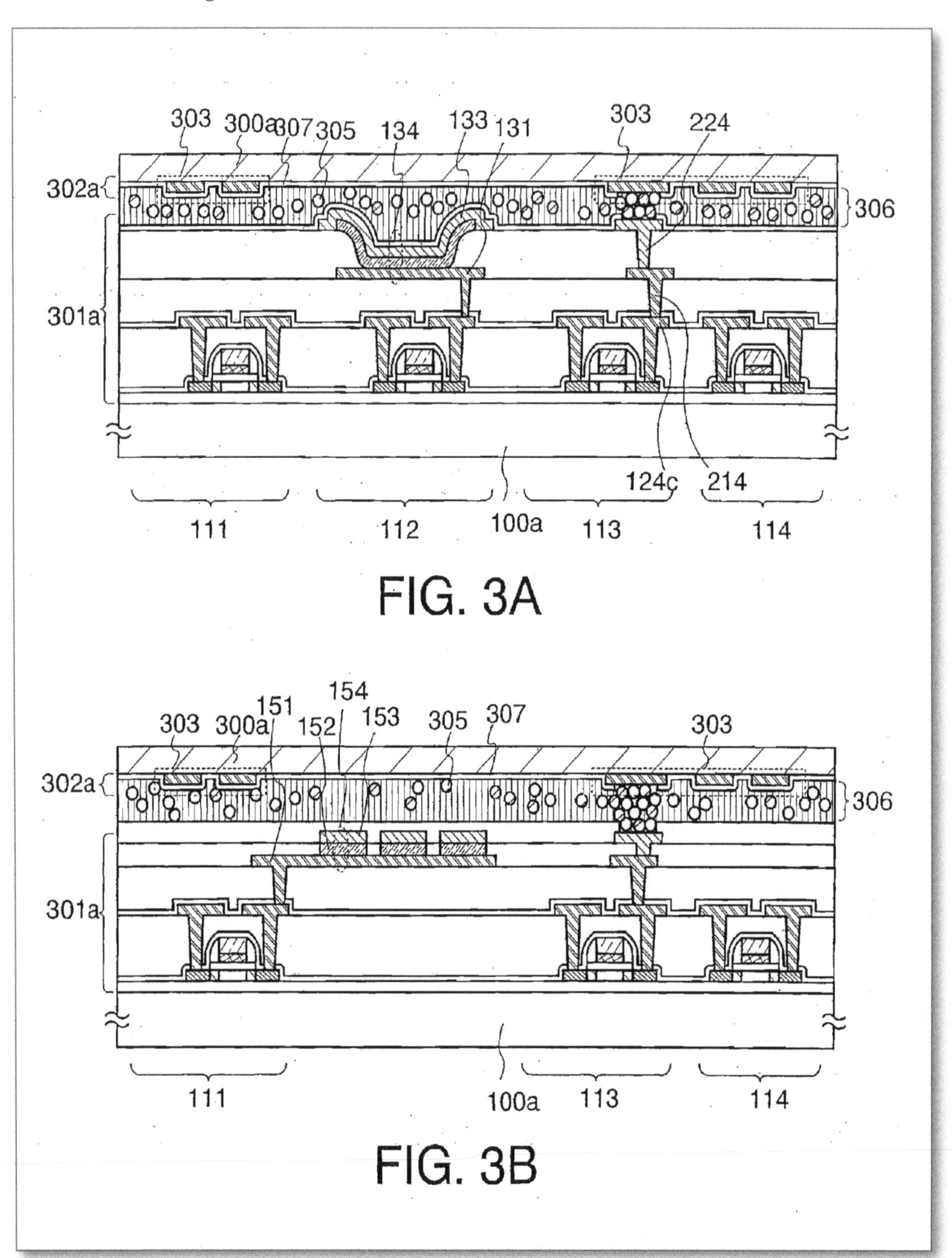

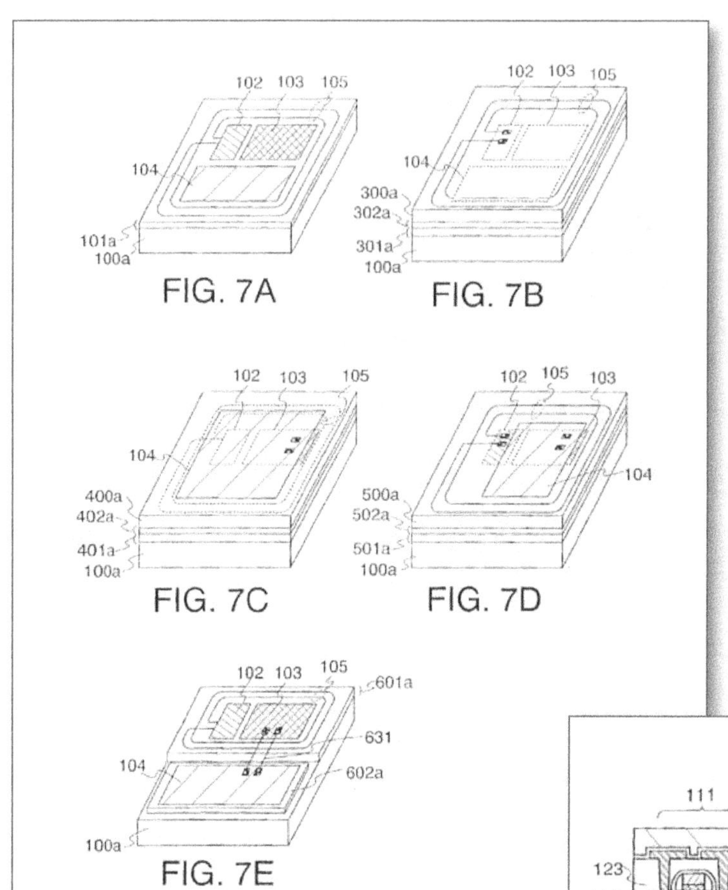

FIG. 7A FIG. 7B FIG. 7C FIG. 7D FIG. 7E

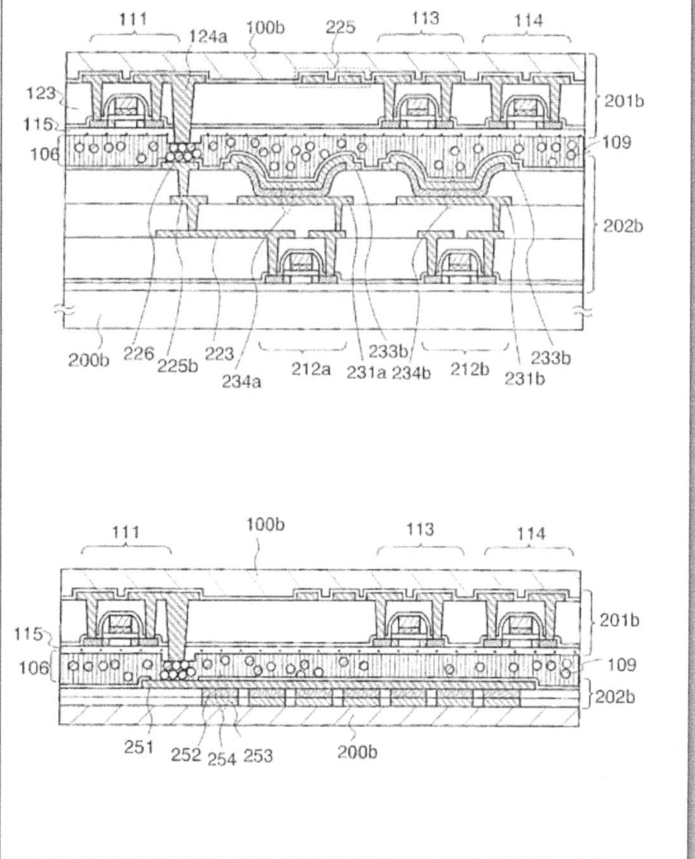

Photographs are more common now and can also provide intriguing images and designs.

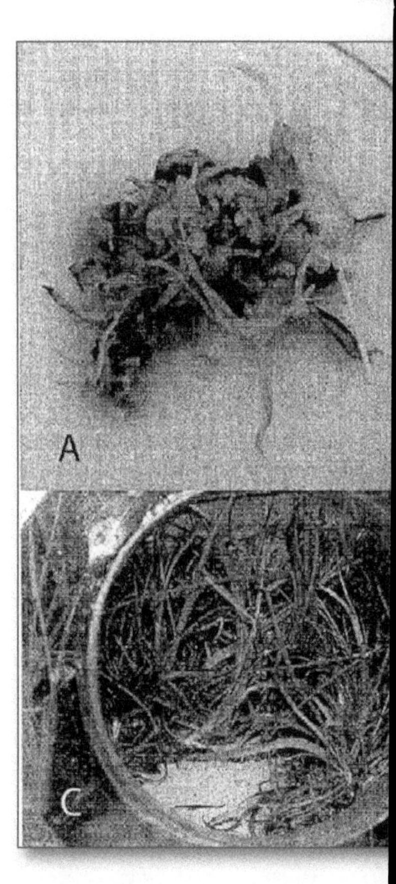

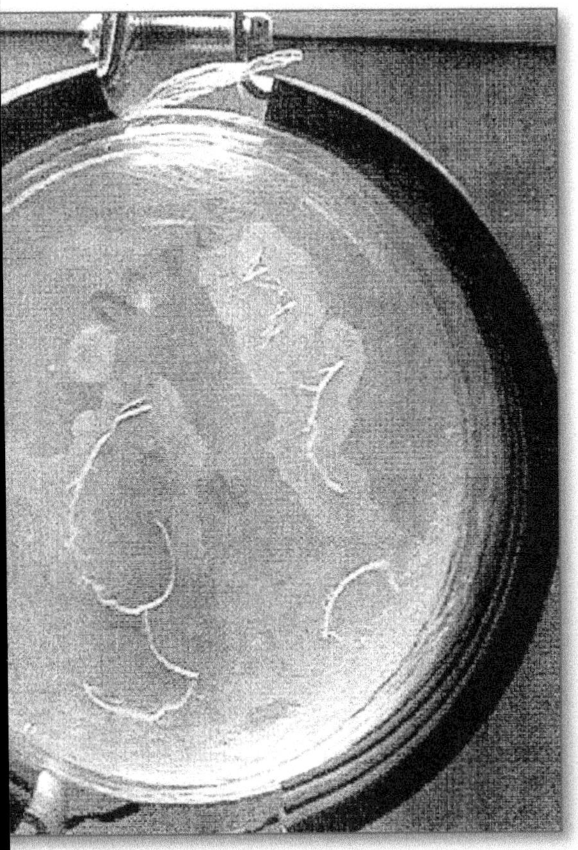

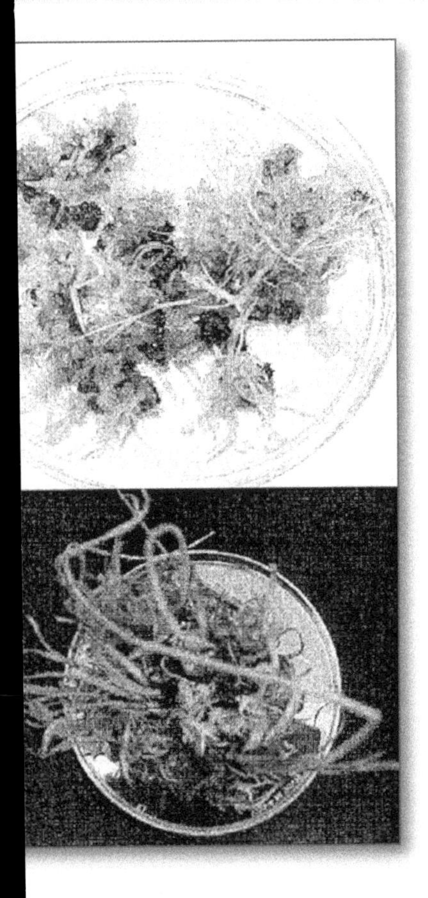

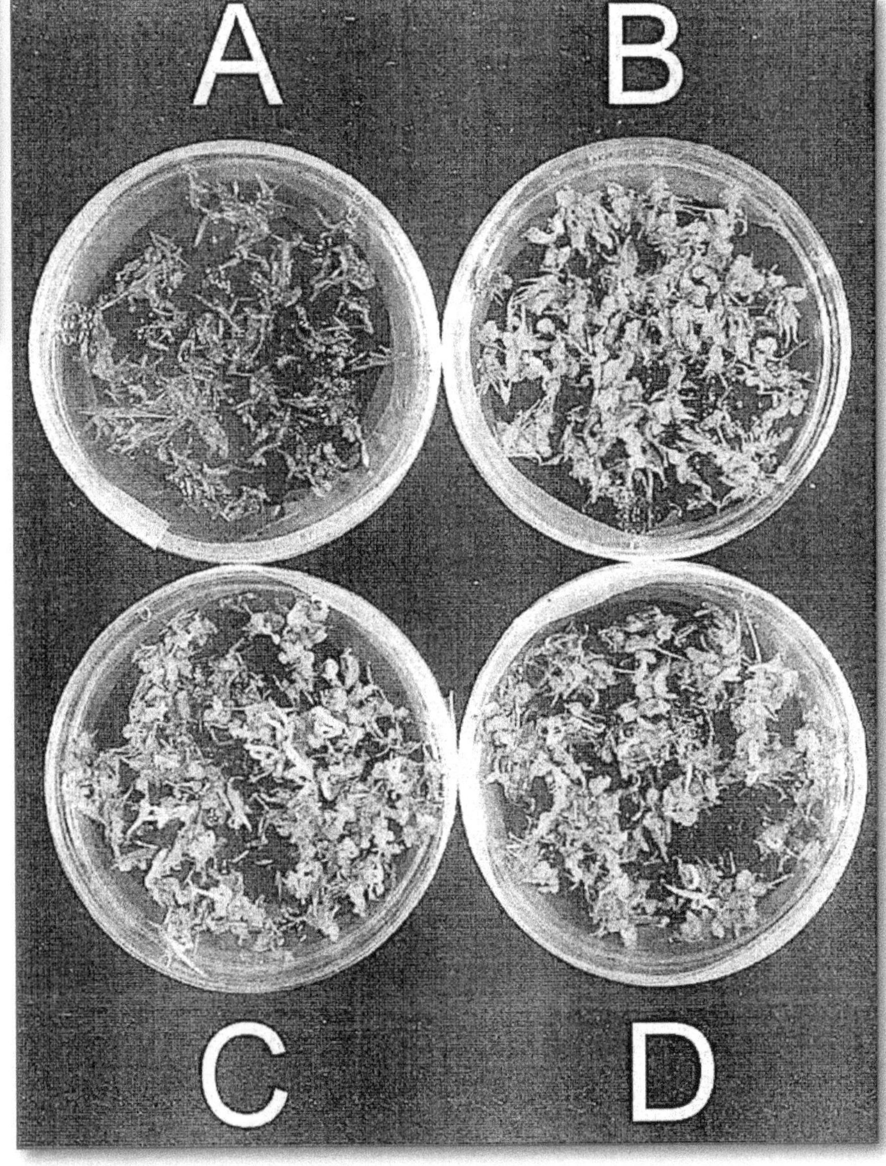
A
B
C
D

Computer drawings also express interesting designs and patterns...

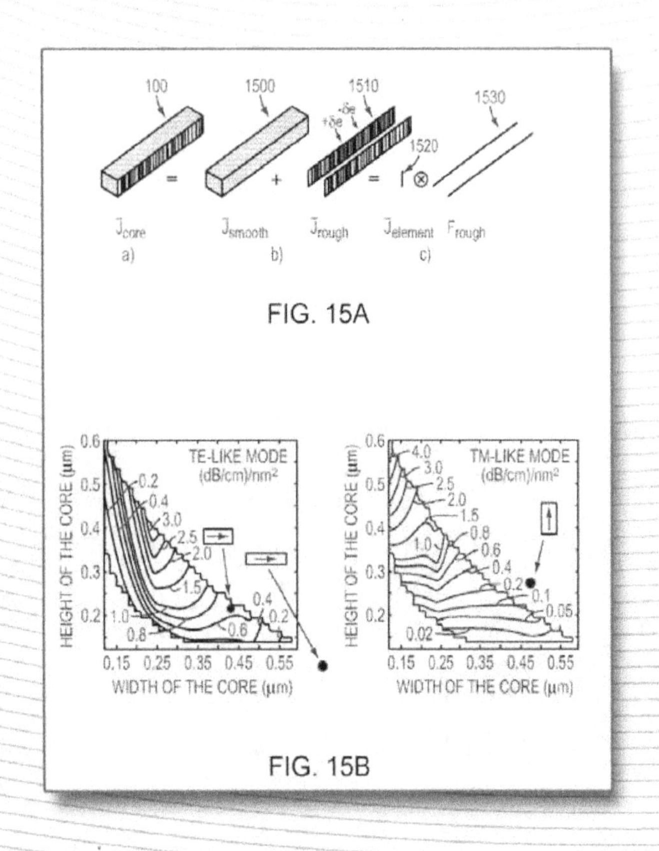

FIG. 15A

FIG. 15B

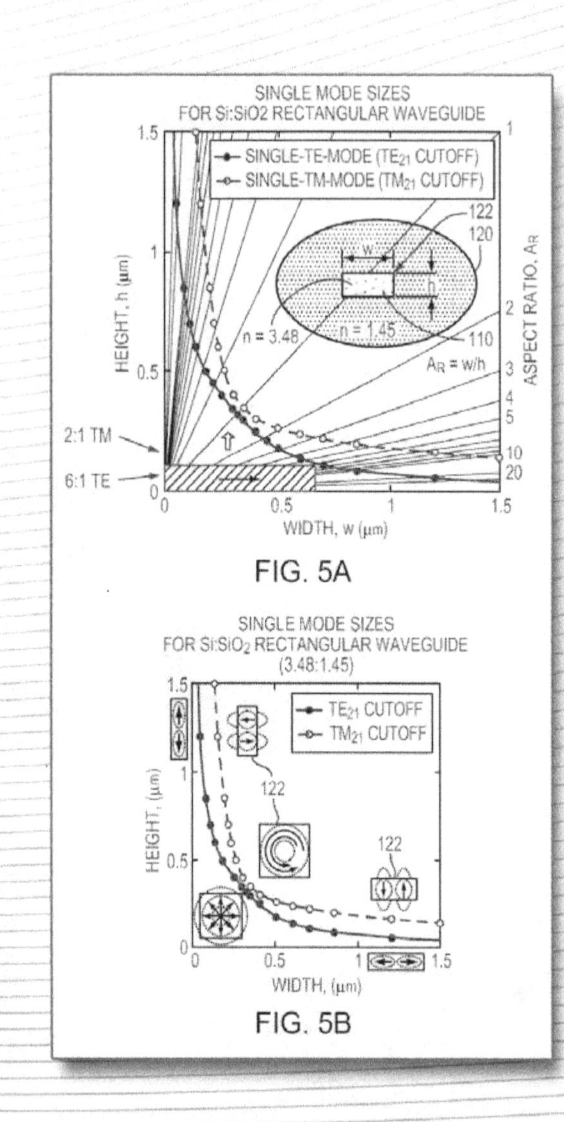

FIG. 5A

FIG. 5B

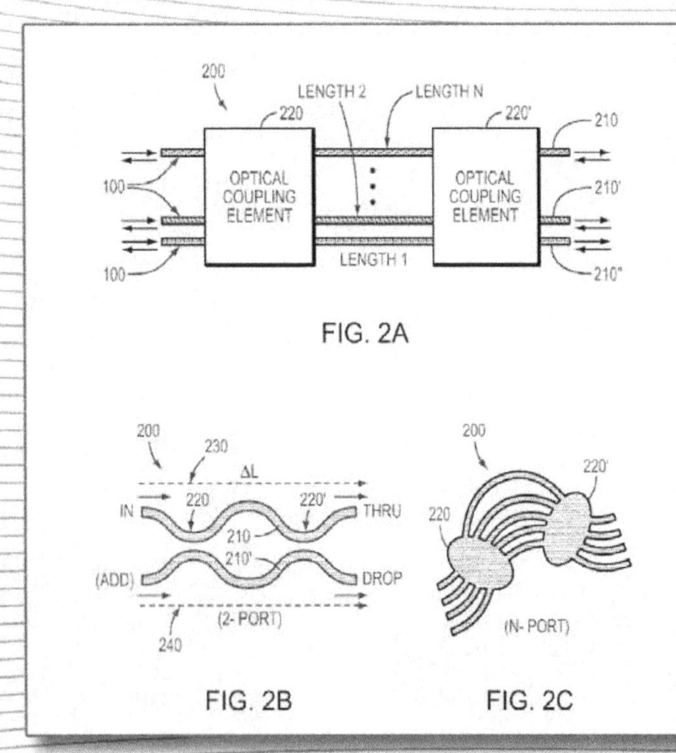

FIG. 2A

FIG. 2B

FIG. 2C

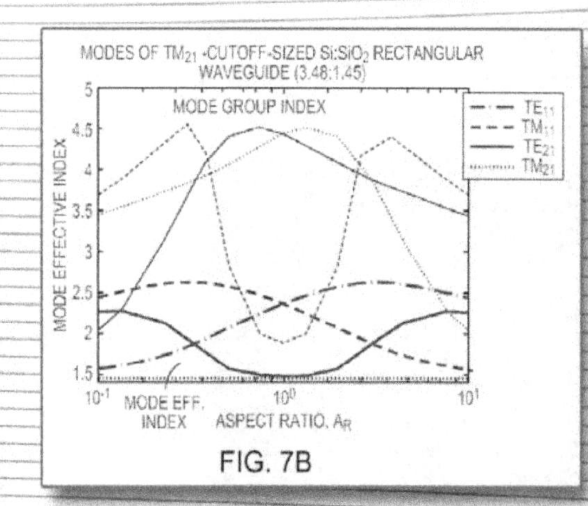

FIG. 7B

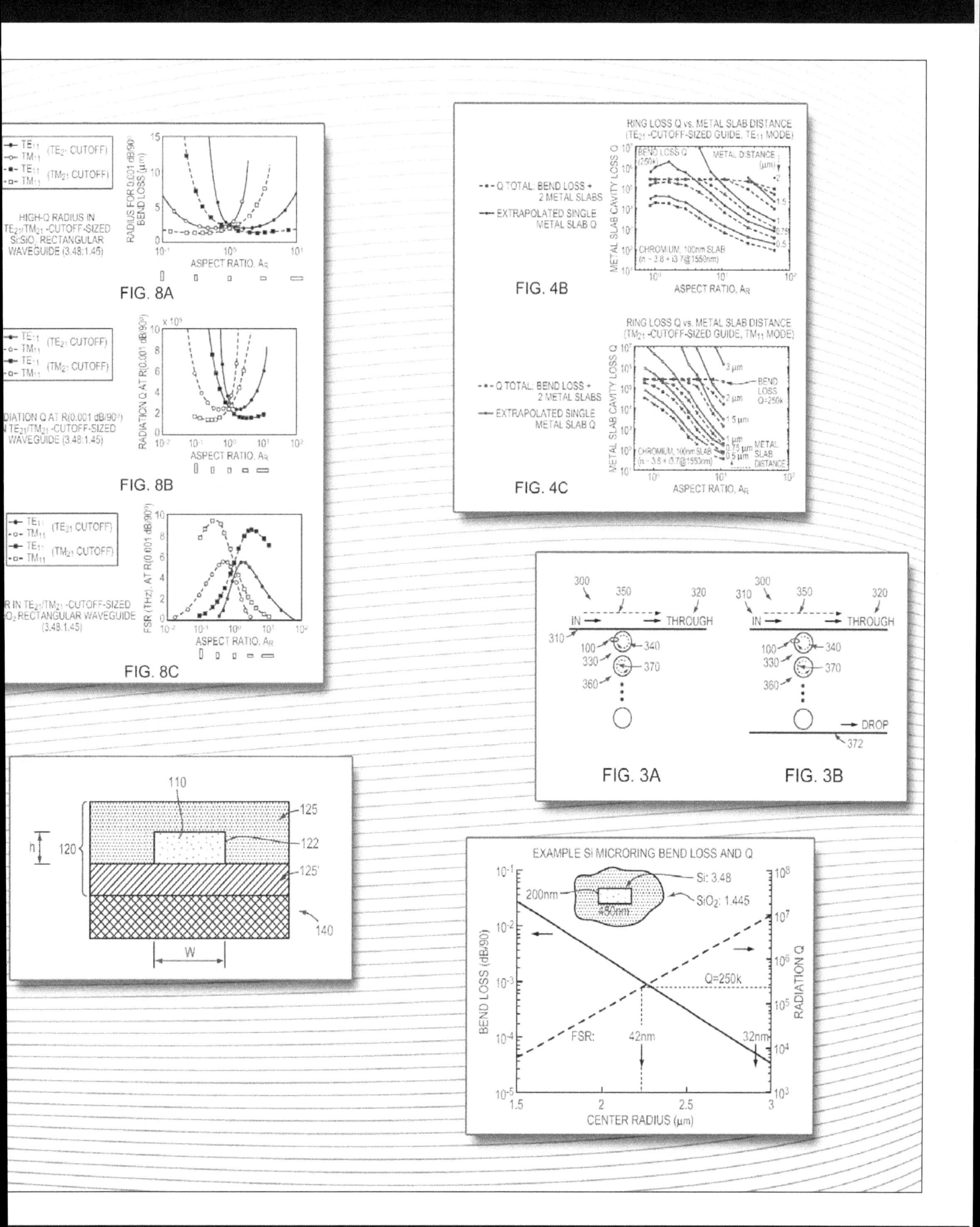

FIG. 8A

FIG. 8B

FIG. 8C

FIG. 4B

FIG. 4C

FIG. 3A

FIG. 3B

As with so much of our world, computer display graphics and interfaces are constantly updated and patentable--one rare case where text can be used (just not for explaining anything about the invention).

Yet sometimes the simplest images are the most appealing.

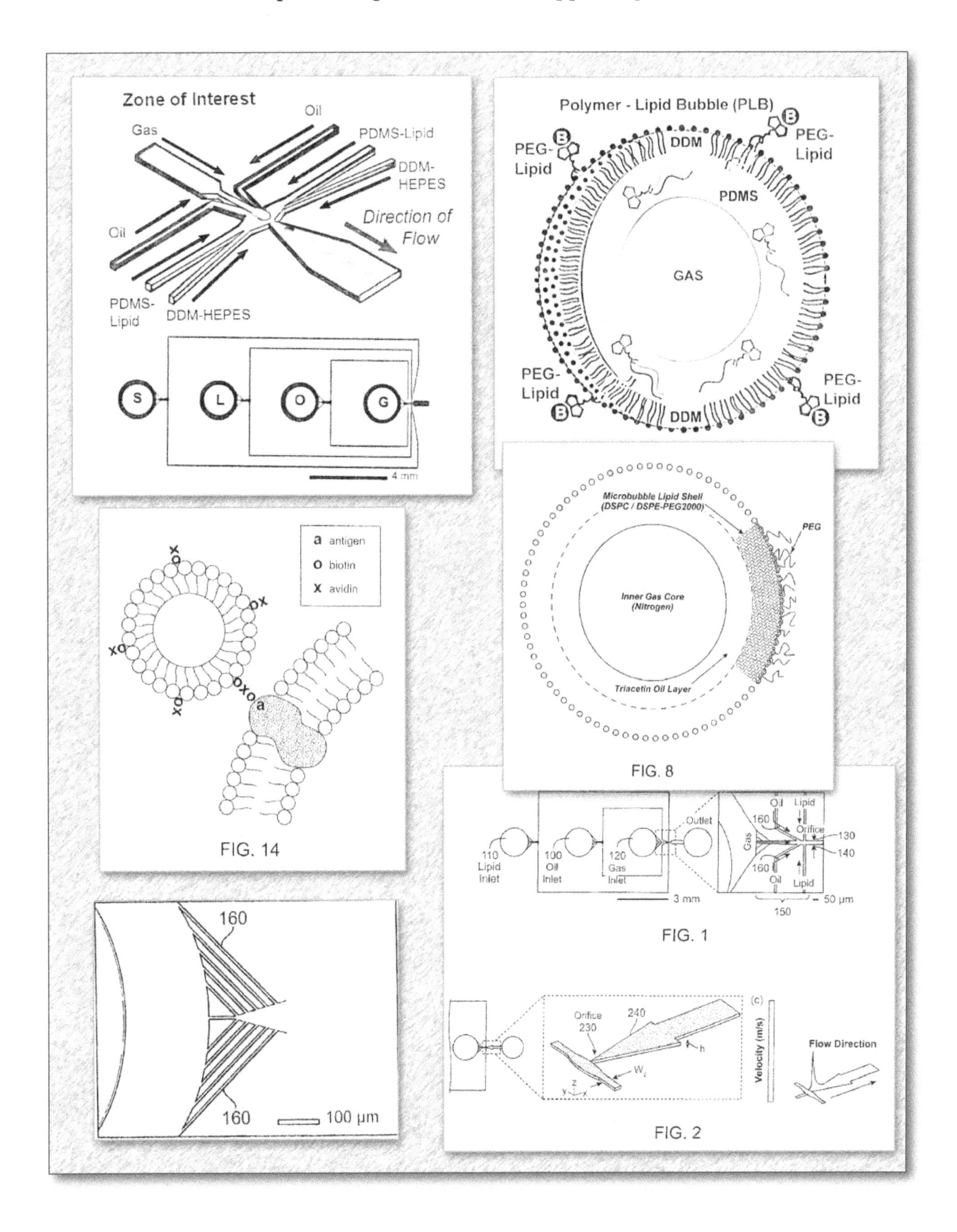

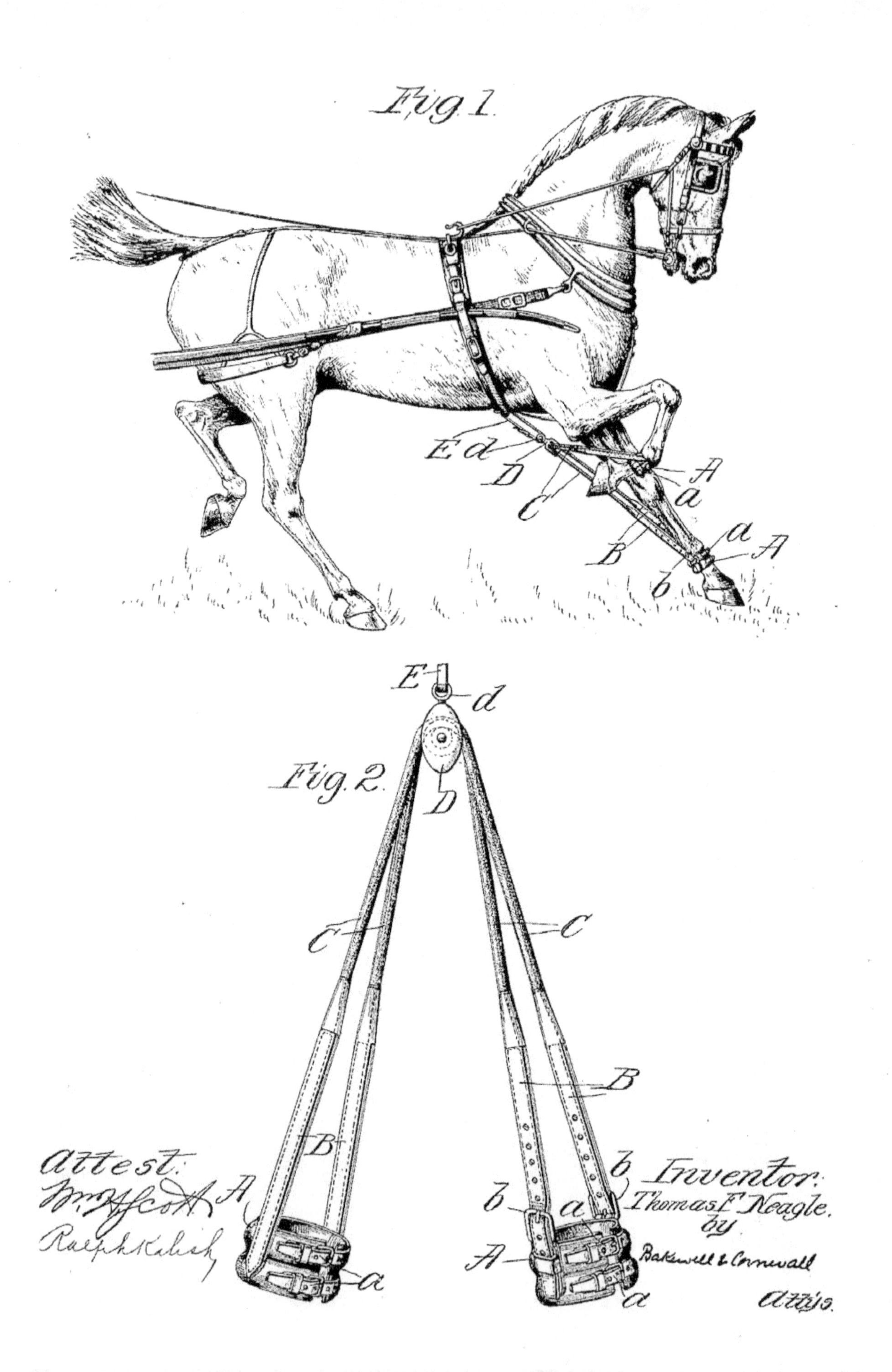

HOBBLE FOR DRIVING HORSES

T.F. NEAGLE Oct. 16, 1900 No. 659,856

Chapter 6

The Art of the Patent

Throughout this book the central theme has been the importance of patent art in line with its sometimes stunning beauty. We've seen how patent drawings track history and preserve those moments, both fleeting and sea changing, that mark the evolution of human technology. Yet they also contain a magic that is often overlooked in the rush to claim our territory. This magic is illustrated in the following drawings. The invention's use may not be of interest to you directly, but don't miss the beauty. Abstract, literal, and anything in between, take a moment to stop and smell the hybrid roses.

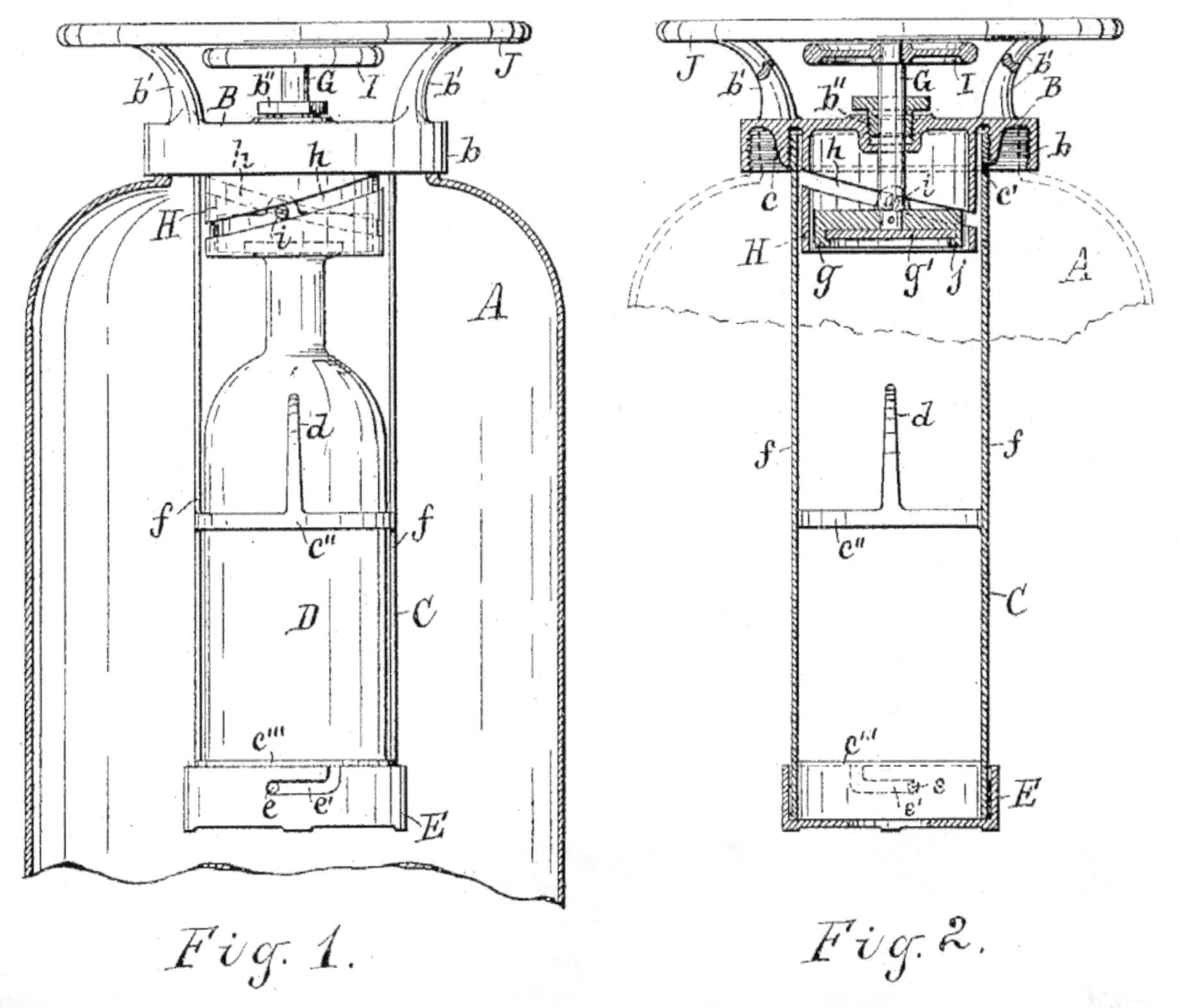

FIRE EXTINGUISHER
J.W. CLARKE May 8, 1900 No. 649,160

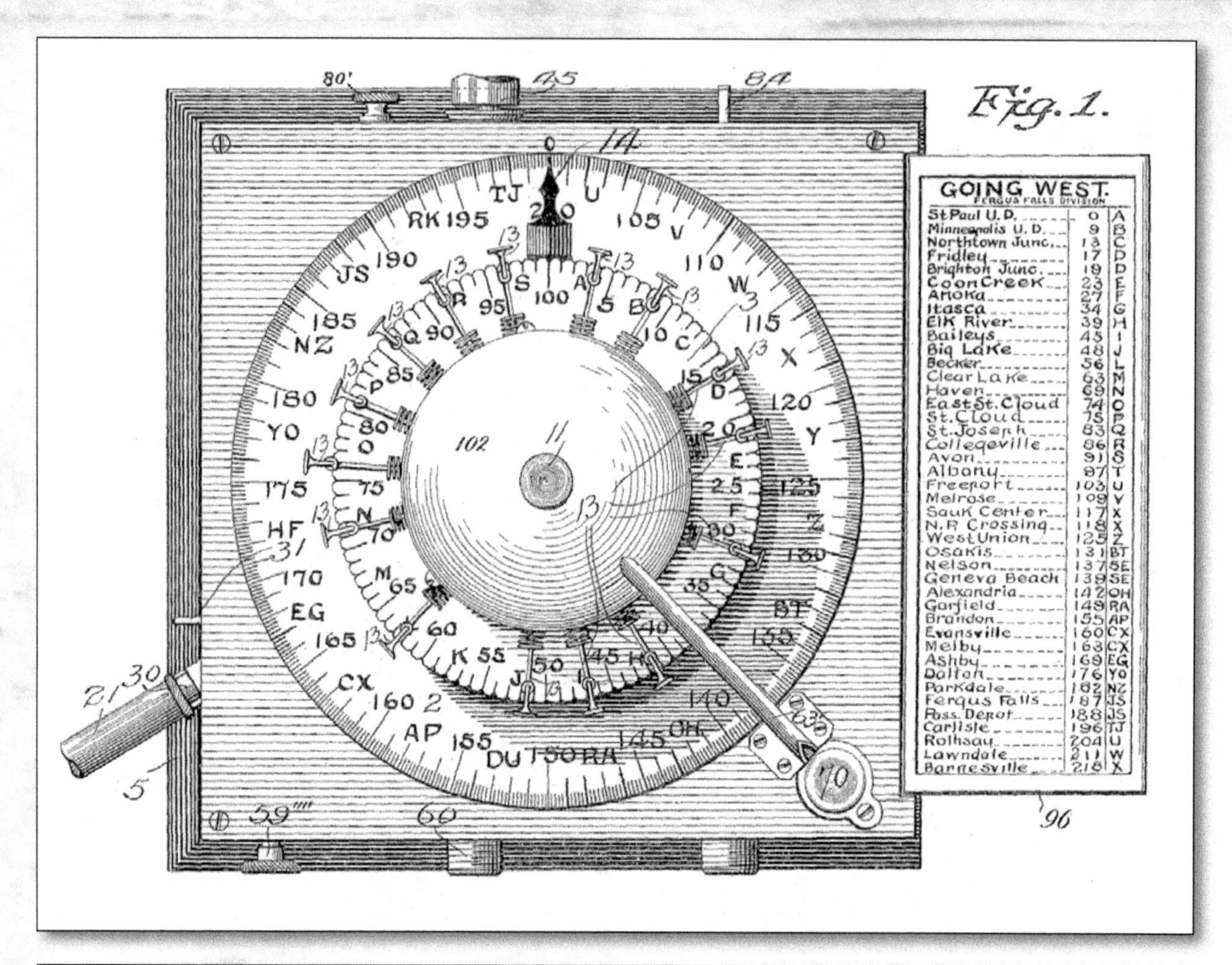

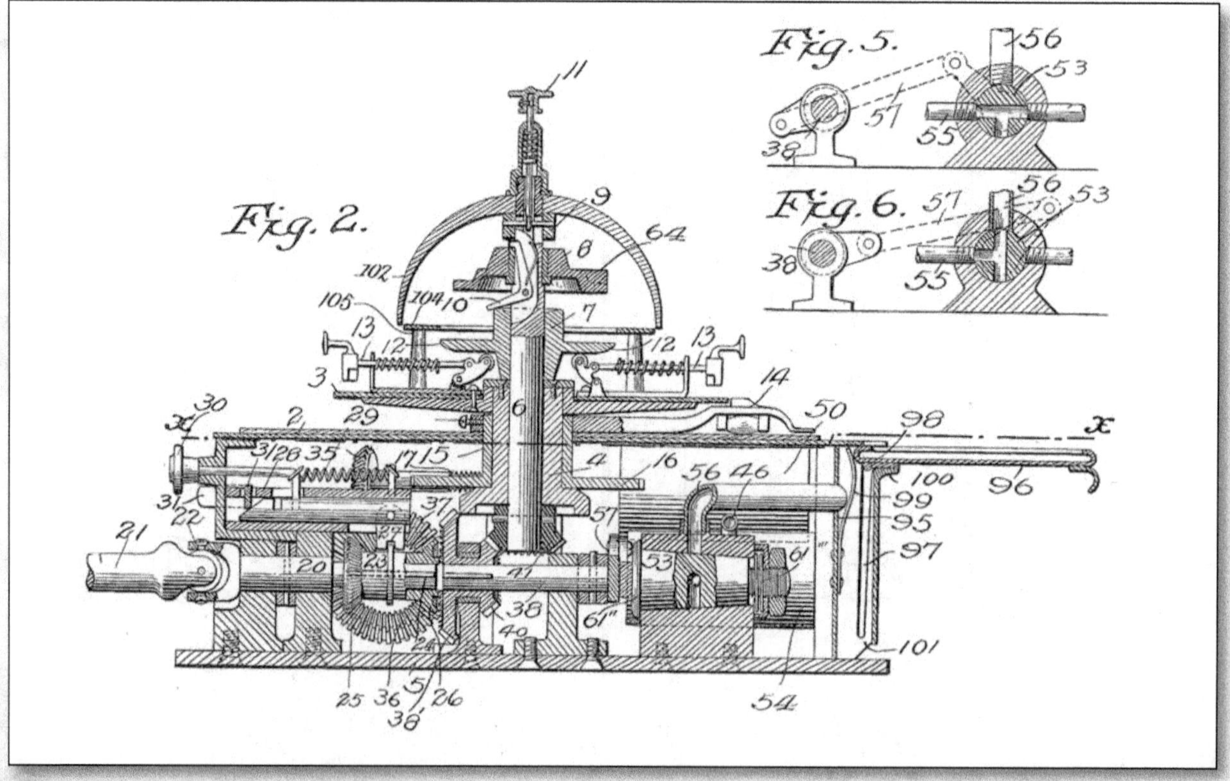

H. DE WALLACE
TRAIN ORDER SIGNAL
Jan. 3, 1899
No. 617,232

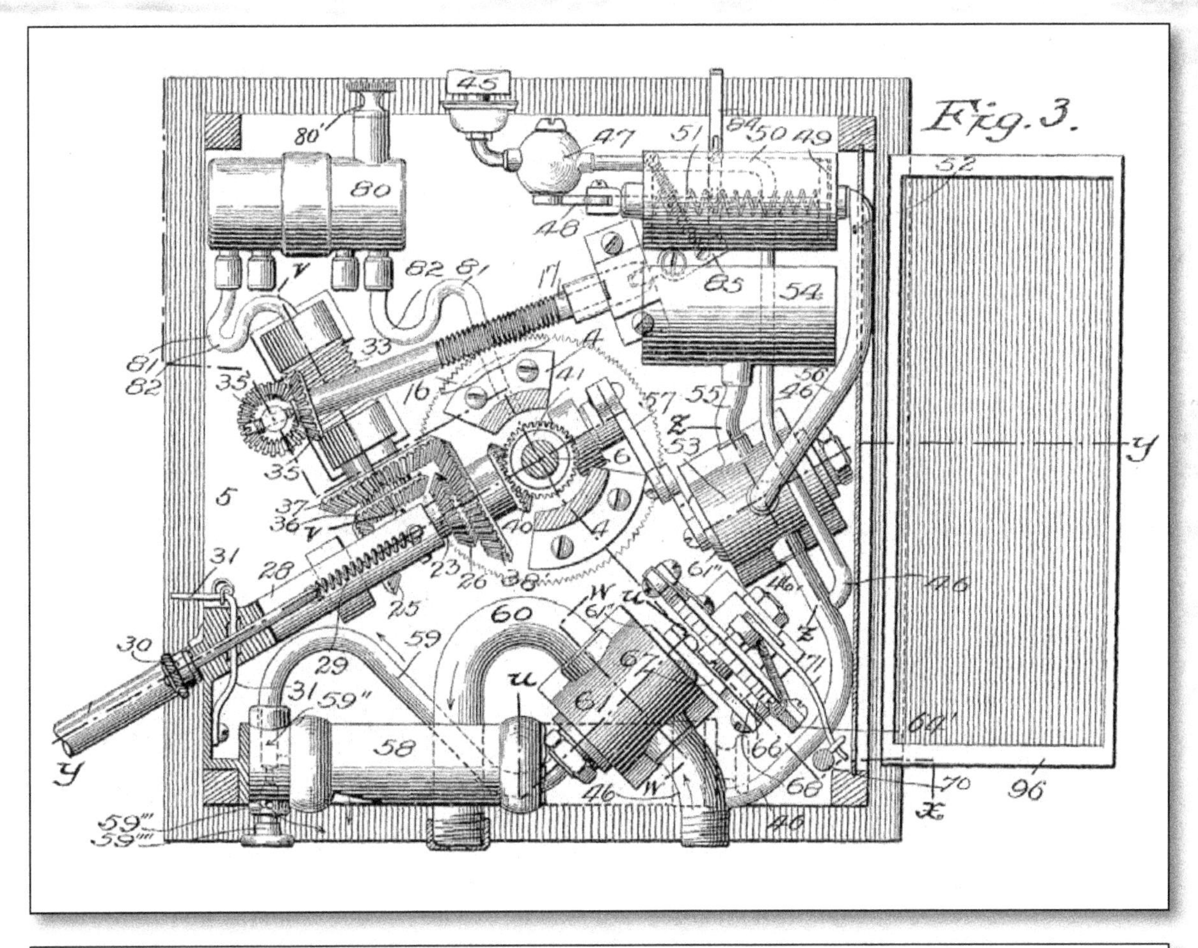
Fig. 3.

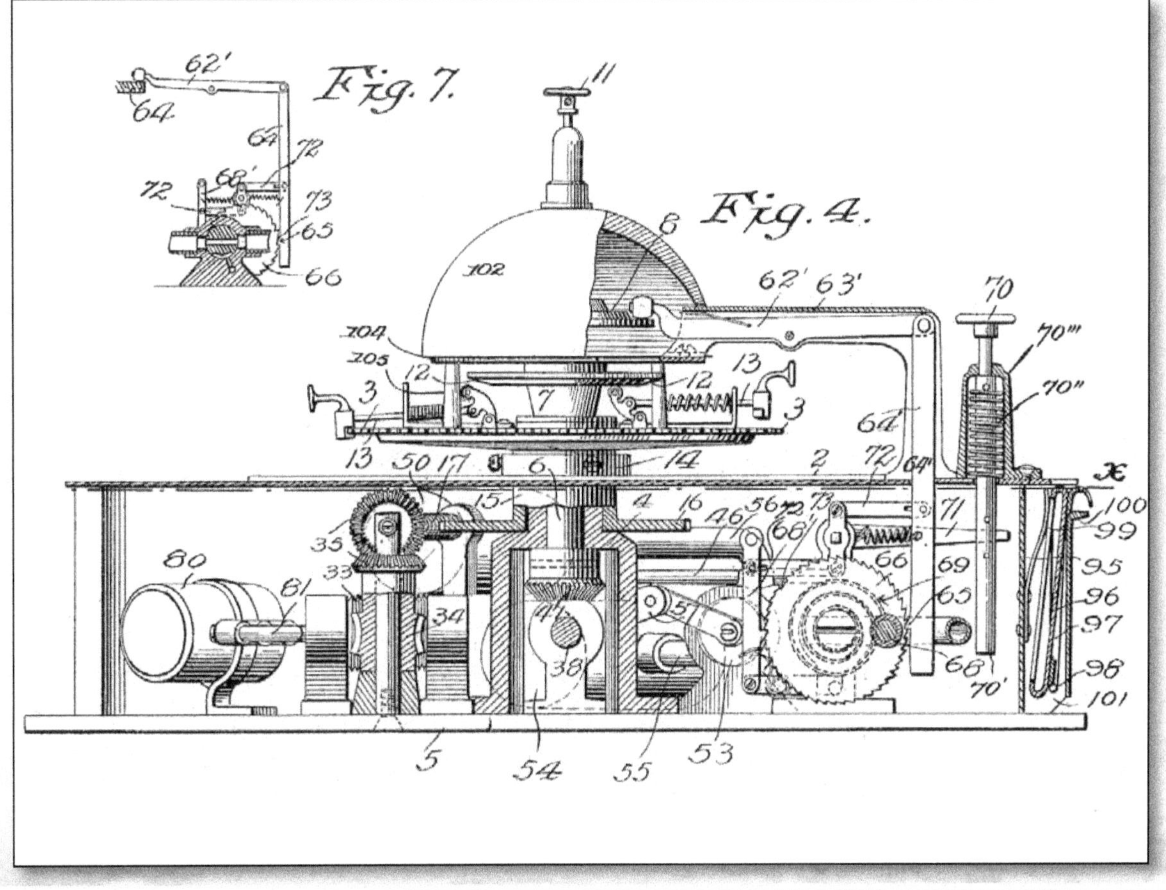
Fig. 7.
Fig. 4.

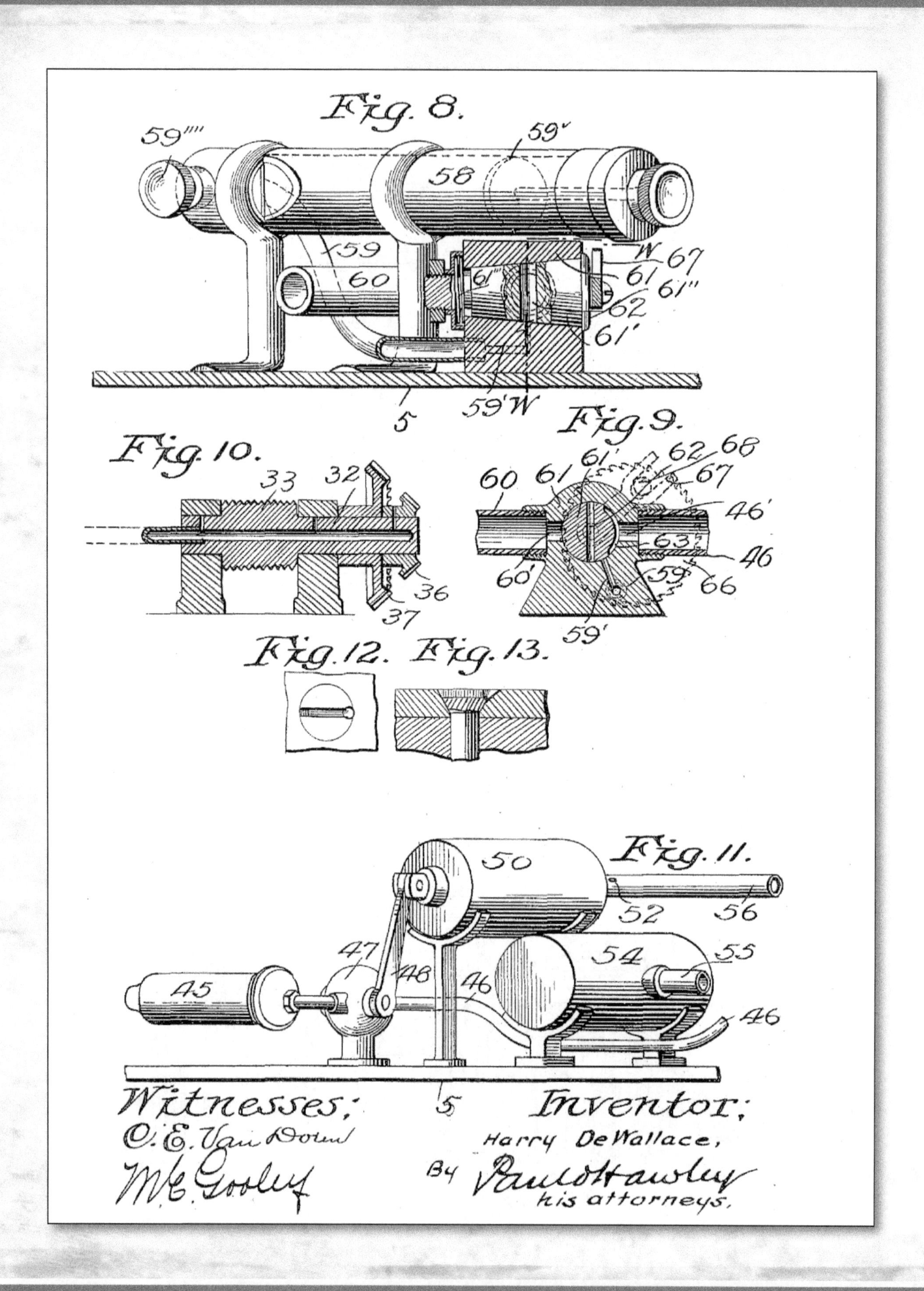

H. DE WALLACE
TRAIN ORDER SIGNAL
Jan. 3, 1899
No. 617,232

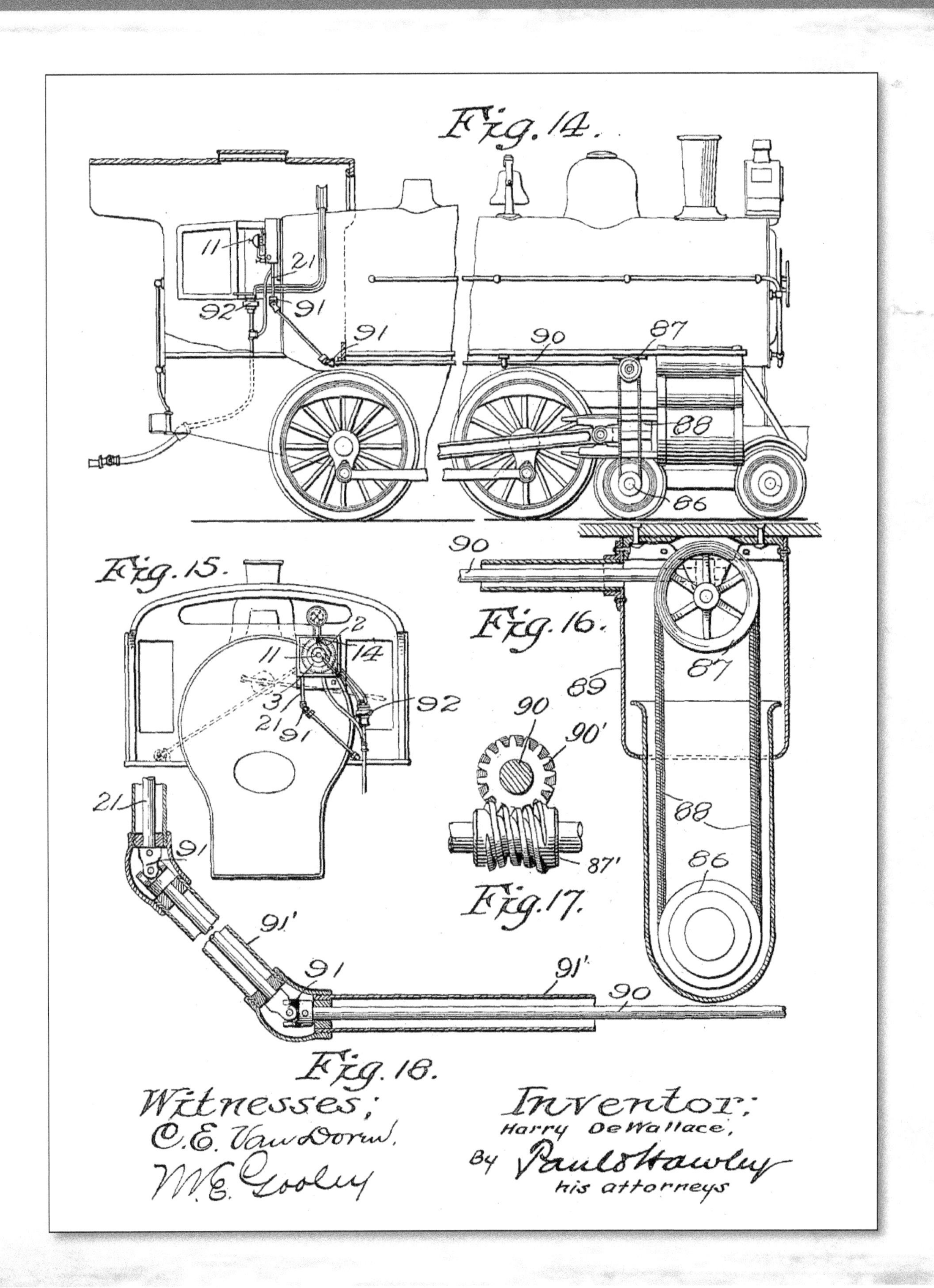
Fig. 14.
11
21
92
91
91
90
87
88
86
90
Fig. 15.
12
11
14
3
92
21
91
Fig. 16.
87
89
90
90'
88
86
87'
Fig. 17.
21
91
91'
91
91'
90
Fig. 18.
Witnesses;
C. E. VanDoren.
M. E. Gooley
Inventor:
Harry DeWallace,
By Paul & Hawley
his attorneys

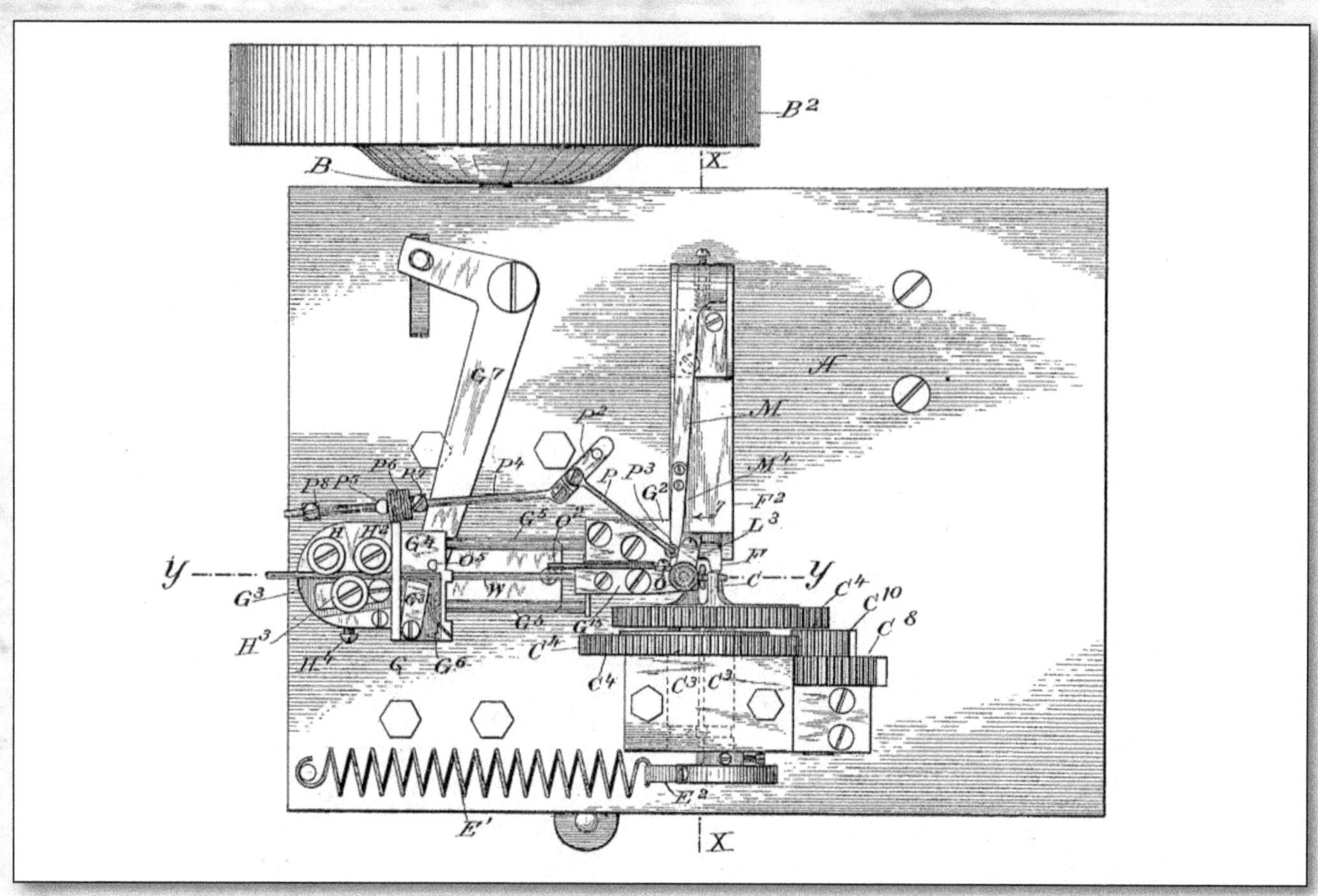

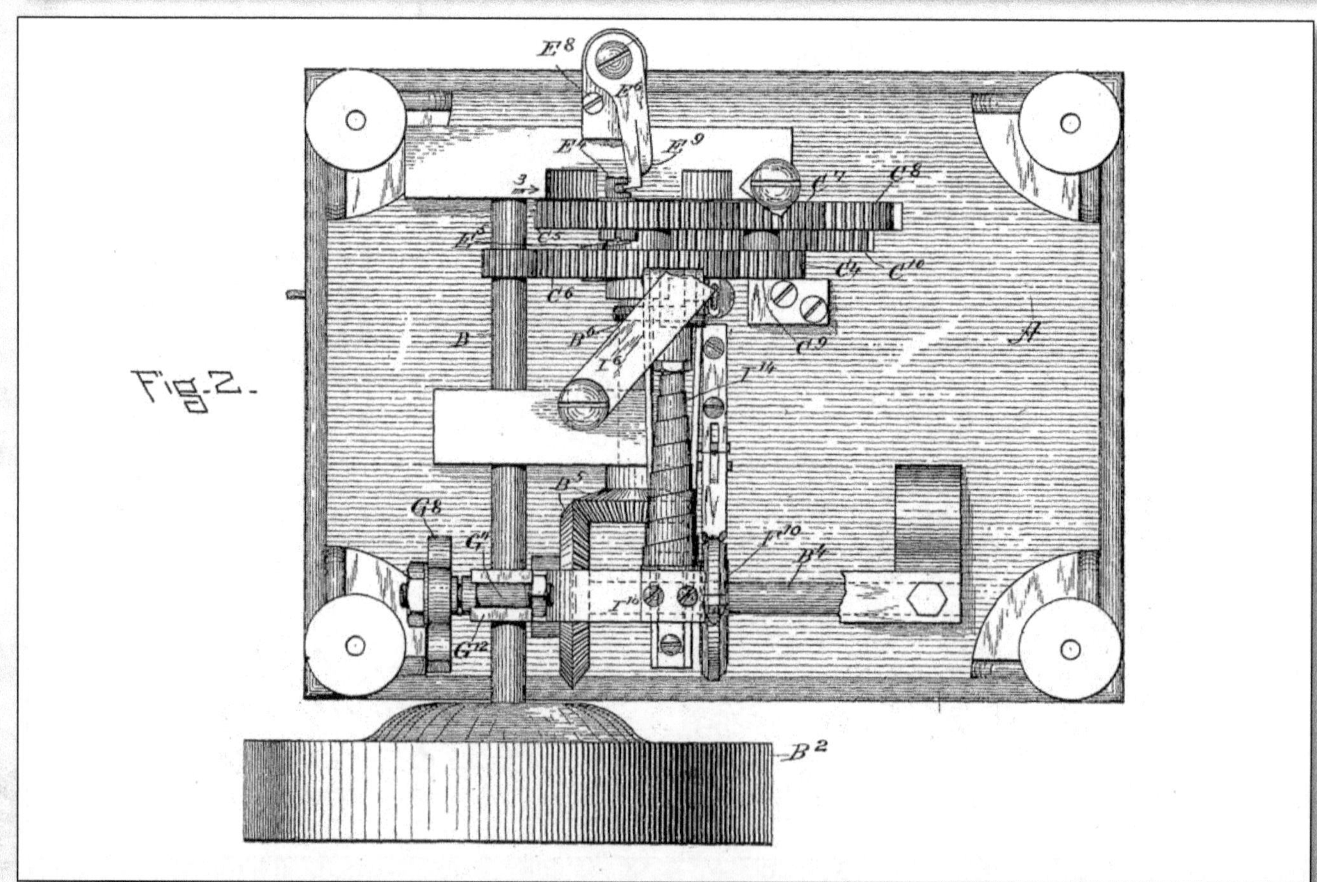

CHAIN MAKING MACHINE

E. THOMSON & C.E. HARTHAN Jan. 16, 1894 No. 512,848

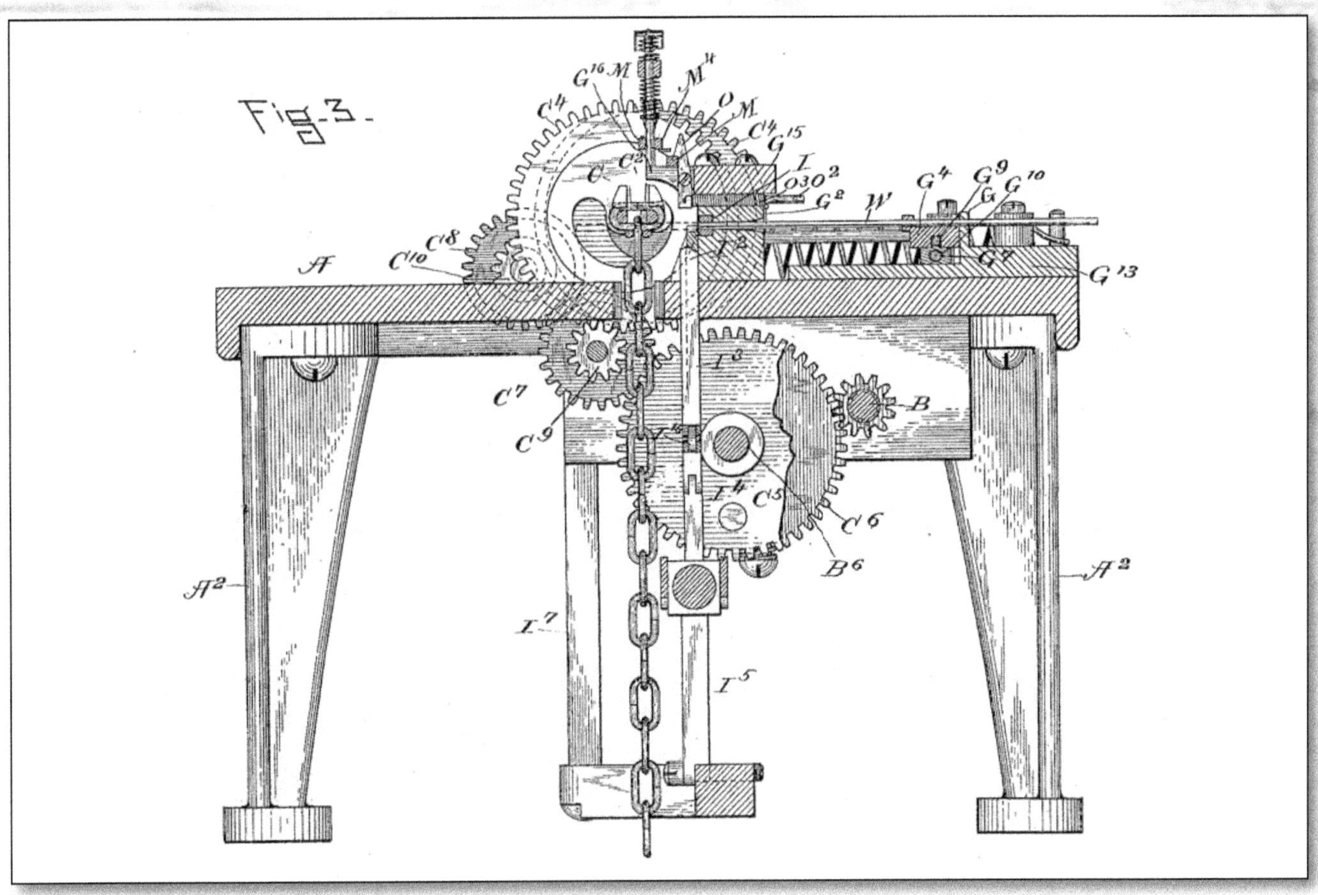

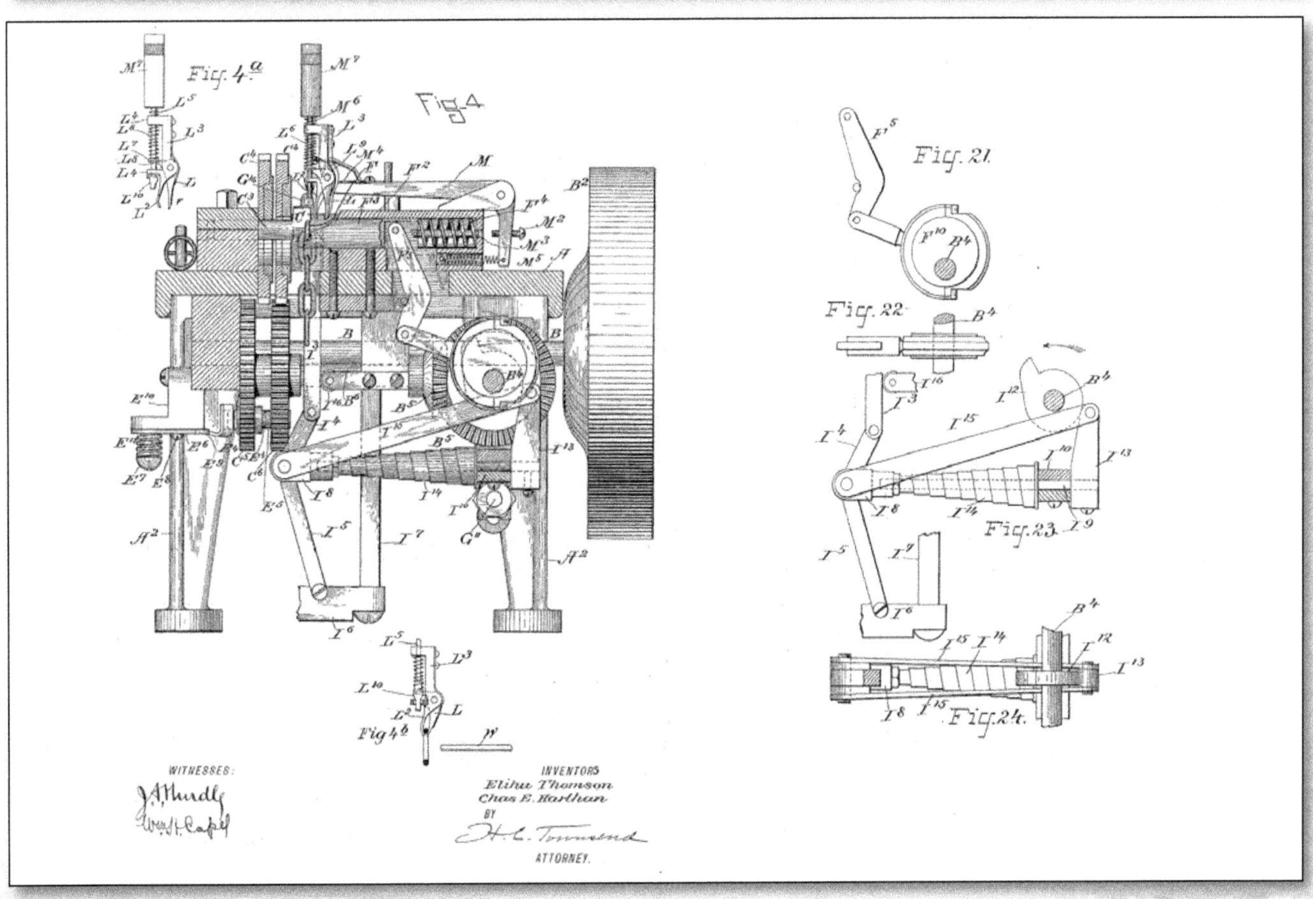

CHAIN MAKING MACHINE

E. THOMSON & C.E. HARTHANJan. 16, 1894 No. 512,848

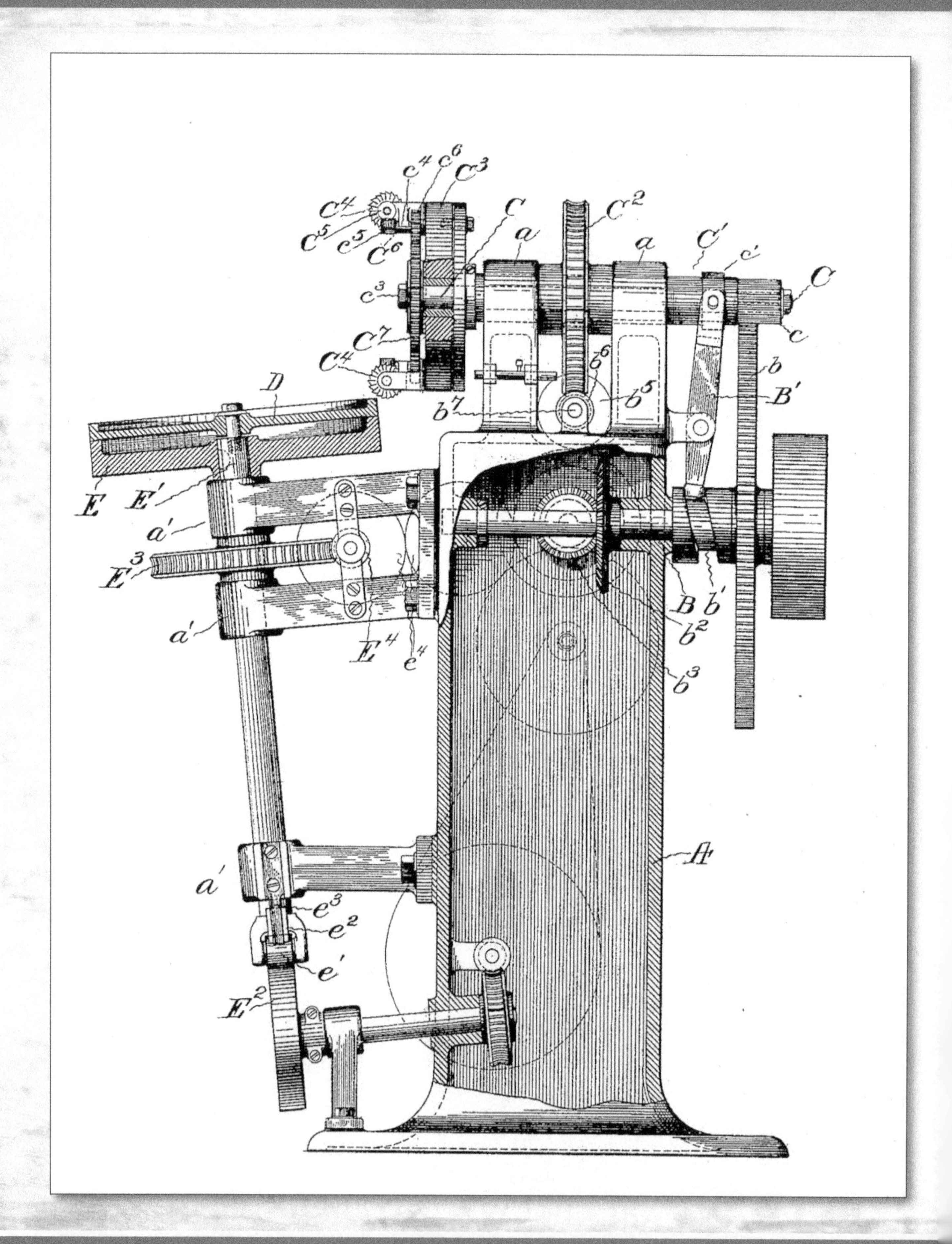

H.F. CONTZ

GEAR CUTTING MACHINE
Dec. 5, 1899

No. 638,563

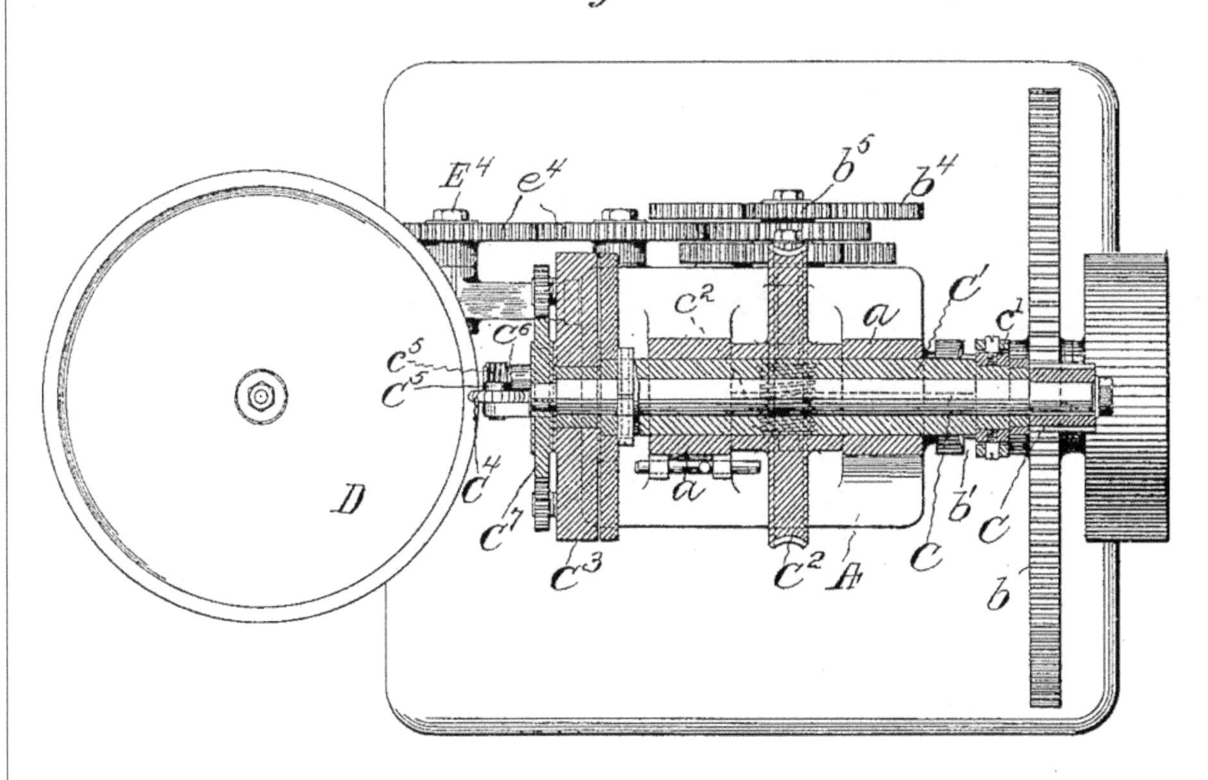
Fig. 2
E4
e4
b5
b4
C2
a
C'
C1
C5
C5
C6
C4
C7
C3
a
C2
A
C
b'
C
b
D

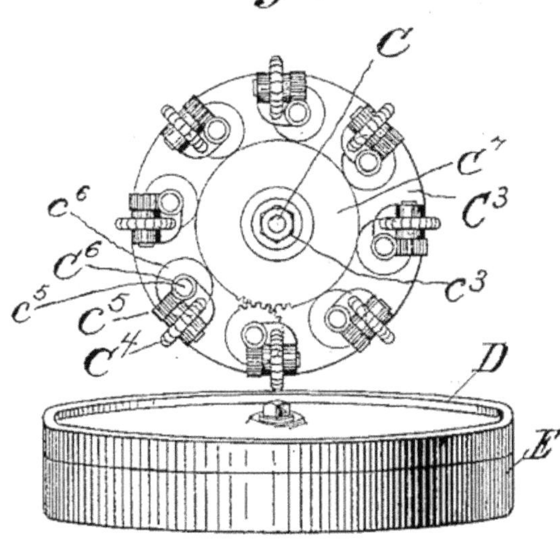
Fig. 3
C
C7
C3
C6
C6
C3
C5
C5
C4
D
E

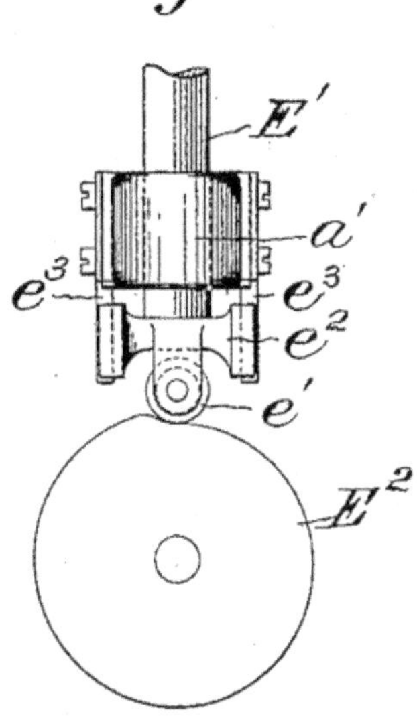
Fig. 4
E'
a'
e3
e3
e2
e'
E2

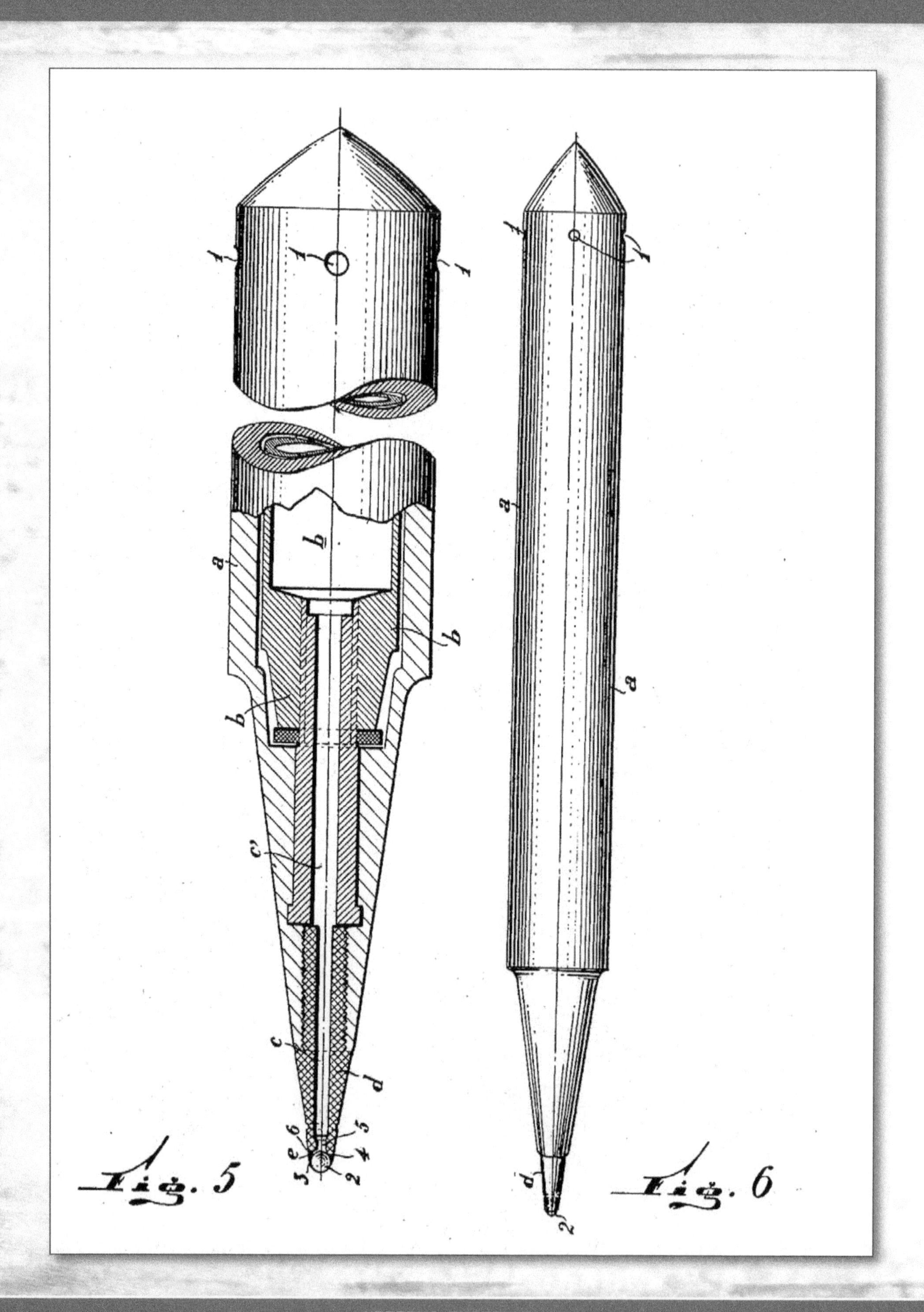

L.J. BIRO

WRITING INSTRUMENT
Dec. 11, 1945

No. 2,390,636

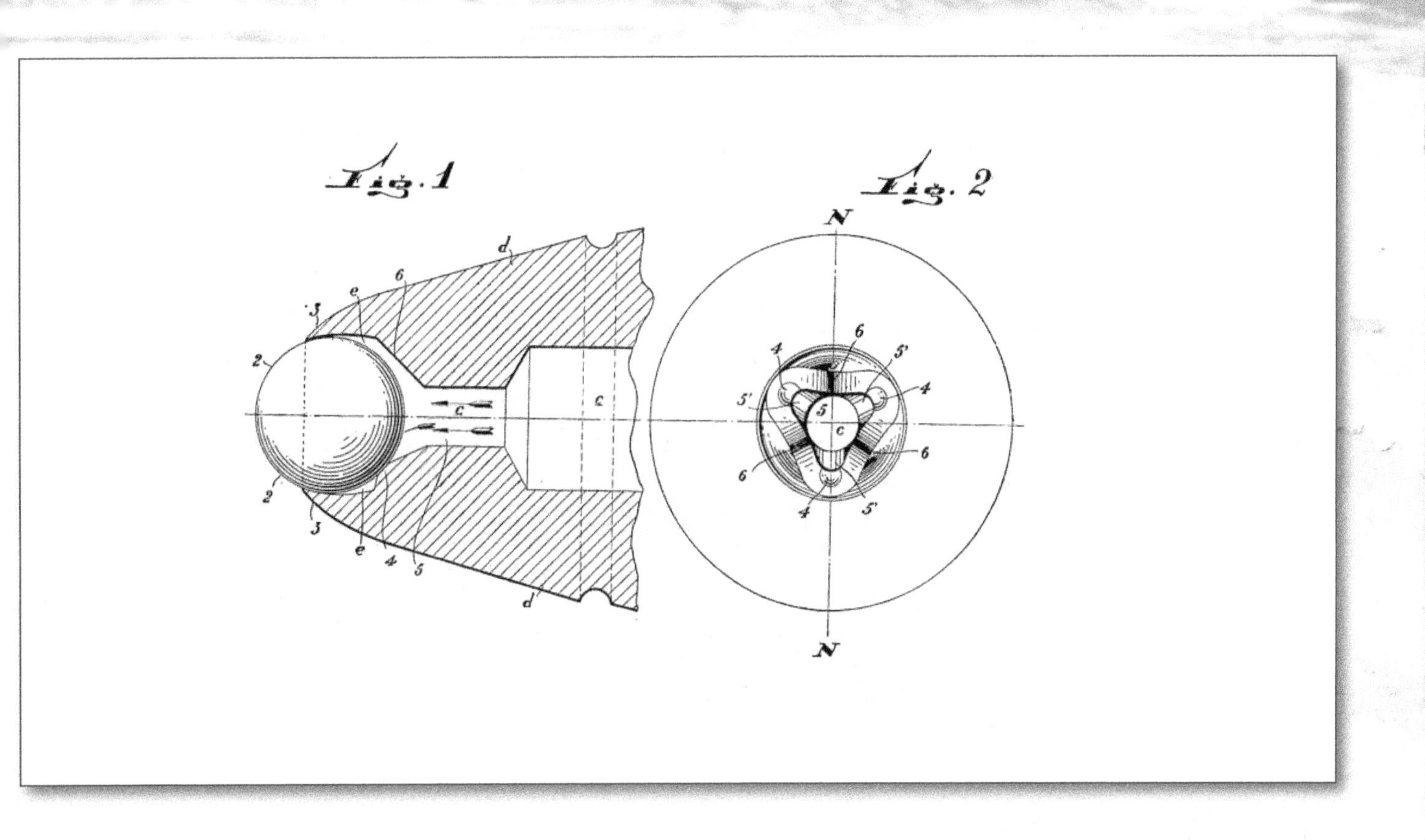
Fig. 1
Fig. 2
N
N

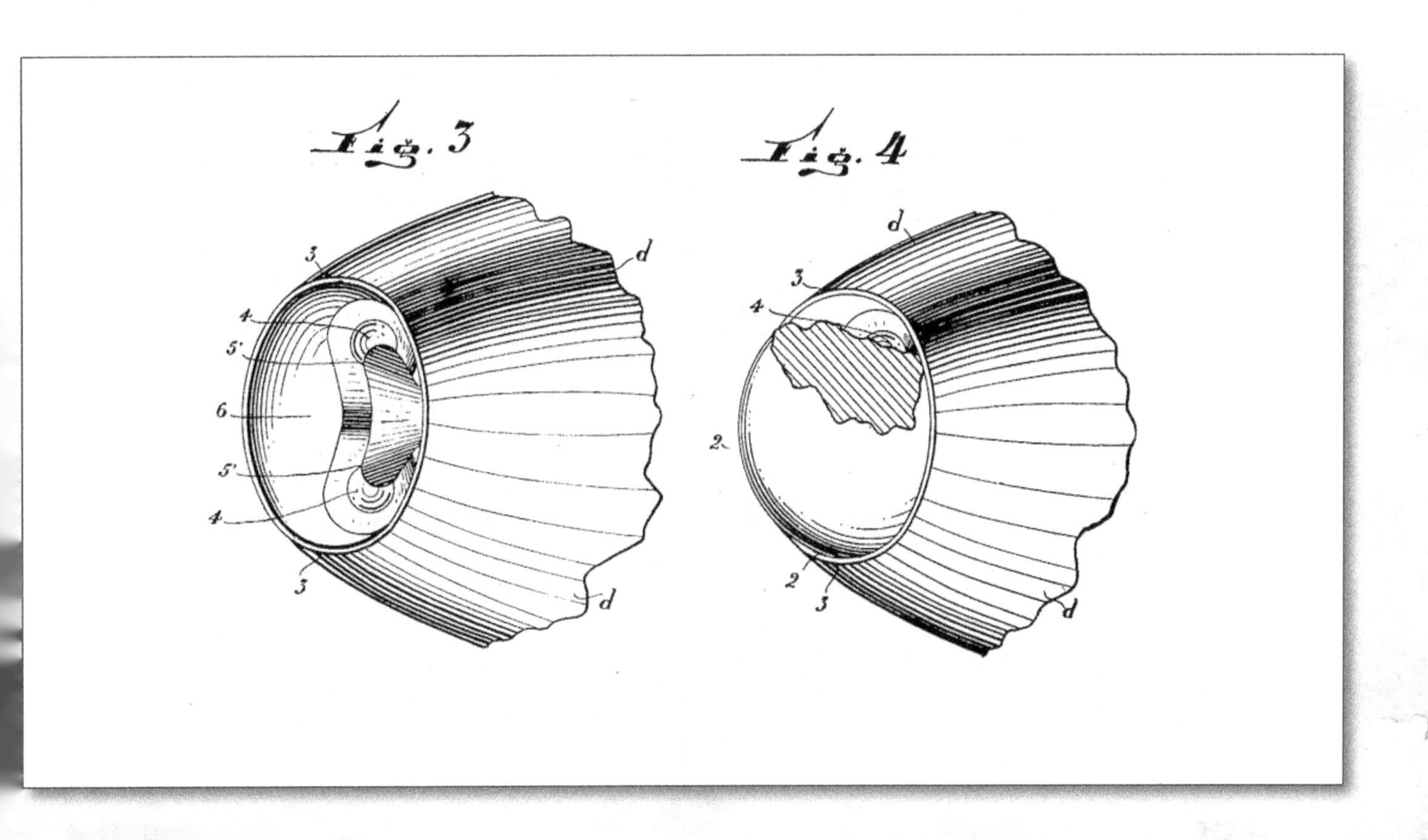
Fig. 3
Fig. 4

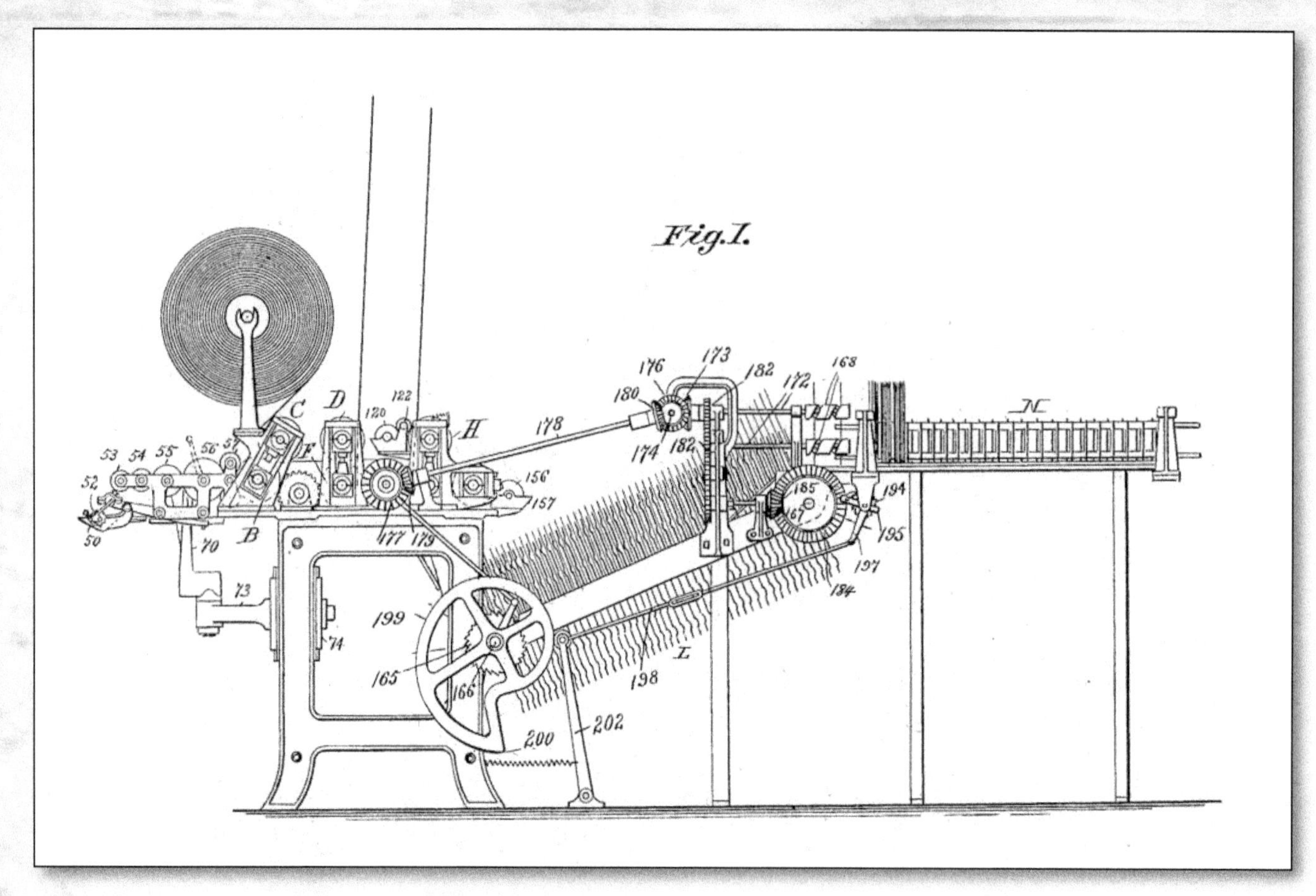

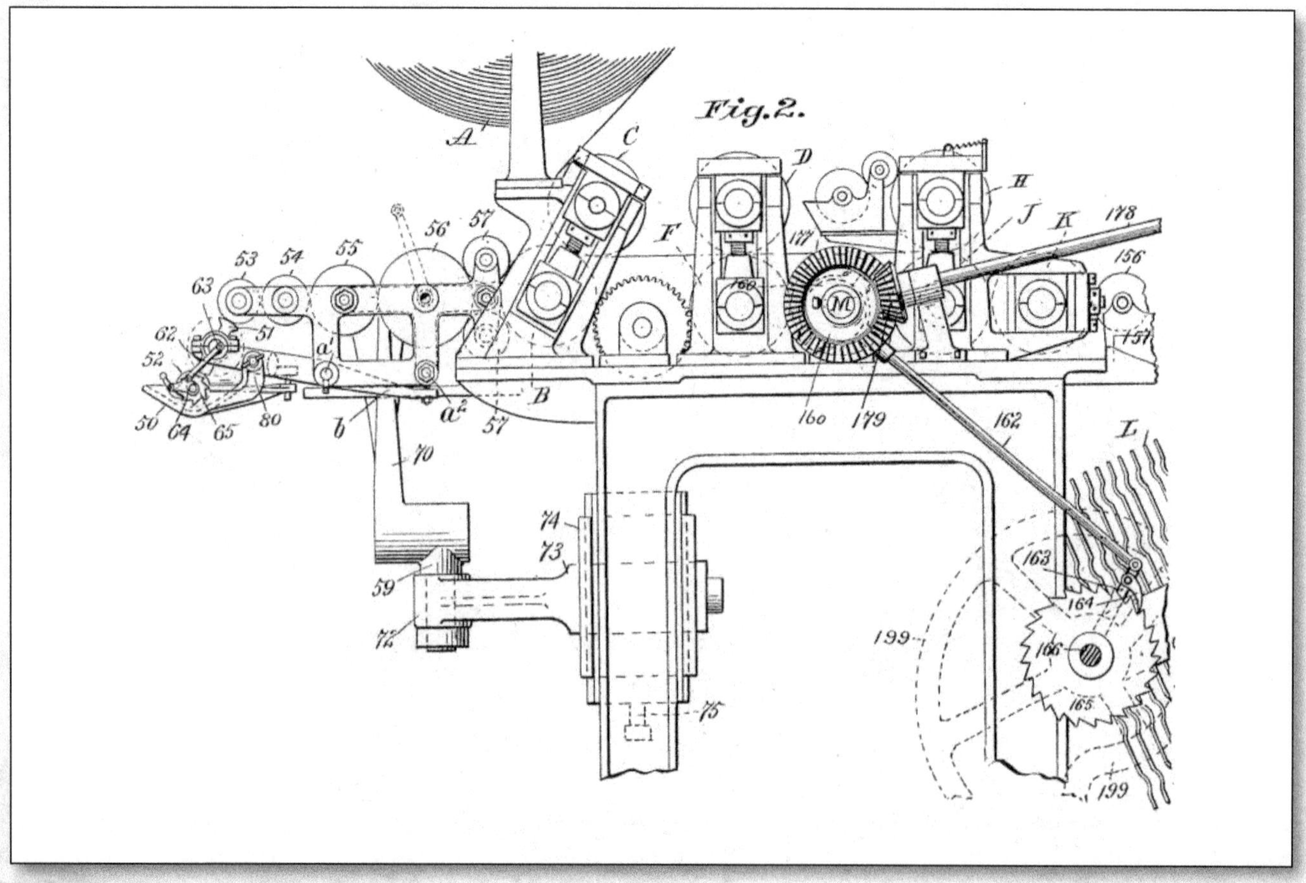

MACHINE FOR MAKING AND PRINTING ENVELOPES
C. A. TEAL AUG. 7, 1894 No. 524,288

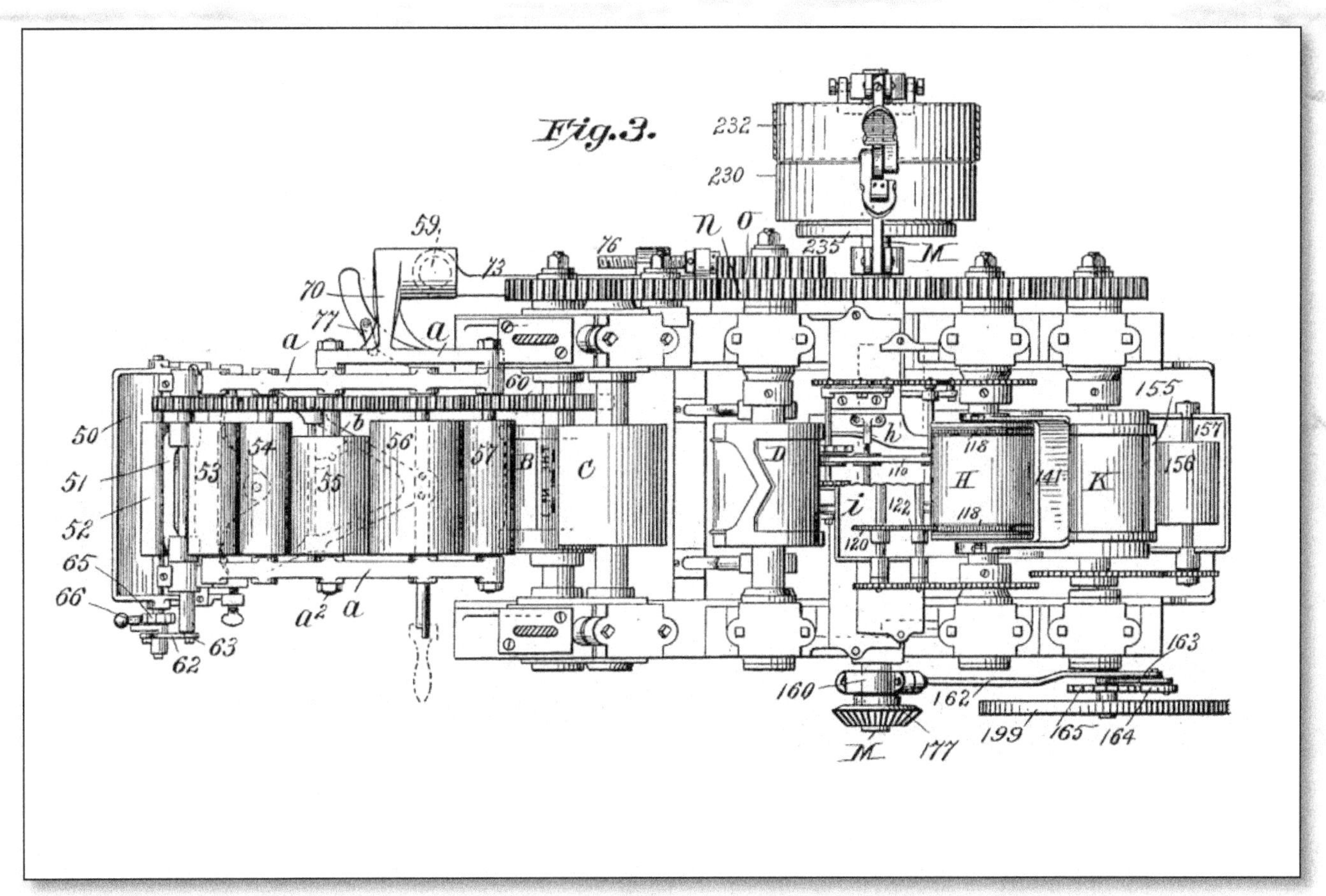

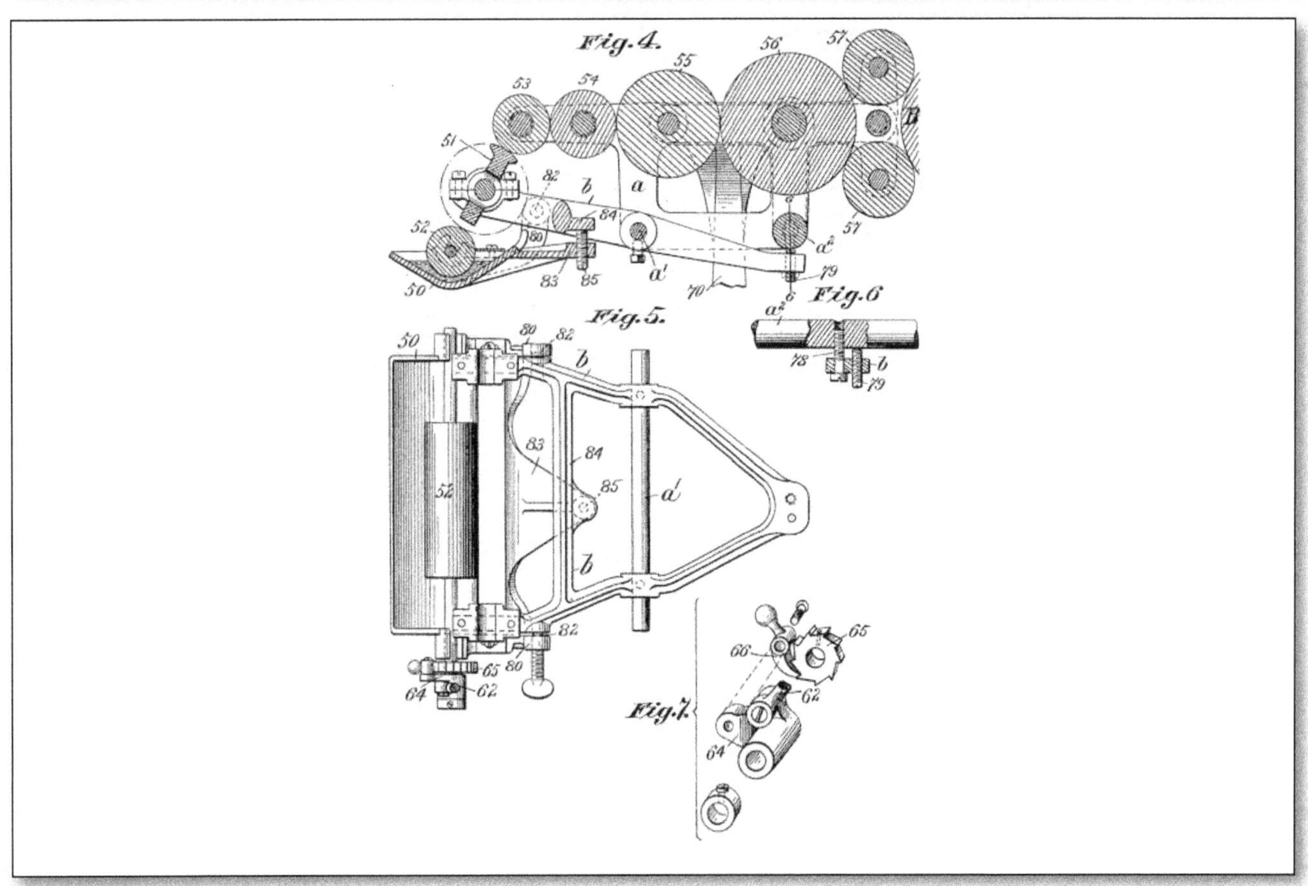

MACHINE FOR MAKING AND PRINTING ENVELOPES
C. A. TEAL AUG. 7, 1894 No. 524,288

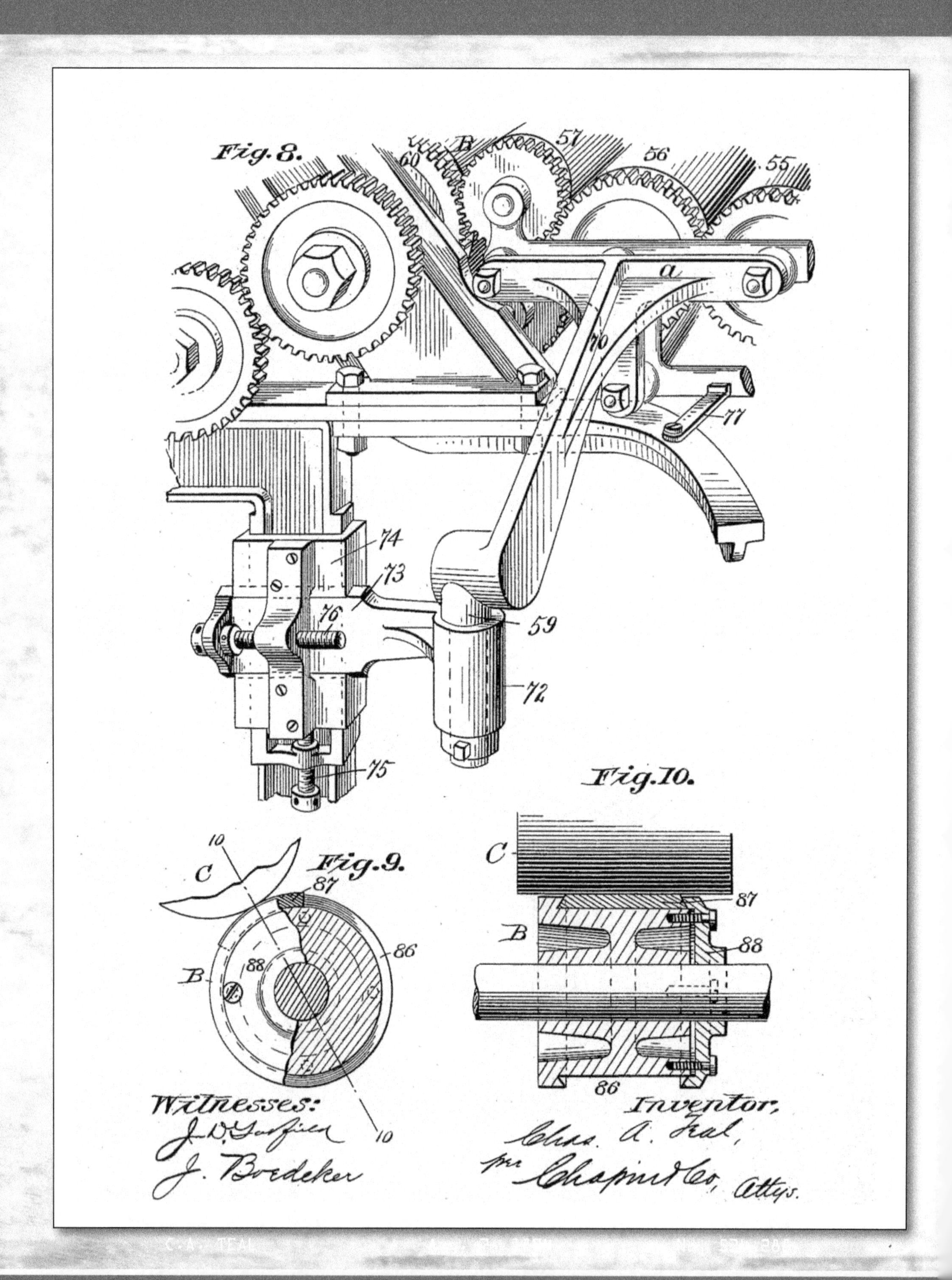

MACHINE FOR MAKING AND PRINTING ENVELOPES
C. A. TEAL AUG. 7, 1894 No. 524,288

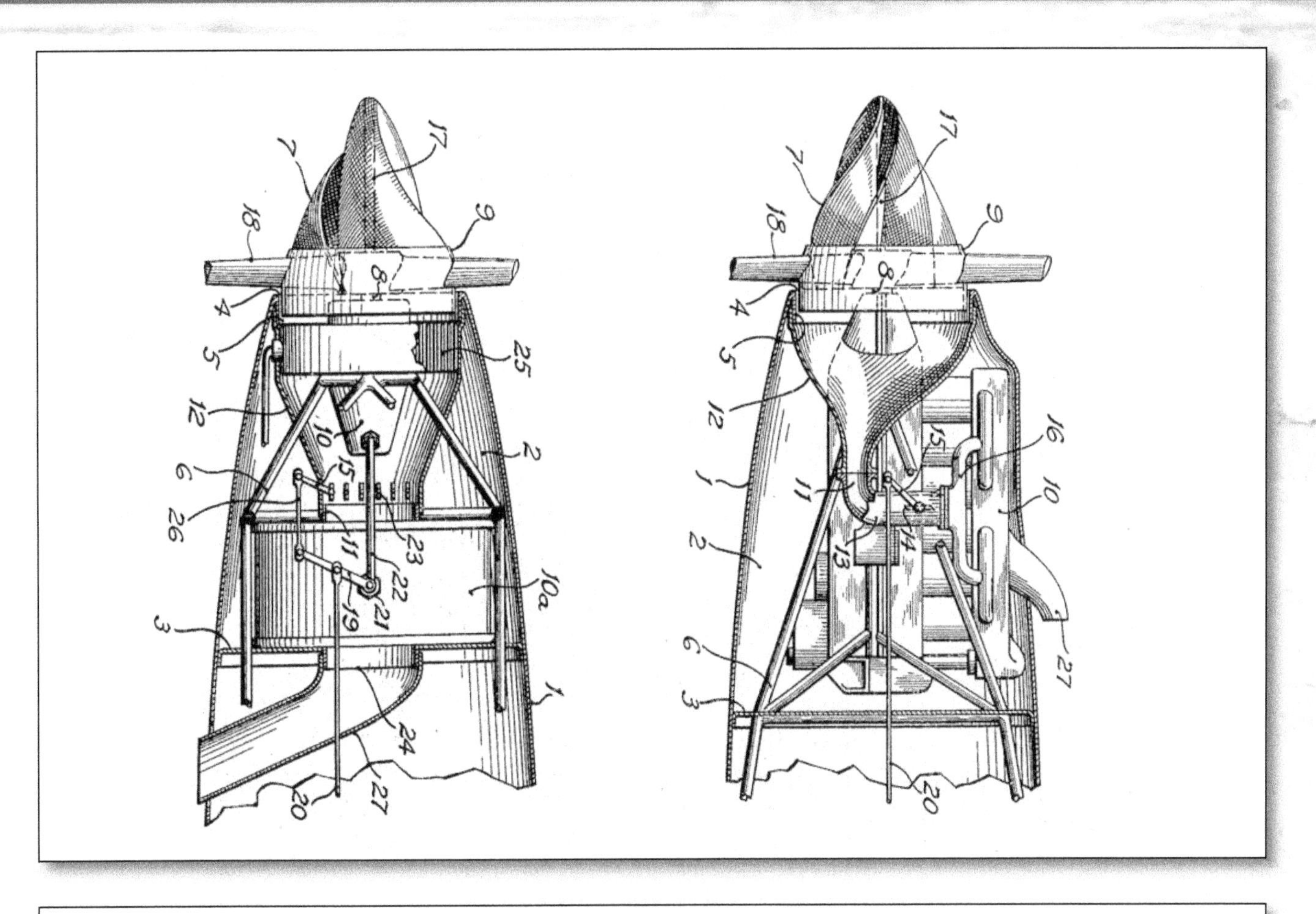

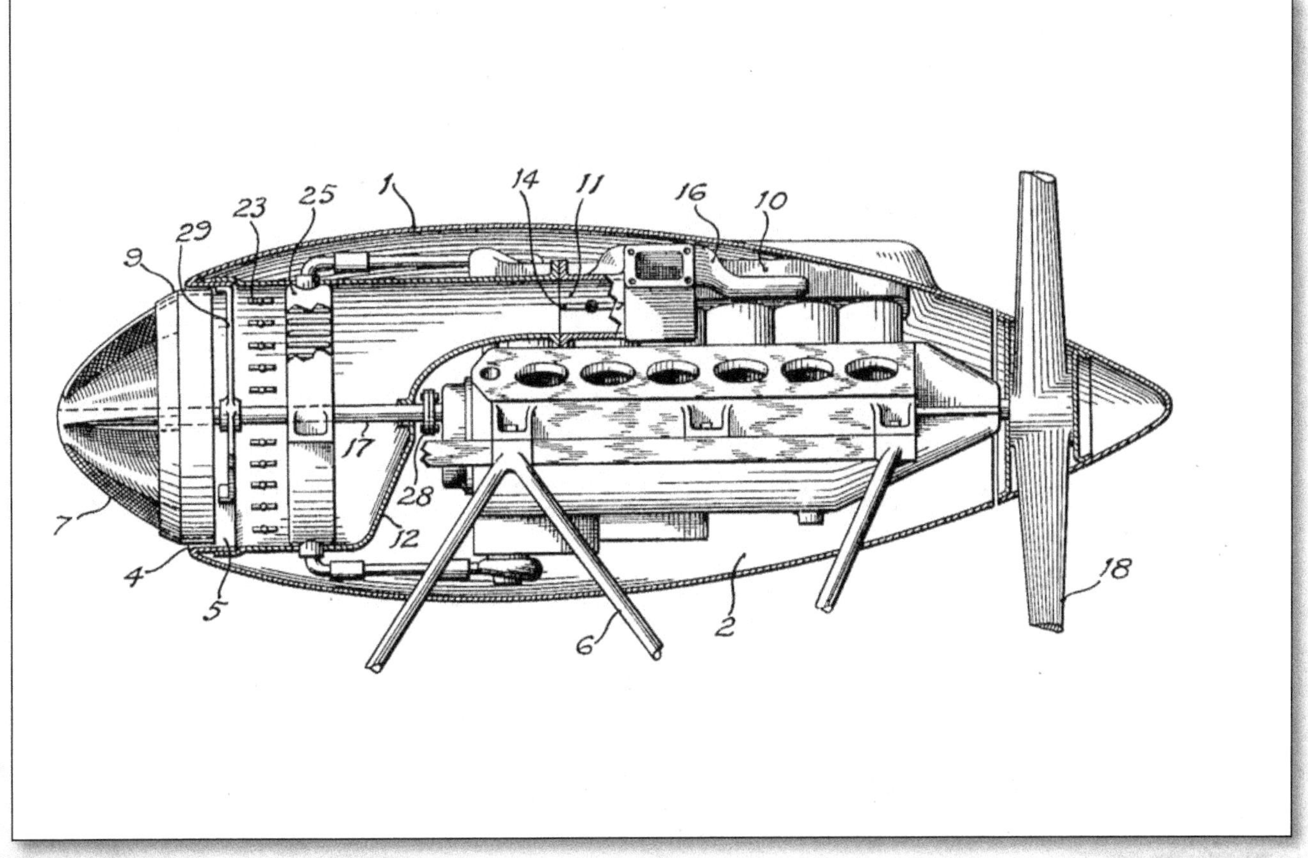
1
2
4
5
6
7
9
10
11
12
14
16
17
18
23
25
28
29

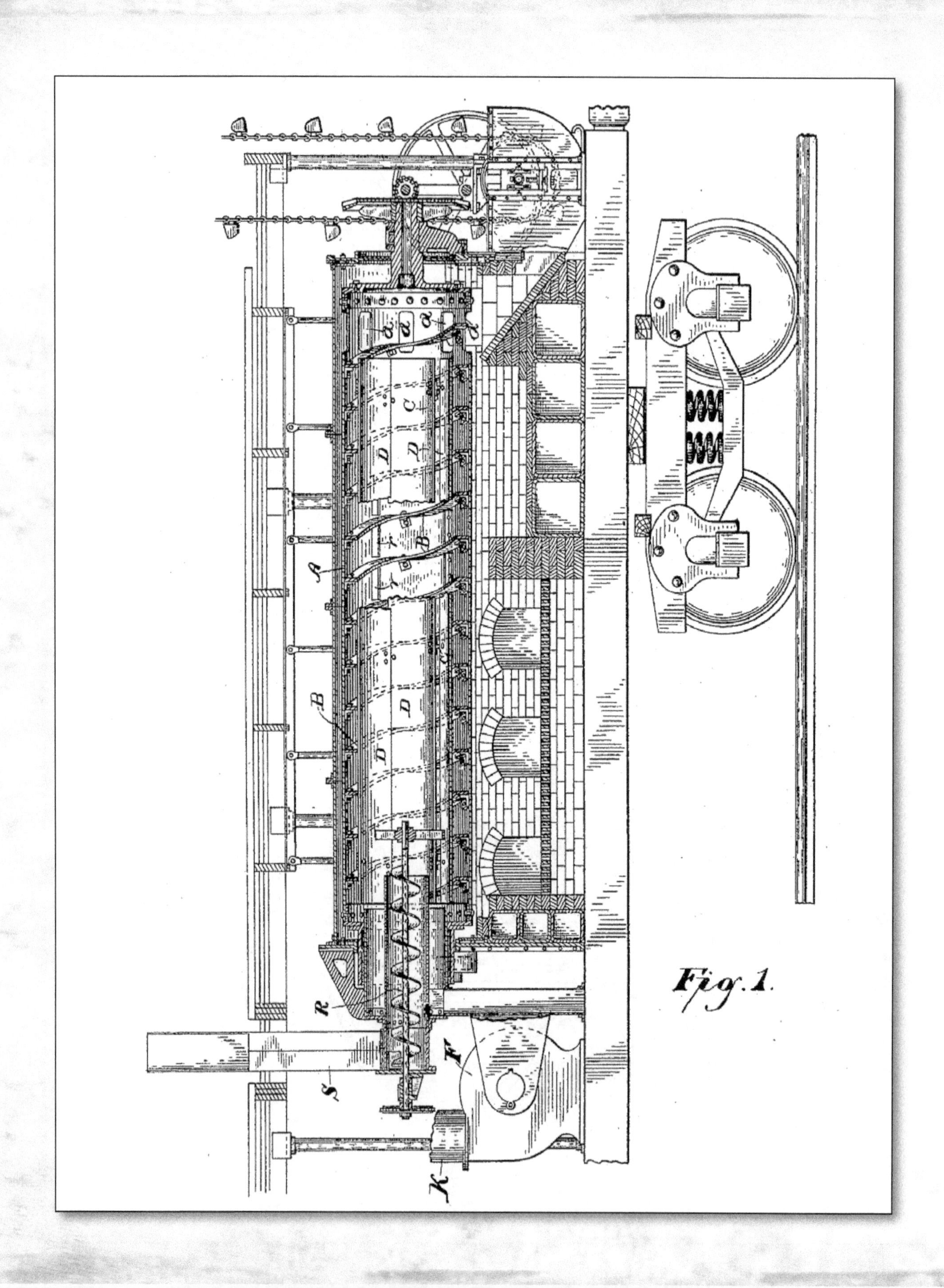

Fig. 1.

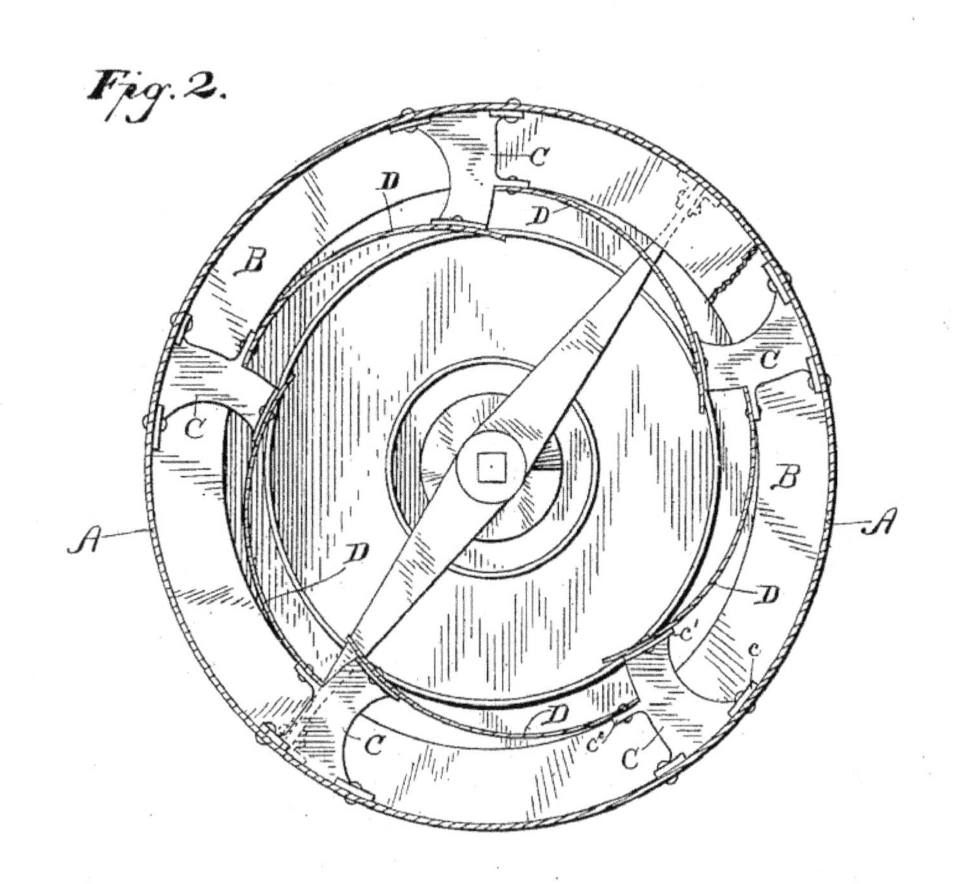

Fig. 3.

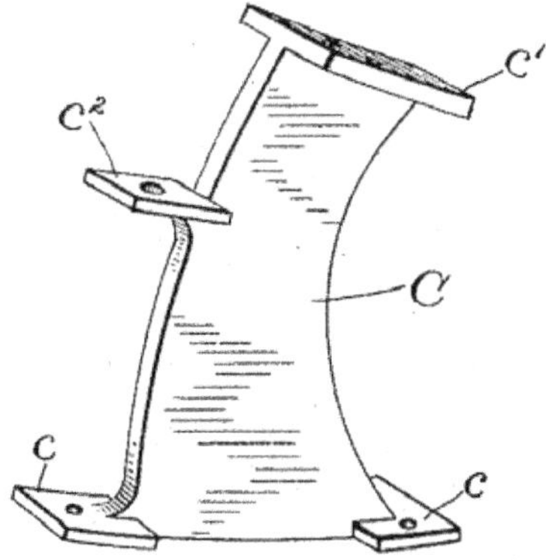

WITNESSES:

C.S. Frye.

J.A. Walsh.

INVENTOR

Frederick Berner, Jr.

BY

Chester Bradford.

ATTORNEY

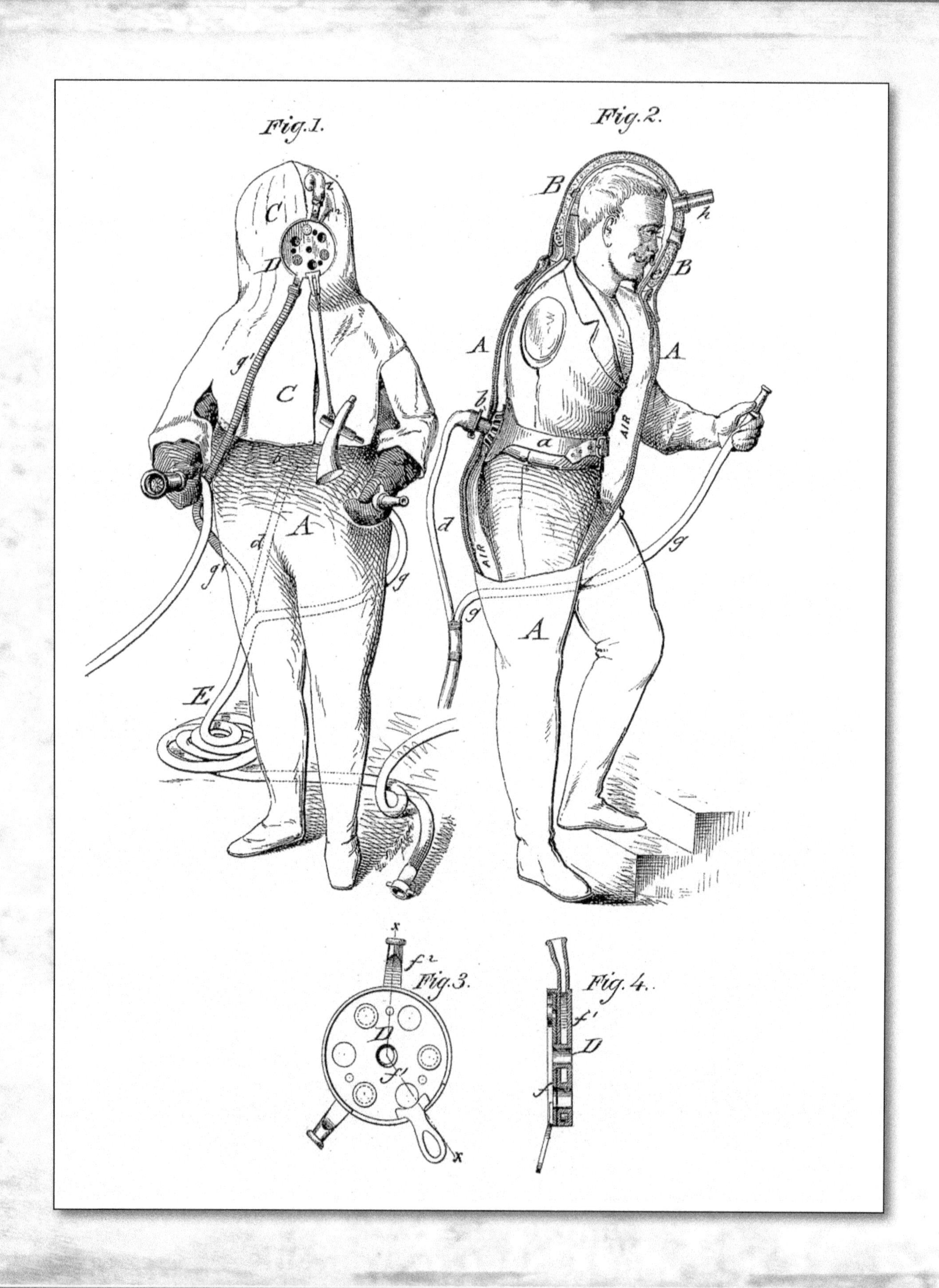

FIREMAN'S SUITS

J.W. OSTBERG

Feb. 29, 1876

No. 174,286

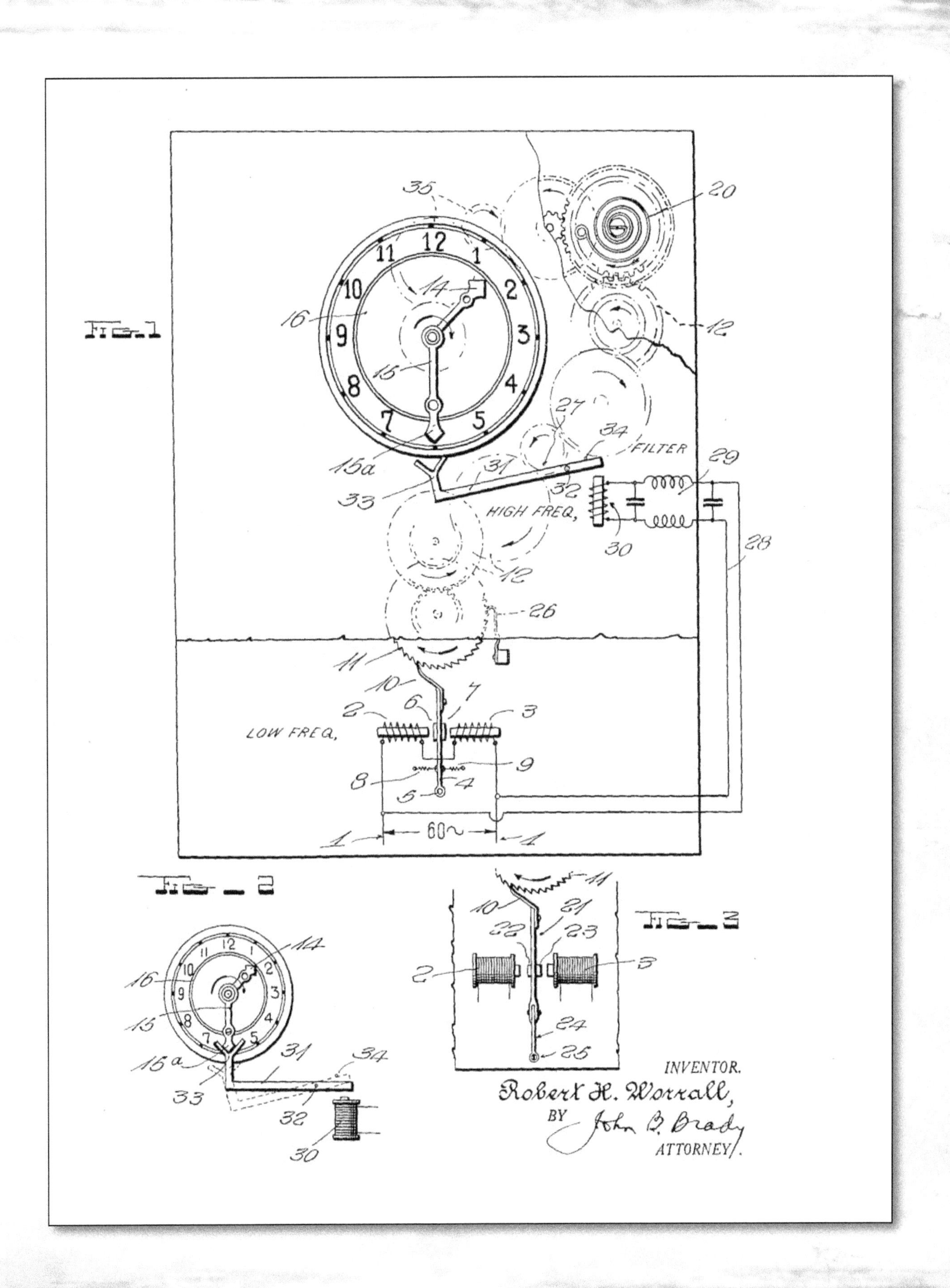

HOROLOGY SYSTEM

R.H. WORRALL June 5, 1934 No. 1,961,320

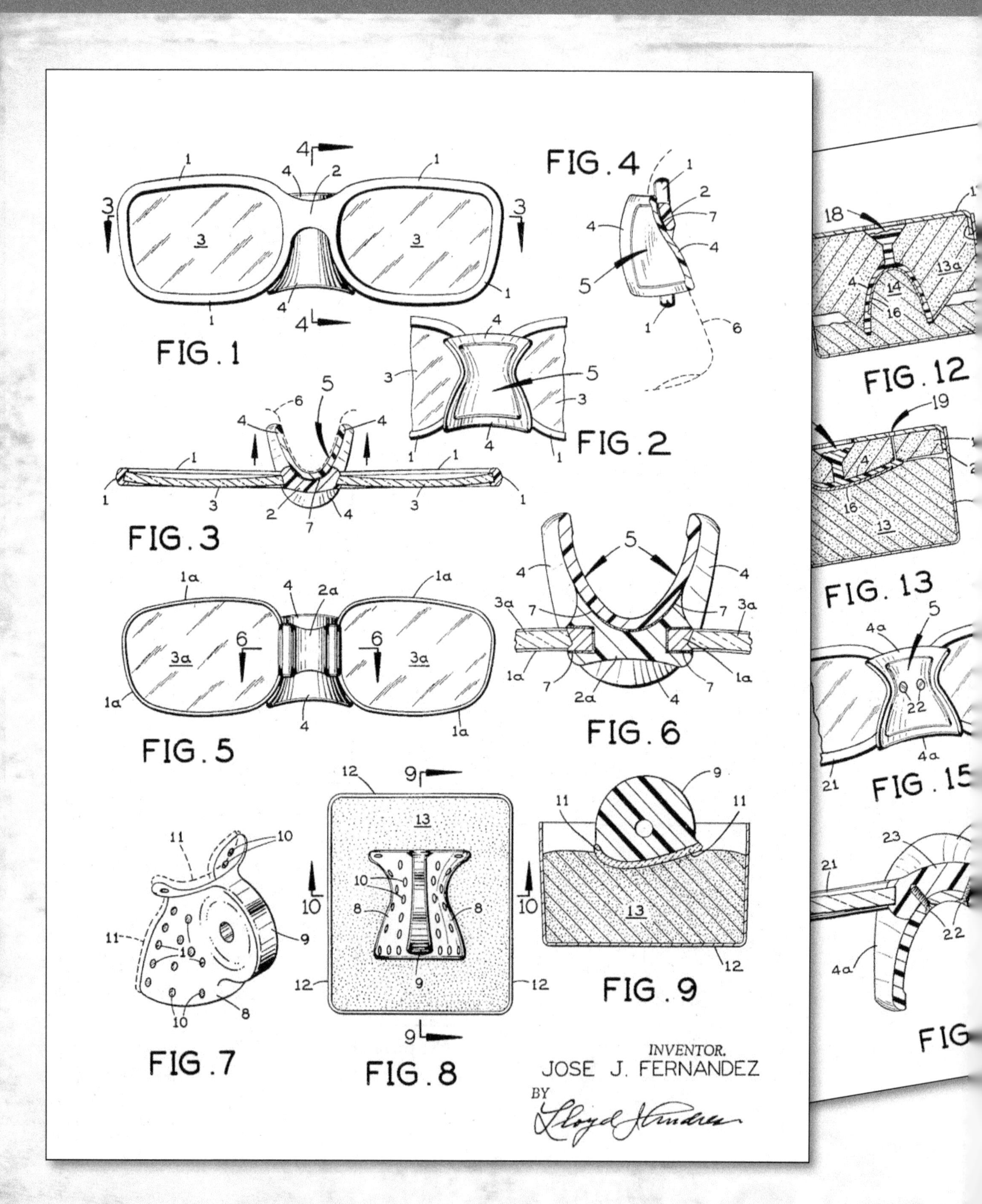

J.J. FERNANDEZ

VACUUM SPECTACLE BRIDGE
Oct. 31, 1972

No. 3,701,592

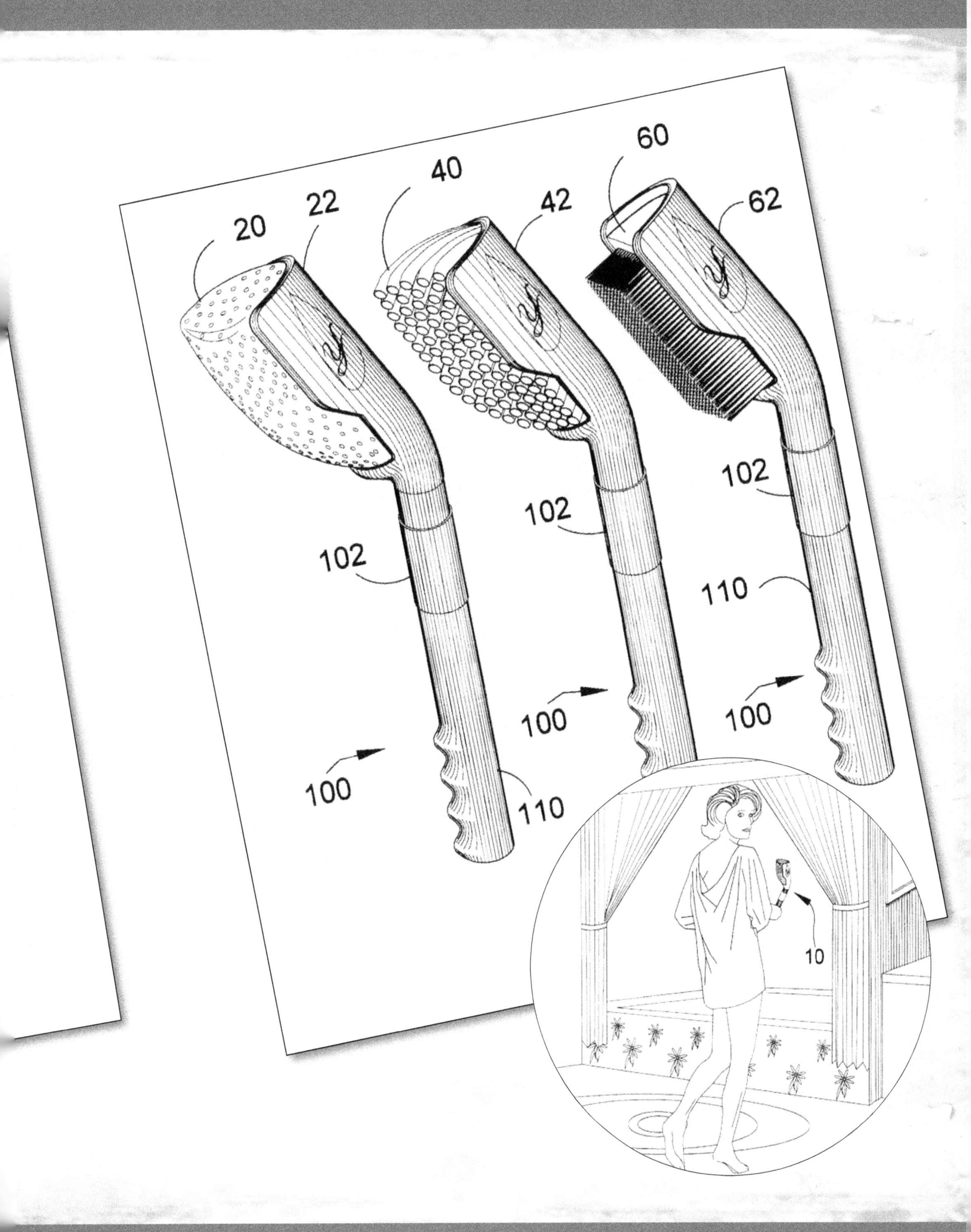
20
22
40
42
60
62
102
102
102
110
110
100
100
100
10

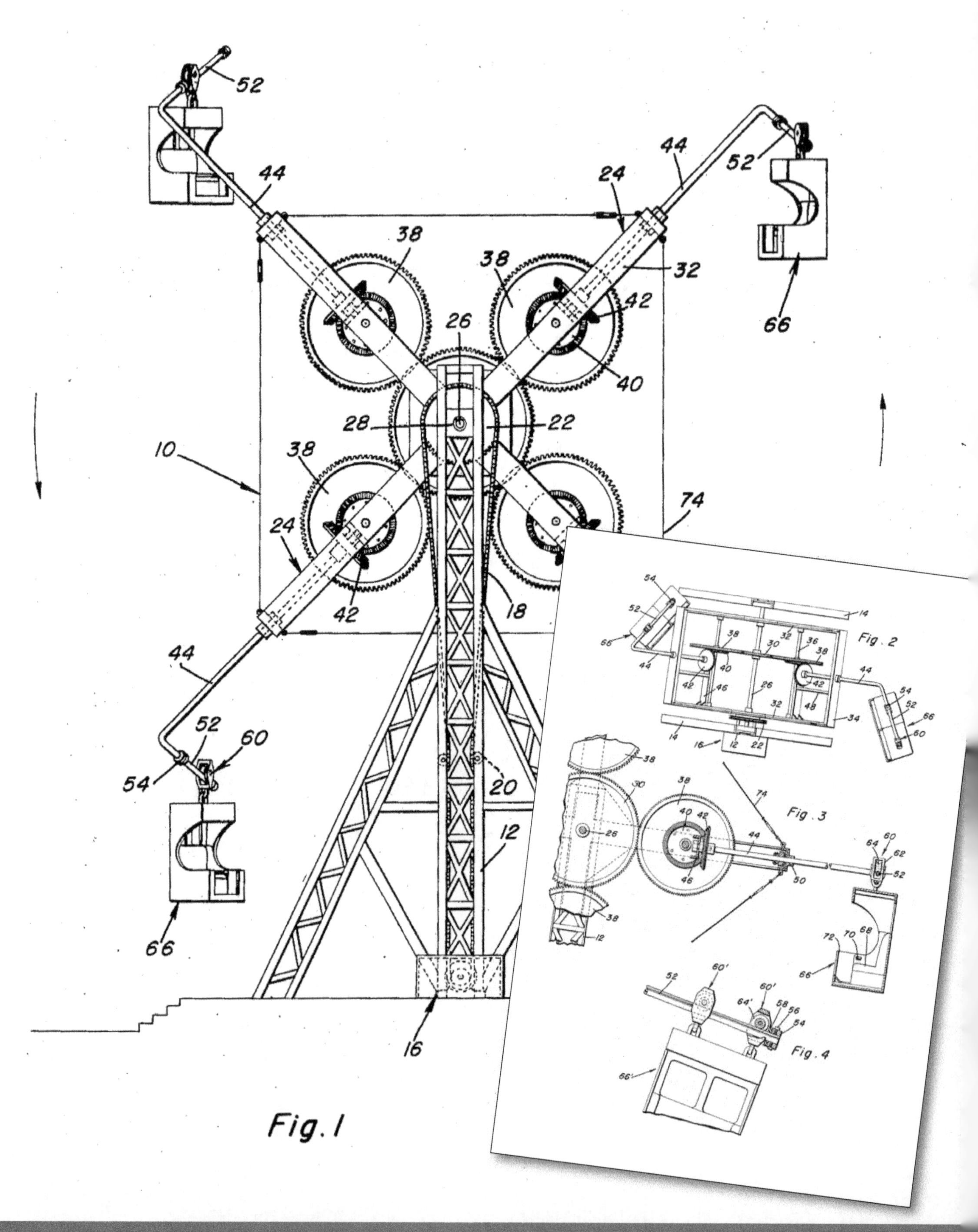

AMUSEMENT RIDE DEVICE
M.R. CASTILLE Mar. 25, 1958 No. 2,828,128

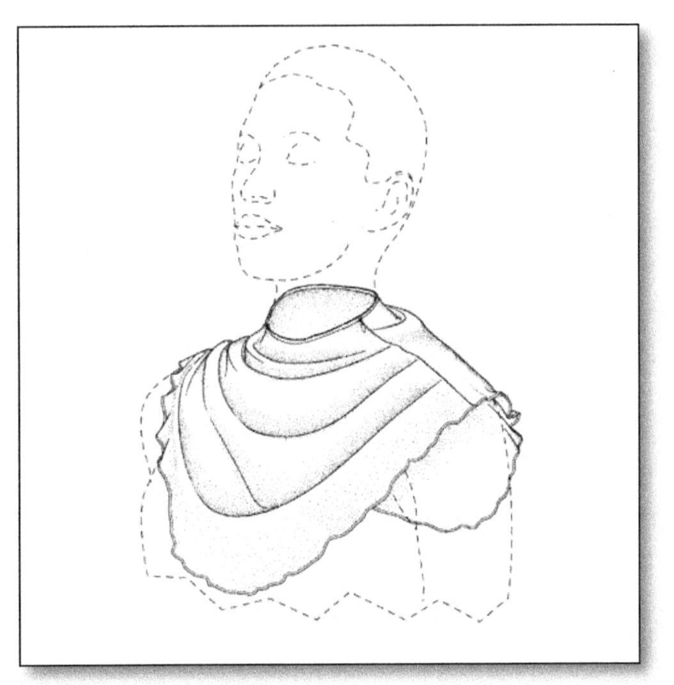

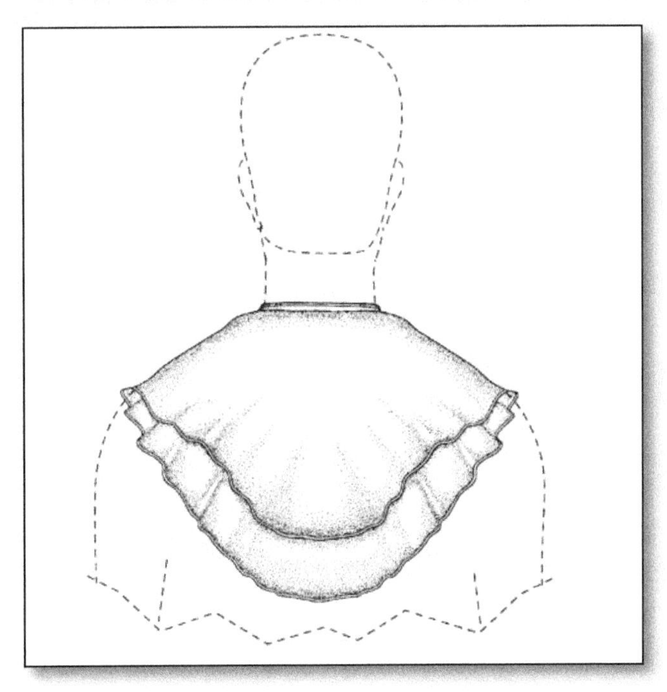

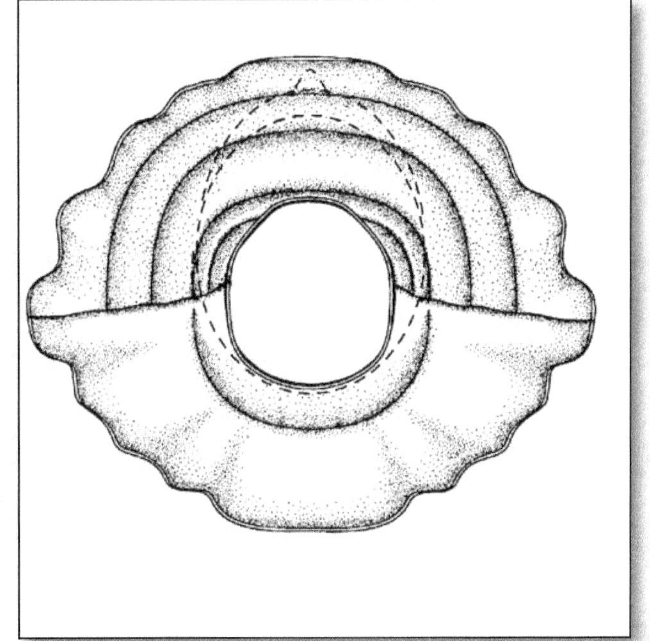

SCARF
R.F. DEMING JR. Jun. 1, 2004 No. D490,591

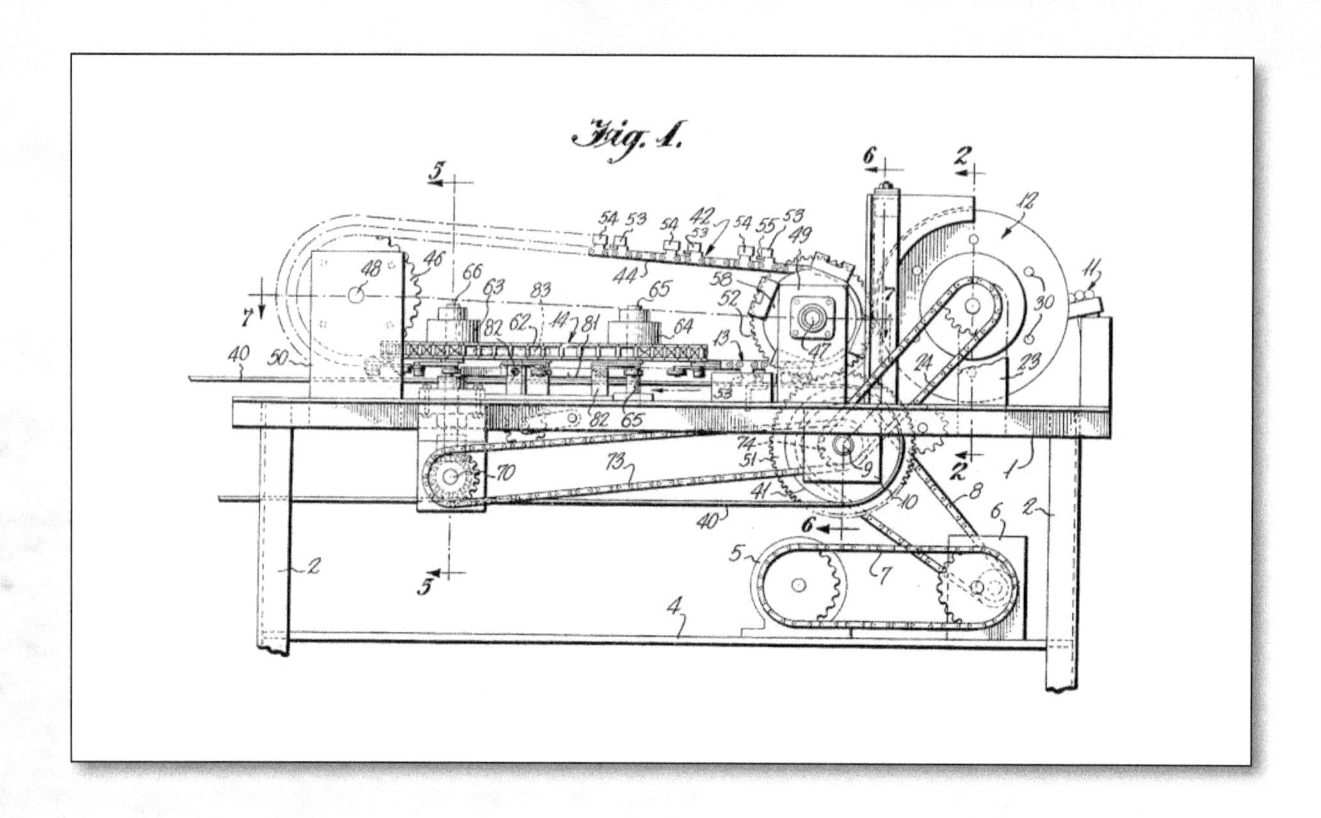

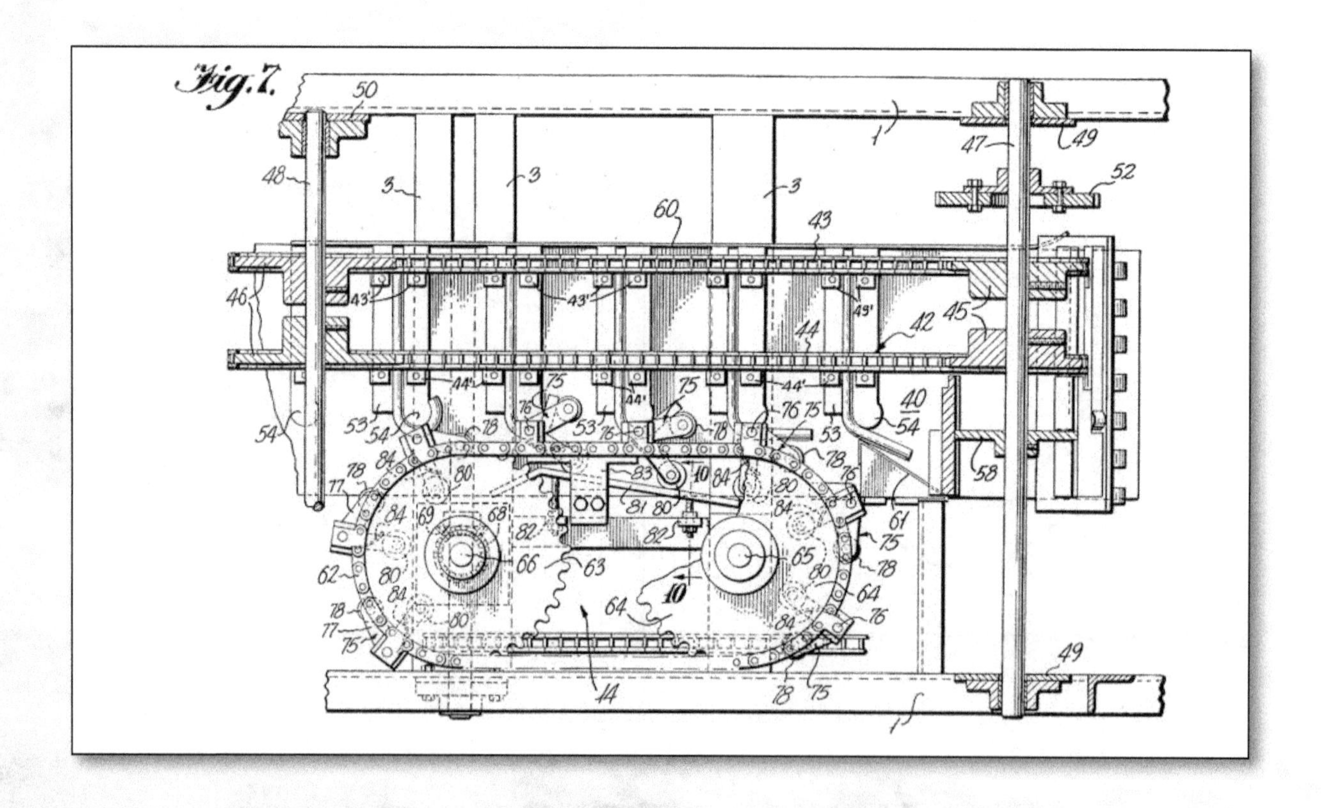

CANDY CANE FORMING MACHINE
G.H. KELLER Oct. 18, 1960 No. 2,956,520

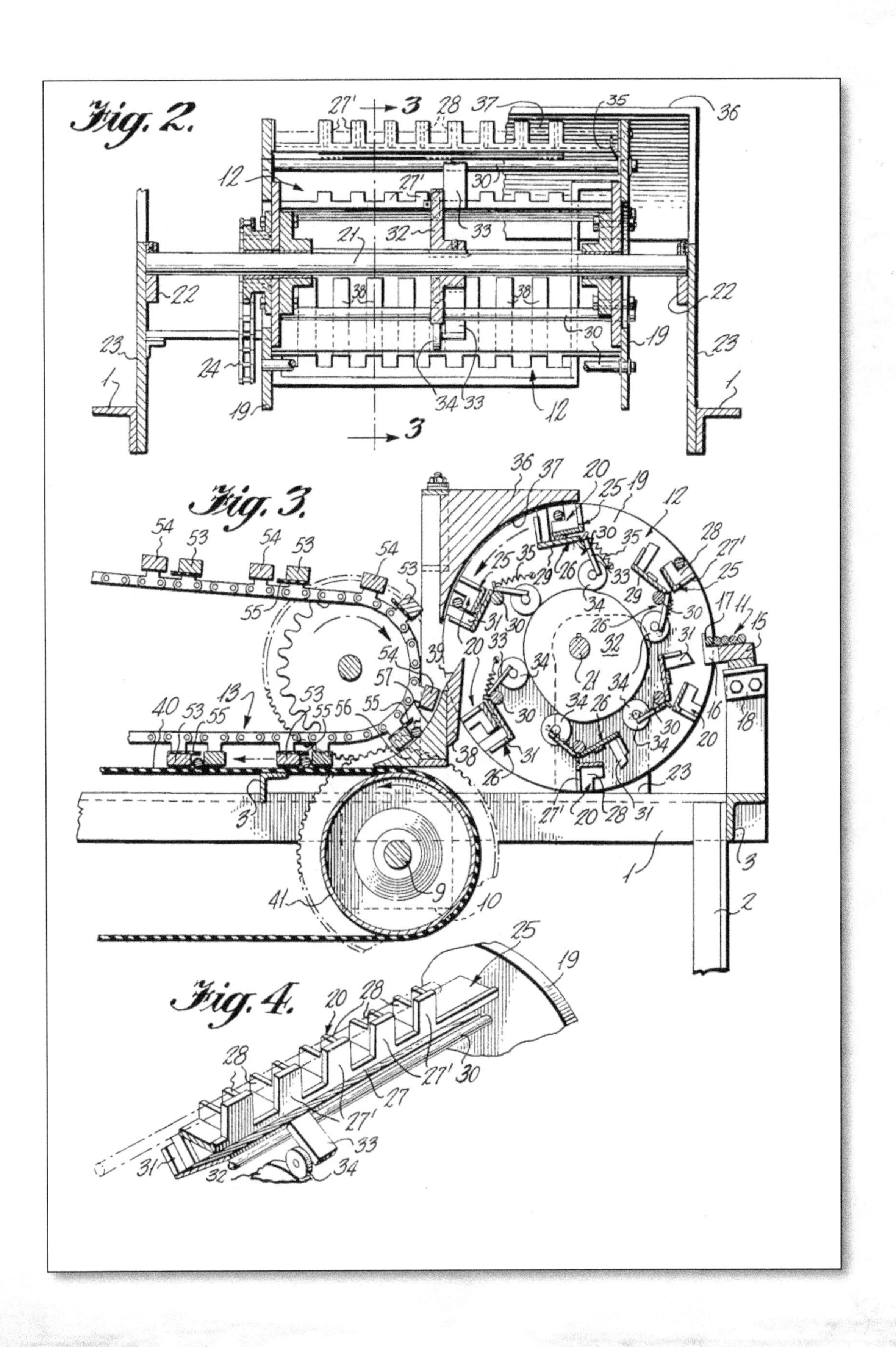

CANDY CANE FORMING MACHINE

G.H. KELLER Oct. 18, 1960 No. 2,956,520

BUOYANT BULLETPROOF COMBAT UNIFORM
N. J. WATERBURY DEC. 30, 1965 No. 3,398,406

FIRE!

BUOYANT BULLETPROOF COMBAT UNIFORM
N. J. WATERBURY DEC. 30, 1965 No. 3,398,406

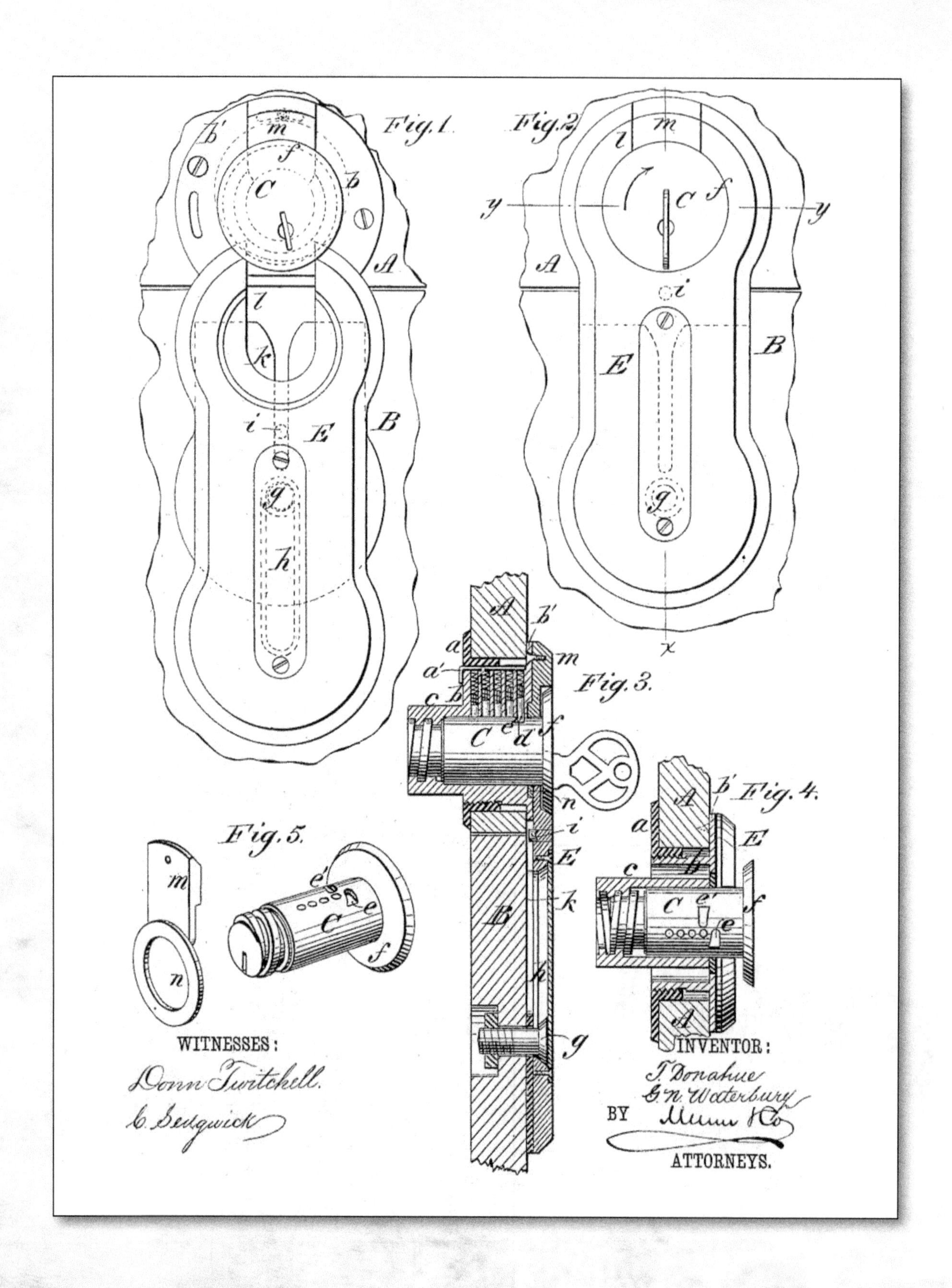

TRUNK LOCK
T. DONAHUE & G.N. WATERBURY Apr. 11, 1882 No. 256,300

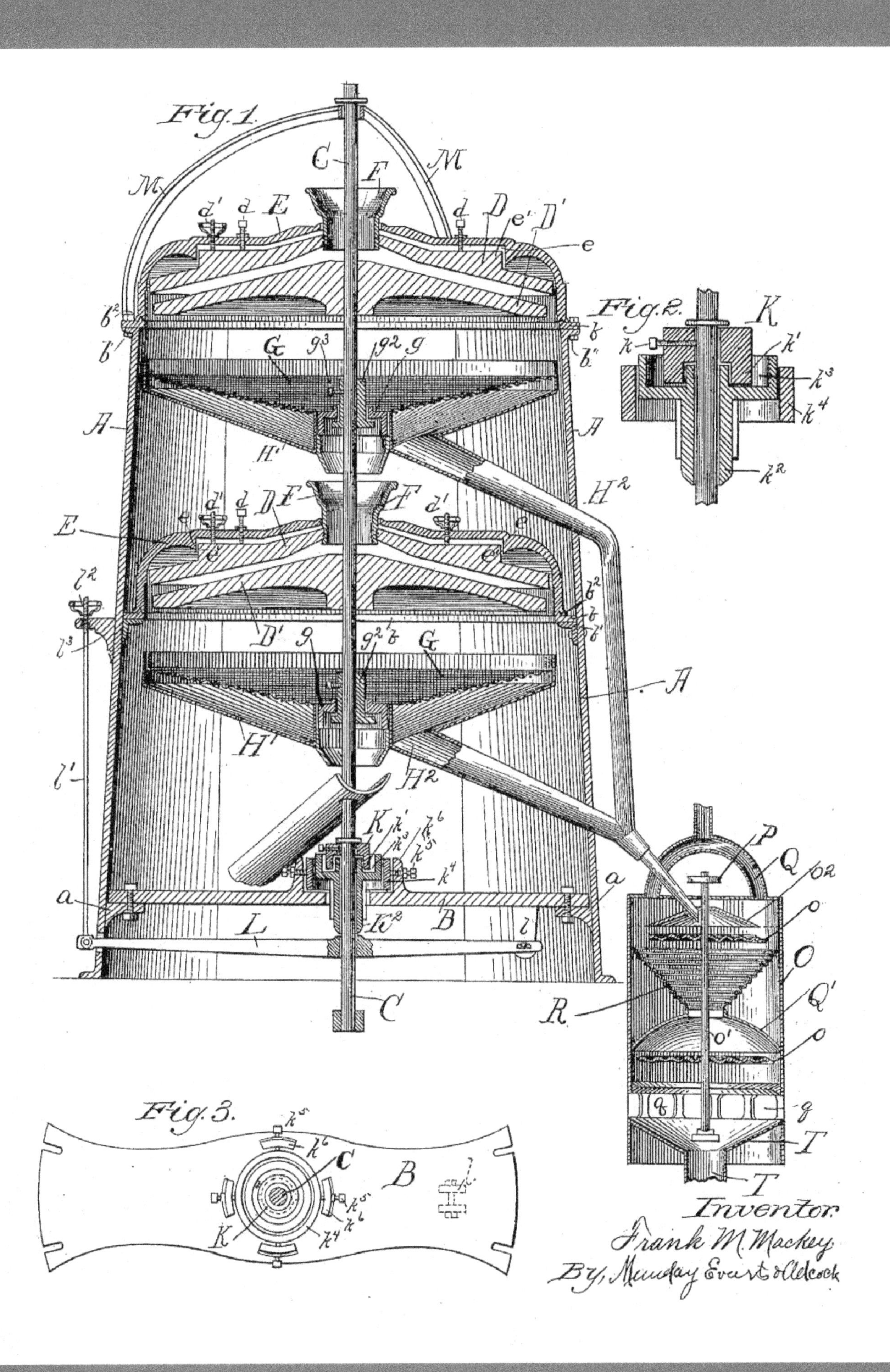

F.M. MACKEY

MILLING APPARATUS
Feb. 5, 1884

No. 293,047

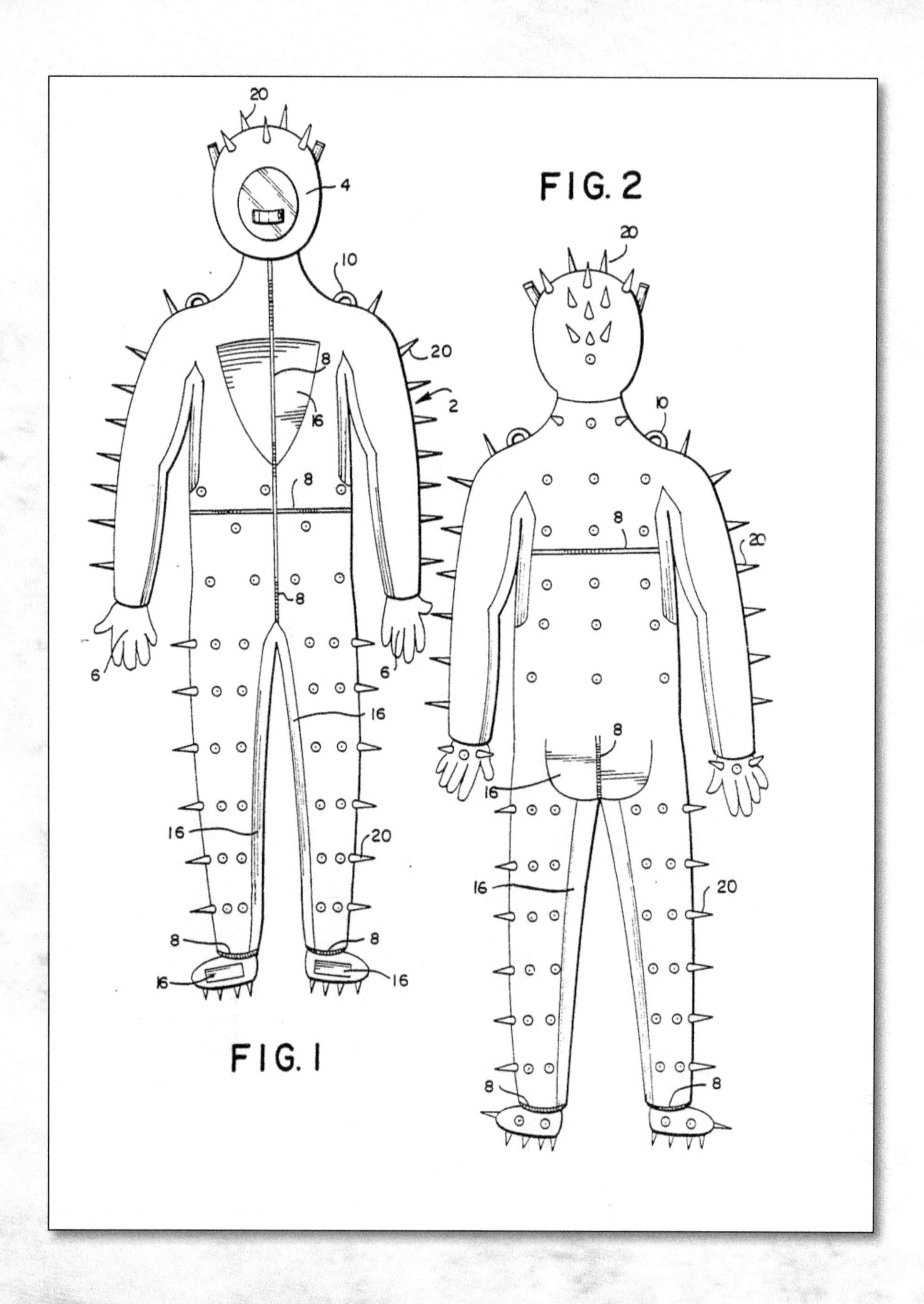
FIG. 2
FIG. 1
20
4
10
8
16
2
6

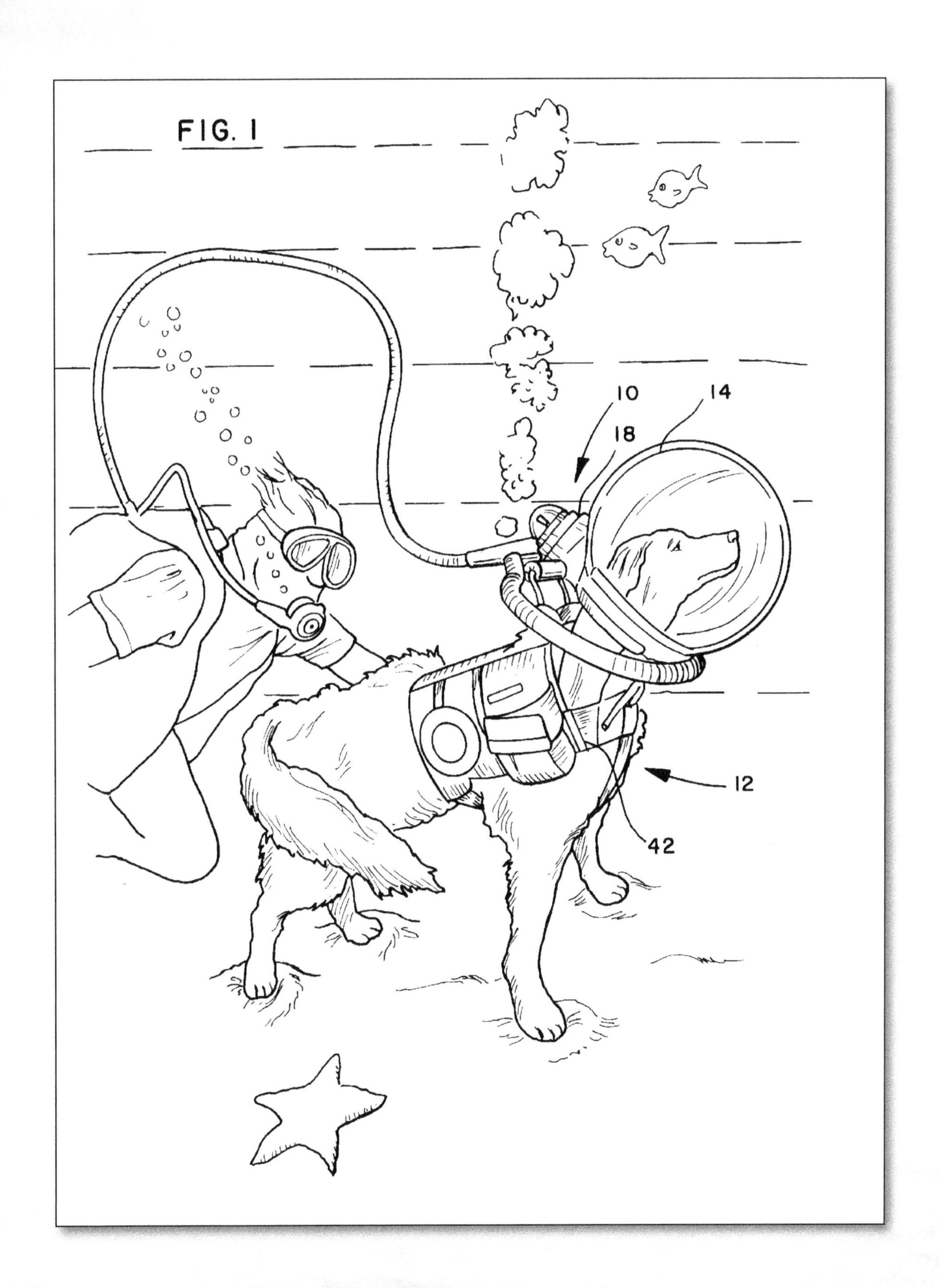
FIG. 1
10
14
18
12
42

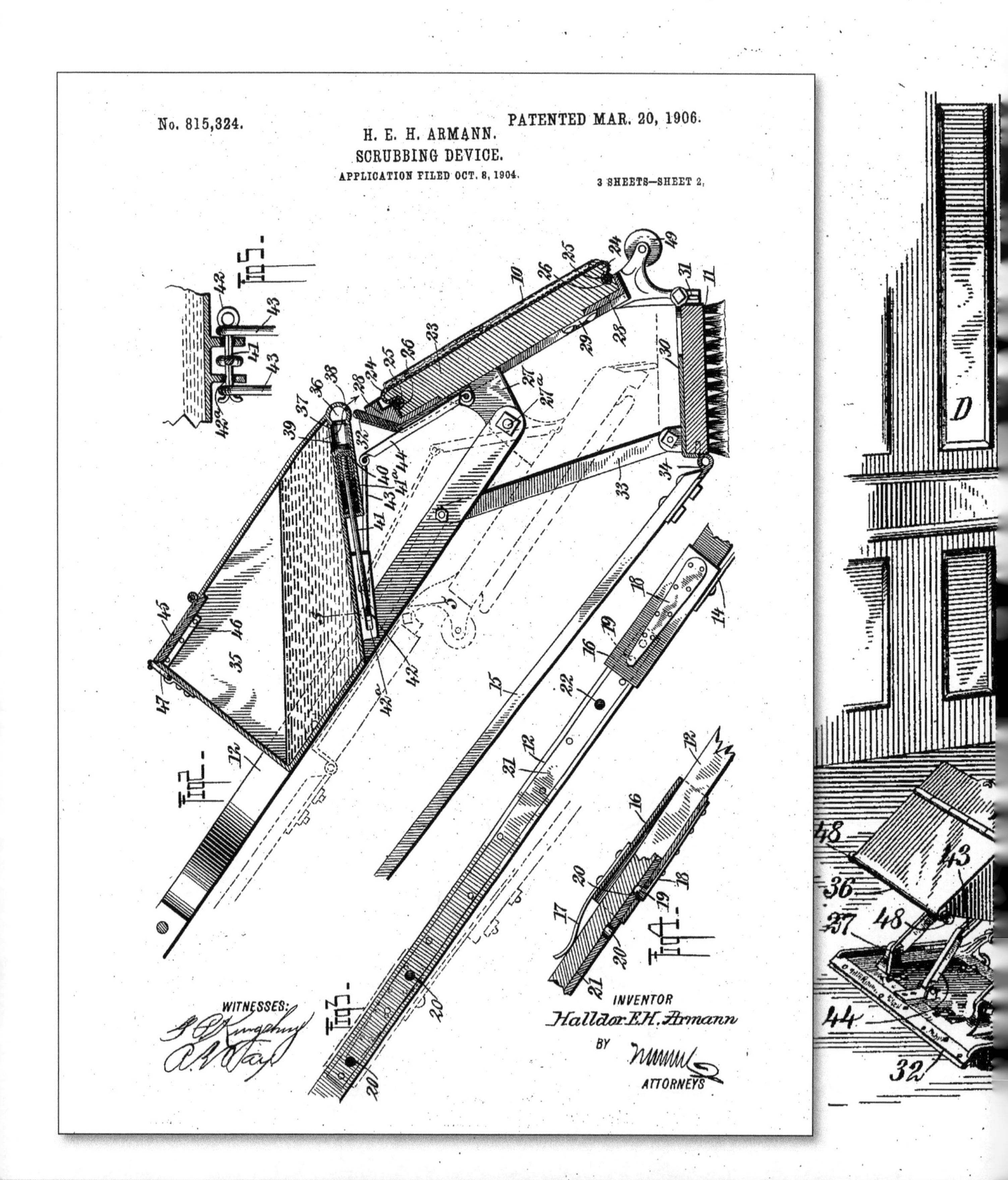
No. 815,324.
PATENTED MAR. 20, 1906.
H. E. H. ARMANN.
SCRUBBING DEVICE.
APPLICATION FILED OCT. 8, 1904.
3 SHEETS—SHEET 2.
WITNESSES:
INVENTOR
Halldor E.H. Armann
BY
ATTORNEYS

SCRUBBING DEVICE
H. E. H. ARMANN MAR. 20, 1906 No. 816,324

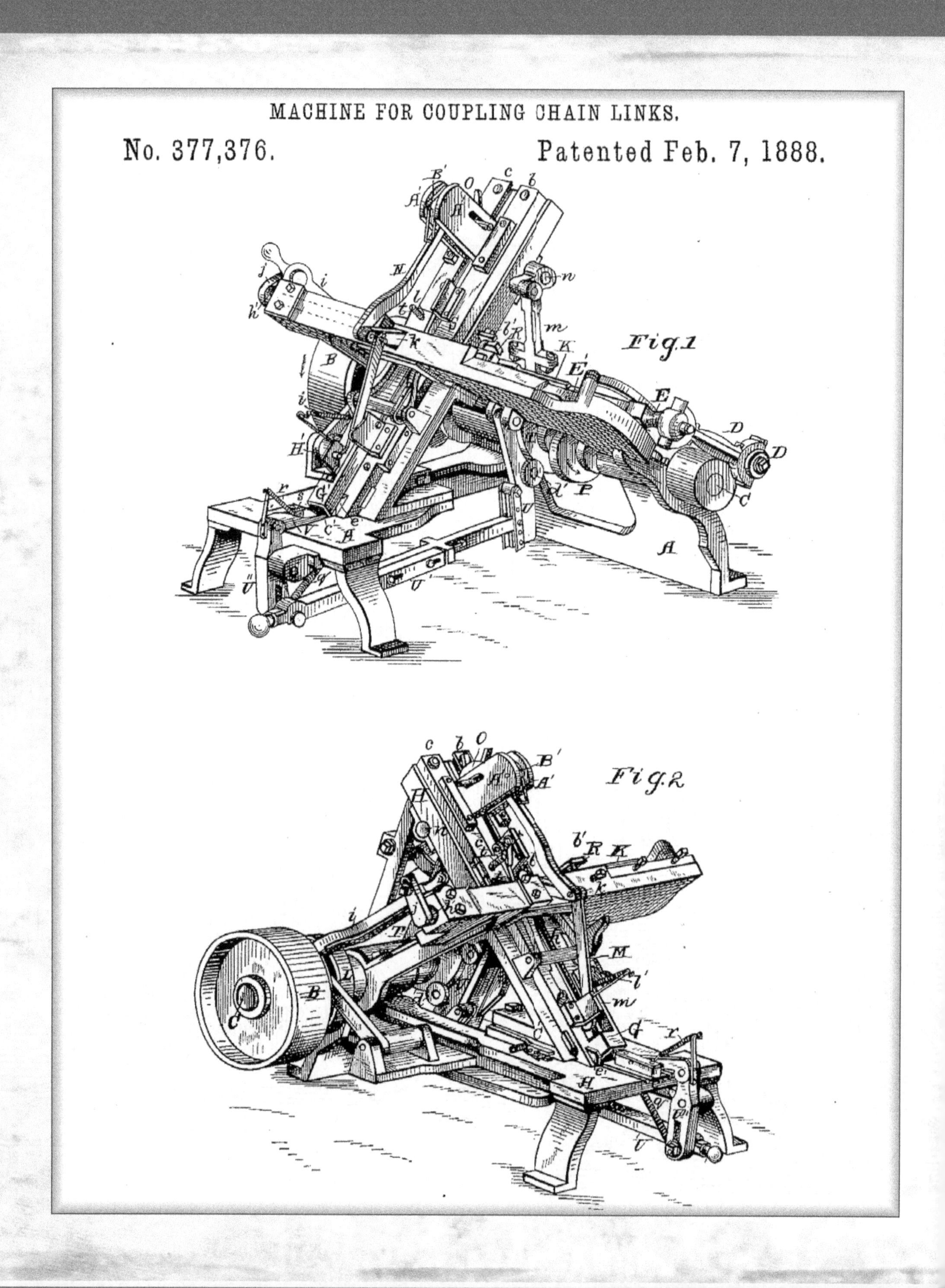

MACHINE FOR COUPLING CHAIN LINKS
N. B. FASSETT FEB. 7, 1888 No. 377,376

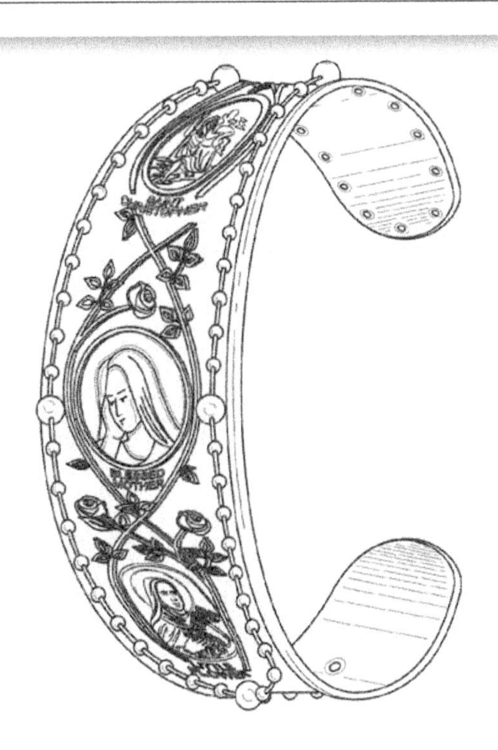

FIG. 1

FIG. 2

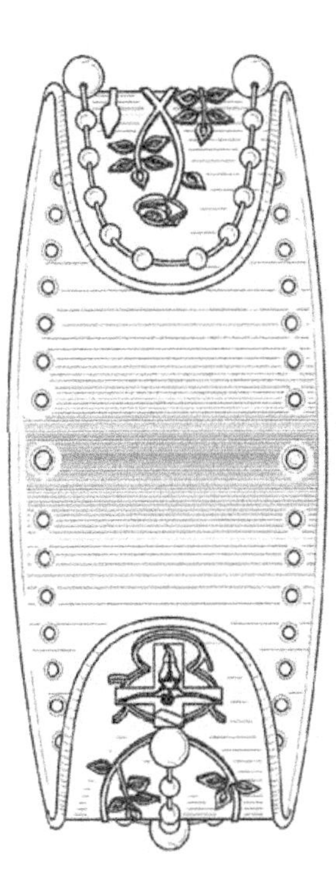

FIG. 3

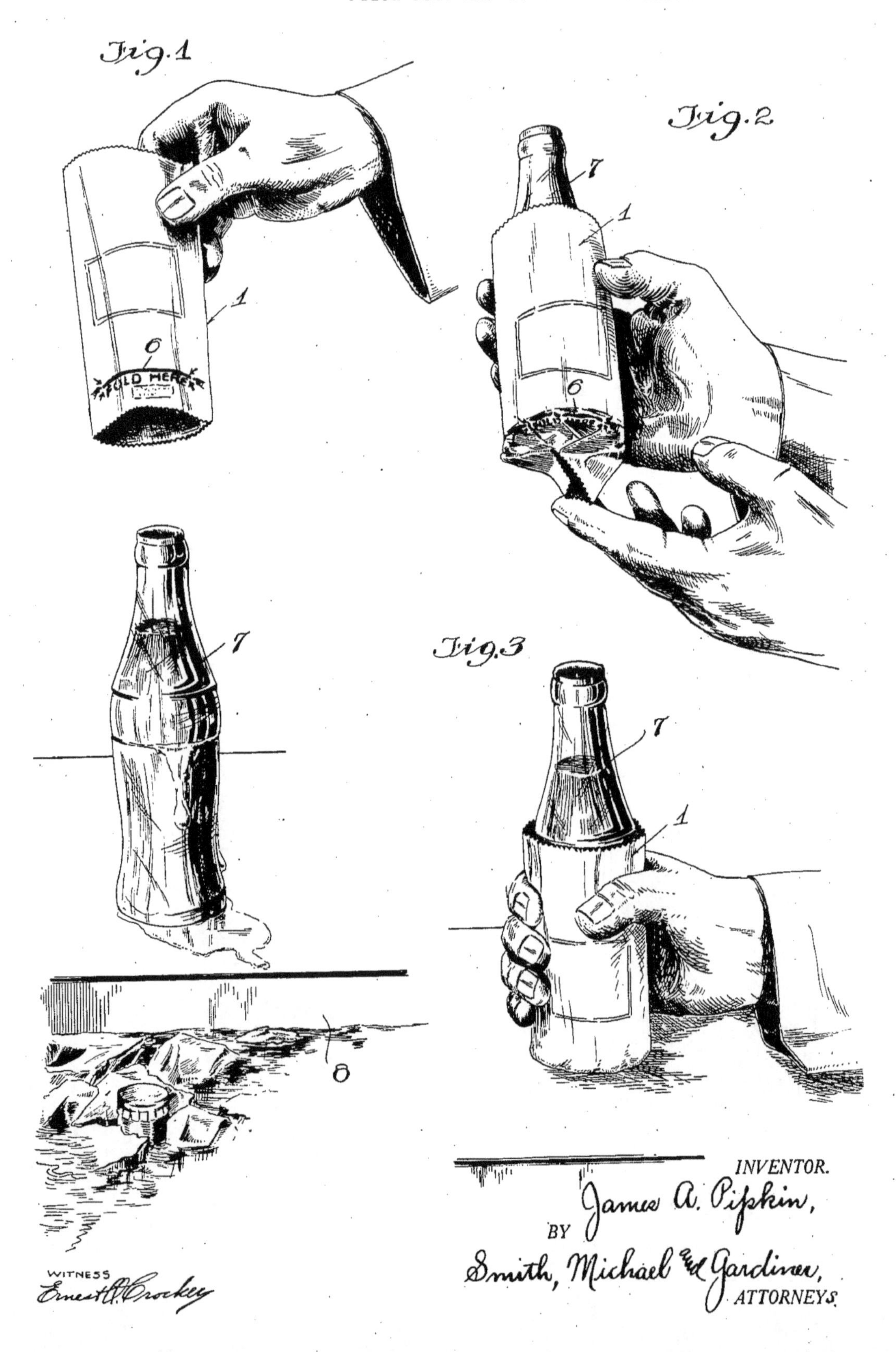
Dec. 20, 1932.
J. A. PIPKIN
1,891,892
DRIP CATCHING ATTACHMENT FOR BOTTLES
Filed Oct. 11, 1929
2 Sheets-Sheet 1
Fig. 1
Fig. 2
Fig. 3
FOLD HERE
INVENTOR.
James A. Pipkin,
BY
Smith, Michael & Gardiner,
ATTORNEYS.
WITNESS
Ernest P. Crockey

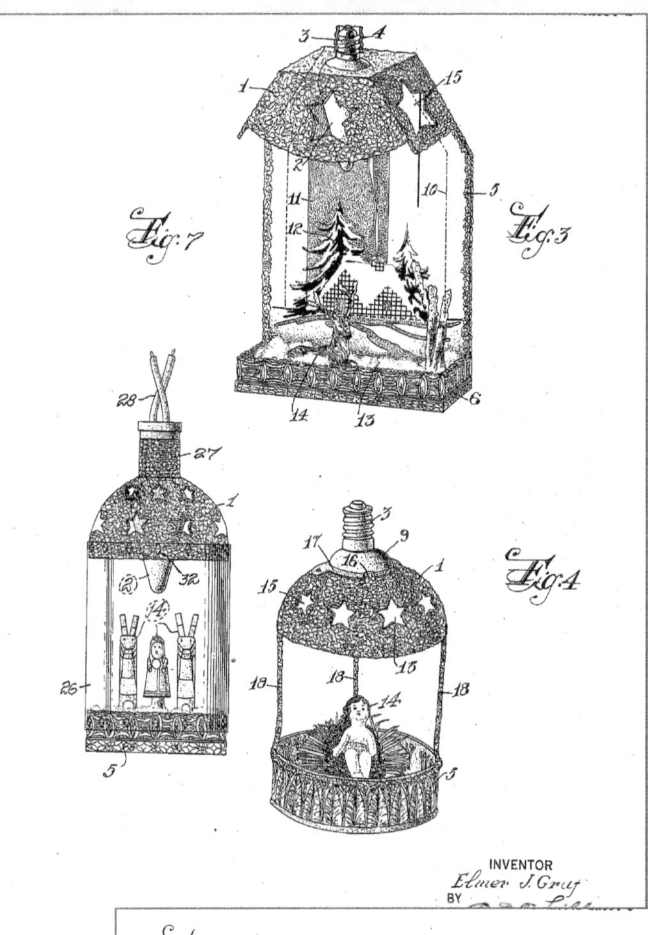

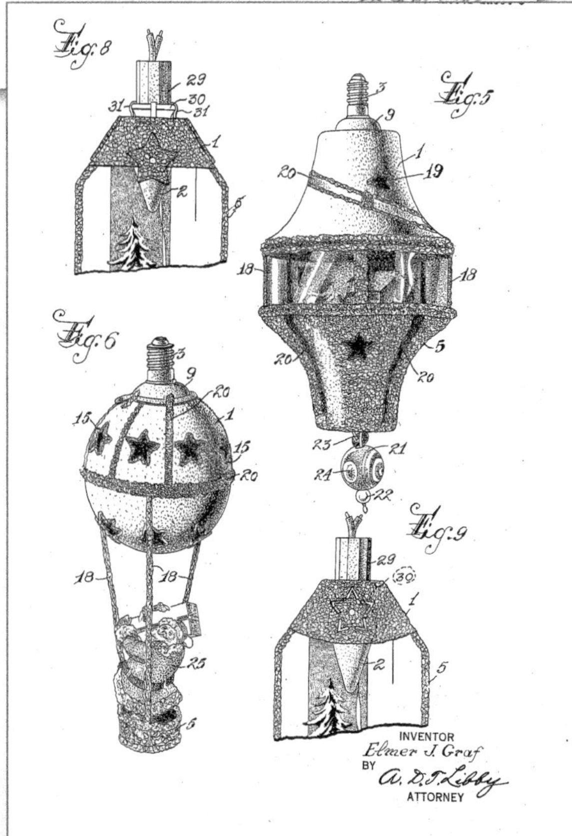

ILLUMINATED DECORATIVE DEVICE

ELMER J. GRAF — OCT. 26, 1937 — No. 2,097,061

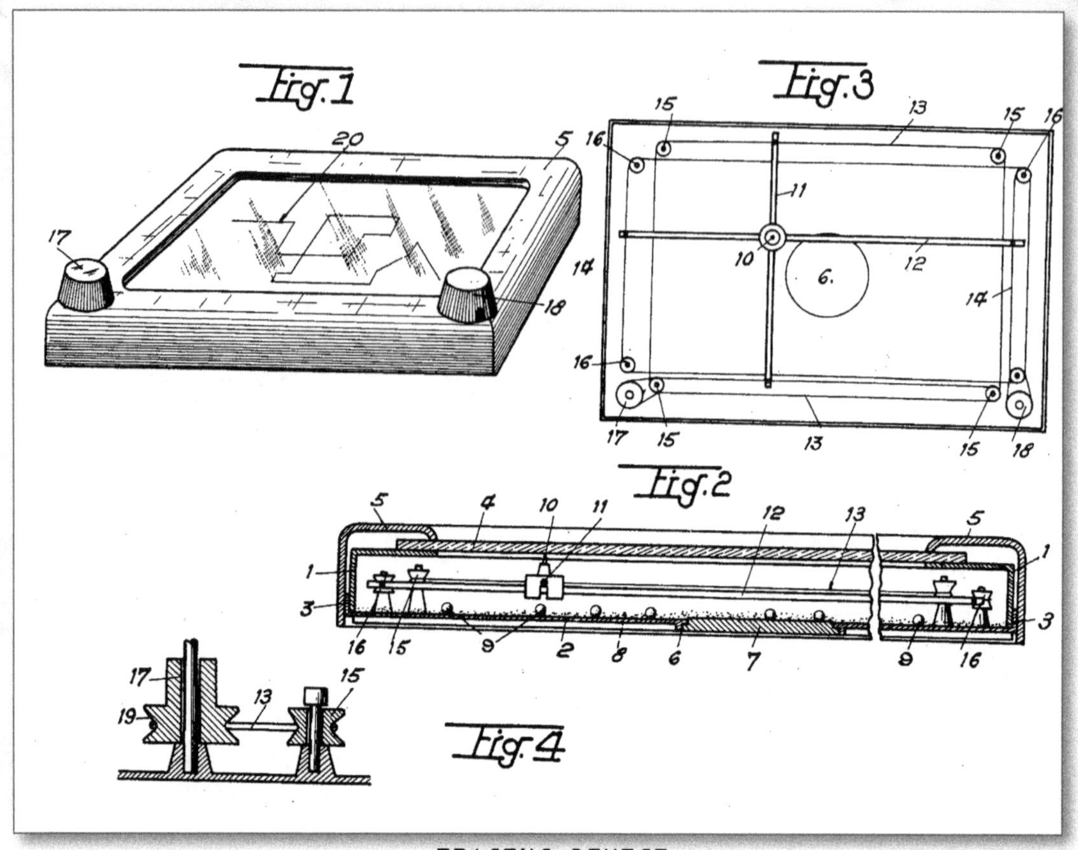

A. GRANDJEAN TRACING DEVICE SEPT. 25, 1962 No. 3,055,113

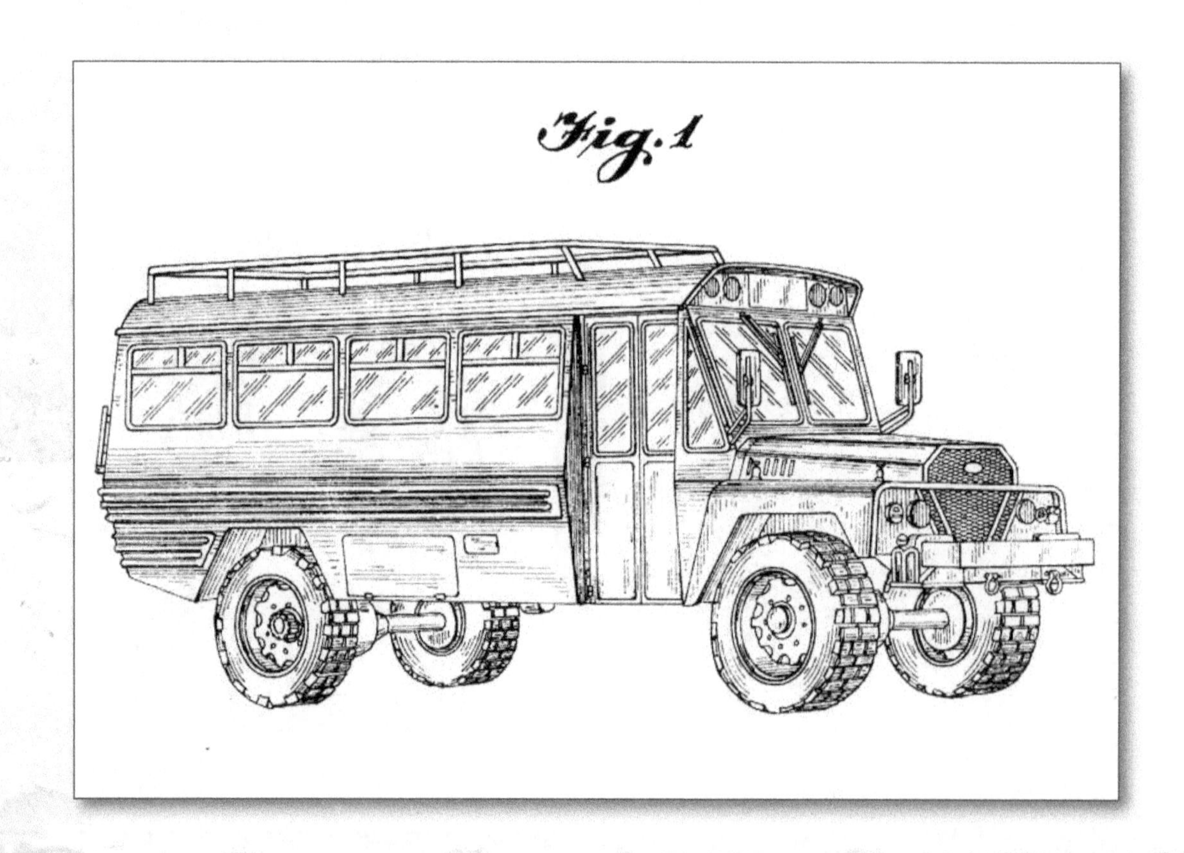

P. LEGUEU AIR TRANSPORT BUS FEB. 7, 1984 No. D272,524

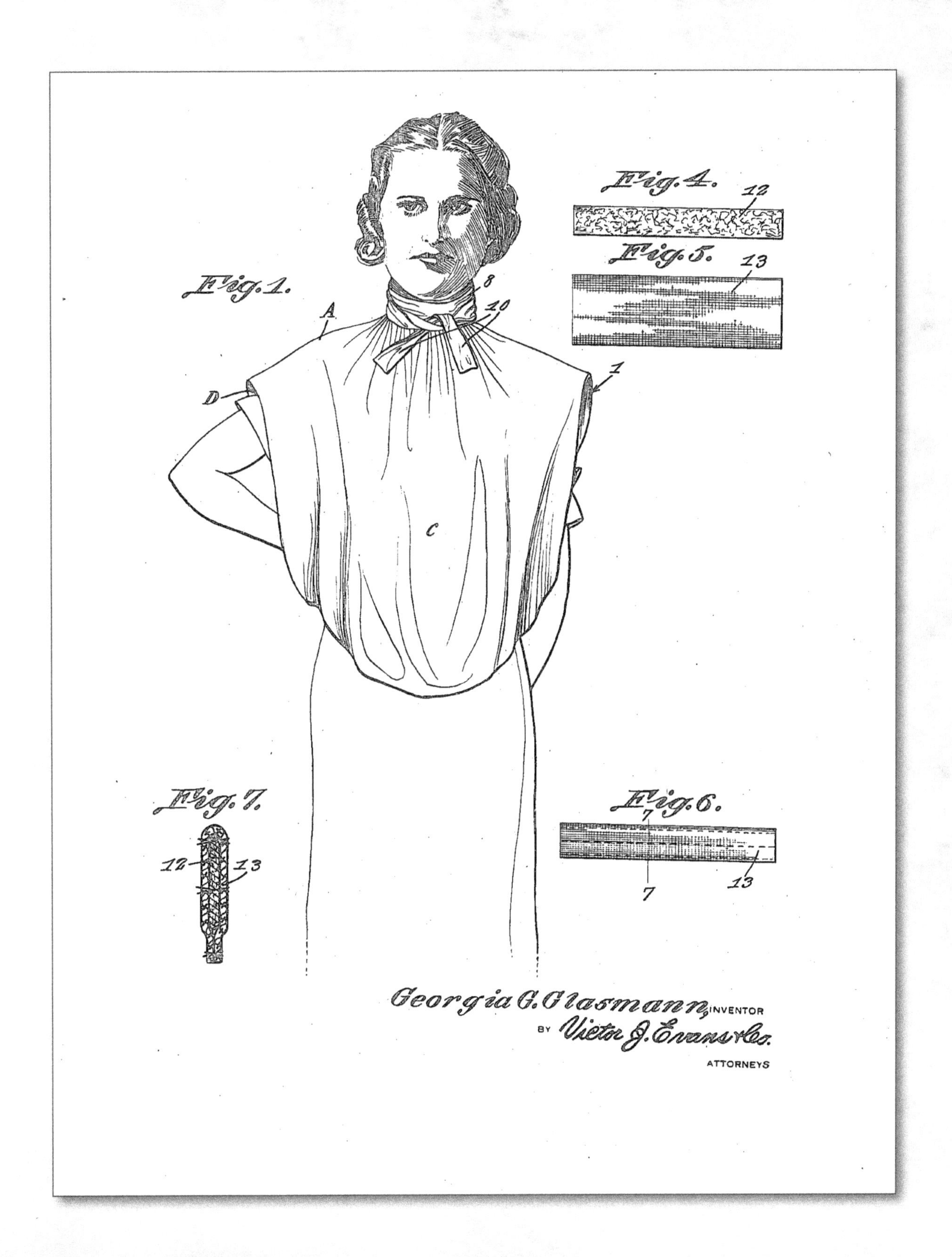

HEAT RESISTING APRON FOR BEAUTY PARLORS
G. G. GLASMANN APRIL 19, 1938 No. 2,114,922

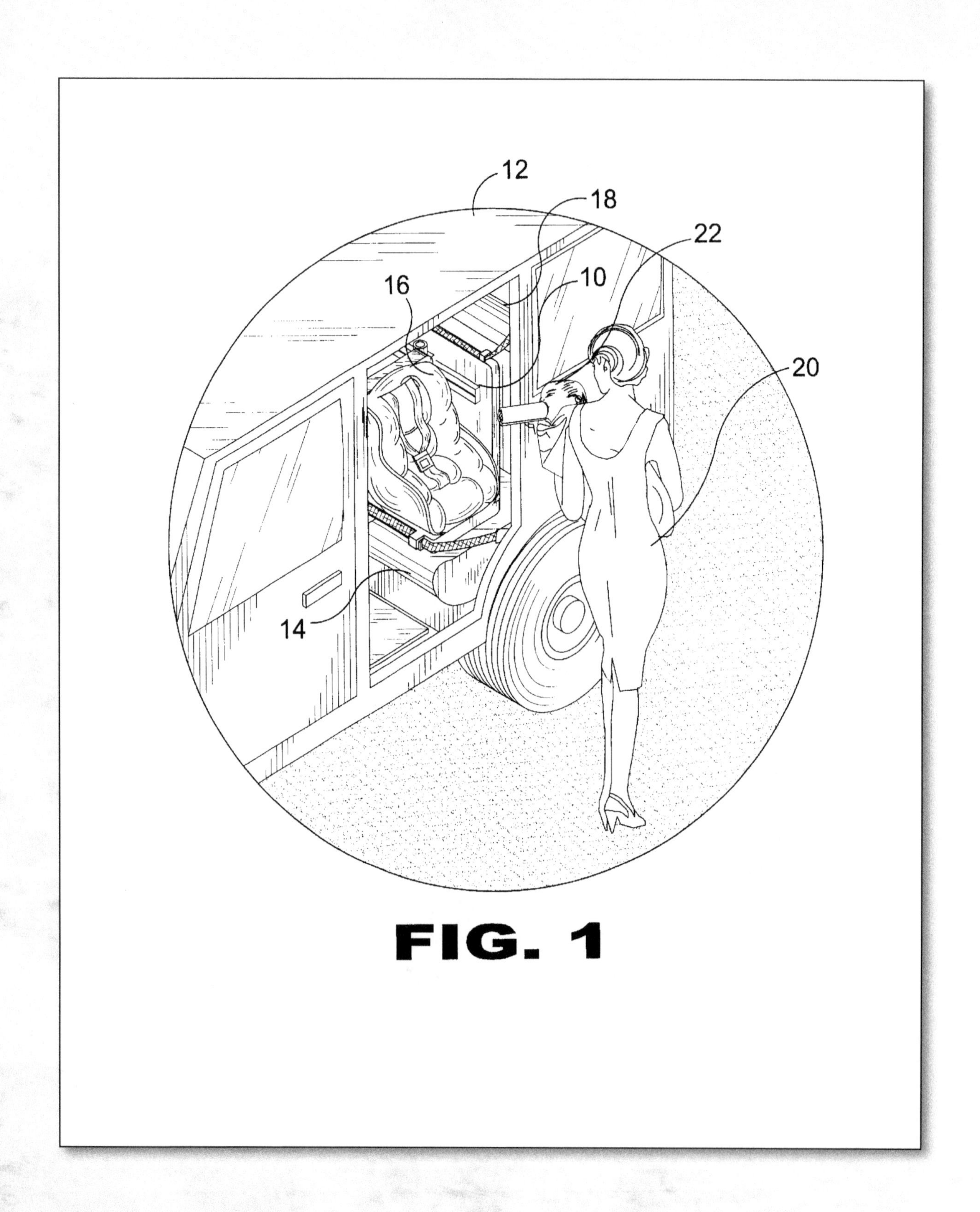

FIG. 1

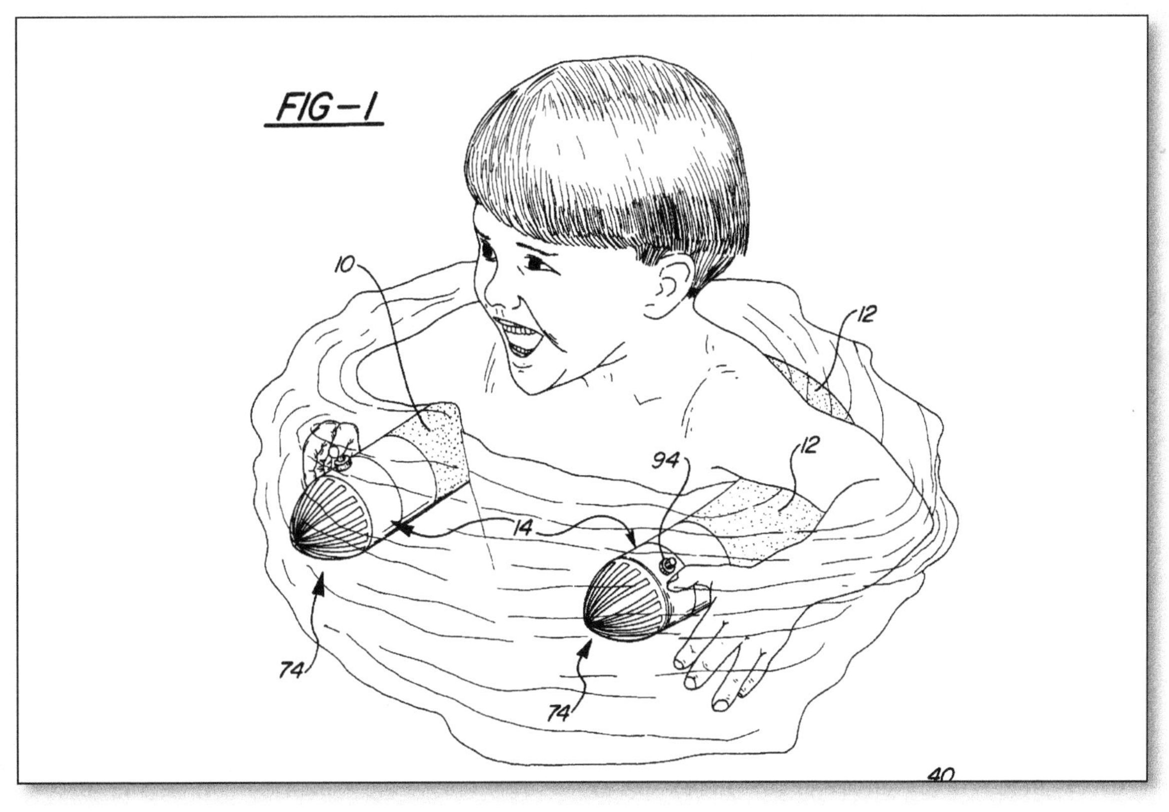

MOTORIZED TUBULAR FLOTATION APPARATUS
SILADKE ET AL. SEPT. 7, 1999 No. 5,947,782

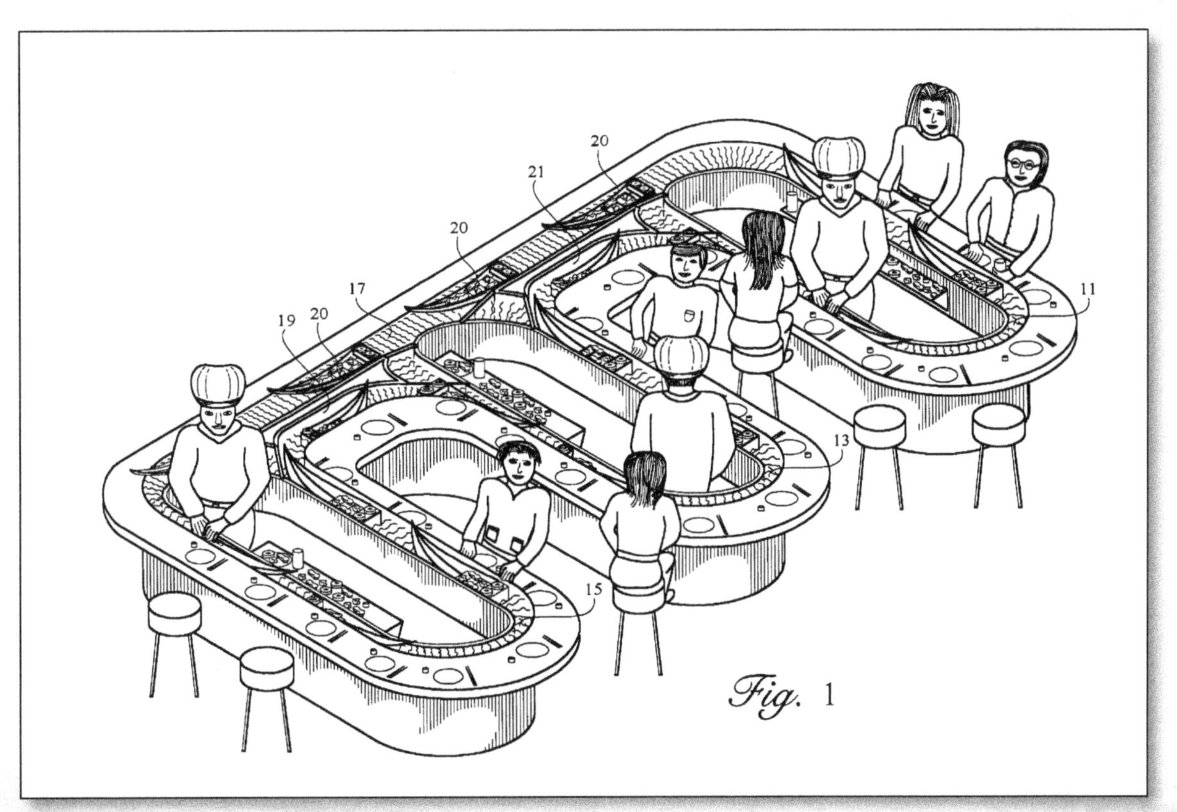

INTERLINKED WATERCOURSES FOR SUSHI BOATS
LAI JAN. 30, 2001 No. 6,179,088

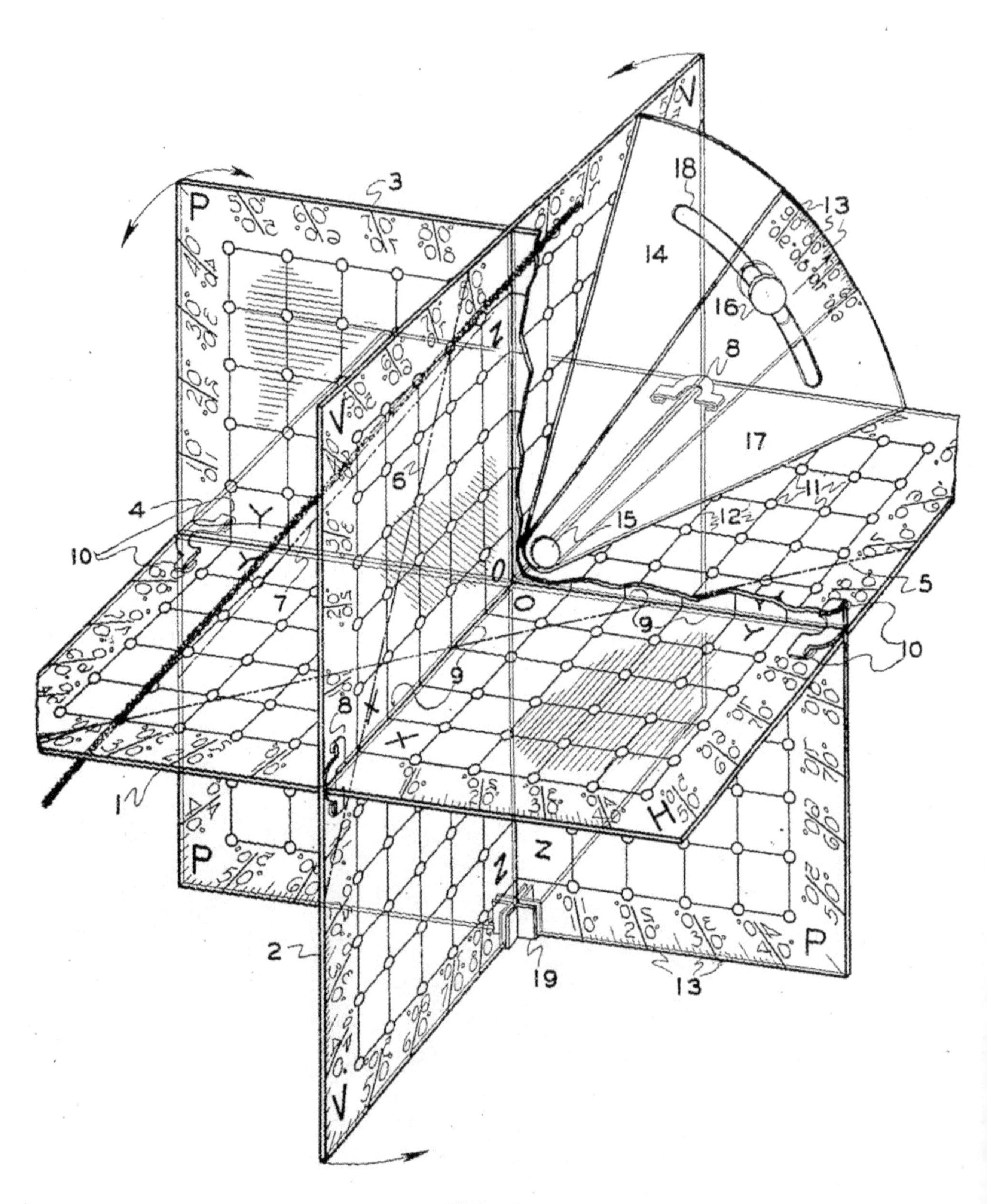

FIG. I

GEOMETRICAL DEVICE

H.M. McCULLY June 6, 1933 No. 1,912,380

G. S. BARKENTIN.
Statuette.

No. 10,513. Patented March 12, 1878.

Witnesses.
J. H. Shumway
H. A. Kitson

Geo. S. Barkentin
Inventor
By Atty.
John E. Earle

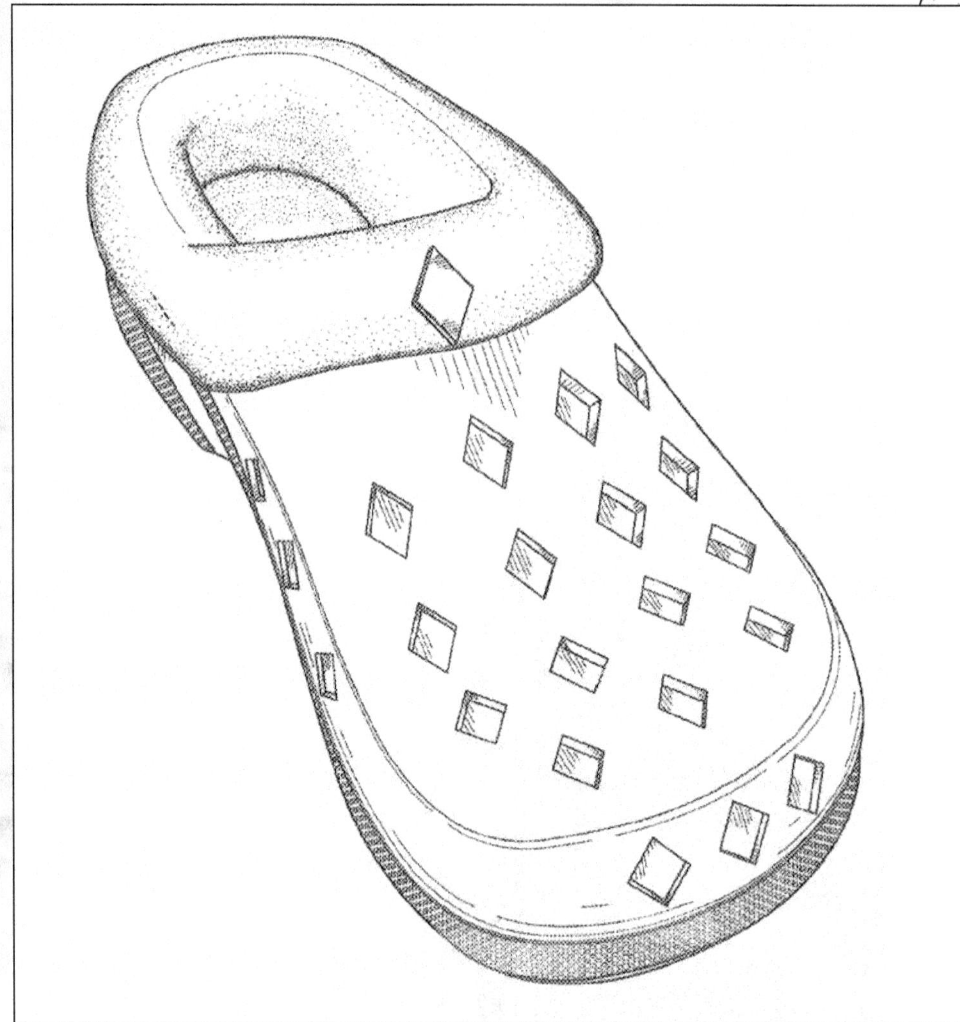

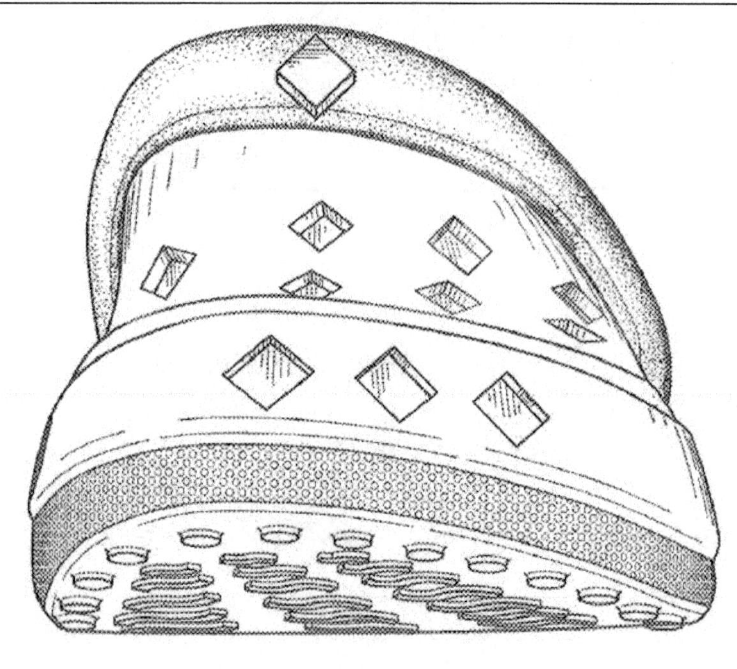

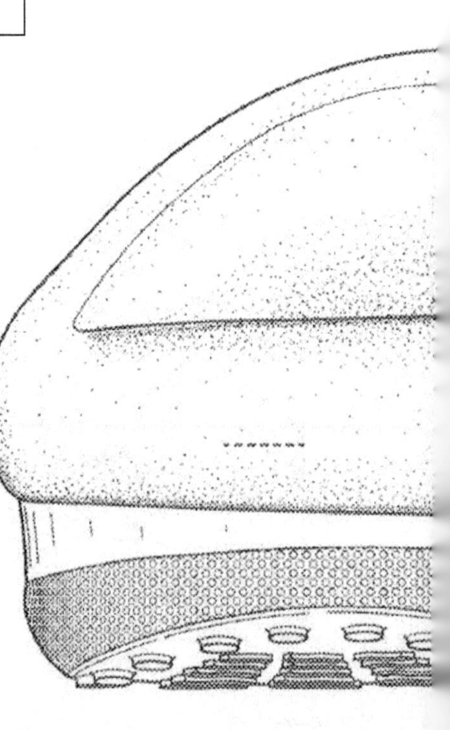

MICHAEL WOLF

WINTER CLOG
Feb. 9, 2010

No. D609,453

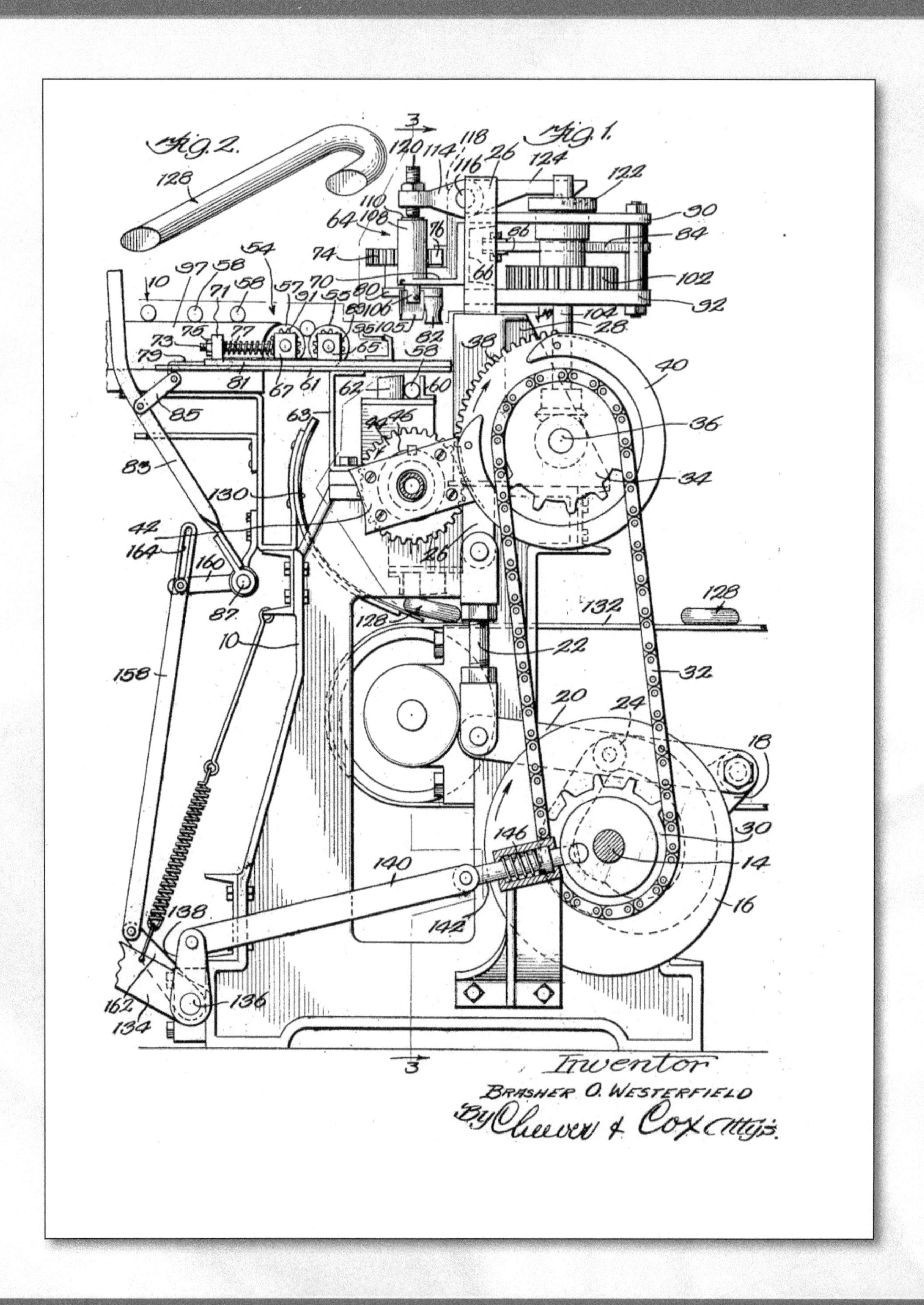

B.O. WESTERFIELD

CANDY FORMING MACHINE
Dec. 15, 1931

No. 1,836,349

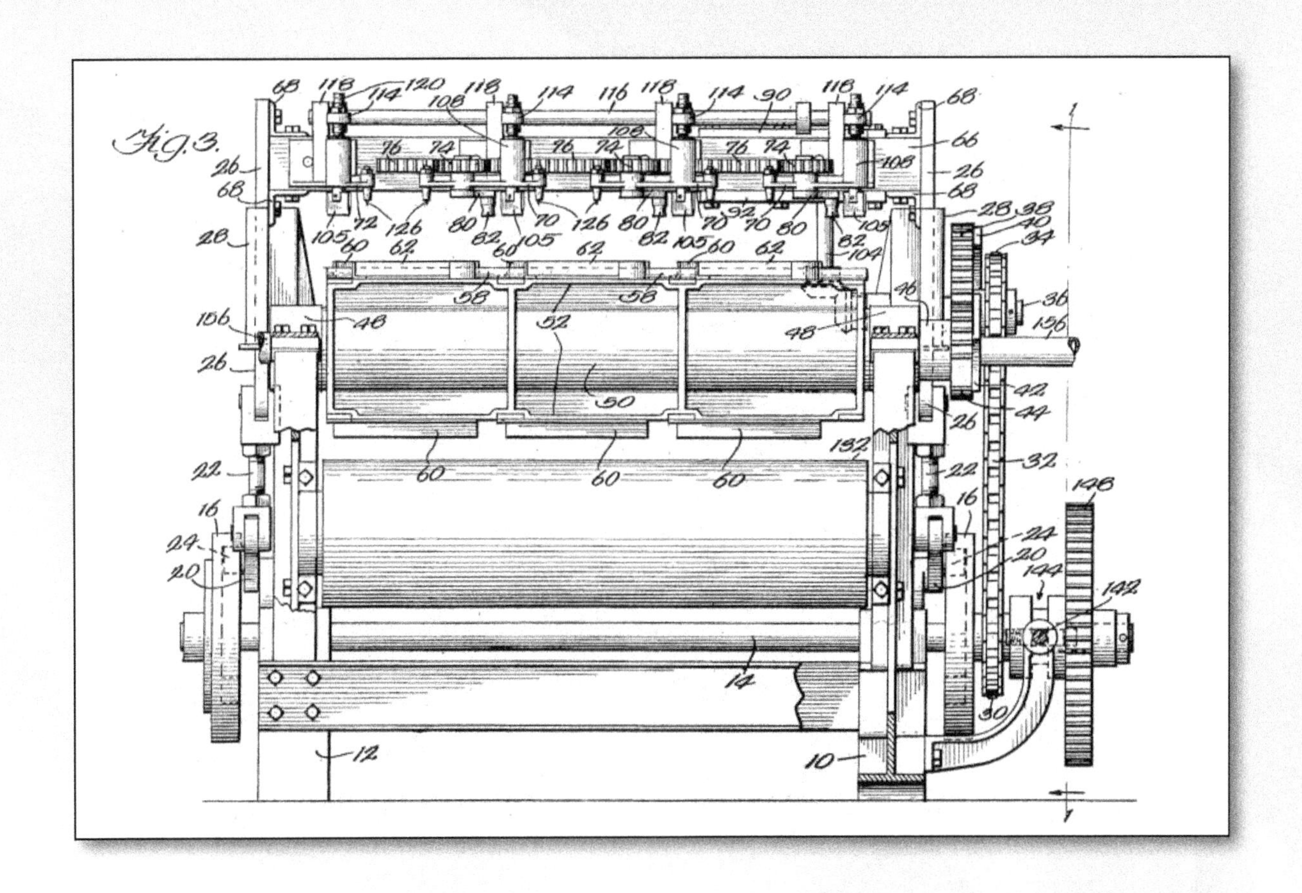
Fig. 3.

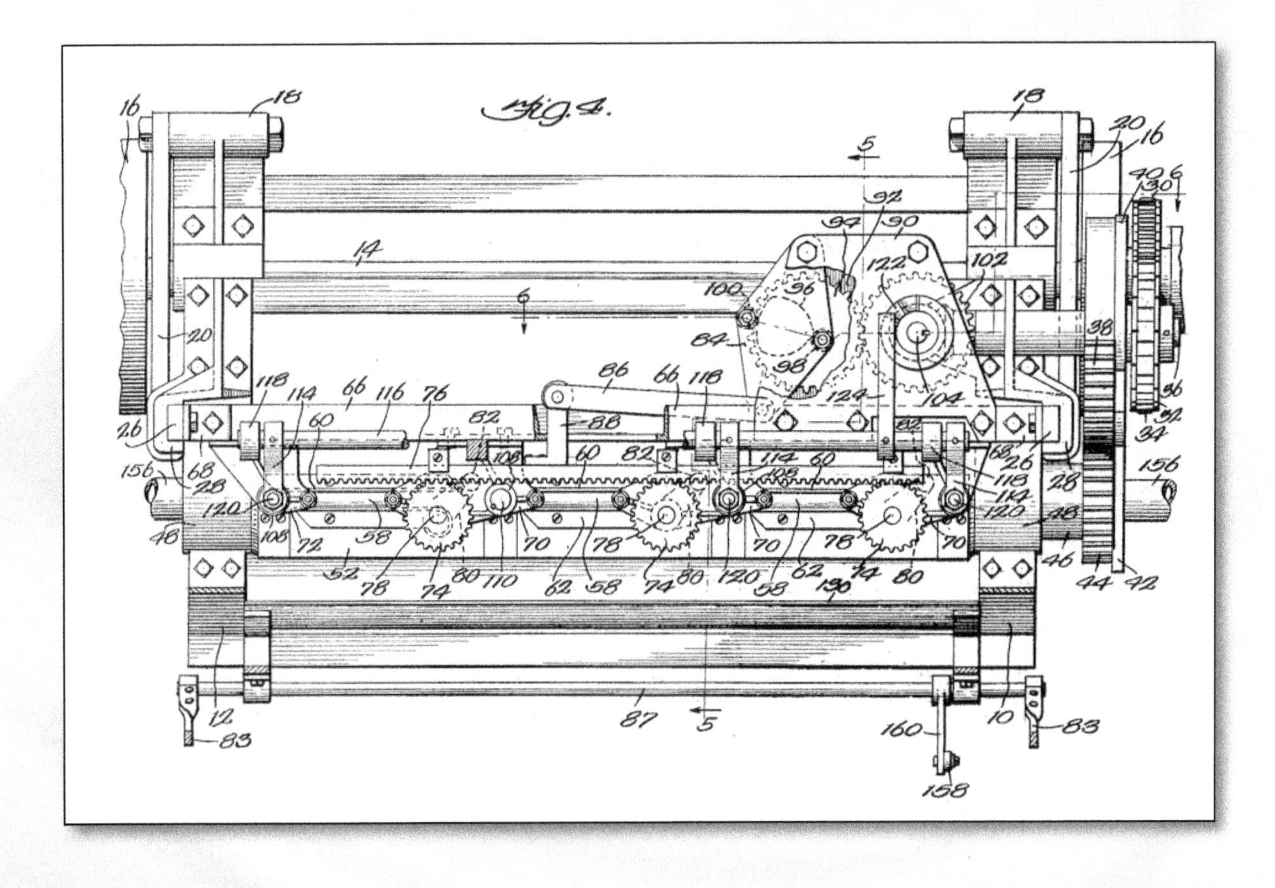
Fig. 4.

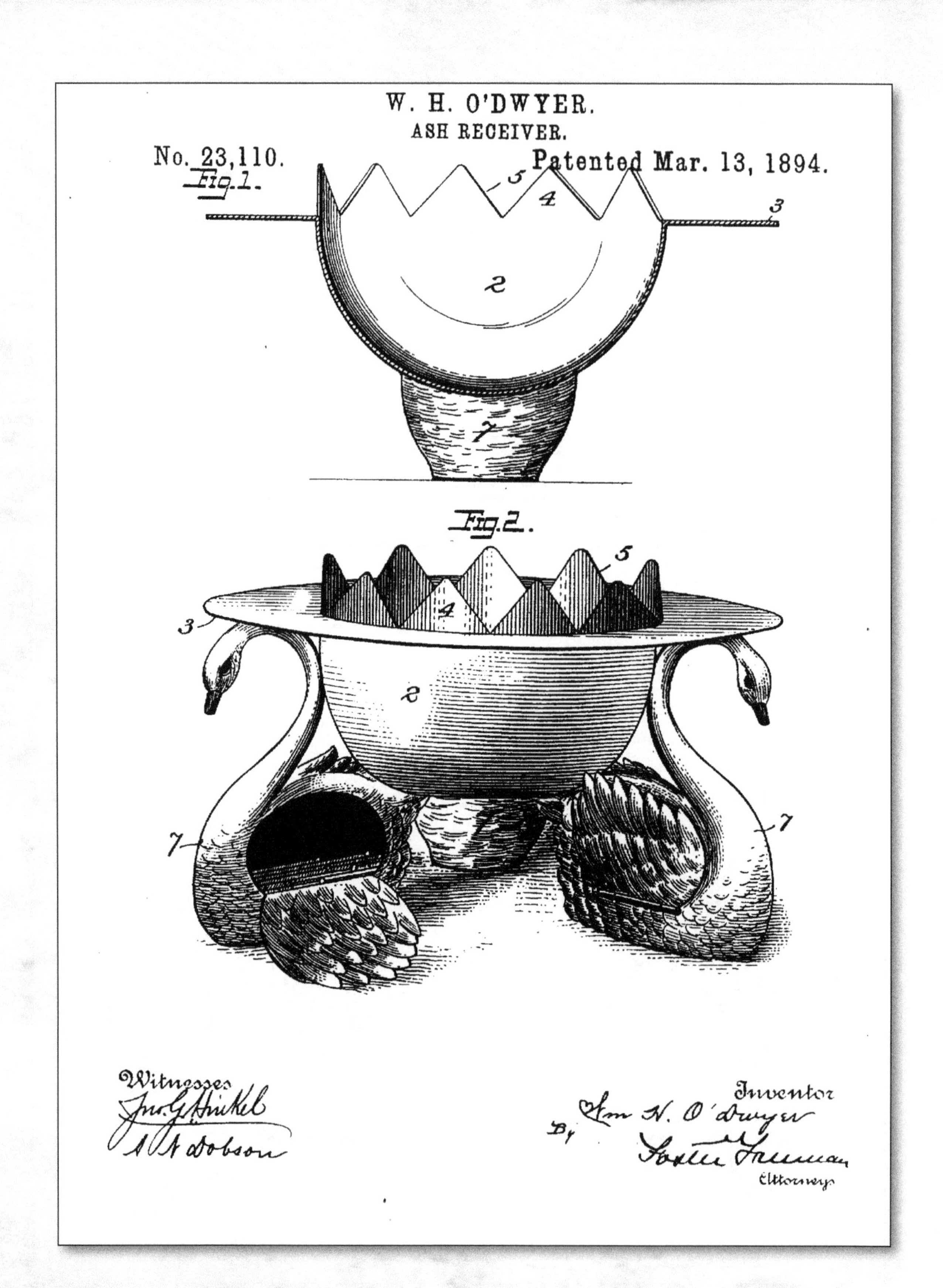
W. H. O'DWYER.
ASH RECEIVER.
No. 23,110.
Patented Mar. 13, 1894.
Fig.1.
Fig.2.
Witnesses
Inventor
Attorneys

WATER BOTTLE
APRIL 3, 2007

WEBB ET AL.

No. D539,656

C. BASTOW.

ARTICLE OF MANUFACTURE.

APPLICATION FILED OCT. 21, 1915.

48,850. Patented Apr. 11, 1916.

WITNESSES

Frank C. Palmer

E. B. Marshall

INVENTOR

Carrodus Bastow

BY *Munn & Co*

ATTORNEYS

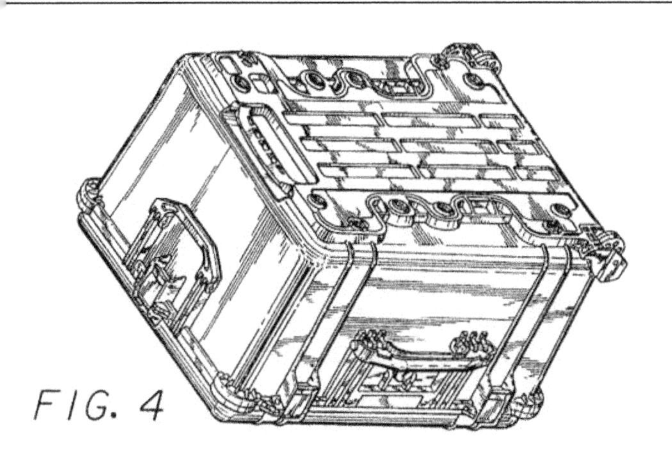
FIG. 4

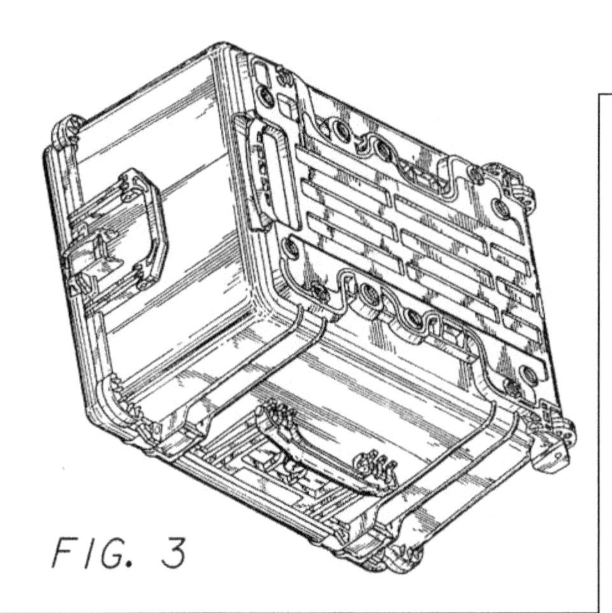
FIG. 3

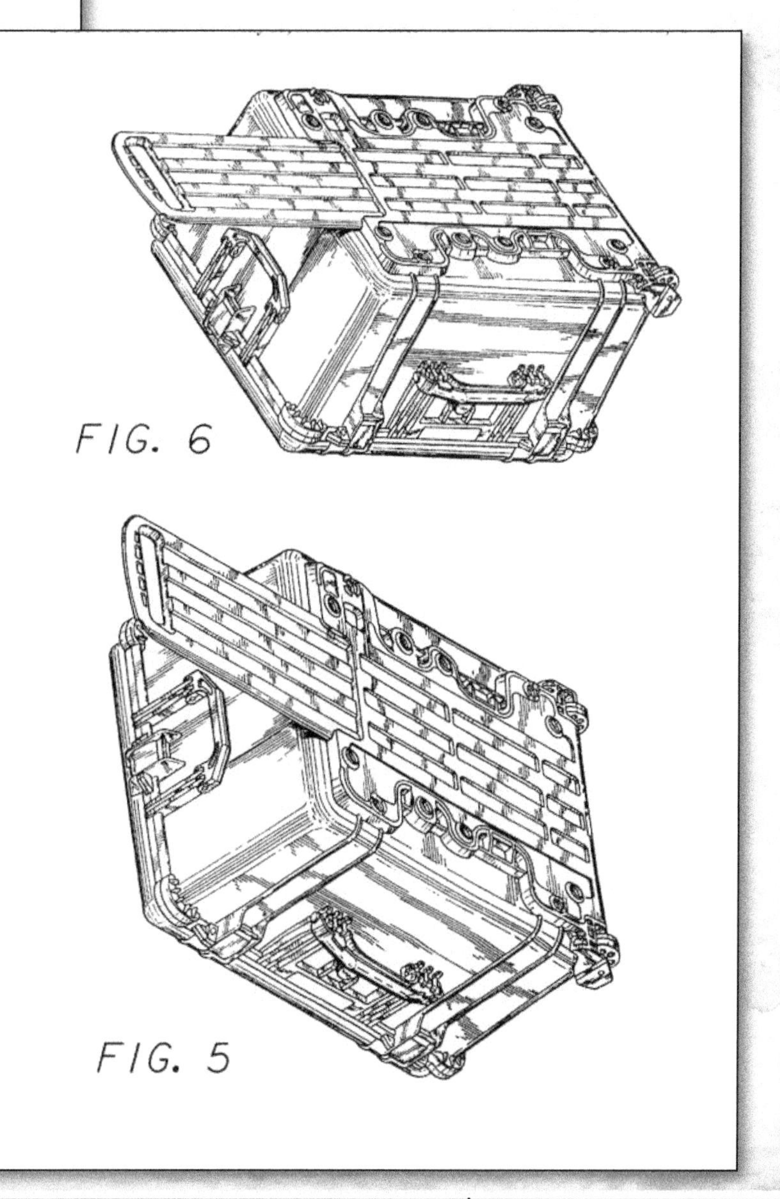
FIG. 6

FIG. 5

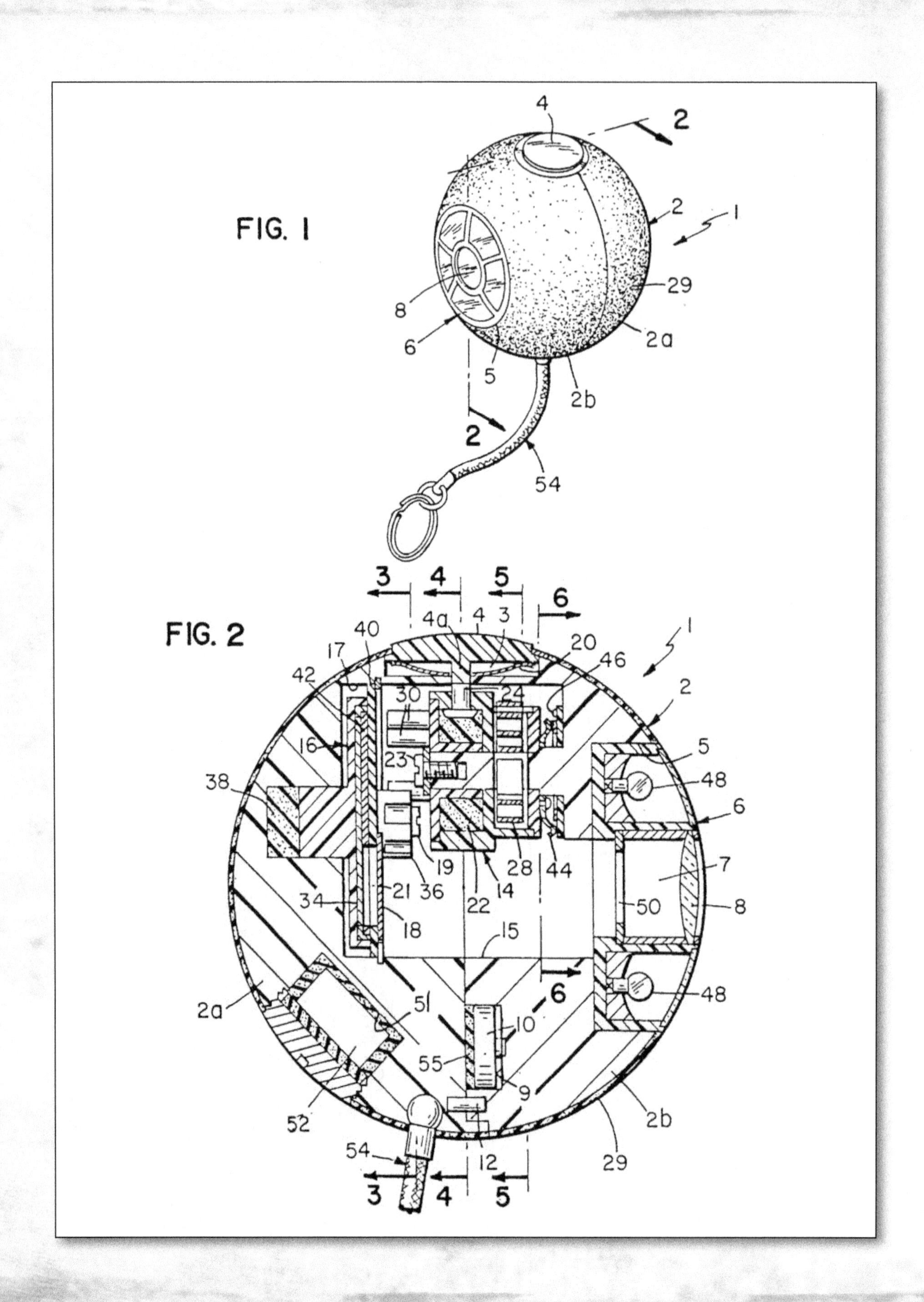
FIG. 1
FIG. 2

STATUE
P. MONTANA July 20, 1920 No. 55,872

Acknowledgements

Wow, a lot goes into writing a book, even one with few words like this one! Most of the work was graphic layout, and for that I thank my graphic artist and brother, Bryan. I must also thank my editors and muses, my wife Tami, Karen Lacey, Tracy Falk (who always knew I'd write a book... although maybe not a coffee table art book), Melissa (author of *The Paci-Fairy* and great encourager and publishing know-it-all), my assistant Jeanette who will undoubtedly be fulfilling book orders, my mom who taught me 1 Corinthians 13:4 through action, and to my kids who wondered what I was writing all those nights after work... thank you for your patience waiting for me to play Legos with you!

I also want to thank Gene Scott, patent agent, who taught me how to write patents and introduced me to this strange thing called "claims." And thanks to Paul Kane, a truly gifted patent draftsman who showed me that this is a field of art as much as it is science.

Several other patent attorneys and PTO Examiners chimed in with suggested patents, many of which I included in these pages. Thank you Phillip Hyder, Susan Krakower, Susan Lee, Stephen Nipper, Greg Kavounas, and Bob Frohwerk.

I have another crowd to thank, and that's my cherished Kickstater.com funding crowd of backers: Joseph Colbert, Adam Thomas, Stan White, David Apatoff, Muthukumar Ramalingam, Gene Quinn, Mussie Sibhatu, Ezekiel Dumke, Vladimir Vayntraub, Peter J. Lennartsson, Aakash Parekh, Prapancha Soekoro, Jeanette & Carey Johnson, Marcia Southwick, Chad Playford, Tom Alexander, Steven Chayer, and Stan Poe. If you don't know about Kickstarter.com, check it out. It's how I funded the initial production run of this book, and how I sold my first 100 copies. Thanks also to Greg Ahoronian, Gene Quinn, Jim Kirk, and Adam Thomas for helping spread the news about the Kickstarter project.

CPSIA information can be obtained
at www.ICGtesting.com
Printed in the USA
BVHW010420050222
627964BV00003B/51

9 780983 964001